PAMPHLETS.

Contents:

EVERETT'S ORATION

DELIVERED AT

Plymouth.

AN

ORATION

DELIVERED AT PLYMOUTH

DECEMBER 22, 1824.

By EDWARD EVERETT.

Boston.

CUMMINGS, HILLIARD & CO. 134 WASHINGTON STREET.

1825.

I. R. Butts, Printer.

Press of the North American Review.

Plymouth, December 23, 1824.

PROFESSOR EDWARD EVERETT,

SIR,—In obedience to a vote of the Trustees of the PILGRIM SOCIETY, I have the honor to make the subjoined communication.

"At a meeting of the Trustees of the PILGRIM SOCIETY, holden in Plymouth, Dec. 22, 1824,

"*Voted*, That the thanks of the Society be presented to Professor EDWARD EVERETT, for his interesting and eloquent Discourse delivered this day; and that a copy be requested for publication."

I am, with due sentiments of respect and regard, sir,

Your obedient servant,
SAMUEL DAVIS,
Corresponding Secretary.

A few passages in the following Discourse were, on account of its length, omitted in the delivery.

Oration.

THERE are occasions on which the employment, best calculated to be pleasing, becomes a source of anxiety; and the most flattering trust grows into a burthen. Amidst all the proud and grateful feelings, which the return of this anniversary must inspire, in the bosom of every child of New England, a deep solicitude oppresses me, lest I should fail in doing justice to the men, to the day, and to the events, which we are met to commemorate. In this solicitude, no personal sentiment mingles. I should be unworthy to address you, on this occasion, could I, from the selfish desire of winning your applause, devote one of the moments of this consecrated day to any cold speculations, however ingenious or original. Gladly would I give utterance to the most familiar commonplaces, could I be so happy in doing it, as to excite or strengthen the feelings, which belong to the time and the place. Gladly would I repeat to you those sentiments, which a hundred times have been uttered and welcomed on this anniversary; sentiments, whose truth does not change in the change of circumstances, whose power does not wear out with time. It is not by pompous epithets or lively antithesis, that the exploits of the pilgrims are to be set forth by their children. We can only do this worthily, by repeating the plain tale of their sufferings, by dwelling on the circumstances under which their memorable enterprise was executed, and by cherishing and uttering that spirit, which led them across the Ocean, and guided them to the spot where we stand.—We need no voice of artificial rhetoric to celebrate their names. The bleak and deathlike desolation of nature proclaims, with touching eloquence, the fortitude and patience of the meek adventurers. On the bare and wintry fields around us, their exploits are written in characters, which will last, and tell their tale to posterity, when brass and marble have crumbled into dust.

The occasion which has called us together is certainly one, to which no parallel exists in the history of the world. Other countries, and our own also, have their national festivals. They commemorate the birthdays of their illustrious children; they celebrate the foundation of important institutions: momentous events, victories, reformations, revolutions awaken, on their anniversaries, the grateful and patriotic feelings of posterity. But we commemorate the birthday of all New England; the foundation, not of one institution, but of all the institutions, the settlements, the establishments, the communities, the societies, the improvements, comprehended within our broad and happy borders.

Were it only as an act of rare adventure; were it a trait in foreign, or ancient history; we should fix upon the achievement of our fathers, as one of the noblest deeds, in the annals of the world. Were we attracted to it, by no other principle than that sympathy we feel, in all the fortunes of our race, it could lose nothing —it must gain—in the contrast, with whatever history or tradition has preserved to us of the wanderings and settlements of the tribes of man. A continent for the first time, effectually explored; a vast ocean traversed by men, women, and children, voluntarily exiling themselves from the fairest regions of the old world; and a great nation grown up, in the space of two centuries, on the foundations so perilously laid, by this pious band:—point me to the record, to the tradition, nay to the fiction of any thing, that can enter into competition with it.—It is the language not of exaggeration, but of truth and soberness to say, that there is nothing in the accounts of Phenician, of Grecian, or of Roman Colonization, that can stand in the comparison.

What new importance then does not the achievement acquire to our minds, when we consider that it was the deed of our fathers; that this grand undertaking was accomplished on the spot where we dwell; that the mighty region they explored is our native land; that the unrivalled enterprise they displayed, is not merely a fact proposed to our admiration, but is the source of our being; that their cruel hardships are the spring of our prosperity; their amazing sufferings the seed, from which our happiness has sprung; that their weary banishment gave us a home; that to their separation from every thing which is dear and pleasant in life, we owe all the comforts, the blessings, the privileges, which make our lot the envy of mankind.

These are the well known titles of our ancestors to our gratitude and veneration.

But there seems to me this peculiarity in the nature of their enterprise, that its grand and beneficent consequences are, with the lapse of time, constantly unfolding themselves, in an extent, and to a magnitude, which, till they are witnessed, are beyond the reach of the most sanguine promise. In the frail condition of human affairs, we have generally nothing left us to commemorate, but heroic acts of valor, which have resulted in no permanent effect; great characters, that have struggled nobly, but in vain, against the disastrous combinations of the age; brilliant triumphs of truth and justice, rendered unproductive, by the complication of opposite events, and by the stern resistance of that system of destiny, of which even the independence of our wills seems an obedient member.—At best, it is a great blessing, when we can point to some bright unclouded character; or some prosperous and well ordered institution; fortunate in rise and progress; grand and glorious at maturity; majestic, peaceful, and seasonable in decay, and piously lamented when no more; and it is to the few spectacles of this kind in human history, that our minds so constantly and fondly revert from the chequered scene of intermediate and troubled times and conditions.

But it is the peculiar character of the enterprise of our pilgrim forefathers—successful indeed in its outset—that it has been more and more successful, at every subsequent point in the line of time.—Accomplishing all they projected; what they projected was the least part of what has been accomplished. Forming a design, in itself grand, bold, and even appalling, for the sacrifices it required, and the risks it involved; the fulfilment of that design is the least thing, which, in the steady progress of events, has flowed from their counsels and their efforts.—Did they propose to themselves a refuge beyond the sea, from the religious and political tyranny of Europe? They achieved not that alone, but they have opened a wide asylum to all the victims of tyranny throughout the world. We ourselves have seen the statesmen, the generals, the kings of the elder world, flying for protection, to the shadow of our institutions. Did they wish only to escape to a remote corner, where the arm of oppression could not reach them? They founded a great realm, an imperial patrimony of liberty, the first effectual counterpoise in the scale of human right. Did they look for a retired spot, inoffensive for its obscurity and safe in its remoteness, where the little church of Leyden might enjoy the freedom of conscience? Behold the mighty regions over which in peaceful conquest—victoria sine clade—they have borne the banners of the cross.—Did they seek, beneath the protection of trading charters, to prosecute a frugal commerce in reimbursement of the expenses of their humble establishment? The fleets and navies of their descendants are on the farthest ocean; and the wealth of the Indies is now wafted with every tide to the coasts, where with hook and line they painfully gathered up their little adventures.—In short, did they, in their brightest and most sanguine moments, contemplate a thrifty, loyal, and prosperous colony—portioned off, like a younger son of the imperial household, to an humble, a dutiful distance? Behold the spectacle of an independent and powerful Republic, founded on the shores where some of those are but lately deceased, who saw the first-born of the pilgrims.

And shall we stop here? Is the tale now told; is the contrast now complete; are our destinies all fulfilled; have we reached the meridian; are we declining; are we stationary? My friends, I tell you, we have but begun; we are in the very morning of our days; our numbers are but an unit; our national resources but a pittance; our hopeful achievements in the political, the social, and the intellectual nature, are but the rudiments of what the children of the Pilgrims must yet attain. If there is any thing certain in the principles of human and social progress; if there is any thing clear in the deductions from past history; if there is any, the least, reliance to be placed on the conclusions of reason, in regard to the nature of man, the existing spectacle of our country's growth, magnificent as it is, does not suggest even an idea of what it must be. I dare adventure the prediction, that he who shall stand where I stand, two centuries hence, and look back on our present condition from a distance, equal to that from which we contemplate the first settlement of the Pilgrims, will sketch a contrast far more astonishing; and will speak of our times as the day of small things, in stronger and juster language, than any in which we can depict the poverty and wants of our fathers.

But we ought to consecrate this day, not to the promise, nor even the present blessings of our condition, except so far as these are connected with the memory of the Pilgrims. The twenty second of December belongs to them; and we ought, in consistency, to direct our thoughts to the circumstances, under which their most astonishing enterprise was achieved. I shall hope to have contributed my mite towards our happy celebration, if I can succeed in pointing out a few of those circumstances of the first emigration to our country, and particularly of the first emigration to New England,* from which, under a kind Providence, has flowed not only the immediate success of the undertaking, but the astonishing train of consequences auspicious to the cause of liberty, humanity, and truth.

* See Note A.

I. Our forefathers regarded, with natural terror, the passage of the mighty deep. Navigation, notwithstanding the great advances which it had made in the sixteenth century, was yet, comparatively speaking, in its infancy. The very fact, that voyages of great length and hazard were successfully attempted in small vessels, a fact which, on first view, might seem to show a high degree of perfection in the art, in reality proves that it was as yet but imperfectly understood. That the great Columbus should put to sea, for the discovery of a new passage across the Western Ocean to India, with two out of three vessels *unprovided with decks*, may indeed be considered the effect, not of ignorance of the art of navigation, but of bitter necessity.* But that Sir Francis Drake, near a hundred years afterwards, the first naval commander who ever sailed round the earth, enjoying the advantage of the royal patronage, and aided by the fruits of no little personal experience, should have embarked on his voyage of circumnavigation, with five vessels, of which the largest was of one hundred, and the smallest of fifteen tons,†

* See Note B.

† Biographia Brittanica, III. 1732.

must needs be regarded as proof, that the art of navigation, in the generation preceding our ancestors, had not reached that point, where the skilful adaptation of means to ends supersedes the necessity of extraordinary intrepidity, aided by not less extraordinary good fortune. It was therefore the first obstacle, which presented itself to the project of the pilgrims, that it was to be carried into execution, across the ocean, which separates our continent from the rest of the world.* Notwithstanding, however, this circumstance, and the natural effect it must have had on their minds, there is no doubt that it is one of those features in our natural situation, to which America is indebted, not merely for the immediate success of the enterprise of settlement, but for much of its subsequent growth and prosperity.

I do not now allude to the obvious consideration, that the remoteness of the country, to be settled, led to a more thorough preparation for the enterprise, both as respects the tempers of those who embarked in it, and the provisions made for carrying it on; though this view will not be lost on those, who reflect on the nature

* See Note C.

of man, by which difficult enterprises (so they be not desperate) are more likely to succeed, than those which seem much easier. Nor do I allude to the effect of our distance from Europe, in preventing the hasty abandonment of the colony, under the pressure of the first difficulties; although the want of frequent and convenient reconveyance was doubtless a considerable security to the early settlements, and placed our fathers, in some degree, in the situation of the followers of Cortez, after he had intrepidly burned the vessels, which conveyed them to the Mexican coasts.

The view, which I would now take of the remoteness of America from Europe, is connected with the higher principles of national fortune and progress.

The rest of the world, though nominally divided into three continents, in reality consists of but one. Europe, Asia, and Africa are separated by no natural barriers, which it has not been easy in every age for an ambitious invader to pass; and apart from this first consequence of the juxtaposition of their various regions, a communication of principle and feeling, of policy and passion, may be propagated, at all times, even to their remote and seemingly inaccessible communities. The consequence has been, on the whole, highly unfavorable to social progress. The extent of country inhabited or rather infested by barbarous tribes, has generally far outweighed the civilized portions; and more than once, in the history of the world, refinement, learning, arts, laws, and religion, with the wealth and prosperity they have created, have been utterly swept away, and the hands, as it were, moved back, on the dial plate of time, in consequence of the irruption of savage hordes into civilized regions. Were the early annals of the East as amply preserved as those of the Roman empire, they would probably present us with accounts of revolutions, on the Nile and the Euphrates, as disastrous as those, by which the civilized world was shaken, in the first centuries of the Christian era.—Till an ocean interposes its mighty barrier, no citadel of freedom or truth has been long maintained. The magnificent temples of Egypt were demolished in the sixth century before our Saviour, by the hordes, which Cambyses had collected from the *steppes* of Central Asia. The vineyards of Burgundy were wasted in the third century of our era, by roving savages from beyond the Caucasus. In the eleventh century, Gengis Khan and his Tartars swept Europe and Asia from the Baltic to the China Sea. And Ionia and Attica, the gardens of Greece, are still, under the eyes of the leading Christian powers of Europe, beset by remorseless barbarians from the Altai Mountains.

Nor is it the barbarians alone, who have been tempted by this facility of communication, to a career of boundless plunder. The Alexanders and the Cæsars, the Charlemagnes and the Napoleons, the founders of great empires and authors of schemes of universal monarchy, have been enabled, by the same circumstance, to turn the annals of mankind into a tale of war and misery. When we descend to the scrutiny of single events, we find that the nations, who have most frequently and most immediately suffered, have been those most easily approached and overrun;—and that those who have longest or most uniformly maintained their independence, have done it by virtue of lofty mountains, wide rivers, or the surrounding sea.

In this state of things, the three united continents of the old world do not contain a single spot, where any grand scheme of human improvement could be attempted, with a prospect of fair experiment and full success, because there is no spot safe from foreign interference; and no member of the general system so insignificant, that his motions are not watched with jealousy by all the rest. The welfare and progress of man in the most favored region, instead of proceeding in a free and natural course, dependent on the organization and condition of that region alone, can only reach the point, which may be practicable in the general result of an immensely complicated system, made up of a thousand jarring members.

Our country accordingly opened, at the time of its settlement, and still opens, a new theatre of human development.—Notwithstanding the prodigious extent of commercial intercourse, and the wide grasp of naval power among modern states, and their partial effect in bringing us into the political system of Europe, it need not be urged, that we are essentially strangers to it;—placed at a distance, which retards, and for every injurious purpose, neutralizes all peaceful communication, and defies all hostile approach. To this it was owing that so little was here felt of the convulsions of the civil wars, which followed in England so soon after the expulsion of our fathers. To this, in a more general view, we are indebted for many of our peculiarities as a nation, for our steady colonial growth, our establishment of independence, our escape amidst the political storms which, during the last thirty years, have shaken the empires of the earth.—To this we shall still be indebted, and more and more indebted, with the progress of our country, for the originality and stability of our national character. Hitherto the *political* effects of our seclusion, behind the mighty veil of waters, have been the most important. Now, that our political foundations are firmly laid; that the work of settlement, of colonization, of independence, and of union is all done, and happily done, we shall reap, in other forms, the salutary fruits of our remoteness from the centres of foreign opinion and feeling.

I say not this in direct disparagement of foreign states; their institutions are doubtless as good, in many cases, as the condition of things now admits; or when at the worst, could not be remedied by any one body, nor by any one generation of men; and the evil which requires for its remedy the accord of successive generations, at the same time that it may generally be called desperate, ought to bring no direct reproach upon the men of any one period.

But without disparaging foreign institutions, we may be allowed to prefer our own ; to assert their excellence, to seek to build them up on their original foundations, on their true principles, and in their unmingled purity. That great word of Independence, which, if first uttered in 1776, was most auspiciously anticipated in 1620, comprehends much more than a mere absence of foreign jurisdiction. I could almost say, that if it rested there, it would scarcely be worth asserting. In every noble, in every true acceptation, it implies not merely an American government, but an American character, an American pride. To the formation of these, nothing will more powerfully contribute than our geographical distance from other parts of the world. The unhealthy air of Europe is purified in crossing the waves of the Atlantic. The roaring of its mighty billows is not terrible,—it does but echo the voices of our national feeling and power.

In these views there is nothing unsocial ; nothing hostile to a friendly and improving connexion of distant regions with each other, or to the profitable interchange of the commodities, which a bountiful Providence has variously scattered over the earth. For these and all other desirable ends, the perfection, to which the art of navigation is brought, affords abundant means of conquering the obstacles of distance. It is idle, in reference to these ends, to speak of our remoteness from the rest of the world, while our commerce is exploring the farthest regions of the earth; while, in exchange for the products or efforts of our industry, the flocks on the western declivity of the Peruvian Andes are supplying us with wool; the north-eastern coasts of Japan furnishing us with oil; and the central provinces of China, with tea. At this moment, the reward of American skill is paid by the Chieftains of inner Tartary, wrapped up in the furs, which, in our voyages of circumnavigation, we have collected on the North Western Coast of our Continent. The interest on American capital is paid by the haughty viziers of Anatolia, whose opium is cultivated and gathered for our merchants. The wages of American labor are paid by the princes of Hindostan, whose plantations of indigo depend on us for a portion of their market. While kings and ministers, by intrigue and bloodshed, are contesting the possession of a few square miles of territory, our commerce has silently extended its jurisdiction from island to island, from sea to sea, from continent to continent, till it holds the globe in its grasp.

But while no one can doubt the mutual advantages of a judiciously conducted commerce, or be insensible of the good, which has resulted to the cause of humanity, from the cultivation of a peaceful and friendly intercourse with other climes, it is yet beyond question, that the true principle of American policy, to which the whole spirit of our institutions, not less than the geographical features of the country, invites us, is *separation from Europe.* Next to union at home, which ought to be called not so much the essential condition of our national existence, as our existence itself, separation from all other countries, in policy, spirit, and character, is the great principle, by which we are to prosper. It is toward this that our efforts, public and private, ought to strain ; and we shall rise or decline in strength, improvement, and worth, as we observe or desert this principle. This is the voice of nature, which did not in vain disjoin our continent from the old world ; nor reserve it beyond the ocean for fifty centuries, only that it might become a common receptacle for the exploded principles, the degenerate examples, and the remediless corruptions of other states. This is the voice of our history, which traces every thing excellent in our character and prosperous in our fortunes, to dissent, nonconformity, departure, resistance, and revolution. This is taught us by the marked peculiarity, the wonderful novelty which, whether we will it or not, displays itself in our whole physical, political, and social existence.

And it is a matter of sincere congratulation, that, under the healthy operation of natural causes, very partially accelerated by legislation, the current of our pursuits and industry, without deserting its former channels, is throwing a broad and swelling branch into the interior. Foreign commerce, the natural employment of an enterprising people, whose population is accumulated on the seacoast, and whose neutral services are called for by a world in arms, is daily reverting to a condition of more equal participation among the various maritime states, and is in consequence becoming less productive to any one. While America remains, and will always remain, among the foremost commercial and naval states, an ample portion of our resources has already taken a new direction. We profited of the dissensions of Europe, which threw her trade into our hands ; and we amassed a capital, as her carriers, before we could otherwise have one of our own. We are now profiting of the pacification of Europe, in the application to our own soil, our own mineral and vegetable products, our water course and water falls, and our general internal resources, of a part of the capital thus accumulated.

This circumstance is, in a general view, most gratifying ; inasmuch as it creates a new bond of mutual dependence, in the variety of our natural gifts, and in the mutual benefits rendered each other by the several sectional interests of the country. The progress is likely to be permanent and sure, because it has been mainly brought about in the natural order of things, and with little legislative interference. Within a few years what a happy change has taken place! The substantial clothing of our industrious classes is now the growth of the American soil, and the texture of the American loom; the music of the water wheel is heard on the banks of our thousand rural streams; and enterprise and skill, with wealth, refinement, and prosperity in their train, having studded the seashore with populous cities, are making their great "progress" of improvement through the interior, and sowing towns and villages, as it were broadcast, through the country.

II. If our remote position be so important among the circumstances, which favored the enterprise of our fathers, and have favored the growth of their settlements, scarcely less so was the point of time at which those settlements were commenced.

When we cast our eyes over the annals of our race, we find them to be filled with a tale of various fortunes; the rise and fall of nations;—periods of light and darkness;—of great illumination, and of utter obscurity;—and of all intermediate degrees of intelligence, cultivation, and liberty. But in the seeming confusion of the narrative, our attention is arrested by three more conspicuous eras at unequal distances in the lapse of ages.

In Egypt we still behold, on the banks of the Nile, the monuments of a polished age; —a period, no doubt, of high cultivation, and of great promise. Beneath the influence of causes, which are lost in the depth of antiquity, but which are doubtless connected with the debasing superstitions and despotism of the age, this period passed away, and left scarce a trace of its existence, beyond the stupendous and mysterious structures,—the temples, the obelisks, and the pyramids,—which yet bear witness to an age of great power and cultivated art, and mock the curiosity of mankind by the records inscrutably carved on their surfaces.

Passing over an interval of one thousand years, we reach the second epoch of light and promise. With the progress of freedom in Greece, the progress of the mind kept pace; and an age both of achievement and of hope succeeded, of which the indirect influence is still felt in the world. But the greater part of mankind were too barbarous to improve by the example of this favored corner; and though the influence of its arts, letters, and civilization was wonderfully extensive and durable,—though it seemed to revive at the court of the Roman Cæsars, and still later, at that of the Arabian Caliphs, yet not resting on those popular institutions and popular principles, which can alone be permanent because alone natural, it slowly died away, and Europe and the world relapsed into barbarity.

The third great era of our race is the close of the fifteenth century. The use of the mariner's compass and the invention of the art of printing, had furnished the modern world, with two engines of improvement and civilization, either of which was far more efficacious than all united, known to antiquity. The reformation also, about this time, disengaged Christianity, itself one of the most powerful instruments of civilization, from those abuses, which had hitherto nearly destroyed its beneficent influence on temporal affairs ; and at this most chosen moment in the annals of the world, America was discovered.

It would not be difficult, by pursuing this analysis, to show that the very period, when the settlement of our coasts began, was peculiarly auspicious to the foundation of a new and hopeful system.

Religious reformation was the original principle, which enkindled the zeal of our pilgrim fathers ; as it has been so often acknowledged to be the master principle of the greatest movements in the modern world.* The religions of Greece and Rome were portions of the political systems of these countries. The Scipios, the Crassuses, and Julius Cæsar himself, were high priests. It was, doubtless, owing in part to this example, that at an early period after the first introduction of Christianity, the heads of the church so entirely mistook the spirit of this religion, that, in imitation of the splendid idolatry, which was passing away, they aimed at a new combination of church and state, which received but too much countenance from the policy of Constantine.† This abuse, with ever multiplying and aggravated calamitous consequences, endured, without any effectual check, till the first blow was aimed at the supremacy of the papal power, by Philip the Fair of France, in the fourteenth century,

* See Note D. † See Note F.

who laid the foundation of the liberties of the Gallican church, of which the Constitution may be called the Catholic Reformation.*

After an interval of two hundred years, this example was followed and improved upon by the Princes in Germany, that espoused the protestant reformation of Luther, and in a still more decisive manner by Henry the Eighth in England; at which period we may accordingly date the second great step in the march of religious liberty.†

Much more, however, was yet to be effected toward the dissolution of the unnatural bond between Church and State. Hitherto a domestic was substituted for a foreign yoke, and the rights of private conscience had, perhaps, gained but little in the exchange. In the middle of the sixteenth century, and among the exiles, whom the frantic tyranny of Queen Mary had driven to the free cities on the Rhine, the ever memorable communion of Puritans arose. On their return to England, in the reign of Queen Elizabeth, they strenuously opposed themselves to the erection and peculiarities of the English national church.

* See Note F. † See Note G.

Nearly as we have now reached, both in simplicity of principle and point of time, to our pilgrim forefathers, there is one more purifying process to go through, one more generation to pass away. The major part of the Puritans themselves, while they rejected some of the forms, and disliked the organization of the English church, adhered in substance to the Constitution of the Genevan church, and their descendants were willing, a century later, to accept of an establishment by law in Scotland.

It remained, therefore, to shake off the last badge of subjection, and in the person of Robert Brown, an individual himself of no very commendable qualities, the last step was taken in the progress of reform, by asserting the independence of each single church. The personal character of Brown was such as to throw no little discouragement on the cause; nor did it acquire firmness till espoused by Robinson, who may be called the father of the *Independent* churches. His own at Leyden was the chief of these, and fidelity to their principles was the motive of their departure from Holland, and the occasion of their settlement at Plymouth.*

* See Note H.

But all may not be disposed to join us, in so exact a specification of the beginning of the seventeenth century, as the period, when religious reform had reached its last perfection, and consequently, as the era most favorable to the establishment of a new and free state. None, however, on a larger view of the subject, will be unwilling to allow that this was the great age of general improvement. It was the age, when the discoveries of the Spanish, Portuguese, and English navigators had begun to exert a stimulating influence on the world at large, and the old continent and the new, like the magnetic poles, commenced those momentous processes of attraction and repulsion, from which so much of the activity of both has since proceeded. It was the period when the circulation of knowledge had become general; and books in all languages were in the hands of a very large class in every country. The history of Europe, in all its states, shows the extent and vehemence of the consequent fermentation. With their new engines of improvement and new principles of right, the communities of men rushed forward in the course of reform; some with firmness and vigor, proportioned to the greatness of the object in view, most with tumult and desperation, proportioned to the duration and magnitude of their injuries, and none with entire success. The most that was effected, in the most fortunate states, was a compromise between the new claims and the old abuses. Absolute kings stipulated to be no longer absolute ; and free men preferred what they called petitions of right. In this way, and after infinite struggles, a tolerable foundation for considerable practical liberty was laid on two principles, in the abstract entirely false ; that of acquiescence on the part of the sovereign, and prescription in favor of the people. So firmly established are these principles, by consent of the statesmen of the freest country in Europe, as the best and only foundation of civil rights, that so late as the last years of the eighteenth century, a work of ingenuity seldom, of eloquence never, surpassed, was written by Mr Burke, to prove, that the people of England have not a right to appoint and to remove their rulers ; and that if they ever had the right, they deliberately renounced it at what is called the *glorious* revolution of 1688, for themselves and their posterity forever.*

It is obvious, therefore, that the meliorations, which have taken place in Europe within the last two centuries, rest on no sound principle, and are but the effect of alteratives on the fatal malady of age, with which her states are sick at heart. It is true that the popular element, such is its sovereign healing power, which, even on the poor footing of a compromise, has been introduced into a portion of their political constitutions, has operated some of the beneficent effects of the fabled transfusion of youthful blood into aged veins. But the principles of prescription and acquiescence unfortunately run as much in favor of abuses and corruptions as of privileges. On the received footing, the acknowledged vices and evils of their institutions are as sacred as the best rights, and the door to any consistent and rational improvement is effectually closed ; because the more degenerate, the more antiquated, the more hostile to the spirit and character of the age, the institution that needs reform may be, the more ancient it will also

* See Note I.

commonly be found, and in consequence, the more strongly fortified by prescription.

While, therefore, the work of social renovation is entirely hopeless in Europe, we cannot but regard it as the plain interposition of Providence, that, at the critical point of time, when the most powerful springs of improvement were in operation, a chosen company of pilgrims, who were actuated by these springs of improvement, in all their strength, who had purchased the privilege of dissent at the high price of banishment from the civilized world, and who, with the dust of their feet, had shaken off the antiquated abuses and false principles, which had been accumulating for thousands of years, came over to these distant, unoccupied shores. I know not that the work of thorough reform could be safely trusted to any other hands. I can credit their disinterestedness, when they maintain the equality of ranks; for no rich forfeitures of attainted lords await them in the wilderness. I need not question the sincerity with which they assert the rights of conscience; for the plundered treasures of an ancient hierarchy are not to seal their doctrine. They rested the edifice of their civil and religious liberties on a foundation as pure and innocent as the snows around them. Blessed be the spot, the only one on earth, where such a foundation was ever laid. Blessed be the spot, the only one on earth, where man has attempted to establish the good, without beginning with the sad, the odious, the too suspicious task of pulling down the bad.

III. Under these favorable auspices, the Pilgrims landed on the coast of New England. They found it a region of moderate fertility, offering an unsubdued wilderness to the hand of labor, with a climate temperate indeed, but compared with that which they had left, verging somewhat near to either extreme; and a soil which promised neither gold nor diamonds, nor any thing but what should be gained from it by patient industry. This was but a poor reality for that dream of oriental luxury, with which America had filled the imaginations of men. The visions of Indian wealth, of mines of silver and gold, and fisheries of pearl, with which the Spanish adventurers in Mexico and Peru had astonished the ears of Europe, were but poorly fulfilled on the bleak, rocky, and sterile plains of New England. No doubt, in the beginning of the settlement, these circumstances operated unfavorably on the growth of the colony. In the nature of things, it is mostly adventurers, who incline to leave their homes and native land, and risk the uncertainty of another hemisphere; and a climate and soil like ours furnished but little attraction to the adventuring class. Captain Smith, in his zeal to promote the growth of New England, is at no little pains to show that the want of mineral treasures was amply compensated by the abundant fishery of the coast; and having sketched in strong colors the prosperity and wealth of the states of Holland, he adds, "Divers, I know, may allege many other assistances, but this is the chiefest mine, and the sea the source of those silver streams of their virtue, which hath made them now the very miracle of industry, the only pattern of perfection for these affairs; and the benefit of fishing is that *primum mobile* that turns all their spheres to this height of plenty, strength, honor and exceeding great admiration."*

While we smile at this overwrought panegyric on the primitive resource of our fathers, we

* Smith's Generall Historie, &c. Vol. II. p. 185. Richmond Edit.

cannot but do justice to the principle, on which it rests. It is doubtless to the untempting qualities of our climate and soil, and the conditions of industry and frugality, on which alone the prosperity of the colony could be secured, that we are to look for a full share of the final success, that crowned the enterprise.

To this it is to be ascribed that the country itself was not preoccupied by a crowded population of savages, like the West India Islands, like Mexico and Peru, who, placed upon a soil yielding almost spontaneously a superabundance of food, had multiplied into populous empires, and made a progress in the arts, which served no other purpose, than to give strength and permanence to some of the most frightful systems of despotism, that ever afflicted humanity; systems uniting all that is most horrible in depraved civilization and wild barbarity. The problem indeed is hard to be solved, in what way and by what steps a continent, possessed by savage tribes, is to be lawfully occupied and colonized by civilized man.* But this question was divested of much of its practical difficulty by the scantiness of the native population, which our

* See Note K.

fathers found in New England, and the migratory life to which the necessity of the chace reduced them. It is owing to this, that the annals of New England exhibit no scenes like those which were acted in Hispaniola, in Mexico, and Peru; no tragedies like those of Anacoana, of Guatimozin, and of Atahualpa; no statesman like Bovadilla; no heroes like Pizarro and Cortes;

> "No dark Ovando, no religious Boyle."

The qualities of our climate and soil enter largely in other ways into that natural basis, on which our prosperity and our freedom have been reared. It is these which distinguish the smiling aspect of our busy, thriving villages from the lucrative desolation of the sugar islands, and all the wide spread, undescribed, indescribable miseries of the colonial system of modern Europe, as it has existed beyond the barrier of these mighty oceans, in the unvisited, unprotected, and unavenged recesses of either India. We have had abundant reason to be contented with this austere sky, this hard unyielding soil. Poor as it is, it has left us no cause to sigh for the luxuries of the tropics, nor to covet the mines of the southern regions of our hemisphere. Our rough and hardly subdued hill sides and barren plains have produced us that, which neither ores, nor spices, nor sweets could purchase,—which would not spring in the richest gardens of the despotic East. The compact numbers and the strength, the general intelligence and the civilization which, since the world began, were never exhibited beneath the sultry line, have been the precious product of this iron bound coast.* The rocks and the sands, which would yield us neither the cane nor the coffee tree, have yielded us, not only an abundance and a growth in resources, rarely consistent with the treacherous profusion of the tropical colonies, but the habits, the manners, the institutions, the industrious population, the schools and the churches, beyond all the wealth of all the Indies.

> "*Man is the nobler growth our soil supplies,*
> And souls are ripened in our northern skies."

Describe to me a country, rich in veins of the precious metals, that is traversed by good roads. Inform me of the convenience of bridges, where the rivers roll over golden sands. Tell me of a thrifty, prosperous village of freemen, in the

* See Note L.

miserable districts where every clod of the earth is kneaded up for diamonds, beneath the lash of the task master. No, never! while the constitution, not of states, but of human nature, remains the same; never, while the laws, not of civil society, but of God are unrepealed, will there be a hardy, virtuous, independent yeomanry in regions where two acres of untilled banana will feed a hundred men.* It is idle to call that *food*, which can never feed a free, intelligent, industrious population. It is not food. It is dust; it is chaff; it is ashes;—there is no nourishment in it, if it be not carefully sown, and painfully reaped, by laborious freemen, on their own fee-simple acres.

IV. Nor ought we omit to say, that if our fathers found, in the nature of the region to which they emigrated, the most favorable spot for the growth of a free and happy state, they themselves sprang from the land, the best adapted to furnish the habits and principles essential to the great undertaking. In an age that speculates, and speculates to important purpose, on the races of fossil animals, of which

* See Note M.

no living specimen has existed since the deluge, and which compares, with curious criticism, the dialects of languages which ceased to be spoken a thousand years ago, it cannot be called idle to inquire which of the different countries of modern Europe possesses the qualities, that best adapt it to become the parent nation of a new and free state. I know not in fact, what more momentous question in human affairs could be asked, than that which regards the most hopeful lineage of a collective empire. But without engaging in so extensive a discussion, I may presume that there is not one who hears me, that does not feel it a matter of congratulation and joy, that our fathers were Englishmen.

No character is perfect among nations, more than among men, nor is the office of the panegyrist more respectable towards the one than the other. But it must needs be conceded, that after our own country, England is the most favored abode of liberty; or rather, that besides our own, it is the only land where liberty can be said to exist; the only land where the voice of the sovereign is not stronger than the voice of the law. We can scarce revolve with patience the idea, that we might have been a Spanish colony, a Portuguese colony, or a Dutch colony; we can scarcely compare with coolness the inheritance of those institutions, which were transmitted to us by our fathers, with that which we must have received from almost any other country; absolute government, military despotism, privileged orders, and the holy inquisition.* What would have been the condition of this flourishing and happy land, were these the institutions, on which its settlement had been founded? There are, unfortunately, too many materials for answering this question, in the history of the Spanish and Portuguese settlements on the American continent, from the first moment of unrelenting waste and desolation, to the distractions and conflicts, of which we ourselves are the witnesses. What hope can there be for the colonies of nations, which possess themselves no spring of improvement; and tolerate none in the regions over which they rule; whose administration sets no bright examples of political independence; whose languages send out no reviving lessons of sound and practical science, afraid of nothing that is true of manly literature, of free speculation; but

* See Note N.

repeat, with every ship that crosses the Atlantic, the same debasing voice of despotism, credulity, superstition, and slavery.

Let us here bring our general conceptions down to an example. The country called Brazil, and till lately subject to the kingdom of Portugal, (a kingdom more nearly of the size of Tennessee than of any other of the United States ;)—the country of Brazil, stretching from the mouth of the Oyapoco, in the fourth degree of north latitude, to the Banda Oriental in the thirty third degree of south, and from Peru to the Atlantic Ocean,* is, by computation, one tenth part more extensive than the entire territory of the United States. Our whole vast possessions, from the most southern point of Florida to the northeastern extremity of Maine, and from the Atlantic to the Pacific Ocean,—possessions which the Surveyor's chain has never marked out, over which tribes of Indians yet roam undisturbed, whose numbers, whose race, whose very names are unknown,—tracts unexplored, in which the wild hunter, half savage, half outlaw, has not yet startled the beaver, on the still and solitary banks of his

* See Note O.

hereditary stream,—I say this mighty territory is one tenth smaller than Brazil. And now name to me a book in the Portuguese language, where a Brazilian could read so much as the elements of liberty. Name to me a law in the Portuguese code, to protect his property from confiscation and himself from the rack or the stake, whenever the minister shall give the nod. Name me an institution in the whole Portuguese system, in the remotest degree favorable to the progress and happiness of man.—And yet it is from this despised corner of Europe, that all the seed must come, to sow this mighty land. It is from this debased source that all the influences have gone forth, which have for three centuries actually decided, and for centuries more must decisively influence the destinies of these all but boundless territories.*

What citizen of our republic is not grateful in the contrast which our history presents? —Who does not feel, what reflecting American does not acknowledge, the incalculable advantages derived to this land, out of the

* See Note P.

deep fountains of civil, intellectual, and moral truth, from which we have drawn in England?—What American does not feel proud that he is descended from the countrymen of Bacon, of Newton, and of Locke?—Who does not know, that while every pulse of civil liberty in the heart of the British empire beat warm and full in the bosom of our fathers; the sobriety, the firmness, and the dignity with which the cause of free principles struggled into existence here, constantly found encouragement and countenance from the sons of liberty there?—Who does not remember that when the pilgrims went over the sea, the prayers of the faithful British confessors, in all the quarters of their dispersion, went over with them, while their aching eyes were strained, till the star of hope should go up in the western skies?—And who will ever forget that in that eventful struggle, which severed this mighty empire from the British crown, there was not heard, throughout our continent in arms, a voice which spoke louder for the rights of America, than that of Burke or of Chatham, within the walls of the British parliament, and at the foot of the British throne?—No, for myself, I can truly say, that after my native land, I feel a tenderness and a reverence for that of my fathers. The pride I take in my own country makes me respect that from which we are sprung. In touching the soil of England, I seem to return like a descendant to the old family seat ;—to come back to the abode of an aged, the tomb of a departed parent. I acknowledge this great consanguinity of nations. The sound of my native language beyond the sea, is a music to my ear, beyond the richest strains of Tuscan softness, or Castillian majesty.—I am not yet in a land of strangers, while surrounded by the manners, the habits, the forms, in which I have been brought up. I wander delighted through a thousand scenes, which the historians, the poets have made familiar to us,—of which the names are interwoven with our earliest associations. I tread with reverence the spots, where I can retrace the footsteps of our suffering fathers; the pleasant land of their birth has a claim on my heart. It seems to me a classic, yea, a holy land, rich in the memories of the great and good; the martyrs of liberty, the exiled heralds of truth; and richer as the parent of this land of promise in the west.

I am not,—I need not say I am not,—the panegyrist of England. I am not dazzled by her riches, nor awed by her power. The sceptre, the mitre, and the coronet, stars, garters, and blue ribbons seem to me poor things for great men to contend for. Nor is my admiration awakened by her armies, mustered for the battles of Europe; her navies, overshadowing the ocean; nor her empire grasping the farthest east. It is these, and the price of guilt and blood by which they are maintained, which are the cause why no friend of liberty can salute her with undivided affections. But it is the refuge of free principles, though often persecuted; the school of religious liberty, the more precious for the struggles to which it has been called; the tombs of those who have reflected honor on all who speak the English tongue; it is the birthplace of our fathers, the home of the pilgrims; it is these which I love and venerate in England. I should feel ashamed of an enthusiasm for Italy and Greece, did I not also feel it for a land like this. In an American it would seem to me degenerate and ungrateful, to hang with passion upon the traces of Homer and Virgil, and follow without emotion the nearer and plainer footsteps of Shakspeare and Milton ; and I should think him cold in his love for his native land, who felt no melting in his heart for that other native land, which holds the ashes of his forefathers.

V. But it was not enough that our fathers were of England: the masters of Ireland, and the lords of Hindostan are of England too. But our fathers were Englishmen, aggrieved, persecuted, and banished. It is a principle, amply borne out by the history of the great and powerful nations of the earth, and by that of none more than the country of which we speak, that the best fruits and choicest action of the commendable qualities of the national character, are to be found on the side of the oppressed few, and not of the triumphant many. As in private character, adversity is often requisite to give a proper direction and temper to strong qualities ; so the noblest traits of national character, even under the freest and most independent of hereditary governments, are commonly to be sought in the ranks of a protesting minority, or of a dissenting sect. Never was this truth more clearly illustrated than in the settlement of New England.

Could a common calculation of policy have dictated the terms of that settlement, no doubt our foundations would have been laid beneath the royal smile. Convoys and navies would have been solicited to waft our fathers to the coast; armies, to defend the infant communities; and the flattering patronage of princes and lords, to espouse their interests in the councils of the mother country. Happy, that our fathers enjoyed no such patronage; happy, that they fell into no such protecting hands; happy, that our foundations were silently and deeply cast in quiet insignificance, beneath a charter of banishment, persecution, and contempt; so that when the royal arm was at length outstretched against us, instead of a submissive child, tied down by former graces, it found a youthful giant in the land, born amidst hardships, and nourished on the rocks, indebted for no favors, and owing no duty. From the dark portals of the star chamber, and in the stern text of the acts of uniformity, the pilgrims received a commission, more efficient, than any that ever bore the royal seal. Their banishment to Holland was fortunate; the decline of their little company in the strange land was fortunate; the difficulties which they experienced in getting the royal consent to banish themselves to this wilderness were fortunate; all the tears and heart breakings of that ever memorable parting at Delfthaven, had the happiest influence on the rising destinies of New England. All this purified the ranks of the settlers. These rough touches of fortune brushed off the light, uncertain, selfish spirits. They made it a grave, solemn, self-denying expedition, and required of those who engaged in it, to be so too. They cast a broad shadow of thought and seriousness over the cause, and if this sometimes deepened into melancholy and bitterness, can we find no apology for such a human weakness?

It is sad indeed to reflect on the disasters, which the little band of pilgrims encountered. Sad to see a portion of them, the prey of unrelenting cupidity, treacherously embarked in an unsound, unseaworthy ship, which they are soon obliged to abandon, and crowd themselves into one vessel; one hundred persons, besides the ship's company, in a vessel of one hundred and sixty tons. One is touched at the story of the long, cold, and weary autumnal passage; of the landing on the inhospitable rocks at this dismal season; where they are deserted before long by the ship, which had brought them, and which seemed their only hold upon the world of fellow men, a prey to the elements and to want, and fearfully ignorant of the numbers, the power, and the temper of the savage tribes, that filled the unexplored continent, upon whose verge they had ventured. But all this wrought together for good. These trials of wandering and exile of the ocean, the winter, the wilderness and the savage foe were the final assurance of success.* It was these that put far away from our fathers' cause, all patrician softness, all hereditary claims to preeminence. No effeminate nobility crowded into the dark and austere ranks of the pilgrims. No Carr nor Villiers would lead on the ill provided band of despised Puritans. No well endowed clergy were on the alert, to quit their cathedrals, and set up a pompous hierarchy in the frozen wilderness. No craving governors were anxious to be sent over to our

*See Note Q.

cheerless El Dorados of ice and of snow. No, they could not say they had encouraged, patronised, or helped the pilgrims; their own cares, their own labors, their own councils, their own blood, contrived all, achieved all, bore all, sealed all. They could not afterwards fairly pretend to reap where they had not strewn; and as our fathers reared this broad and solid fabric with pains and watchfulness, unaided, barely tolerated, it did not fall when the favor, which had always been withholden, was changed into wrath; when the arm, which had never supported, was raised to destroy.

Methinks I see it now, that one solitary, adventurous vessel, the Mayflower of a forlorn hope, freighted with the prospects of a future state, and bound across the unknown sea. I behold it pursuing, with a thousand misgivings, the uncertain, the tedious voyage. Suns rise and set, and weeks and months pass, and winter surprises them on the deep, but brings them not the sight of the wished for shore. I see them now scantily supplied with provisions, crowded almost to suffocation in their illstored prison, delayed by calms, pursuing a circuitous route;—and now driven in fury before the raging tempest, on the high and giddy waves. The awful voice of the storm howls through the rigging. The laboring masts seem straining from their base;—the dismal sound of the pumps is heard;—the ship leaps, as it were, madly, from billow to billow;—the ocean breaks, and settles with engulphing floods over the floating deck, and beats with deadening, shivering weight, against the staggered vessel.—I see them, escaped from these perils, pursuing their all but desperate undertaking, and landed at last, after a five months passage, on the ice clad rocks of Plymouth,—weak and weary from the voyage,—poorly armed, scantily provisioned, depending on the charity of their ship-master for a draught of beer on board, drinking nothing but water on shore,—without shelter,—without means,—surrounded by hostile tribes. Shut now the volume of history, and tell me, on any principle of human probability, what shall be the fate of this handful of adventurers. —Tell me, man of military science, in how many months were they all swept off by the thirty savage tribes, enumerated within the early limits of New England? Tell me, politician, how long did this shadow of a colony, on which your conventions and treaties had not smiled, languish on the distant coast? Student of history, compare for me the baffled projects, the deserted settlements, the abandoned adventures of other times, and find the parallel of this. Was it the winter's storm, beating upon the houseless heads of women and children; was it hard labor and spare meals;—was it disease,—was it the tomahawk,—was it the deep malady of a blighted hope, a ruined enterprise, and a broken heart, aching in its last moments, at the recollection of the loved and left, beyond the sea; was it some, or all of these united, that hurried this forsaken company to their melancholy fate? —And is it possible that neither of these causes, that not all combined, were able to blast this bud of hope?—Is it possible, that from a beginning so feeble, so frail, so worthy, not so much of admiration as of pity, there has gone forth a progress so steady, a growth so wonderful, an expansion so ample, a reality so important, a promise, yet to be fulfilled, so glorious?

Such, in a very inadequate statement, are some of the circumstances under which the settlement of our country began. The historian of Massachusetts, after having given a brief notice of Carver, of Bradford, of Winslow, of Brewster, of Standish, and others, adds, "These were the founders of the colony of Plymouth. The settlement of this colony occasioned the settlement of Massachusetts Bay; which was the source of all the other colonies of New England. Virginia was in a dying state, and seemed to revive and flourish from the example of New England. I am not preserving from oblivion," continues he, "the names of heroes whose chief merit is the overthrow of cities, of provinces, and empires; but the names of the founders of a flourishing town and colony, if not of the whole British empire in America."* This was the judicious reflection of Hutchinson sixty years ago, when the greatest tribute to be paid to the Fathers of Plymouth was, that they took the lead in colonizing the British possessions in America. What then ought to be our emotions, as we meet on this anniversary, upon the spot, where the first successful foundations of the great American republic were laid?

* Hutchinson's History of Massachusetts Bay, Vol. II. Appendix. page 463.

Within a short period, an incident has occurred, which of itself connects, in the most gratifying association, the early settlement of New England with the present growth and prosperity of our wide extended republic. Within the past year, the sovereign hand of this great confederacy of nations has been extended for the restoration and security of the harbor, where, on the day we celebrate, the germ of the future growth of America was comprehended within one weather beaten vessel, tossing upon the tide, on board of which, in the words of Hutchinson, the fathers of New England, by a solemn instrument, "formed themselves into a proper democracy." Two centuries only have elapsed, and we behold a great American representation convened, from twenty four independent and flourishing republics, taking under their patronage the local interests of the spot where our fathers landed, and providing in the same act of appropriation, for the removal of obstacles in the Mississippi and the repair of Plymouth beach. I know not in what words a more beautiful commentary could be written, on our early infancy or our happy growth. There were members of the national Congress which made that appropriation, I will not say from distant states, but from different climates; from regions which the sun in the heavens does not reach in the same hour that he rises on us. Happy community of protection! Glorious expansion of brotherhood! Blessed fulfilment of that first timorous hope, that warmed the bosoms of our fathers!

Nor is it even our mighty territory, to which the influence of the principles and example of the fathers of New England is confined. While I utter the words, a constitution of republican government, closely imitated from ours, is going into operation in the states of the Mexican confederation, a region more extensive than all our territories east of the Mississippi.* Farther south, the provinces of central America, the republic of Guatimala, a country equal in magnitude to our Atlantic states, has sent its envoys to solicit an union with us. Will posterity believe that such an offer was made and refused, in the age that saw England and Spain rushing into war, for the possession of a few uninhabited islets on the coast of Patagonia? Pass the isthmus of Darien, and we behold the sister repub-

* See Note R.

lic of Colombia, a realm two thirds as large as Europe, ratifying her first solemn treaty of amity and commerce with the United States; while still onward to the south, in the valleys of the Chilian Andes, and on the banks of the La Plata, in states not less vast than those already named, constitutions of republican government are in prosperous operation, founded on our principles, and modelled on our forms. When our commissioners visited those countries in 1817, they found the books most universally read among the people, were the constitutions of the United States, and of the several states, translated into the language of the country; while the public journals were filled with extracts from the celebrated "Defence" of these constitutions, written by that venerable descendant of the Pilgrims, who still lives to witness the prosperous operation of the governments, which he did so much to establish.*

I do not fear that we shall be accused of extravagance in the enthusiasm we feel at a train of events of such astonishing magnitude, novelty, and consequence, connected by associations

* See Note S.

so intimate, with the day we now hail; with the events we now celebrate; with the pilgrim fathers of New England. Victims of persecution! how wide an empire acknowledges the sway of your principles! Apostles of liberty! what millions attest the authenticity of your mission! Meek champions of truth, no stain of private interest or of innocent blood is on the spotless garments of your renown! The great continents of America have become, at length, the theatre of your achievements; the Atlantic and the Pacific, the highways of communication, on which your principles, your institutions, your example are borne. From the oldest abodes of civilization, the venerable plains of Greece, to the scarcely explored range of the Cordilleras, the impulse you gave at length is felt. While other regions revere you as the leaders of this great march of humanity, we are met on this joyful day, to offer to your memories our tribute of filial affection. The sons and daughters of the Pilgrims, we have assembled on the spot where you, our suffering fathers, set foot on this happy shore. Happy indeed, it has been for us. O that you could have enjoyed those blessings, which you prepared for your children. Could our comfortable homes have shielded you from the wintry air; could our abundant harvests have supplied you in time of famine; could the broad shield of our beloved country have sheltered you from the visitations of arbitrary power! We come in our prosperity to remember your trials; and here on the spot where New England began to be, we come to learn of our pilgrim fathers a deep and lasting lesson of virtue, enterprise, patience, zeal, and faith!

NOTES.

Note A. Page 13.

The object of this Discourse is of course more immediately confined to New England, as the part of the country most directly affected by the settlement of Plymouth. Some of the topics, however, apply equally to all parts of America; others to all the English Colonies on this Continent. It was not thought necessary to interrupt the train of remark, in each single case, to modify it in reference to this qualification. New England alone is generally mentioned, and the more or less extensive application of each separate topic of observation is left to be made by the intelligent.

Note B. Page 14.

It is stated by Peter Martyr, the *first writer* on the discovery of America, that two of the vessels of Columbus were without decks. "Ex regio fisco destinata sunt tria Navigia; unum onerarium caveatum, alia duo levia mercatoria *sine caveis*, quæ ab Hispanis caravelæ vocantur." *(De rebus Oceancis*, p. 2.) Peter Martyr,* who had lived and served long, as soldier and ambassador, in Spain, cannot be supposed to have been ignorant of the sense, in which the word *Caravel* was used by the Spaniards. At the same time, it must be allowed to be a circumstance almost incredible, that an expedition, like that of Columbus, should be fitted out, with two out of three vessels unprovided with decks. In Bossi's *Vita di Cristofero Colombo*, published at Milan in 1818, is an able annotation on the subject of the Caravels. It is there asserted, on the credit of an Italian Marine Dictionary, (published at Milan in 1813, in three vols. 4to. and bearing a high character,) that the word "Caravella is known in the Mediterranean, as indicating the larger Turkish ships of war, with a high poop; but that in Portugal it denotes a vessel of from 120 to 140 tons." Du Cange in his Glossary expresses the opinion, that it is a word of Italian origin, an opinion, which de Bossi condemns, regarding it rather as Turkish or Arabic, and probably introduced into the

---

* He must be carefully distinguished from Peter Martyr, the Reformer, who taught for some time in England, and who flourished near a half century after the historian. The name of Peter Martyr is in either case the Christian name only, and to avoid the confusion, it might be expedient to use their family names. That of the reformer was Vermigli, that of the historian d'Anghiera. An account of the former is given in Tiraboschi, VII. 327; of the latter, in the same author, VIII. 366.

European languages by the Moors. These authors, however, are apparently both in an error. The true origin of the term is, no doubt, given in Ferrarii origines linguæ Italicæ, as follows; " *Caravela* navigii minoris genus: *Carabus; Græce* Καράβιον." The primitive meaning of the Latin *Carabus* and the Greek Καράβιον is *Crab*, a word, in fact, derived from them. In either language, the word was used to signify a *vessel* or a *boat*. The word Καράβιον has descended to the modern Greeks, who use Καράβι for a *vessel*, in general; and Isidore, a late Latin writer, in his *Origines*, lib. xix. c. 1, defines a *Carabus* to be a " small skiff made of osiers, which, covered with raw leather, forms a sort of boat." There seems, therefore, much reason to respect the authority of the historian first quoted, who describes the Caravel of the Spaniards as a light open vessel. This minuteness of criticism will, I hope, be pardoned on a subject so closely connected with the discovery of America.

Having in the beginning of this note called Peter Martyr d'Anghiera the first writer, who commemorates Columbus, (and so he is generally reputed,) it should be observed, that he is entitled to this credit of precedence, by a very slight priority. The dedication of his Decades bears date Prid. Calend. October, or September 30, 1516. In November of the same year, was published a Polyglott Psalter, at Genoa, containing the Psalms in Hebrew, Greek, Arabic, and Chaldee, in which, in the form of a note on Psalm xix. 5. *Their line is gone out through all the earth, and their words to the end of the world*, is given an account of Columbus and his discoveries, filling seven octavo pages, as copied in a work of de Murr. This is doubtless the first account of Columbus, for P. Martyr d'Anghiera introduces him simply as " Ligur vir." The editor of this Psalter and author of the note in question, was Guistiniani, a bishop, and as he speaks of Columbus as a native of Genoa, at a period so early, and mentions the bequest made by Columbus of the tenth part of his estates to the city of Genoa, his authority is of great weight in settling the contested points of the place of the birth of Columbus, and the authenticity of his will. Since the appearance, however, of the important and curious work entitled Codice diplomatico Colombo-Americano ossia raccolta di documenti originali e inediti, spettanti a Christofero Colombo, alla scoperta e allo governo dell' America, Genoa, 1823, these questions may be considered as put at rest.

This last very curious work, which has not yet attracted a due degree of notice from the public, though containing more *official* details relative to Columbus than all the other works hitherto published relative to America, was printed by order of the magistrates of Genoa. An account of the English translation of it may be found in the North American Review for April last, page 415. Two manuscripts, copies of the grants, patents, &c. of the Spanish government to Columbus (from one of which the work is now at length printed) were made by order of Columbus himself, and sent to his friend Oderigo, in Genoa. In 1670, the descendant of Oderigo presented the two manuscripts to the magistracy at Genoa. During the French Revolution one of the manuscripts was taken to Paris, and has not yet been restored to Genoa. The other was supposed to be lost, till on the death of Count Micheloni Cambiasi, a Senator of Genoa, it was advertised for sale among his books, but immediately claimed as public property. It has since been deposited in a monument erected for the purpose, and from it the work in question is printed.

Whether the two manuscripts thus mentioned be the only ones in existence may admit of doubt. When I was in Florence in 1818, a small folio manuscript was brought to me, written on parchment, apparently two or three centuries old, in binding once very rich, but now worn, containing a series of documents in Latin and Spanish, mostly the latter, with the following title on the first blank page, "Treslado de las Bullas del Papa Alexandro VI, de la Concession de las Indias y los titulos, privilegios, y cedulas reales, que se dieron a Christoval Colon."—I was led by this title to purchase the work; but, deterred by the abundant use of abbreviations and a limited acquaintance with the language, I made no attempt for several years to read it. My attention having been turned again to it, by the publication of the work at Genoa, and having had an opportunity, by the kindness of a friend, of seeing a copy of it, the only one perhaps in this part of the country, I was surprised to find my manuscript, as far as it goes, *nearly* identical in its contents with that of Genoa, supposed to be one of the only two in existence. My manuscript consists of about *eighty* closely written folio pages, which coincide precisely with the text of the first *thirty seven* documents, contained in two hundred and forty pages of the Genoese volume. A few more documents, wanting in my manuscript, are found in the Genoese work; and a second Bull of Alexander VI, in Latin, is contained in the former, and is wanting in the latter.

In the last of the documents, contained in the Genoese volume, and wanting in my manuscript, we read as follows;

"Los originales destos privillegios y cartas y cedulas y otras muchas cartas de sus Altezas e otras escripturas, tocantes al Señor Almirante, estan en el monasterio de Sancta Maria de las Cuevas de Sevilla.

"Otrosy esta, en el dicho Monasterio un libro traslado de los privilegios e cartas susodichos, semejante que esto.

"Otro traslado levo este año de M. D. II. y tiene Alonso Sanchez de Carvajal a las Yndias, escripto en papel e abtorizado.

"Otro traslado en pergamino tal como este."

Mention is here accordingly made of four copies of these documents, three on parchment and one on paper. Two of them were sent by Columbus himself to Genoa. Whether that procured by me at Florence be a third; whether it be that supposed to be at Paris; or, what is more probable perhaps, another copy, there are at present no means of deciding. I hope to have in my power, on some other occasion, to describe it more accurately, particularly in those respects, in which it differs from the Genoese volume.

Note C. Page 15.

It is probable that the great extent, to which the business of fishing on the banks of Newfoundland and the New England coasts was early carried, was one chief cause of the familiarity of men with the idea of the passage across the Atlantic, and consequently of the readiness of our forefathers to undertake it. It appears, that as early as 1578, there were employed in this fishery, of Spaniards 100 sail, besides 20 or 30 in the whale fishery on the same coasts; of Portuguese 50; of French 150; of English from 30 to 50. (*Hakluyt*, Vol. III. p. 132, cited in the *North American Review* for July, 1824, p. 140.) Captain Smith remarks, that according to "Whitbourne's discovery of Newfoundland," the banks and coasts in that region were visited by 250 sail of English fishermen annually. (Vol. II. p. 246, Richmond Edition.) So important was this work of Whitbourne esteemed for the encouragement of the British fisheries that, by an order in Council, dated 12th of April, 1622, it was ordered to be distributed to every parish in the kingdom. (Ancient Right of the English Nation to the American Fisheries, &c. London, 1764.) The last cited valuable treatise contains (page 50) an important statement of the amount of the French fishery in 1745, "made in that year, at the desire of the Governor of the Massachusetts province, by Mr Thomas Kilby." By this account, it appears that "564 ships in all, and 27,500 men were yearly employed from France on the banks of Newfoundland." The extent of the British fisheries, in this quarter, on an average of three years ending 1773, may be seen in Lord Sheffield's Observations on the Commerce of the American States, 6th Ed. p. 64. From one of the documents in the work entitled, "The Fisheries and the Mississippi," by the present Secretary of State, it appears that before 1810, there were annually employed from the United States 1232 vessels in the Bank, Bay, and Labrador fisheries, navigated by 10,459 men.—See also *Seybert's Statistics*, p. 333.

Note D. Page 29.

"From the commencement of the *religious war* in Germany to the peace of Westphalia, scarce any thing great or memorable occurred in the European political world, with which the reformation was not essentially connected. Every event in the history of the world in this interval, if not directly occasioned, was nearly influenced by this religious revolution, and every state, great or small, remotely or directly experienced its influence." *Schiller's* Geschichte des dreissigjährigen Krieges. I. 1.

Note E. Page 29.

The close connexion of the religious and political system of Rome is sufficiently shown by the authority of Cicero.—He begins the Oration pro domo sua, in these words, cum multa divinitus, Pontifices, a majoribus nostris inventa atque instituta sunt; tum nihil præclarius quam quod eosdem et religionibus deorum immortalium et summæ Reipublicæ præesse voluerunt; ut amplissimi et clarissimi cives rempublicam bene gerendo religiones sapienter interpretando conservarent. Whence is it that a principle should be commended by so wise a statesman as Cicero, and in point of experience have been found so salutary in Rome, which has been uniformly productive of evil in modern states and condemned by the soundest politicians?—The cause of the apparent anomaly is no doubt to be found in the organization of the church as a separate institution, having its own principles of growth and decline; and the organization of the clergy as a body having its own interest.—Such a body, when entrusted with power in the state, will be apt to exercise it under the influence of the esprit du corps for its own advancement. In Rome, the public religion rested upon no other sanction than any other part of the public system and the ministers of religion, not belonging to a separate consecrated body, were not liable to be influenced by any other than reasons of state in the administration of their religious functions. Although such a state of things might seem unfriendly to religious influence, it produced not that effect on the Romans, who may be characterized, during the Republic, as a religious people.—

A list of the Pontifices Maximi may be found at the close of the learned treatise of Bosii *de pontifice maximo Romæ veteris.* It contains the most familiar names in the civil history of Rome. After the fall of the Republic, the Emperors regularly assumed the title of Pontifex Maximus, as is shown in another treatise of the same author, *Bosii de Pontificatu maximo imperii Romani exercitatio.* What is somewhat singular is, that this title of *High Priest*, originating in the ancient Roman paganism, should have been retained by the Christian emperors down to Gratian. It was afterwards adopted by the Popes, a circumstance which appears to have escaped Middleton in his letter from Rome.

The oft quoted exclamation of Dante, shows at how early a period the principle of the reformation had suggested itself to the independent thinkers.

Ahi, Costantin, di quanto mal fu madre,
Non la tua conversion, ma quella dote,
Che da te prese il primo ricco padre.

Note F. Page 30.

The treatment which Pope Boniface VIII received from Philip the fair in the fourteenth century, was as much more audacious than any thing in the recent history of the Papal see, as the power of Boniface was greater than that of Pius VII. Philip not only returned the most contemptuous answers to the Pope's letters, but sent William de Nogaret, (justly called by Mosheim, the most intrepid and inveterate enemy of the Pope before Luther) into Italy to excite a sedition, to seize the person of Boniface and bring him in chains to Lyons. This he so far effected as to get possession of the Pope, whom he loaded with indignities, and even struck on the head with an iron gauntlet. Though rescued by the citizens of Anagni, from the hands of de Nogaret, he died soon after "of the rage and anguish into which these insults threw him." It is useful to recal these traits of history, to enable us to judge more impartially of contemporary events.

Note G. Page 30.

The progress of religious reform, to which I have alluded, concerns only the connexion of church and state. As this connexion was more intimate in the Catholic church, than in any other, that church was so far the most corrupt. And as this connexion was unquestionably as prejudicial to the church, as to the state, the catholics have really as much reason to rejoice in the reformation as the protestants. There can be but little doubt, in the mind of any one who reads the history of the middle ages, that the interests of no communion of Christians have been more advanced by the reformation, than of that which regards the Pope as its head.

In like manner, in speaking of the reform carried on in England by the dissenters and puritans, no other reference is had than to the political question of the union of church and state. This union, as existing in England, I consider a great political abuse. As to the doctrinal points agitated between the catholics and protestants; the church of England and dissenters; however important they may have been at different times thought, so long as they rested within the limits of speculative theology, their settlement, one way or the other, could have had but little effect on the condition of states.

Note H. Page 31.

Bishop Burnet has discriminated the Presbyterians and Independents, in the following manner. "The main difference between these was, that the Presbyterians seemed reconcilable to the church; for they loved episcopal ordination and a liturgy, and upon some amendments seemed disposed to come into the church; and they liked the civil government and limited monarchy. But as the independents were for a commonwealth in the state, so they put all the power in the church in the people, and thought that their choice was an ordination: nor did they approve of set forms of worship." *History of his own Times*, II. 406.

This character, it must be remembered, was given of the Indepen dents, after the times of the commonwealth in England. At the period of the first emigrations to New England, there is no reason for accusing the independents of disaffection to the civil government.

In 1619, Mr. Robinson published, at Leyden, " Apologia pro exulibus Anglis qui Brownistæ vulgo appellantur." Mosheim conjectures that the name of *Independents* may have grown out of a word in the following sentence, in which the leading principle of their religious peculiarities is expressed, " Cœtum quemlibet particularem esse totam, integram, et perfectam ecclesiam ex suis partibus constantem, immediate et *independenter* (quoad alias ecclesias) sub ipso Christo." *Apologia, Cap.* V. *p.* 22. Cited in *Mosheim*, V. 388.

Note I. Page 34.

A considerable, and the most elaborate part of Burke's Reflections on the Revolution in France, is occupied in refuting the assertion of Dr Price, that by the Revolution in 1688, the English people acquired " the right to choose their own governors, to cashier them for misconduct, and to frame a government for themselves." It is certainly too much to say, in unlimited terms, that the English Constitution, as fixed at the Revolution, gives a right of choosing or removing the king. On the other hand, it is equally certain that both at, after, and before the Revolution, Parliament claimed and exercised the right of choosing and deposing the king and limiting the succession. Burke expresses himself thus : " So far is it from being true that we acquired a right, by the Revolution, to elect our kings, that if we had possessed it before, the English nation did, at that time, most solemnly renounce and abdicate it for themselves, and for all their posterity forever. These gentlemen [Dr Price and his party] may value themselves as much as they please on their whig principles ; but I never desire to be thought a better whig than Lord Somers," &c.

Lord Somers is thus particularly appealed to by Mr Burke, in support of his construction of the Constitution, because the declaration of right was drawn by him. But it is somewhat remarkable that Burke should have insisted so much on this authority, for Lord Somers printed a work in 1710, of which the title sufficiently shows the object :—" A brief history of the succession of the Crown of England ; wherein facts collected from the best authorities are opposed to the novel assertors of indefeasible hereditary right." After having in this work, gone through with a masterly deduction of the history of the English crown from the establishment of it, Lord Somers sums up, as follows : " I shall leave every man to make his own observations on this historical deduction. But this one observation I believe all men must make from it ; that it hath been the constant opinion of all ages, that the Parliament of England had an unquestionable power to limit, restrain, and qualify the succession as they pleased, and that in all ages they have put their power in practice ; and that the historian* had reason for saying, that seldom or never the third heir in a right descent enjoyed the crown of England !"

Note K. Page 38.

The settlements made by civilized Europeans on the coasts of America and of other countries occupied by savages, have evidently proceeded on the assumption of peculiar principles of national or rather social law.

* 'Daniel, fol. 5. in vita H. I.'

Not only the arbitrary kings of Spain and Portugal, but the constitutional king of England, claimed a right of occupying, possessing, and granting to individuals or companies, all newly discovered heathen lands; nor was it admitted that the natives had any right to the soil, in the same sense that citizens of one country acknowledge each other's rights, and the governments of friendly nations the rights of each other's subjects. There does not seem to be any principle of natural law, by which savage tribes can claim *full right* to the whole of the widest region, which they wander over in the chase, and to the perpetual exclusion of civilized settlers. If then savage nations have not a full right, what right have they; and to how much territory have they any right? These are questions not yet well settled.—What is the ground and extent of the obligation, which a civilized community is under, by inalienable reservations of land and by liberal appropriations of money, to introduce the arts of civilized life among border tribes of a different race and language, with whom no intermixture of blood can take place without degeneracy?—As modes of diffusing civilization most widely, is the choice well established between the increase of a civilized population and civilizing a barbarous one? These questions present themselves in their most delicate form, in the present controversy in the state of Georgia, and it may be doubted whether they are fully solved on the general notions of humanity usually applied to them, however strong and natural the prepossession felt at a distance in favor of a weaker party.

Note L. Page 40.

As it is now generally admitted that a *temperate climate* is essential to the attainment of the highest degrees of civilization, (*Heeren's Ideen Th. V. Allgemeine Vorerinnerungen*,) there is more reason than ever to depart from the ancient phraseology of *Zones*, in the use of which we almost unconsciously connect the idea of certain degrees of heat or cold with certain parallels of latitude. The remarks in the text, relative to tropical regions, must of course be confined to tropical climates. Our own continents present the most striking instances of the change of climate; and of natural productions, state of civilization, and social character, as affected by climate; in travelling, on the same parallel, from the coasts to the summits of the mountains.

The Atlas of Humboldt contains a curious comparative view of the different altitude of the limit of perpetual congelation in different latitudes. And his *Essay on Isothermal lines*, as well as various parts of his large works, furnish the most instructive illustrations of the same subject. See particularly his *Relation Historique*, Tom. II p. 350.

Note M. Page 41.

"I doubt if there be another plant upon the face of the earth, which, on a small space of soil, produces a quantity of nutritious substance so considerable as the banana. Eight or nine months after the sucker is planted, the banana tree begins to develope its cluster, and the fruit may be gathered the tenth or eleventh month. When the stalk is cut, there is constantly found among the numerous shoots, which have sprung from the roots, a sprout (*pimpollo*) which with two thirds the height of the parent plant, bears fruit three months later. It is thus that a plantation of banana, which is called in the Spanish colonies a *Platanar*, perpetuates itself without any other care than that of cutting the stalks, whose fruit has ripened, and digging the earth slightly about the roots once or twice a year. A spot of ground of one hundred square metres (about one tenth more than so many square yards) in surface, is sufficient to contain at least from thirty to forty banana plants. This spot of ground, reckoning the weight of the cluster only at from about thirty five to forty five pounds, would yield nearly four thousand five hundred weight of food. What a difference between this product and that of the cereal gramina, in the most fertile parts of Europe. Wheat, supposing it sown and not planted, in the Chinese way, and calculating on the basis of a tenfold increase, does not produce, on a hundred square metres, more than about thirty three pounds weight of grain. In France the legal acre of 54,995 square feet, is sown broadcast in very good land, with about 160 pounds of grain, on medium and poor land with from 200 to 220 pounds ; and the produce varies from 1000 to 2500 pounds the acre. The potato, according to M. Tessier yields in Europe, on one hundred square metres of land well manured, about one hundred pounds of the root; or from four to six thousand pounds on the acre of France. The product of the banana is consequently to that of wheat as 133 to 1 ; and to that of potatoes as 44 to 1."

"In an eminently fertile country, a legal French acre cultivated with banana of the larger kind (*Platano Arton*) would feed more than fifty persons for a year; while in Europe the same acre, on the principle of an eight fold increase, would yield but about twelve hundred pounds of wheat, a quantity not equal to the support for a year of two persons."—*Humboldt Essai Politique sur le Royaume de la Nouvelle Espagne.* Tom. III. 28, 35.

Note N. Page 43.

It need not be said, that the remarks, which are made in the text, relative to the colonial establishments of different nations on the American soil, can be intended to convey no disrespectful insinuation toward the free states now rising upon those colonial foundations.—The very magnitude of the abuses of the ancient system is among the causes of the convulsive efforts, which have been made, in our days, against those abuses; and the Patriots, who, under infinite discouragements, have effected thus far the political regeneration of those vast regions, are entitled to the greater praise for the difficulties incident to their enterprise. But that they are under no obligation to principles and examples derived from the mother country ; that the institutions established in the Spanish and Portuguese colonies, instead of serving as a school of freedom—like the colonial institutions in the North American colonies—were of a nature to retard the growth of independence, cannot be doubted.—Even in establishing a form of free government, the leaders of the revolution in Colombia, have been obliged to express their regret that the state of the country and of its population did not allow them to prefer the *Federative* System of the United States to the less perfect *Central* System, which they have adopted.—See the opinions of Bolivar and M. de Salazar as quoted in the North American Review for Jan. 1825. p. 79.

Note O. Page 44.

Few questions in Geography have been the subject of more important controversies than the limits of Brazil. It is not a little astonishing to see states like Spain and Portugal, which had respectively by the discovery of America and the passage of the Cape of Good Hope, made the acquisition of new territory larger than Europe, contesting with bitterness a few square leagues of morass on the banks of the Amazon and its tributaries.—The facts, on which the controversies alluded to turned, are principally these. Pope Nicholas V, in 1454, granted to Alfonso King of Portugal, in full sovereignty, all the countries, which he should discover from Cape Non in Africa to India.* About the time of this grant the navigators of Portugal discovered the Cape de Verde Islands, and the Azores. In 1486, the Portuguese navigator Diaz discovered the Cape of Good Hope. In 1492 Columbus discovered America ; and controversies immediately arose between the Courts of Spain and Portugal, relative to the interference of their several discoveries. To settle this controversy the Spanish Court procured of Pope Alexander VI, (himself a Spaniard,) the famous bull bearing date May 1493, in which he gives to the king of Spain, in full sovereignty, " All the islands and continents which are or may be found, (Omnes insulas et terras firmas inventas et inveniendas, detectas et detegendas,) to the south and west of a meridian line drawn one hundred leagues south of the southernmost of the Azores or Cape de Verde Islands.—This is the famous " *line of demarcation;*" for though, (contrary to the popular representation) nothing is said, in this bull, of the right of the Portuguese to all discoveries east of the line, yet the former Papal grant to Portugal, already mentioned, had given to that kingdom the sovereignty over its discoveries in the east. The Portuguese having shortly after acquired Brazil, by the discoveries of Pinzon, who had been of the company of Columbus on his first voyage, it was perceived that it lay to the *westward* of the line of demarcation, and of course was subject to the Spanish claim. By the treaty of Tordesillas, in 1494, these conflicting rights were compromised, and the sovereigns of Spain and Portugal agreed to run the line three hundred and seventy leagues west of that prescribed by the Pope's bull. This memorable line, by which the territory of three fourth parts of the globe was divided, was to be run by skilful geographers, within ten months. Herrera *(Decad.* III. *lib.* VI.) describes, in a manner approaching the ludicrous, the array of maps, charts, globes, and instruments, which the geographers brought to this discussion ; and Humboldt justly remarks in reference to these and other kindred contests, (Relation Historique, Tom. II. p. 441,) that the interests of science alone have been served by them. While the question was keenly agitated between the Portuguese and Spanish geographers, the former striving to run the line as far west and the latter as far east as possible, the discovery and occupation of the Moluccas by the Portuguese, completely inverted the policy of both parties. These valuable islands were perceived to be nearly opposite the Cape de Verdes, on the other side of the globe ; and the farther to the west of the Cape de Verdes the line of demarcation was run, so much more of the Moluccas and other neighboring islands would fall within the Spanish hemisphere. The Portuguese geographers *now* contended that the line of demarcation should be counted 370 leagues from a line running through the isle of *Salis*, the easternmost of the Cape de Verdes, while the Spaniards counted the 370 leagues from a line running through St Antonio, which was ninety leagues more to the west, and was the most western of the group ;—each party being anxious to lose in Brazil, that it might gain in the Spice islands.—The controversy was protracted for many years, till in 1580, it was, for a time, settled by the union of the two crowns of Spain and Portugal. (De Laet, Novus Orbis, p. 541.)

---

* See the original document in the great Corps Diplomatique. Tom. III. p. 200.

After their separation in 1640, the contest was revived. But the Spice islands having been wrested from the Portuguese by the Dutch, the controversy between the Portuguese and the Spaniards was now reduced to the limits of Brazil. The parties accordingly again changed sides; the Portuguese geographers, at the conferences held at Puente de Caya in 1682, maintained that the 370 leagues must be counted from the most western point of St Antonio, while the Spaniards insisted on the centre of the isle St Nicholas. Two or three commissions, at great expense, were sent out, in the course of the last century, to settle the possession of the uninhabited swamps on the banks of the Tuamini;—the region which was constituted debateable ground by the uncertainty of the point, through which the meridian line should be run.—(*Humboldt Relation Historique*, Tom. II. p. 442.)

In the first volume of M. Martens' supplement to the *Recueil des Traites*, p. 372, the treaty of Tordesillas is contained, and in no previous collection of treaties. The limit of the Oyapok, Oyapoco, or Iapoc, was finally settled by the 107th Article of the Act of the Congress of Vienna; and by a separate convention therein provided for, between Portugal and France.

Note P. Page 45.

A more than ordinary identity of interest and character was effected between Portugal and Brazil; and this vast region was even called by the name of Portugal. "On the banks of the Rio Negro," says Humboldt, in the chapter cited in the last note, "the neighboring country beyond the Amazon is called, in the language of the Spanish Missions, neither Brazil nor the *Capitania general* of Grand Pará, but *Portugal*. The copper colored Indians and the Mulattos, which I have seen ascending from Barcelos to the Spanish fort San Carlos, are *Portuguese*. This denomination prevails among the people even to the coasts of Cumana. A favorite anecdote relates, how the imagination of one of the commandants in the expedition of Solano to settle the limits, in 1754, was struck, by hearing the inhabitants of these regions called *Portuguese*. The old soldier, as ignorant as brave, was provoked at having been sent to the banks of the Orenoque by sea: "If" said he, "as I hear, this vast province of Spanish Guyana reaches all the way to Portugal, (a los Portugeses,) why did the king make us sail from Cadiz. I should have preferred travelling a little farther by land."—"These expressions of *näive* ignorance," adds Humboldt, "remind one of a strange opinion of Lorenzana the distinguished archbishop of Mexico. This prelate, a person of great historical research, observes in his edition of the letters of Cortes, published so late as 1770, that the possessions of the king of Spain in New California and New Mexico, border by land on *Siberia!*"

These anecdotes alone may serve as an index to the colonial systems of Spain and Portugal, whose archbishops and commissioners for settling limits supposed, in the middle of the last century, that Brazil was bounded by Portugal and New Mexico by Siberia.

Note Q. Page 52.

The sentiment in the text is very strongly illustrated by the statements contained in Pringle's account of the present state of "the English settlers at the Cape of Good Hope." From that work, it appears that ninety thousand persons besieged Earl Bathurst's office, with applications to embark in the government expedition, to found the colony in question. The calamitous consequences are detailed in the work alluded to.

Note R. Page 58.

The constitution of the Mexican confederacy was adopted by the general constituent Congress Oct. 4. 1824, and may be found translated in the National Journal for Dec. 10 and 11th.

The Mexican confederacy consists of the following states and territories; the states of Chiapas, Chihuahua, Coahuila y Tejas, Durango, Guanajuato, Mexico, Michoacan, Nuevo Leon, Oajaca, Puebla de los Angeles, Queretaro, San Luis Potosi, Sonara y Sinaloa, Tabasco, Tamaulipas (?) Vera Cruz, Ialisco, Yucatan, and Zacatecas; the territories of upper and lower California, Colima, and Santa Fe of New Mexico. The character of Tlaxcala is to be fixed by a constitutional law.

It will be observed that the division into states and territories does not precisely correspond with the old division into intendencies.

Note S. Page 59.

"The following are a few of the subjects of the political essays of the Censor (a periodical paper published at Buenos Ayres) in 1817: an explanation of the Constitution of the United States, and highly praised—The Lancastrian System of Education—on the causes of the prosperity of the United States—Milton's essay on the liberty of the press—A review of the work of the late President Adams, on the American Constitution, and a recommendation of checks and balances, continued through several numbers and abounding with much useful information for the people—brief notice of the life of James Monroe, president of the United States—examination of the federative system—on the trial by Jury—on popular elections—on the effect of enlightened productions on the condition of mankind—an analysis of the several state constitutions of the Union, &c.

"There are in circulation, Spanish translations of many of our best revolutionary writings. The most common are two miscellaneous volumes, one, containing Paine's common sense and rights of man, and declaration of Independence, several of our constitutions, and General Washington's farewell address. The other is an abridged history of the United States down to the year 1810, with a good explanation of the nature of our political institutions, accompanied with a translation of Mr Jefferson's inaugural speech, and other state papers. I believe these have been read by nearly all who can read, and have produced a most extravagant admiration of the United States, at the same time, accompanied with something like despair."—Breckenridge's South America, Vol. II. pp. 213, 214.

REMARKS

AT THE

PLYMOUTH FESTIVAL,

ON

THE FIRST OF AUGUST, 1853,

IN COMMEMORATION OF

THE EMBARKATION OF THE PILGRIMS.

BY

EDWARD EVERETT.

BOSTON:
CROSBY, NICHOLS, AND COMPANY,
111 WASHINGTON STREET.
1853.

CAMBRIDGE:
METCALF AND COMPANY, PRINTERS TO THE UNIVERSITY.

REMARKS.

You have been good enough, Mr. President, to intimate that, among our numerous honored guests, (to whom your complimentary remarks, with possibly a single exception, might have applied with as much justice as to myself,) I am the individual to whom you look, to respond to the toast that has just been announced. I rise to obey the call. It is true that there is a single circumstance for which it is possible that the allusion may be more exclusively applicable to me than to any other gentleman present. It is most true, that, on one pleasant occasion on which I have been at this delightful and beloved Plymouth, I suggested that it might be expedient, not always, but occasionally, to transfer the celebration of the great day from the winter to the summer season. Supposing that to be the allusion which you had in your mind, I feel that I may without impropriety obey your call by rising to respond to the toast that has just been given.

It is now hard upon thirty years since I had the honor, on the 22d of December, to address the sons and daughters of the Pilgrims, assembled at this place. I deemed it a peculiar privilege and honor. I deem it, sir, a still greater privilege to find myself here on this joyous occasion, and to be permitted to participate in this happy festival, where we have an attendance of so many distinguished friends and fellow-citizens from distant parts of the country, — from almost every State in the Union, sir, you have already told us ; where we are favored with the company of the representatives of the New England Society of New York, one of those institutions which are carrying the name and principles of the Pilgrims to the farthest ends of the land; where we are gratified with the presence of our military friends from the same city, the great commercial emporium of the United States; where we are honored by so much of the gravity, the dignity, and the character of the community, and are favored with the presence of so much of its beauty, grace, and loveliness.

I do indeed, sir, feel it to be a privilege to be here under these circumstances, and I deem myself most highly honored in being called upon to respond to the toast which you have just announced, in commemoration of the embarkation of the Pilgrims, and its results. The theme is vast; I shrink from it; I know not where to begin, or where to end. It seems to me, sir, that you yourself, in the remarks with which you have favored the company, struck the key-note of this great theme, in alluding to the state of this vast continent before the Pilgrims came, and to the situation of its primitive inhabitants. There is the beginning. I could not but feel it, as I saw one or two of them, poor wanderers, as we came into Plymouth, seated by the road-side, wondering spectators of the pageant which was passing before their eyes.

A few days ago, as I saw in the newspapers, two light birch-bark canoes appeared in Boston Harbor, containing each a solitary Indian. They seemed, as they approached, to gaze in silent wonder at the city of the triple hills, rising street above street, and crowned with the dome of the State-House, and at the long line of villas stretching far into the background; — at the numerous small vessels outward bound, as they dropped down the channel and spread their broad wings to the breeze, and those which were returning weather-beaten from the ends of the earth; — at the steamers, dashing in every direction across the harbor, breathing volumes of smoke from their fiery lungs. They paddled their frail barks with dexterity and speed through this strange, busy, and to them, no doubt, bewildering scene; and having made the circuit of East Boston, the Navy Yard, the city itself, and South Boston, dropped down with the current, and disappeared among the Islands.

There was not a human being of kindred blood to utter a word of welcome to them, in all the region which on the day we now commemorate was occupied by their forefathers in Massachusetts. The race is gone. It would be a mistaken sentimentality to regret the change; to regret that some thousand uncultured barbarians, destitute of all the improvements of social life, as we understand it, and seemingly incapable of adopting them, should have yielded gradually to the civilized millions who have taken their place. But we must, both as men and as Christians, condemn whatever of oppression and wrong has marked the change, (as is too apt always to be the case when strong and weak are brought into contact with each other,) and without affectation we may indulge a heartfelt sympathy for the feeble and stricken relics of once powerful and formidable tribes of fellow-men.

On the 1st of August, 1620, the circumstances of the two races, as far as this part of America is concerned, presented very nearly the reverse of the picture we have just contemplated. On that day, the territory now forming the States of New England was occupied by numerous Indian tribes, some of which were strong and warlike. They were far behind the natives of Mexico and Peru, but they had added some simple agriculture to their hunting and fishing,—their moccasons, and snow-shoes, and stone hatchets, and arrow-heads, and wampum-belts, evinced their aptitude for the humble arts of savage life; they retained unimpaired their native independence, ignorant of the metaphysical claims to sovereignty which powerful governments three thousand miles off founded upon the right of discovery; and neither the arts, nor the arms, nor the diseases, nor the vices of civilized life, had commenced that terrible warfare against them, which has since been pushed nearly to their extermination.

On that day, and in this condition of the American races, a handful of careworn, twice-doomed English exiles set sail from Delft Haven, in Holland, with the intention, after being joined by a few brethren of the faith in England, to encounter the then much-dreaded perils of the Atlantic, and the still more formidable uncertainties of their projected settlement on the outer edge of the New World. Two centuries and a third have passed, the momentous ages of national infancy, childhood, and youth have been rapidly lived through, and six prosperous republics, parents of a still increasing family of States in the boundless West, have grown up in the wilderness. In the mean time, in this part of the continent, the native inhabitants have sunk far below the point of comparative weakness, down to the verge of annihilation; and we have assembled now and here to celebrate the day on which this all-important change commenced.

I allude, Mr. President, to this revolution in the condition of this continent, and the races occupying it, not as introducing a narrative of familiar incidents or a train of commonplace reflections, but as pointing directly to the great problem which first presented itself on the discovery of America, and the agency of the Pilgrim Fathers in its solution, — an agency whose first public manifestation might be said to commence with the ever-memorable embarkation at Delft Haven, to which I have just referred.

The discovery itself of the American continent may, I think, fairly be considered the most extraordinary event in the history of the world. In this, as in other cases, familiarity blunts the edge of our perceptions; but much as I have meditated, and often as I have treated this theme, its magnitude grows upon me with each successive contemplation. That a continent nearly as large as Europe and Africa united, spread out on both sides of the equator, lying between the western shores of Europe and Africa and the eastern shore of Asia, with groups of islands in either ocean, as it were stopping-places on the march of discovery,—a continent not inhabited indeed by civilized races, but still occupied by one of the families of rational man,—that this great hemisphere, I say, should have lain undiscovered for five thousand years upon the bosom of the deep,—a mystery so vast, within so short a distance, and yet not found out,—is indeed a marvel. Mute nature, if I may so express myself, had made the discovery to the philosopher, for the preponderance of land in the eastern hemisphere demanded a counterpoise in the west. Dark-wooded trees, unknown to the European naturalist, had from age to age drifted over the sea and told of the tropical forests where they grew. Stupendous ocean currents, driven westward by the ever-breathing trade-winds, had wheeled their mighty flexures along the American coast, and returned to Europe with tidings of the everlasting breakwater which had stopped their way. But the fulness of time had not yet come. Egypt and Assyria, and Tyre and Carthage, and Greece and Rome must flourish and fall, before the seals are broken. They must show what they can do for humanity before the veil which hides its last hope is lifted up. The ancient civilization must be weighed in a balance and found wanting. Yes, and more. Nature must unlock her rarest mysteries; the quivering steel must learn to tremble to the pole; the astrolabe must climb the arch of heaven, and bring down the sun to the horizon; science must demonstrate the sphericity of the earth, which the ancients suspected, but could not prove; the press must scatter the flying rear of mediæval darkness; the creative instincts of a new political, intellectual, and social life must begin to kindle into action; and then the Discoverer may go forth.

He does go forth. The discovery is made; the balance of the globe is redressed. A continent nearly equal in extent to one half the ancient hemisphere is brought to light. What momentous questions present themselves! Another world! Is it a twin sister of the ancient world? It has mountains, and rivers, and lakes, and forests, but does it contain the homes of kindred man; — of cultivated races, who have pursued, independently of their Eastern brethren, separate, perhaps higher paths of civilization? In a word, has the great cause of Humanity made an immediate gain by the wonderful event which has added so much to the geography of the world as before known?

The first contact answered these questions in the negative. The native races, apparently incapable of assimilation, seemed doomed by a mysterious Providence to pass away. The Spaniard came upon them, borne on winged monsters, as they thought, from beyond the sea; careering on strange quadrupeds,—horse and rider, as they supposed, forming but one animal; and he advanced under cover of that fearful ordnance, which they mistook for the three-bolted artillery of the skies. He came in all these terrors and he brought them death. Those that escaped have borrowed little from us but the poisonous cup, —the loathsome malady,—the murderous weapon. The skies are mild, the soil is fertile, there is every variety of climate,—a boundless theatre for human enjoyment and action,—but the appointed agent was not there. Over the greater part of the new-found continent, society, broken down by eternal wars between neighboring tribes,—at once in its decrepitude and infancy,—had not yet risen even to the pastoral stage. Nature, in fact, had not bestowed upon man the mute but faithful partners of his toil,—the horse, the ox, the sheep, and other still humbler associates, whose aid (did he but know it) lies at the basis of his civilization; who furnish so much of his food and clothing, meat, milk, eggs, wool, skins, and relieve his weary muscles of their heaviest burdens. In a word, there was no civilized population to stand up and enter into equal comparison and generous rivalry with Europe. The discoverer has come; but the settler, the colonist, the conqueror, alas that I must add! too often the oppressor and destroyer, are to follow in his train. By these various agencies, joyous and sorrowful, through these paths of triumph and woe, the culture of the Old World, in the lapse of successive generations reformed of its abuses, enriched with new arts, animated by a higher spirit of humanity, transferred from the privileged few to the mass of the community, is to be reproduced and perfected in the West.

I need not say to this company, assembled on the shore of the haven for which so many noble hearts on that terrible voyage throbbed with sickening expectancy, — that quiet haven where the Mayflower furled her tattered sails, — that a greater, a nobler work was never performed by man. Truly, the *opus magnum*, *the* great work of humanity. You bid me speak of that portion of it which devolved on the Pilgrims. Would to heaven I could find words to do justice even to my own poor conceptions, and still more that I could find conceptions not far below the august reality! A mighty work of improvement, in which (not to speak of what has been done in other portions of the continent) the poor, solitary Mayflower, so to say, has multiplied herself into the thousand vessels that bear the flag of the Union to every sea; has scattered her progeny through the land, to the number of nearly a quarter of a million for every individual in that drooping company of one hundred; and in place of the simple compact which was signed in her cabin, to which you, sir, [Governor Clifford,] have just alluded, has exhibited to the admiration of mankind a constitution of republican government for all this growing family of prosperous States. But the work is in its infancy; my honored friend will indulge me in the bright vision of its certain progress. It must extend throughout the length and breadth of the land; and what is not done directly by ourselves must be done by other governments and other races, by the light of our example. The work — the work must go on. It must reach at the North to the enchanted cave of the magnet, within never-melting barriers of Arctic ice; it must bow to the lord of day on the altar-peaks of Chimborazo; it must look up and worship the Southern Cross. From the easternmost cliff on the Atlantic, that blushes in the kindling dawn, to the last promontory on the Pacific, which catches the parting kiss of the setting sun, as he goes down to his pavilion of purple and gold, it must make the outgoings of the morning and evening to rejoice, in the gladsome light of morals, and letters, and arts. Emperors, and kings, and parliaments, — the oldest and the strongest governments in Europe, — must engage in this work in some part or other of the continent, but no part of it shall be so faithfully and successfully performed as that which was undertaken on the spot where we are now gathered, by the Pilgrim Fathers of New England.

Providence from the beginning strewed their path with salutary hardships. Formidable difficulties beset them from the first. Three years of weary negotiation had failed to procure for these noble adventurers the express sanction of the British government; they scarcely obtained its reluctant and tacit permission to banish themselves to the ends of the earth; and their shattered private fortunes allowed but the meanest outfit; but on the 1st of August, 1620, under these poor auspices, they embarked, a handful of Pilgrims, to lay upon this spot the foundation, not only of this our beloved New England, but of all that portion of United America which traces its descent to this venerated stock.

When we contrast the heart-stricken company which on that day wept and knelt on the quay at Delft Haven, till the impassive spectators, ignorant of the language in which their prayers were offered, and the deep fountains of grief from which their sorrows flowed, were yet fain to melt into sympathetic tears, — when we compare them with the busy, prosperous millions of our present New England, — we seem to miss that due proportion between results and their causes which history delights to trace. But a deeper and more appreciative study reveals the secret.

There are two Master Ideas, greatest of the spiritual images enthroned in the mind of man, the only ideas, comparatively speaking, which deserve a name among men, springs of all the grand beneficent movements of modern times, by whose influence the settlement of New England may be rationally explained. You have anticipated me, descendants of the Pilgrims, these Great Ideas are God and Liberty. It was these that inspired our Fathers; by these that their weakness was clothed with power, that their simplicity was transmuted to wisdom; by these that the great miracle of their enterprise was wrought.

I am aware that to ascribe such a result, even in

part, to the influence of religion, will sound like weakness and superstition in this material age; — an age at once supremely sceptical and supremely credulous, which is ready to believe in every thing spiritual rather than God, and admits all marvels but the interposition of his providence; — an age which supposes it a thing of every day's occurrence to evoke from their awful rest the spirits of the great and good, and believes that master intellects, who while they lived, obstructed with these organs of sense, ravished the ear with the tongues of men, and, having now cast off "this muddy vesture of decay," are gone where they speak with the tongues of angels, can yet find no medium of communication from the eternal world but wretched inarticulate rappings and clatterings, which pot-house clowns would be ashamed to use in their intercourse with each other, — as if our matchless Choate, for instance, who has just electrified the land with a burst of eloquence not easily paralleled in the line of time, and worthy of the illustrious subject of his eulogy, if sent with a message from a higher stage of being, would creep skulking and rapping behind the wainscot, instead of coming in robes of light, with a voice like the music of the spheres; — an age, I say, that believes all this, and yet doubts and sneers at the wonder-working fervors of earnest men, swayed by the all-powerful influence of sincere faith.

It believes — yes, in the middle of the nineteenth century, it believes that you can have the attraction of gravitation, which holds the universe together, suspended by a showman for a dollar, who will make a table dance round the room by an act of volition, — forgetful of the fact, that, if the law of gravitation were suspended for the twinkling of an eye, by any other Power than that which ordained it, every planet that walks the firmament, yea, all the starry suns, centres of the countless systems, unseen of mortal eyes, which fill the unfathomed depths of the heavens, would crumble back to chaos, — but it can see in the Pilgrims nothing but a handful of narrow-minded bigots, driven by discontent from the Old World to the New; and can find nothing in the majestic process by which United America has been established as a grand temple of religious and civil liberty, — a general refuge of humanity, — but a chapter in political history, which neither requires nor admits explanation.

Mr. President, this may sound like philosophy, but it is the philosophy of the Sadducee; it is a text on which Isaac Laquedem himself might lecture. It quenches the brightest glory of our nature. The Pilgrims were actuated by that principle, which, as I have just said, has given the first impulse to all the great movements of the modern world, — I mean profound religious faith. They had the frailties of humanity. This exalted principle itself was combined with human weakness. It was mingled with the prejudices and errors of age, and country, and sect; it was habitually gloomy; it was sometimes intolerant; but it was reverent, sincere, all-controlling. It did not influence, it possessed the soul. It steeled the heart to the delights of life; it raised the frame above bodily weakness; it enabled the humble to brave the frowns of power; it triumphed over cold and hunger, the prison and the scaffold; it taught uneducated men to speak with persuasive fervor; it gave manly strength and courage to tender and delicate women. In the admirable letter of Robinson and Brewster, — whom I call great men, Mr. President, — written, in 1617, to Sir Edwyn Sandys, — whom, they pathetically say, "under God, above all persons and things in the world, we rely upon," — among the suggestions which they make to encourage him to further their undertaking is this: —

"We do verily believe and trust that the Lord is with us, unto whom and whose service we have given ourselves in many trials, and that he will graciously prosper our endeavors, according to the simplicity of our hearts."

The men who can utter these words with sincerity, and who have embarked in a just cause, have already succeeded. They may not gather the fruit, but they have planted the seed; others may build, but they have laid the foundation. This is the spirit which in all ages has wrought the moral miracles of humanity, — which rebuked and overturned the elegant corruption of the classical polytheism, as it did the darker and fiercer rites of Thor and Woden, — which drove back the false and licentious crescent into Asia, and held Europe together through the night of the Middle Ages, — which, limited neither to country, communion, nor sex, despite of human weaknesses and errors, in the missions of Paraguay and the missions of the Sandwich Islands, in Winthrop, in Penn, and in Wesley, in Eliza Seton and Mary Ware, has accomplished the beneficent wonders of Christian faith and love.

But, sir, our fathers embraced that second grand idea of civil liberty with not less fervor than the first. It was a kindred fruit of the same stock. They cherished it with a zeal not less intense and resolute. This is a topic for a volume, rather than for the closing sentence of a speech at the dinner-table. I will only say that the highest authorities in English history, Hume, Hallam, Macaulay, neither of them influenced by sympathy with the Puritans, concur in the opinion that England was indebted to them for the preservation of her liberties in that most critical period of her national existence, when the question between prerogative and law, absolute authority and constitutional government, was decided for ever.

In coming to this country, our fathers most certainly contemplated, not merely a safe retreat beyond the sea, where they could worship God according to the dictates of their own conscience, but a local government founded on popular choice. That their foresight stretched onward through the successive stages of colonial and provincial government which resulted in the establishment of a great republican confederacy, it would be extravagant to pretend, but from the primitive and venerable compact signed on the 11th of November, 1620, on board the Mayflower, while she yet nestled in the embrace of Provincetown Harbor, after her desolate voyage, like a weary child at evening in its mother's arms, through every document and manifesto which bears on the question, there is a distinct indication of a purpose to establish civil government on the basis of republican equality.

In a word, Mr. President, their political code united religion and liberty, morals and law, and it differed from the wild license which breaks away from these restraints, as the well-guided railway engine, instinct with mechanical life, conducted by a bold, but skilful and prudent hand, and propelled in safety towards its destination, with glowing axle, along its iron grooves, differs from the same engine when its speed is rashly urged beyond the point of safety, or when, driven by criminal recklessness or murderous neglect, it leaps madly from the track, and plunges with its crushed and shrieking train into the jaws of destruction.

Die Ansiedlungen der Normanen

— in —

Island, Grönland u. Nord-Amerika

im 9., 10. und 11. Jahrhundert.

Ein Vortrag von Emil Ulrici.

—o—

Meine Herren!

Wenn Sie irgend ein Kind welches die Schule besucht fragen: wer hat Amerika entdeckt, so wird es Ihnen antworten: Christoph Columbus und wird sogar noch die Jahreszahl 1492 hinzufügen Dennoch war Columbus keineswegs der erste Entdecker Amerikas, wie fast ein Jeder weiß; —es giebt eben Thatsachen, die zwar fast allgemein bekannt sind, die aber so selten Erwähnung finden, daß sie dem Gedächtniß leicht vollständig entschwinden. Dahin gehört auch die Entdeckung Amerikas durch die Normannen fast ein halbes Jahrtausend vor der Zeit des Columbus. Wenn ich mir deshalb heute erlaube, jene früheren Entdeckungen in Ihr Gedächtniß zurückzurufen, so kann es natürlich nicht in meiner Absicht liegen, anerkannte Verdienste zu schmälern. Was jener große Genuese geleistet, bleibt ihm unbenommen, umsomehr, da ja erst durch seine Entdeckung Amerika der Civilisation erschlossen ist. Allein unsere Anerkennung dürfen wir jenen harten unverzagten Männern nicht versagen, die vor nahezu 1000 Jahren ohne Compaß und die neueren Hülfsmittel, welche der Schifffahrt gegenwärtig zu Gebote stehen, sich viele hunderte von Meilen auf das offene Meer hinauswagten und ihren Zeitgenossen neue bis dahin unbekannte Gebiete erschlossen.—

Die früheste Entdeckung Amerikas ging von Norwegen aus, allein nicht direkt, sondern Schritt für Schritt gingen jene alten Seehelden — oder zum Theil wohl auch Seeräuber — westlich und entdeckten so zuerst die Faröer, dann Island, später Grönland und endlich das amerikanische Festland. — Lassen Sie uns deshalb den westlichen Zügen der alten Normannen schrittweise folgen und wir werden es dann ganz natürlich finden, daß jene alten Wickinger schon um das Jahr 1000 unserer Zeitrechnung das Land entdeckten, welches fast 500 Jahre später Columbus wieder auffand und welches inzwischen vollständig vergessen war.—Zur heutigen Zeit wäre dies freilich nicht möglich, allein vor 1000 Jahren war die Buchdruckerkunst noch nicht erfunden, der Verkehr der Völker unter einander war sehr beschränkt und besondere Ereignisse erfuhr man selbst in dem Lande, in dem sie stattgefunden oft erst nach Jahren.—

Es war im Jahre 861 als Naddod, ein berühmter Wiking, aus Norwegen, der die kürzlich von Grim Gamle aufgefundenen Faröer Inseln aufsuchen wollte, durch Stürme nach Island verschlagen wurde. Er nannte das Land, welches zum großen Theil mit Schnee bedeckt war, Snjoland (Schneeland) und kehrte in seine Heimath zurück; 3 Jahre später, im Jahre 864 ging es einem Schweden Namens Gardur ähnlich; auch er wurde nach Island verschlagen, ohne das Land näher zu betrachten. Im Jahre 867 endlich suchte Flocke aus Norwegen, die Insel, von der er gehört hatte, auf, verließ sie jedoch wieder und erst im Jahre 874 ließ sich Ingolf, der in Norwegen einen Mord begangen und deshalb fliehen mußte dauernd auf der Insel nieder; im Vorbeifahren hatte er die Insel schon 870 gesehen; in seiner Begleitung befand sich sein Schwager Leif. — In Norwegen war inzwischen im Jahre 863 Harald mit dem Zunamen Harfagar (Schönhaar) der Sohn Halfdan des Schwarzen, zur Herrschaft gelangt; er unterjochte die kleineren Herrscher und warf sich zum alleinigen Könige von Norwegen auf; die von ihm unterworfenen Fürsten nicht an Dienstbarkeit gewöhnt, so wie deren Anhang, verließen in Folge dessen der Mehrzahl nach Norwegen und siedelten zum großen Theil nach Island über, ja die Auswanderung nach der neuentdeckten Insel nahm so zu, daß Harald bangte, Norwegen werde entvölkert, er verbot die Auswanderung gänzlich und legte jedem Islandfahrer eine Buße von 5 Oeren ($5.00) auf; übrigens zogen damals nicht nur Norweger, sondern auch Dänen, Schweden, Irländer und Bewohner der Hebriden nach Island und etwa 50 Jahre später, im Jahre 930 war fast die ganze Insel angesiedelt und bebaut, besonders die West- und Nordküste.—Da jene Auswanderer nicht zu den mittellosen Flüchtlingen gehörten, sondern meistentheils angesehene, begüterte, gleichberechtigte Männer waren, die mit allen ihren Gütern und Familiengliedern übersiedelten, so bildete sich in Island im Laufe der Zeit eine außerordentlich freisinnige Verfassung aus; Anfangs nahm ein Jeder so viel Land in freien Besitz, wie er nöthig zu haben glaubte, und lebte dort frei und unabhängig unter Freien. Ausgenommen hiervon waren natürlich, wie es damals selbstverständlich, die mit hinübergebrachten Knechte, denen man jedoch später ebenfalls volle Freiheit bewilligte.—

Die Normänner waren zu jener Zeit noch Heiden, und sie fanden (wie es heißt) in Island bei ihrer Ankunft bereits eine, wenn auch sehr spärliche Bevölkerung vor. Diese frühesten Ansiedler sagten aus, sie seien von Westen herübergekommen, sie sprachen die irländische Sprache und waren Christen.—Als die Zahl der Normannen überhand nahm, verließen jene das Land und kehrten in ihre frühere westliche Heimath, muthmaßlich nach Amerika zurück. — Auf diese frühesten Bewohner Islands werde ich später noch zurückkommen.—

Die Bekehrungsversuche christlicher Missionäre blieben in Island lange vergeblich und erst im Jahre 1000 gelang es Thorgeier das Christenthum einzuführen; daß übrigens dies sogenannte Christenthum etwas rein äußerliches war und auf die Sitten und Gebräuche nicht den mindesten Einfluß hatte, ging schon aus den 5 Punkten hervor, über die man sich schließlich einigte. Es waren folgende:

1. Alle Einwohner werden getauft.
2. Die Götterbilder und Tempel werden zerstört.
3. Wer öffentlich den Göttern opfert und ihre Bilder anbetet, wird des Landes verwiesen.
4. Dies im Geheimen zu thun ist jedoch gestattet.
5. Die alten Gesetze betreffs Aussetzen der Kinder, Essen von Pferdefleisch &c. überhaupt Alles, wodurch das nominelle Christenthum nicht geradezu umgestoßen wurde, blieb in voller Kraft.

Im Jahre 1056 bekam Island in Isleif den ersten Bischof, sein Nachfolger wurde 1096 sein Sohn Gizor (beide waren natürlich nach damaliger Sitte verheirathet) und bereits 1104 wurde ein zweiter Bischofssitz für Nord Island gegründet.— Ehe wir von Island weiter westlich wandern, will ich noch bemerken, daß im Jahre 1118 das älteste und umfassendste Gesetzbuch des skandinavischen Alterthums, die sogenannte Graugans verfaßt und angenommen wurde. — Die Blüthezeit isländischer Cultur und Literatur fällt in das 12. und 13. Jahrhundert; zu dieser Zeit entstanden wahrscheinlich die ältere und jüngere Edda und die Heimskringla (Weltkreis), norwegische Königssagen.—Die ältere Edda hat wohl Sämund Sigfuson († 1133) zum Verfasser, während die jüngere Edda und Heimskringla dem Vater der skandinavischen Geschichte Snorre Sturlason (geboren 1179 † 1241) zugeschrieben werden. (Im Jahre 1262 endlich unterwarf sich Island, durch innere Unruhen erschüttert und zerrüttet, dem Könige Hakon *VI.*) Hakonson von Norwegen.—

Während wir bisher den verbürgten Pfaden der Geschichte gefolgt sind und auch fernerhin uns nur an verbürgte Thatsachen halten wollen, möchte ich Sie bitten, mir einen Augenblick auf das Gebiet der

Sage zu folgen; sie ist ja eine Stiefschwester und stete Begleiterin der frühesten Geschichte. — Ich habe bereits erwähnt, daß zur Zeit, als die Normänner von Island Besitz nahmen, sich dort, wie es scheint, bereits weiße christliche Bewohner vorfanden, die von jenen Westmänner genannt wurden, weil sie von Westen aus über den Ocean gekommen waren (Komnir lit vestan un haf—wie es in den alten Membranen heißt). Sie sprachen irländisch, oder wenigstens ein der irländischen Sprache sehr nahe stehendes Idiom und wir sind deshalb genöthigt die dunkeln und mangelhaften Spuren zu verfolgen, welche in allerfrühesten Zeiten die Bewohner Irlands der Sage nach über das Meer nach Westen führten.—

Im Jahre 432 predigte der Britte Succath als Bischof Patricius das Christenthum in Irland und es entstanden daselbst eine Menge Klöster, deren Bewohner, von der dem Irländer noch heut innewohnenden Reiselust durchdrungen wurden; im Eifer das Christenthum zu predigen, fuhren viele derselben nicht nur hinüber nach Frankreich wie Fridolin † 514 und Columbian † 597, im 7. Jahrhundert Gallus † 640, sondern sie wandten sich auch nördlich und westlich, bevölkerten die Faröer und andere Inseln. — Der heilige Brendanus soll der erste gewesen sein, welcher eine größere Entdeckungsreise nach Westen gemacht, Amerika erreicht und von 562—572 dort geblieben sein soll.—Es wird in den alten Membranen von einem Großirland (Irland hit mikla) auch Weißmännerland (Hvitramannaland) gesprochen, das der Beschreibung nach etwa da gelegen haben muß, wo sich jetzt die Staaten Virginien, Nord- und Südcarolina befinden; auch erzählten die im Jahre 1010 von Karlsefne bei seiner Reise nach Vinland gefangenen beiden Knaben der Skraelinger, (Eskimos) ihrem Lande gegenüber, also südlich, gegenüber der jetzigen Cheasepeakebai, befände sich ein Land, in welchem hellfarbige Menschen wohnten, die weiße Kleider anhätten, Stangen mit Tüchern vor sich herträgen und mit lauter Stimme schrien. Es scheint dies auf katholische Processionen zu deuten; auch die Schawanesen, ein Indianerstamm, der früher Florida bewohnte, haben eine Sage, daß lange vor ihrer Zeit, ihre früheren Wohnsitze von Weißen bewohnt gewesen seien, von denen hier und da noch Spuren vorhanden, ja es zeigten sich sogar zur Zeit, als die Spanier landeten, noch schwache Spuren von Christenthum.—Von hier also, von Hvitramannaland, kamen vielleicht die frühesten Bewohner Islands, die nach Ankunft der Normannen, in ihre westliche Heimath zurückkehrten; daß sie Christen, zum Theil Geistliche und irländischen Ursprunges waren, schloßen die Normannen aus irländischen Schriften, Meßglocken und Krummstäben, die sie auf Island zurückgelassen hatten. —Daß die Irländer sowohl wie die Normannen, schon in frühester Zeit auf ihren primitiven Fahrzeugen weite Seereisen unternahmen, ist ja allbekannt; wir finden letztere schon im 5. Jahrhundert im Besitz der Inseln an der Mündung der Loire; 845 fuhren sie mit 120 Boten die Seine hinauf und brandschatzten Paris. Wenig später finden wir sie sogar in Spanien und Italien, und es hat deshalb durchaus nichts Unwahrscheinliches, daß diese kühnen wettergehärteten Piraten sich schon vor mehr wie 1000 Jahren westlich wandten und das amerikanische Festland erreichten, umsomehr, da das westliche Vorgebirge von Irland nur etwa 540 Seemeilen also ca. 2000 englische Meilen von der südwestlichen Spitze Neu Fundlands entfernt liegt, eine Entfernung, welche die Normännen bei günstigem Winde in 16—20 Tagen zurücklegen konnten. — Allein, wenn es hiernach auch möglich, ja wahrscheinlich erscheint, daß Amerika bereits im 6. oder 7. Jahrhundert von Europäern besucht wurde, so haben wir doch darüber keine positive Gewißheit. Anders dagegen verhält es sich mit jenen Reisen, welche um das Jahr 1000 und kurze Zeit nachher nach Amerika unternommen wurden. Ueber diese sind wir, wie Sie sogleich sehen werden, fast vollständig unterrichtet, ja es ist der Forschung sogar gelungen, mit ziemlicher Genauigkeit die Punkte zu bezeichnen, wo die Reisenden vor mehr wie 800 Jahren landeten und ihre Niederlassungen gründeten.—

Wenden wir uns nach dieser Abschweifung zurück nach Island, als der ersten Station zwischen Europa und dem Festlande von Amerika.

Daß die seekundigen Bewohner Islands, ihre alten Gewohnheiten das Meer zu durchforschen, nach ihrer Uebersiedlung auf die Insel nicht aufgegeben haben, ist wohl selbstverständlich. Es erscheint deshalb ganz natürlich, daß sie sehr bald nach ihrer Niederlassung die gegenüberliegende Küste von Grönland, welche sie mit ihren Schiffen in etwa 3 Tagen (85 Seemeilen) erreichen konnten, zu erforschen suchten. Und in der That wurde Grönland schon im Jahre 976 von Gunbjörn gesehen,—wirklich betreten wurde es im Frühjahre des Jahres 986 von Erik dem Rothen, der über 2 Jahre an der Westküste zubrachte und seine Wohnung während der ersten Zeit in Brattalid im Eriksfjord, nahe dem jetzigen Cap Farewell, während des letzten Winters auf einer der Inseln vor der Mündung des Eriksfjord aufschlug. Während des Sommers umschiffte er Cap Farewell, so wie einen Theil der Westküste und kehrte 988 nach Island zurück. Im folgenden Jahre lief er abermals und diesmal mit 25 Fahrzeugen von Island aus, von denen 14 Grönland erreichten und die ersten wirklichen Ansiedler dorthin brachten, denen bald andere folgten. — Schon im Jahre 1000 zählte man in Grönland 190 Höfe (Wohnsitze) und mehrere Klöster, die in 2 Bezirke zerfielen, den Westbau und den Ostbau.—Letzterer stieß bei Cap Herjuflsnaes (jetzt Ikigeit unter dem 60. Grad n. B.) mit dem Westbau zusammen, lag übrigens nicht, wie man früher wohl annahm an der Ostküste, sondern umfaßte den südlichsten Theil von Grönland und einen in der Mitte des Landes, von Süden nach Norden zu gelegenen Streifen.—Wenig später wurde bereits in Gardar in der Gegend des jetzigen Frederikshaab ein Bischofssitz errichtet und so wie Island 1262 wurde Grönland im Jahre 1264 in politischer Beziehung mit Norwegen vereinigt. — Im Jahre 1379 finden wir des Bischofs Alf von Grönland erwähnt. Er war der letzte grönländische Bischof, welcher im Grönland selbst residirte; wenngleich bis in das 16. Jahrhundert Bischöfe ernannt wurden, die jedoch nie dorthin gelangten. Der zuletzt ernannte Bischof von Grönland war Vinzens; er starb 1540 in Maribo auf der dänischen Insel Laaland.— Zur Zeit des Bischofs Alf waren im Westbau 4 Kirchen und 110 Höfe, im Ostbau eine Kathedrale, in Gardar 11 andere Kirchen, 3 oder 4 Klöster und 190 Höfe; man schlägt danach die Zahl der Bewohner auf mindestens 6000 an. — Im Jahre 1379 machten die Eskimos von den Normannen Skrälinger genannt, Einfälle in das Land, tödteten einen Theil der Bewohner und zerstörten viel Eigenthum; 1408 endlich wollte Andres, der 17. Bischof der grönländischen Kirche von seinem Stuhle Besitz nehmen, konnte Grönland aber nicht mehr erreichen, weil das Land rings von Eisfeldern besetzt war. Wenige Jahre vorher geschieht Gränlands auch Erwähnung in einem vom Bischof Alf (dem 16. Bischof) ausgestellten Dokument.— Im Jahre 1418 wurde Grönland durch eine feindliche Flotte heimgesucht und die Bewohner größtentheils getödtet; man war lange der Meinung, daß jener Angriff von Eskimos herrührte, bis es sich später herausstellte, daß jene Flotte eine englische gewesen. — Reste der grönländischen Colonie waren wohl noch bis um die Mitte des 15. Jahrhunderts vorhanden; das letzte geschichtlich wichtige Dokument, in welchem Grönlands Erwähnung geschieht, ist ein Brief von Pabst Nicolaus *V.* vom Jahre 1448, in welchem derselbe unter Anderem sagt: Es ist beklagenswerth, daß die Bewohner der Insel Grönland, die an der äußersten Grenze des großen Oceans im Norden des Königreichs Norwegen liegen soll, und die mir viele Jahrhunderte christliche Treue bewahrt, vor 30 Jahren von heidnischen Ausländern räuberisch überfallen, theils getödtet, theils fortgeschleppt wurden &c. Er befiehlt dann den nächstgelegenen Bischöfen, einen geeigneten Mann als Bischof dorthin zu senden und fügt bei, daß der berühmte Lehrer, der Grönländer König Olai das Christenthum unter ihnen errichtet. — Im Jahre 1484 soll es in Bergen noch viele Leute gegeben haben, die mit der Fahrt nach Grönland vertraut waren; dann schwand das Andenken an dies einst bekannte und viel besuchte Land, welches man erst zu Ende des 16. Jahrhunderts wieder zu finden versuchte, bis endlich im Jahre 1721 Egede dort aufs Neue mit 50 Personen in der Nähe des Fjord Godthaab unter dem 64. Grad n. B. landete.—

Die Hauptschuld, daß die Colonie zu Grunde ging, trug ohne Zweifel die norwegische Regierung. Sie erklärte den Handel mit Grönland für ein königliches

Regal, schloß dadurch Privatunternehmungen dorthin vollständig aus und begnügte sich im Anfang alle Jahre 2,— später 1 Schiff dorthinzusenden, um die Producte der Colonie gegen nothwendige Lebensbedürfnisse einzutauschen. Dadurch wurde der Handel vollständig gelähmt, war selbst für die Krone nicht mehr einträglich und es vergingen oft 3 Jahre bis ein Schiff nach Grönland gesandt wurde. So litten die Bewohner oft den allerbittersten Mangel und während der mannigfachen Wirren in Norwegen unterblieb die Schifffahrt ganz, die Colonie ging zu Grunde und selbst das Andenken an sie verschwand aus dem Gedächtniß späterer Generationen. — Erst Christian *III.* hob das Verbot der Fahrt nach Grönland auf.—

Die früheren Bewohner Grönlands, alte Seefahrer — beschränkten sich nicht darauf ruhig im Lande zu leben, sondern versuchten, nach allen Seiten hin Entdeckungen zu machen, besonders auf der Westseite in der jetzigen Davisstraße damals Giunnugagap genannt, bis hinauf in die Baffinsbay. Es geht dies aus vielen Ruinen und anderen Zeichen hervor, die zum Theil erst in neuerer Zeit bei den Nordpolfahrten entdeckt wurden; der nördlichste Punkt, den sie erreicht haben, scheint der 73. Grad n. B. zu sein; man fand im Jahre 1824 unter 72 Grad 55′ n. B.und 56 Grad 05′ w. L. von Gr. auf dem höchsten Punkte der Insel King Storsoak, einer der Womansinseln der Baffinsbay (4 Meilen nordwestlich von der nördlichsten der heutigen dänischen Niederlassungen) nahe der Reste dreier Grenzsäulen, — einen äußerst merkwürdigenRunstein, dessen schwarzgrüne Oberfläche vermittels eines anderen Steines und Sand polirt zu sein scheint. — Die Inschrift lautet nach Finn Magnusen's und Rafu's Uebersetzung: Erling Sighvats Sohn—Bjarne Thords Sohn und Einride Odds Sohn errichteten an dem Samstage vor dem Siegestage diese Säulen und reinigten diesen Ort im Jahre 1135.—Der Siegestag oder das Siegesopfer war eines der Hauptfeste der alten Skandinavier, das sie am 21. April feierten.—

Nachdem wir gesehen, wie von Europa aus zuerst Island im Jahre 867, von da aus Grönland im Jahre 982 besiedelt worden, lassen Sie uns jetzt den Schiffen folgen, welche von Grönland aus südwestlich steuernd, zuerst das Festland von Amerika entdeckten.

Bjarne Herjulfsson war der erste, welcher von Island nach Grönland segelnd von nordöstlichen Winden verschlagen im Jahre 986 (996?) zuerst das amerikanische Festland sah, allein er landete nicht, sondern suchte seinen Weg nach Grönland zurück, wo man ihm Vorwürfe machte, daß er das neue Land nicht näher erforscht. Es wurde längere Zeit von dieser Entdeckung gesprochen, bis endlich im Jahre 1000 Leif der Sohn Eriks des Rothen, des ersten Ansiedlers von Grönland BjarnesSchiff kaufte und mit35Männern unter denen ein Deutscher Namens Pyrker, in See ging und südwestlich steuernd zuerst an eine niedrige steinige Küste gelangte, über welche hinaus in mäßiger Entfernung Gletscher und schneegekrönte Berge sich erhoben; hier landete er zwar, allein das Land war so wenig einladend, daß er es verließ und es H e l l u l a n d (Steinland) nannte.—Nachdem er wieder in das offene Meer hinausgefahren, kam er südlich segelnd, an eine mit dichten Wäldern bedeckte Küste, deren breiter mit weißem Sand bedeckter Strand sanft gegen das Meer hin abfiel; wegen der Wälder nannte er es M a r k l a n d (Waldland). — Auch hier landeten die Seefahrer, erquickten sich an süßen Beeren, die dort reichlich wuchsen, lichteten jedoch bald wieder die Anker und gingen in die offeneSee. Nachdem sie zweiTage mit Nordostwind gefahren, gelangten sie an eine Insel, die östlich vor dem festen Lande lag. Zwischen dieser Insel und einem Vorgebirge, das sich östlich und nördlich von dem Lande aus erstreckte, segelten sie in einen Sund und warfen Anker an einem Platz, wo ein Fluß, nachdem er durch einen See gegangen sich in das Meer ergoß. Nach dieser Wahrnehmung lichteten sie aufs Neue, führten ihre Schiffe den Fluß hinauf und ankerten in dem See; das Land war meist mit Waldung bedeckt und bot Ueberfluß an schönem kleinen Obst. Hier beschlossen sie zu überwintern, bauten sich geräumige Wohnungen, die später den Namen Leifsbudir (Leifs Häuser) erhielten und erforschten das Land nach allen Richtungen; dabei entdeckte derDeutsche PyrkerWeintrauben, die nur er kannte, weil sie auch in seiner alten Heimath wuchsen, und Leif nannte in Folge dessen das Land Vinland (Weinland).—Nach Leifs Berichten ging hier die Sonne am kürzesten Tage um ½8 Uhr auf und um ½5 Uhr unter. — Im nächsten Frühjahr (1001) segelten sie mit Bauholz und getrockneten Weintrauben beladen nach Grönland zurück. - - Im Jahre 1002 segelte Erichs zweiter Sohn Thorwald mit 30 Gefährten nach Vinland. In den folgenden Jahren erforschte er die nächstliegenden Küsten, fand viel sandige Eilande, aber auch dichtbewaldetes Hochland; 1005 endlich traf er mit seinen Gefährten auf kleine dunkelfarbige Leute, die sie Skrälinger nannten (von skräl klein) und die ohne Zweifel Eskimos waren. Er tödtete dieselben, wurde jedoch später mit seinen Gefährten von großen Mengen angegriffen, wobei er eine tödtliche Wunde erhielt und wurde, wie er es gewünscht, auf einem Vorgebirge in der Nähe (später Krossaner genannt) begraben; die Gefährten kehrten 1005 nach Grönland zurück.—

Es kann nicht in meiner Absicht liegen, Sie mit der Erzählung der zahlreichen, zum Theil auf das Genaueste beschriebenen Fahrten der Grönländer nach Amerika zu ermüden. In aller Kürze will ich nur noch bemerken, daß auch Erich's dritter Sohn Thorstein mit Frau und 25 Gefährten im Jahre 1007 und eine große Menge Anderer im Laufe des 11. Jahrhunderts nach Amerika fuhren und sich längere oder kürzere Zeit dort aufhielten. Im 12. Jahrhundert unter der Regierung Heinrich *II.* von England soll Fürst Madoc von Wales mit 10 Schiffen und einer Schaar von Männern, Weibern und Kindern nach Amerika gegangen sein. Man hat im Mutterlande nie wieder von ihm und seinen Gefährten gehört, doch wird versichert, daß früher Indianer von hellerer Hautfarbe getroffen wurden, in deren Sprache Walesche Worte vorkamen und noch heut ist der Indianerstamm der Mandaus (zu den Dakotas gerechnet) die früher an der Ostküste Amerikas wohnten, in vieler Beziehung von den übrigen Indianern verschieden. Sie sind von ziemlich heller Hautfarbe und man trifft häufig, besonders unter den Frauen, solche mit blondem Haar und blauen Augen.— Die letzte, Amerika betreffende Nachricht ist vom Jahre 1347; 17 Männer segelten von Grönland nach Markland (Neu Braunschweig) um Bauholz zu holen. Auf der Reise wurde das Schiff verschlagen und kam mit Verlust seiner Anker nach Stramfjord im westlichen Island; die Reise wurde von einem Zeitgenossen 9 Jahre nach der Begebenheit beschrieben und es heißt ausdrücklich, das Schiff sei nach Markland gesegelt. Es bestand also in der Mitte des 14. Jahrhunderts noch eine Verbindung zwischen Island, Grönland und dem amerikanischen Festlande.—Lassen Sie mich hier noch eines sonderbaren Zufalles erwähnen, der bekannte, noch jetzt lebende Geschlechter in engste Verbindung mit Amerika bringt.— Im Herbste des Jahres 1007 wurde dem bereits erwähnten Thorfin Carlsefne und seiner Frau Gudrid in Vinland ein Sohn geboren, der den Namen Snorre erhielt. Von ihm stammen durch seine Tochter Hallfried nachweislich in direkter Linie ab — der 1844 verstorbene berühmte Bildhauer Thorwaldson; der durch seine Forschungen auf dem Gebiete der Archäologie ausgezeichnete 1847 gestorbene Gelehrte Finn Magnusen; beide geborene Isländer und die dänischen Grafen und Barone von Hof Rosenkrone;—der früheste Urahn der Genannten war also ein geborener Amerikaner.

Nachdem wir von den Thatsachen selbst Kenntniß genommen haben, lassen Sie uns nun mit Hülfe der Karte die Wege verfolgen, welche die damaligen Seefahrer von Grönland nach Amerika einschlugen; damit wir uns möglichst klar werden über die Bezeichnung und Lage von Helluland, Markland und Vinland und legen wir dabei hauptsächlich die Berichte Leifs und Thorfinns als der ausführlichsten zu Grunde. — Was den Bericht des zuerst an die Küste Amerikas verschlagenen Bjarne anlangt, so möchte ich demselben kein besonderes Gewicht beilegen, da derselbe nirgends landete, nur aus der Entfernung von seinem Schiffe aus, also ohne Zweifel mangelhaft beobachtete. Das Land, welches er zuerst sah, war wohl eine Gegend zwischen dem 40. und 42. Grad nördlicher Breite; er segelte dann an der Küste entlang an Neu Schottland vorbei, gelangte nach Neu Fundland und auch hier die Küste verfolgend, traf ihn ein reißender Südweststurm, durch welchen er innerhalb 4 Tagen an die Küste Grönlands geworfen wurde; Labrador hat er wohl kaum gesehen. Leif, der die erste Reise unternahm und den Ländern Namen beilegte, baute sich Häuser in Vinland und diese wurden später das Ziel aller Reisen.— Diese Häuser, Leifsbudirs genannt, lagen, wie schon früher bemerkt, in der Nähe des Meeres, an einer Stelle, wo ein Fluß, nachdem er durch einen See gegangen, sich in das Meer ergoß. Eine Insel war östlich vor dem Lande gelegen und die Sonne ging an dem kürzesten Tage um 7½ Uhr auf und um 4½ Uhr unter. Aus letzterer Angabe läßt sich die geographische Breite auf 41 Grad 24′ bestimmen, und hierauf gestützt, erkennen wir aus der detaillirten Beschreibung fast mit Sicherheit die Gegend gegenüber der Insel Marthas Vineyard, wo der Taunton, durch die Narraganset Bay fließend, in der Mounthope Bay endigt; umsomehr, da nach der Angabe etwas nordöstlich ein Cap lag, welches Leif Kjalarnes, schiffskielartig, nannte und in dem wir Cap Cod erkennen, welches die Gestalt eines Schiffsschnabels der Vorzeit hat. Wir können sonach über die Bezeichnung Vinland (Weinland) nicht im Zweifel sein. Es wurde darunter der nördlichere Theil der Vereinigten Staaten verstanden, etwa jene Gegend welche jetzt die Staaten Massachusetts, Rhode Island, Connecticut und New York einnehmen, wo man auch noch heut wilden Wein in Menge findet.— Ebenso wenig zweifelhaft ist für uns die Bezeichnung Markland (Waldland). Dasselbe lag nach den Angaben 2 Tagereisen, also 54—60 Seemeilen nordöstlich von Vinland, kann also nur das mit reichem Wald bestandene jetzige Neu-Schottland gewesen sein.—Etwas anders verhält es sich mit Helluland (Steinplattenland). Halten wir uns nur an die angegebene Richtung der späteren Fahrten, so kann unter Helluland nur Neu Fundland verstanden sein, doch paßt die Beschreibung des Landes weit mehr auf Labrador, und Leif, der von Grönland aus südwestlich steuerte, stieß ohne Zweifel auf Labrador, fand das Land öde, mit Schnee, Gletschern und großen Steinen bedeckt und nannte es infolge dessen Helluland, Steinland. Er fuhr dann in das offene Meer hinaus und kam—in welcher Zeit ist nicht angegeben—nach Markland, also nach Neu Schottland. Später, als man mit der Fahrt mehr vertraut war, kürzte man den Weg wohl dadurch ab, daß man mehr südlich hielt und also ohne Labrador zu berühren, nach Neu Fundland kam, welches man für die südlichste Spitze des von Leif Helluland genannten Landes hielt. Der Name paßte zwar für diesen Theil des Landes nicht, indeß er war einmal da; erst als Neu Fundland als Insel erkannt wurde, unterschied man zwischen Helluland it mikla (das große Helluland) und litla Helluland (klein Helluland). —Wir sind deshalb wohl genöthigt, unter dem Helluland der Alten die ganze östliche Küste von Labrador und Neu Fundland zu verstehen, wenngleich der Name ursprünglich nur Labrador beigelegt wurde. Wo jedoch später von Helluland die Rede ist, bezieht sich der Name unzweifelhaft nur auf Neu Fundland; da man bei der Fahrt von Grönland aus wohl nicht mehr nach Labrador, sondern über Neu Fundland nach Vinland gelangte.—

Wir haben gesehen, daß in der Mitte des 14. Jahrhunderts noch eine Verbindung zwischen Island und Amerika bestand. Das Andenken an dies Land erlosch aber nicht mit den Fahrten dorthin, es dauerte Jahrhunderte lang fort unter dem Volke, und die Gelehrten kannten die alten Handschriften, welche über jene Reisen berichteten, und so ist es wohl kaum zweifelhaft, daß Columbus, der Ende Februar 1477 von England aus Island besuchte und durch Gespräche, welche er in lateinischer Sprache mit dortigen Geistlichen und Gelehrten führte, von jenem südwestlich gelegenen Lande hörte und dies dazu beitrug, ihn zu seiner großen Entdeckungsreise zu veranlassen, welche uns das einst so wohl bekannte Land aufs Neue erschloß.—

Druckerei des „Herold.“

RECORDS OF MASSACHUSETTS

UNDER ITS

FIRST CHARTER.

By CHARLES W. UPHAM.

RECORDS OF MASSACHUSETTS

UNDER ITS FIRST CHARTER:

A LECTURE

OF A

COURSE BY MEMBERS OF THE MASSACHUSETTS HISTORICAL SOCIETY,

Delivered before the Lowell Institute,

JAN. 26, 1869.

BY

CHARLES W. UPHAM.

BOSTON:
PRINTED FOR THE AUTHOR.
1869.

One Hundred copies printed.

RECORDS OF MASSACHUSETTS

UNDER ITS

FIRST CHARTER.

THE design of the lecture this evening is to consider the Records of Massachusetts, under its first charter, from the point of view in which they illustrate the formation of a body-politic.

The organization of families and communities into some established order is demanded by the conditions of our nature. More than any other temporal concern, it merits and compels the attention of thoughtful minds; and the questions relating to it have always been acknowledged to rank in the highest department, as subjects of inquiry and meditation. Through the entire range of history, the greatest minds have been turned to it. But a glance at the condition of the nations of the earth shows how unsatisfactory have been the results. The experience of ages has effected little; and the theories of philosophers, not much more. The human race in all lands, and all ages, has groaned under the crushing weight of institutions constructed on false principles. Governments everywhere are upheld by military force; and depend for continuance upon ignorance and superstition. So far as we are an exception, it becomes us to inquire to what we owe the degree of our exemption.

Enlightened views on the subject of government are especially important to a people that governs itself. We can hardly expect to obtain them from treatises and essays, however ingenious and learned. There is, indeed, an inherent obstacle in the way of attaining to the truth by these means. Attempts to reason and speculate concerning it are thwarted by the influence on the mind of pre-existing usages and ideas. Every suggestion of reform is encountered by the necessity of adapting it to a surrounding state of things, and by well-grounded fear, that, however specious the theory, it may not work well in practice. The elements of motive, sentiment, and association, that actuate mankind, are so infinitely diversified that they cannot be calculated. Casual events, and complicated circumstances, not to be foreseen, may bring to naught the best considered schemes.

On this subject, the world craves and needs, not what theorists have conjectured, or philosophers propounded, but what has been tried, and found sufficient. The question is — Has a fair experiment ever been made, under favorable auspices, of laying the foundation, and building the fabric of a government of men? and, if so, let it be brought before us.

As answering this question, and meeting this demand, I cite the colony of Massachusetts, during its first half-century, as more to the purpose than any other instance in history.

In pursuance of the recommendation of Governor Clifford, in a special message of Feb. 12, 1853, the Legislature of Massachusetts ordered the first and second volumes of the "Records of the Governor and Company of the Massachusetts Bay in New England," to be printed, embracing the proceedings in London prior to the transfer of the patent; and continued after that event, under the style of "Colony Records," to 1649. The next year a resolve was passed, approved by Governor Washburn, February 17, for printing the third, fourth, and fifth volumes, carrying the record to 1686, and covering, altogether, the entire period of the government under the first charter. The form and manner in which they were printed do honor to the Commonwealth, and to the distinguished member of our society, intrusted with the responsible duty of editing them, Nathaniel Bradstreet Shurtleff. The copying was done, under his appointment, by David Pulsifer, whose thorough acquaintance with the chirography of early colonial times gives assurance of exactness.

These volumes supply the most important instruction anywhere to be found, on the formation of a civilized State. They are the text-book on the subject; and stand alone in their character, and the value of their contents, as I proceed to show.

On the 3d of November, 1620, James I. granted by letters-patent all that section of North America, between the fortieth and forty-eighth parallels of latitude, from sea to sea, to the "Council established at Plymouth, in the County of Devon, for the Planting, Ruling, Ordering, and Governing of New England in America."

The Council at Plymouth conveyed by a contract, indented March 14, 1628, so much of the territory, included in their aforesaid patent, as was between lines, three miles north of Merrimack River and three miles south of Charles River, running from sea to sea, to Sir Henry Rosewell and Sir John Young, Knights, Thomas Southcott, John Humphries, John Endicott, and Simon Whitcomb, their heirs, assigns, and associates.

One year afterwards, namely, on the 4th of March, 1629, in the fourth year of the reign of Charles I., letters-patent passed the seals, confirming to the above-named six persons, and twenty others, severally named, who had become associated with them, and their heirs, and assigns, "to their only proper and absolute use and behoof forevermore," the territory purchased from the Council at Plymouth. These twenty-six individuals thus came into complete possession, and were owners, so far as the crown of England could give title, of the continent within the limits described. The vocabulary of ordinary language, and of the law, was exhausted in expressing, in every possible iteration and reiteration, the fulness, absoluteness, and perpetuity of the feofment and jurisdiction thus conveyed. In three particulars only was any limitation imposed.

The company was forbidden, in ruling its vast American domain, to make regulations repugnant to the laws of England. But this was merely nominal, as no provision was made, or required to be made, for redress of any wrong done by the company to a planter, or to any outside party. There was, indeed, no way left open, through which the regulations of the company could be brought to adjudication on this point. No political powers, or rights whatever, were given by the patent to the people of the settlement; for the negative protection implied in the language, that no laws should be imposed upon them in conflict with the statutes of the realm, was a mere shadow of a shade, as events proved.

The company was required to pay to the crown one-fifth part of all ores of gold or silver found in the country. This amounted to nothing.

There was one other condition, which also, in practice, hardly amounted to any thing. The patent exempted the settlements, to be made by the company, from all duties of any kind, "inward or outward," for seven years; and, after that, for twenty-one years more, with this exception only, that, during the latter period, they were to be subject to a duty of five per cent upon goods shipped from the plantations to any other part of the dominions of England. But this had no sensible effect here, for the duty was to be exacted at the outer end of the voyage, in the port of discharge; and was there imposed upon all alike, foreigners as well as other colonists. Further, it was pledged by the crown, that on the re-exportation, at any time within thirteen months, of goods upon which this duty had been paid, to any country whatever, no further duty of any kind should be levied on them. The whole arrangement was justly to be regarded as the assurance of a privilege rather than the imposition of a burden. No provision was made relating to the subject, on the expiration of the twenty-one years, but the whole matter left, as between the crown and the company; for it must be noticed that there is no reference whatever, in the patent, to the authority, or even the existence, of Parliament, except as implied in the clauses requiring the regulations of the company not to be repugnant to the laws of England. The duty on goods was not in deference to any acts of Parliament, but carefully described, as "according to the ancient trade of merchants." In order that it might be made clear and certain, that the territories embraced in the patent should not be subject to Parliament, but exclusively connected with the personal private property of the crown, the device was adopted, as in the patent to the Council at Plymouth, of repeating over and over again, that they were appendages of the royal demesnes, "to be holden of us, as of our manor of East Greenwich." They were to be regarded as an enlargement of the grounds of one of the favorite residences of the sovereign. While thus protecting them from interference by any other parts of the government, the King bound himself, and his heirs and successors, to the end of time, not to encroach upon, but, on the contrary, to uphold the administration of the grantees in governing their territory; and enjoined the same upon all exercising authority, civil or military, throughout his dominions.

The persons to whom the patent was issued, were constituted a body-politic. They were to choose, annually, from among themselves, a governor, deputy governor, and eighteen assistants. Any seven or more of the assistants, together with the governor or deputy governor, were to hold a monthly court, for disposing of questions arising from time to time, and requiring immediate attention. There were to be quarterly meetings, held at specified times, by the whole body of the members, or "freemen," as they were called, of the company. These were for making laws or regulations, and the transaction of weighty business. They are spoken of in the patent as "great, general, and solemn assemblies," and termed the "four Great and General Courts" of the company. At the quarterly meeting, occurring in Easter term, that is, in the latter part of May, the annual elections were required to be made.

The King, in the patent, named the persons who were to fill the offices of the company, until the time fixed for an election should arrive. It is remarkable, that, although there were several knights among the grantees, he selected an untitled one for governor. "We do, by these presents, for us, our heirs, and successors, nominate, ordain, make, and constitute our well-beloved Matthew Cradock, the first and present Governor of the said company." Cradock was a London merchant of great wealth, and, as the Records show, of eminent practical ability, energy, and wisdom. He is said to have been connected by family ties, in some way, with Endicott, which accounts, perhaps, for his having been drawn in as an associate of the six original proprietors, and for the deep interest he took in the enterprise. It can hardly be doubted, I think, that he was the same Matthew Cradock, son of a wool merchant in Stafford, who, in the reign of James I., became the owner of the baronial estate in Staffordshire, called Caverswall. The castellated mansion, built as early as the Norman conquest, was reconstructed by him, under the superintendence of Inigo Jones. It is still standing in the form Cradock gave to it, and justly regarded as "one of the most striking, picturesque, and interesting remains of a distant age. A venerable and "solemn fortress-like structure," it demands special attention, as "presenting the ideal of the great architect of the transition from the ancient castle to the baronial mansion." To an American it has a deeper interest. If its possessor and occupant was the "well-beloved" Matthew Cradock, of the patent, it will appear, as we proceed, that to us that noble mansion will ever be invested with sacred memories and associations. Within its massive walls the thought, perhaps, was conceived which has made Massachusetts and our country what they are to-day. Cradock was returned to Parliament from the city of London, in 1640, and died not long after.[1]

It is important to bear in mind that the patent conferred upon the company, in the most emphatic language, all political power whatever, without any reservation that touched the substance of the grant. This is so vital to the case, as I am presenting it, that the expressions used may be quoted, —

> "We do, of our further grace, certain knowledge, and mere motion, give and grant to the said governor or deputy governor, and such of the assistants and freemen of the said company, for the time being, as shall be assembled in any of their General Courts, or in any other courts to be specially summoned and assembled for that purpose, or to the greater part of them, that it shall and may be lawful to and for them, from time to time, to make, ordain, and establish all manner of wholesome and reasonable orders, laws, statutes, and ordinances, directions, and instructions, not contrary to the laws of this our realm of England, as well for settling of the forms and ceremonies of government and magistracy fit and necessary for the said plantation and the inhabitants there, and for naming and styling of all sorts of officers, both superior and inferior, and setting forth of the several duties, powers, and limits of every such office and place, and for impositions of lawful fines, mulcts, imprisonment, or other lawful correction, and for the directing, ruling, and disposing of all other matters and things."

Some dozen or two knights and gentlemen, more or less, sitting in the parlors of Matthew Cradock, in Swithen's Lane, within the ancient limits of London, by virtue of powers thus granted, held absolute sway over this part of America, from

[1] Baronial Halls and Ancient Picturesque Edifices of England, by S. C. Hall, F.S.A. London, 1858. Proceedings of Essex Institute, vol. i. p. 242: Memoir of Cradock, by David Roberts.

Massachusetts Bay to the Pacific Ocean; and they proceeded to administer their government by transporting settlers forthwith.

Very soon it was found expedient to send some one over to superintend affairs here on the spot, and John Endicott, an original purchaser of the country from the Council at Plymouth, was despatched accordingly. Some months after his departure, the company, on the 30th of April, 1629, elected him "Governor of the Plantation in the Massachusetts Bay," and a commission was duly forwarded to him with the form of an oath of office. This was, however, an arrangement, whereby no power was parted with by the company. It was a limited appointment. Endicott's office was to terminate in one year from the day when he took the oath, and the right was expressly reserved of removing him at any time within the year. His authority was limited by sundry conditions, and reports of all his doings were required to be transmitted to London for approval. He executed his functions with fidelity, energy, and ability. But, notwithstanding all his efforts and those of his employers, the affairs of the company were getting into embarrassment, and its operations threatened with ruin.

Cradock, a thorough business man, appreciated the condition of things. He saw the impending catastrophe; and, being of a bold and courageous spirit, with the comprehensive views of a statesman, proved himself competent to discover and apply the only remedy that could save the enterprise. That which had been fatal to colonial success in other attempts, was the difficulty in the Massachusetts plantation. It was managed by a distant administration. Deliberations and determinations by a body sitting in London could not meet the exigencies of a community, with an ocean between, and the interlapse of months in the transmission of orders and intelligence. Forming a plan by which all concerned might be extricated from the responsibilities in which they were becoming more and more involved, he was so fortunate as to secure the co-operation of parties competent to carry it through. A number of gentlemen of property, character, and influence, were found willing to join the company and assume its burdens, with the understanding that they would personally transport themselves and families to America, and make it their permanent home, provided they were allowed to carry the patent with them, hold its offices, execute its functions, and possess all its rights and powers. This was Cradock's proposal, and the arrangement was consummated.

John Winthrop, Thomas Dudley, and others, took their seats in the company, at a meeting, Oct. 15, 1629. At a meeting, five days afterwards, Cradock vacated the chair, and Winthrop was elected governor, with a new board of assistants, all to hold office for one year from that date. Early the next spring, he embarked for Massachusetts Bay, with the patent, and the frame and body of the government. Not a vestige of it was left in England.

There were undoubtedly great and daring irregularities in these proceedings, which could not have escaped notice, and would have been summarily arrested, had there been the slightest suspicion of their ultimate consequences. There is no pretence of authority in the patent for the removal of the company out of the realm, or for the relinquishment of his office by Cradock, in the time and manner. His stepping out of the chair, on the 20th of October, without even going through the ceremony of a resignation, and the election of Winthrop to serve an annual term, when by the patent he could only fill out an unexpired term, were equally without justification. Indeed, no provision is made in that instrument for the resignation of any office, and it is a procedure inadmissible by English usage. The transfer of the company to America brought with it another violation of the patent, inasmuch as they were on the passage across the Atlantic at the date fixed in express terms for the annual election, which was pretermitted in consequence altogether. These departures from and violations of the implied meaning and explicit requirements of the patent were necessities involved in the operation of the transference of it from England to America. Those engaged in it, faced the responsibilities of the occasion without shrinking. No stricture, or comment of any kind, appeared from any quarter; and the thing was done.

From the Records, Matthew Cradock alone appears as the originator and manager of this business; but from the nature of the whole proceeding, it is evident that Winthrop shared with him, as a principal co-actor. Let them each have the glory of the transaction. It is a glory that will become brighter through all time. History sheds no purer lustre upon any names than belongs to the men whose wisdom and statesmanship led to the bold and decisive step that enabled the colony of Massachusetts to bear its great part in teaching how a republic can be built up on a solid and permanent foundation.

The patent of Charles I. to the Massachusetts colony is what is called our First Charter; and, from this point, I shall speak of it under that appellation.

When Winthrop's fleet came to anchor in the harbor of Salem, he, and such members of the company as had accompanied or preceded him, found themselves in absolute and uncontrolled possession of the country, within the limits of their charter. Their jurisdiction and powers were complete; and had they been actuated by selfish motives, or a low ambition, and retained the character of a close corporation, the fortunes of the plantation, and their own fame, would have had the same fate, that of a brief duration and an ignoble end.

The charter gave to them, in express and repeated terms and without limitation, the right to admit new associates. Persons thus admitted became full partners and equal members of the company, called, as has been stated, Freemen. The exercise of this right was the magic by which they converted what was originally a royal act of incorporation for business and commercial purposes, into the constitution of a free and noble Commonwealth. In the year 1631, one hundred and twenty-six of the resident population were admitted, and in the next ten years twelve hundred more.

By this generous and enlightened policy, the PEOPLE here acceded to the rights and powers given in the charter. The Colony of Massachusetts became an independent State. Parliament could not touch it, and the crown had bound itself to keep its hands off.

The result of the proceedings thus far may be restated, at this point, in a few words: The charter gave to the Massachusetts Company sovereignty over its territory. The admission of the people of the plantation into the company gave that sovereignty to them. Having the charter in their possession, and rightfully holding under it, they claimed and exercised absolute self-government.

One hundred and forty-six years before the Declaration of the Independence of the United States, this was an independent government, and continued so for more than half a century, — more independent, in fact, than it has ever been since. Between the period of the First Charter and the war of the Revolution, it was a dependent province, its governors appointed by the British monarch, and the royal assent needed to give validity to its laws. Since the opening of the Revolutionary conflict, to this hour, it has been, in many respects and to a considerable extent, subject to the old Congress of the Confederation, and subsequently to the Government of the United States. But during the fifty-eight years of the First Charter, the people were as free to rule themselves as if they had been on another planet. They chose all their own officers, asked no approval of their laws, suffered no appeal in any case to the mother country, and bowed to no tribunals but of their own erection. This was, and ought to be considered, the first era of American independence.

In this respect, that is, in exemption from foreign interference, the situation of the original colonists of Massachusetts was all that could be desired; in other respects it was equally favorable. All the requisite conditions for the formation of a good government existed. A country lay before them, unoccupied, open, and free; sufficiently large to give room for the experiment, and comprising features and resources adapted to the uses of an industrious and intelligent people, with only here and there a solitary previous settler, or remnants of Aboriginal tribes in no way fastened to the soil. They had among them many persons of large experience in affairs, conversant with the laws and customs, not only of their own native country, but of the nations of Continental Europe, and well read in ancient history. Some of them had held eminent social position, and were of enlarged culture; and not a few, having enjoyed the advantages of the highest schools and seats of academic learning, and of Inns of Court, were remarkably qualified to act the part of statesmen. There probably was a greater amount of practical wisdom and energy among them than in any community, of equal numbers, ever brought together. What they had endured in the old country, and the sacrifices they had encountered in getting away from it, and in opening their wilderness homes, had given them an individual force and independence of character, and liberated their minds from the influence of all sentimental associations and traditional attachments to the usages, institutions, and social fixtures of all kinds in the old country.

An opportunity was thus given to solve the problem of government; to ascertain and determine the true method of forming a political organization in accordance with nature, reason, justice, and right, not to be paralleled elsewhere in the old or new world.

The colony of Plymouth, although dating ten years earlier than Massachusetts and extending its distinct history to the close of the era of our First Charter, cannot, in some respects, be regarded as standing on the same level. Its territory was not large enough to form the basis of a State, developed to its full dimensions and ramifications. Until after the process of political organization was under way here, the older colony could hardly give its attention to any thing else than the struggles required to extricate itself from financial entanglements with parties in England. It was long before they could feel that the houses they had built, and the lands they had cleared, were their own. The infant community springing from Plymouth rock demands, however, the sympathy, veneration, and imitation of the friends of freedom and virtue.

Before landing, on the 11th of November, 1620, the Pilgrims executed a written instrument, known as "The Compact," covenanting and combining themselves together "into a civil body politick," subscribed by forty-one persons. Among the names are those of several who were servants, some who were sailors, and one, at least, who could have had no pretensions to consideration on the ground of personal merit, for he is spoken of by Bradford as having been "shuffled into their company." From the first, he appears to have incurred censure for his "miscarriages." In 1621, he was tied together "neck and heels" for contempt of authority and "opprobrious speeches," and in 1630, hanged for murder.

In view of these facts we must consider the compact, drawn up in the cabin of the "Mayflower," as an instance of universal suffrage, announcing the cardinal principle of a government resting upon the whole people, and deriving its authority from the voices of all descriptions of persons, without distinction of rank, condition, or character, with a comprehensiveness which Massachusetts was long in reaching, and to which the United States could only have been brought by passing through the Red Sea of our recent intestine war.

The public documents and records of the colony of Plymouth have justly been regarded as among the chief historical treasures of the Commonwealth in which it was merged. In 1836, a resolve of the Massachusetts Legislature was approved by Governor Everett for the publication of the Laws of the Old Colony; and by his appointment they were prepared for the press and edited by our esteemed associate who, in a preceding lecture of this course, has done justice to the legislation of that colony. The result of his labors appeared in a valuable and interesting volume entitled " The Compact, with the Charter and Laws of the Colony of New Plymouth." In 1855, a resolve was passed, approved by Governor Gardner, to publish the " Records of the Colony of New Plymouth;" which was executed by printing them in the same beautiful shape as the Massachusetts Records, during the period of the First Charter. The work was performed under the superintendence of the same editor, Dr. Shurtleff. They show in detail the proceedings of a community, of a comparatively small population, on a limited area, conducting its affairs wisely and justly. Its institutions were simple and unpretentious, and administered by enlightened men, with as righteous purposes and free a spirit as the world ever saw. But when we consider government, as branching out in the directions demanded by a people in the exigencies of an expanding growth, requiring complicated arrangements and functions to meet its wants, it is obvious that such an opportunity to develop it was not afforded in Plymouth as in Massachusetts. It was not, for instance, until 1640 that any thing like a House of Deputies appeared, representing towns in a General Assembly in the older colony. In such respects it fell in our rear, even in the order of time.

Rhode Island originally consisted of several plantations, conflicting with each other, and carrying their contentions to the notice of the mother country, thereby keeping their affairs more or less within its jurisdiction. Its first General Court, in which towns were represented, was held in 1647. Nothing, however, can impair its glory, in having first planted and ever sacredly cherished the immortal principle of religious liberty.

What is now Connecticut consisted, for some time, of distinct jurisdictions. Their affairs, like those of Rhode Island, were dependent upon decisions looked for from the mother country; and finally, in 1665, they were consolidated, by the authority of the crown, extinguishing the colony of New Haven, into one government. The gallant rescue of the charter obtained at that time, from the grasp of Sir Edmund Andros, at Hartford in 1687, is justly regarded one of the most memorable incidents of American history. It continued in force to the time of the Revolution, and saved Connecticut from experiencing the fate to which Massachusetts was subjected, after the loss of its First Charter privileges, of a dependent province. It remained, in fact, the constitution of the State of Connecticut until 1818.

What are now Maine and New Hampshire were claimed by conflicting proprietors; a large part of the former, more or less, under a foreign jurisdiction, and both of them much of the time under that of Massachusetts.

As this colony was organized, and in full action, as a civil government, before the other New-England plantations; as it was central to them, to a great degree their common mother, and so much more populous than either, — its history is of larger significance and importance. In many instances, — indeed, for the most part, — they followed in its track and conformed to its practices.

New York was a Dutch dependency until 1664; and its first legislative Assembly was in 1683. New Jersey, Pennsylvania, Delaware, and the Carolinas were proprietary provinces. Maryland had a legislative Assembly in 1639; but remained a proprietary government. The early colonial condition of Virginia was much interrupted, and long in an unsettled state.

The records and memorials of all the colonies are, however, of great value, presenting many features worthy of study, and, in some particulars, severally having claims to special credit.

Massachusetts alone, was all along, for more than half a century, left unmolested to form a government, at her leisure, and as she saw fit. The Records that tell how she did it, possess, therefore, a value altogether unique. They exhibit precisely what a student of political science needs to know, and what can nowhere else be found. I proceed to note a few of the stages in the progress of eliminating the elements, and shaping the forms, of an effective, natural, and well-adjusted social and political organization, narrated in them.

After admitting the people to the freedom and power of the company, the founders of Massachusetts applied themselves slowly and cautiously, but with decisive measures, to their work. For some time, the company, at its meetings, which were all called Courts, took the entire management of affairs, however trivial, into its own immediate hands, acting directly on all matters whatsoever relating to person or property. At their first meeting, the governor and assistants were invested with the necessary powers to execute orders and decisions. At the next meeting, a beadle, afterwards dignified with the title of marshal, was sworn in, whose duty it was to attend the governor and execute his commands; also to be present at the Court, to maintain and enforce respect for its authority. The character and functions of justices of the peace were conferred upon the governor, deputy governor, and six of the assistants. Constables were appointed in the principal settlements.

It soon became apparent, that it was impracticable for assemblies of the whole body of the freemen, or for the Governor and assistants at their monthly meetings, to attend to the multifarious matters constantly demanding adjudication, in settlements as yet without known laws or established customs, and separated from each other by pathless forests. Cases could not reach the Court, with all the evidence required to decide upon them justly; and the Court, therefore, had to go to the cases. Certain persons were appointed in several localities, with limited jurisdiction, "to end small causes," as they expressed it. The body of the freemen, in General Court assembled, having thus begun to part with a portion of their power, and entered upon the path that separates judicial from legislative functions, carefully felt their way along, creating local tribunals in the towns, establishing counties with courts of trial within them, and gradually developing a comprehensive system of judicature.

In 1630, certain persons, their number not always being twelve, were appointed by the General Court to find and report to it the facts relating to particular cases, thus originating here the institution of a jury, as it has come down to us. The General Court continued, however, in most cases, to examine and decide matters directly. In 1635, grand juries were provided to present cases to the General Court.

The administration of estates, and the distribution of property, whether of testates or intestates, the General Court, for some time, kept in its own hands, heeding the law and practice in England, as far as it saw fit; but at a very early period, the policy was discussed, and finally carried into effect, of passing the whole business over to special functionaries. Probate officers were provided. Special care, however, was taken to divest this branch of the law of the ecclesiastical character given to it in the mother country. In arranging the judicial department, the General Court, consisting as it did, immediately or by representation, of the whole people, seems during the entire period of the First Charter, to have retained in its own hands an ultimate control. An appeal to its revising and final judgment was kept open from all tribunals and in all descriptions of cases. Although subsequent experience has shed great additional light upon the subject of the true position of the judiciary, the records, now under review, may well be studied, conveying, as they do, much pertinent instruction and matter for reflection.

As the plantations multiplied, and spread into the interior, it became inconvenient for the people to be fully present at the meetings of the General Court, and the transaction of business was embarrassed by an irregular and unreliable attendance. In 1632, the expedient was adopted of advising the appointment of two persons in each plantation to confer with the Governor and assistants, about the raising of a public stock. In 1634, it was made lawful for the freemen of the several settlements, to choose two or three of their number to attend the Court, to confer about public affairs generally, and to "have the full power and voices of all the said freemen derived to them for the making and establishing laws, granting lands," &c. The principle of representation was thus gradually introduced. All the plantations fell into the practice of appointing such delegates, who were called deputies. For a few years they sat with the assistants in the same room, the Governor or deputy governor presiding over the joint body. It seems to have become the custom for the deputies, to vote separately from the assistants; and a concurrence of the votes of the two portions of the assembly was required to carry a measure. Finally, it was concluded to have them sit in different rooms; and the deputies were organized as a distinct house, choosing their own speaker. In this way a double legislature was established. The fact that it has been adopted in all our States, and in the United States government, would seem to prove that it is founded on sufficient reasons, and essential to good legislation. In this, as in all things else, where the practice established here resembled that of the mother country, the resemblance was not the result of a spirit of conformity, or in deference to authority from that quarter, but solely because, in the natural progress of events, it was found expedient.

At an early day the General Court parted with a very considerable portion of its sovereignty to the several plantations, together with the fee of the lands within the limits of the same, thereby calling into existence what has always been regarded one of the chief elements of our political civilization, — Towns. John Adams declared, that to them, in a great degree, was to be attributed the preparation of this people to engage in, and carry through, the conflict of the Revolution. They are the nurseries of freedom, schools of universal education in popular rights, and alone can fit a people to make, obey, and execute the laws. No country can take the true start, or secure reliable progress in political reform, without them; and there is no race so degraded, as not to be redeemed to a capacity for self-government, if trained by such an institution to the exercise of control over affairs, by local communities in distinct neighborhoods.

Similar arrangements had existed for centuries in the mother country; and to them can be traced the characteristics which have made the English people competent to uphold a constitutional government. The encroachment upon these small local jurisdictions, — by modern Parliamentary interference and the establishment of central commissions or bureaus, — is regarded as having already lowered the character of the population of the rural districts of the kingdom. Towns were the basis of what are called hundreds; and in different sections of England, at different times, had different appellations, as thorp, now village, or hamlet; burgh, now borough; and town. The last, being probably the original name, was the prevalent one;[1] although when our fathers left England, it had become superseded, in some localities, by ville, and parish. But, under the latter designation, the institution had been perverted from its original character, which was purely secular, brought under the power of the Church, and made to receive an ecclesiastical impress.[2] The lawgivers of Massachusetts were too true to their British ancestry to call them villes, and their repugnance to associations, connected with the hierarchy at home, forbid their calling them parishes. They went back to the old Anglo-Saxon name. They made the jurisdiction of towns quite limited at first, gradually enlarging it, until it reached the dimensions still retained, embracing powers the most momentous, and constituting by far the greatest portion of what we feel to be the government under which we live.

When the public exigencies demanded it, a confederation of colonies was effected at the suggestion of the Connecticut plantations, but under the lead of Massachusetts. The entries contained in the Records on this subject, and the documents connected with its organization and operation, may be safely said to stand the test of comparison with the State papers of the originators of the Confederation of the Revolutionary age, and of the founders of our Federal Constitution, as showing the legitimate boundaries between the powers of separate States and of any general government that may be established among them.

The elements that give energy to a commonwealth, in peace or war, are strikingly disclosed and illustrated in the history of Massachusetts under the First Charter. A more efficient government for the preservation of order, security, and the common welfare, has never existed; and the rapidity with which the public resources were brought to bear in military movements, while it was repeated at the opening of the war of Independence, has never been surpassed, even in our day, which has witnessed

[1] A Restitution of Decayed Intelligence in Antiquities concerning our Nation, by Richard Verstigan, 1605, chap. ix. p. 295.

[2] The Parish, its Obligations and Powers; its officers and their duties, with illustrations of the practical workings of the institution in all secular affairs, by Toulmin Smith. London, 1854.

the uprising in their might of a great people to save the national life.

The early records of Massachusetts shed light upon all subjects that relate to the development of the moral as well as physical strength of a State, particularly the diffusion of knowledge, and of a public spirit ready to assume burdens and face danger; and to sacrifice ease, property, and life, for the common weal.

The promptitude, boldness, and impartiality of the internal administration of the government are particularly noticeable. Offences were rebuked and disorder suppressed by sure and decisive measures: no rank or station, no popular affection or habitual reverence for particular persons, however eminent or honored, could obstruct the course or embarrass the movements of even-handed power. The General Court, in the exercise of its sovereignty, treated all men alike, in as well as out of its own body. Sir Richard Saltonstall was fined; Endicott was admonished, disqualified temporarily for holding office, and committed for contempt of the authority and dignity of the Court; and even Winthrop, once in a while, was dropped from his high place.

In the administration of external affairs, the General Court was equally disregardful of all weak and timid considerations. Nothing can surpass the spirit, courage, ability, and success, with which it withstood and repelled attempts of encroachment from the mother country.

There was always a powerful party busily at work in the Court at London, bent upon the suppression of the Massachusetts colony; but by skilful diplomacy on the part of the Court and its able agents in England, following the policy comprehended by Winthrop in two words, — "Avoid and protract;" by standing tenaciously and resolutely upon their charter, particularly that feature of it which left no opening for an appeal to the mother country, and provided no process by which complaints could legitimately be brought against the company; by the opportune diversion of attention from colonial matters to occurrences in England, especially those connected with the controversy between the King and Parliament; and by the blessing of Providence, — every blow was warded off, until two generations had laid the foundations of the political fabric too deep to be moved.

It became, indeed, quite early a general feeling, among sensible people in England, that it was about as well to let the unmanageable and spunky little colony alone.

Collier, in his "Ecclesiastical History of Great Britain," quotes at length the Order in Council Archbishop Laud issued, June 17, 1634, to all places of trade and plantation where the English were settled, enjoining the establishment of the national church in them, and remarks, that, while that order was extended to all the four great divisions of the world, and generally received and obeyed in all colonies and settlements, "New England was somewhat of an exception. The Dissenters," he continues, "who transported themselves thither, established their own fancy."

Charles II., however, was prevailed upon by the enemies of the colony to send over, in 1664, Commissioners to reduce it to subordination; but they went back as they came, disconcerted by the firmness and outgeneralled by the strategy of the colonial authorities. The records containing the communications that passed between these gentlemen and the General Court, show the wonderful sagacity, wariness, and ability of the latter. The royal commissioners were allowed to gain no advantage in the encounter, but were drawn into false positions and exposed attitudes by the expert fencing of their adversary, until they were utterly discomfited and disarmed. The whole affair, as we read its particulars, becomes absolutely amusing, from the superior wisdom and adroitness of the Court. Every attempt to bring the administration here under the control of the mother country, ended in equally humiliating failure.

It cannot, indeed, be doubted, that, if matters had come to extremities at any time, even at the earliest period, when the population scarcely reached up into the thousands, they would have resisted in arms any hostile force that should have ventured to land on their shores, from whatever quarter it might come; relying on the justness of their cause, and the Divine aid, on which they cast themselves with prayer and faith, as no other people ever did. Winthrop informs us, that in January, 1635, in the prevalence of an apprehension that a General Governor was about to be sent over from England, the Court asked the ministers, convened on the occasion, what ought to be done in that event? and they replied, with one voice, that he ought not to be received. The fort at Castle Island was immediately built, and a large *commission* appointed, consisting of the principal inhabitants, of which Winthrop was at the head, for "military affairs," to organize and arm the whole strength of the country for either "offensive or defensive war." The idea was familiarly expressed by all, that they would no sooner relinquish their rights under the charter than their estates, that they would fight for both; and, if driven from their houses and lands on the seashore, they would withdraw deeper and deeper into the forests, carrying their charter, the ark of their covenant, with them. And finally, when James II. abrogated the charter and took ruthless possession of the country, with a design, as the colonial statesmen believed, in pursuance of a secret treaty, to cede it to France, the people of Boston and the vicinity rose in their wrath. Sir Edmund Andros found himself, the next morning, in the lock-up at Fort Hill. He was removed for safer keeping to Castle Island, which, by holding as a prisoner the deposed royal governor, fairly won a right to the title, subsequently given it, of Fort Independence. Finally, he was shipped back to England. In the mean time, old Simon Bradstreet, in his eighty-seventh year, who, fifty-nine years before came over with Winthrop, and was the first secretary and the last governor under the First Charter in Massachusetts, was recalled to his place by an insurgent people, and for three more years affairs were administered as in the days of the old charter. The bold procedure was acquiesced in at home and abroad, no one was called to account for it, and Andros got no redress. The First Charter history of Massachusetts thus closed in glory.

The study of these records will help us avoid errors into which the Fathers of Massachusetts were led. A large department of their legislation, that embracing sumptuary laws and police regulations, is now considered as passing beyond the boundaries of the legitimate power of government, and trenching upon the rights of private life, and the domain of personal freedom. The severities of their penal code are condemned by the sentiments of a more enlightened age; but, in reference to this point, allowance must be made for their circumstances. In the prevention and punishment of crime, they had not what we possess in philanthropic, reformatory, and penitentiary establishments.

In initiating and organizing a government, errors were committed, but they were readily rectified when discovered. In 1636 and 1637, the General Court was led into a measure singularly in conflict with its usual policy and the spirit of the people : a council for life was established, and Winthrop, Dudley, and Endicott elected to it. The prevalence of sounder views prevented any further proceedings, and the plan was dropped.

There is one branch of their administration exposed especially to stricture, and universally condemned, at the present day, which must not be overlooked; for their views and designs in relation to it are proved to have been fallacious and impracticable. They came here with a purpose most dear to their hearts, of establishing and enjoying a system of society and government in which all would be of one mind, in the reception of a particular theological creed and ecclesiastical order. This did not, in their view, involve any violation of the rights of conscience. The New World, as they reasoned, could accommodate persons of all persuasions. They had purchased and planted their territory, and cherished the hope of enjoying it in peace and unity. This idea had captivated their imaginations. The agitations and dissensions arising from conflicting religious theories were distasteful to their feelings. They had left the Old World to get rid of them, and thought it no wrong to ask those who desired to establish and propagate opinions in conflict with theirs, as there was room enough for all, to go elsewhere. To preserve peace, tranquillity, and order, they undertook to keep out Anabaptists, Antinomians, and Quakers. It was an error to expect to succeed in such a policy, and the attempt involved them in the follies and mischiefs of intolerance and persecution. As followers of the divine Word, and disciples of the Great Teacher, they ought to have known better. Tares will spring up with the wheat. LET THEM BOTH GROW TOGETHER UNTIL THE HARVEST. The Lord of the harvest, and he alone, has the right or the power to separate them. In this, then, — it cannot too emphatically be affirmed, — the founders of Massachusetts were in the wrong, and their example is to be held up as a warning. For having pursued the opposite policy, in opening a shelter for all sorts of opinions, and patiently enduring the turmoil of wrangling bigots and fanatical enthusiasts, rather than suffer the hand of the civil power to be lifted against them, the name of Roger Williams will be illustrious, and the peculiar honor of Rhode Island secure for ever.

At the very first meeting of the Massachusetts General Court, after the transfer of the charter, at which a governor and assistants were chosen, on the 18th of May, 1631, it was voted, that "no man shall be admitted to the freedom of this body-politic, but such as are members of some of the churches within the limits of the same;" and they suffered no churches to be gathered, but such as were sound in doctrine, according to the estimation of the General Court. Admitting that the policy announced in this vote was erroneous, and rejoicing, as we all do, that it has long ago been repudiated, it is but fair to give heed to what may be offered in its palliation. It was, in part, suggested by their peculiar situation. It was necessary, by all means, to keep their government from falling into the hands of persons who might appear among them with a disposition to win favor from the parties hostile to them around the royal court; and this seemed the most sure way to keep them out. Further, in spite of all precautions to prevent it, here, as in all first settlements, there were individuals of loose and profligate lives, wholly unfit to share in the government. It was an effectual bar against them. And, after all, it must be conceded, that there was one good feature in it. It ignored the distinction between high and low, rich and poor, bond and free; and was, as far as it went, in this view, a liberal measure. It is due to the Church, Catholic and Protestant, to give it the credit, in every age and every communion, whatever other barriers it has raised, of having welcomed to its bosom persons of all ranks and races, without reference to their position in the scale of society. It has been in advance of the State in this particular.

While we condemn the policy of the Fathers in reference to religious opinions, we must not charge them with having contemplated an established religion as a part of the frame of their government. To that they were utterly opposed. They often, it is true, sought the advice of the ministers concerning public affairs, appreciating their learning and wisdom, but never allowed them to participate in the government. They went further in this respect than we do. No minister, or church officer of any kind, not even a lay-elder, was permitted to hold any legislative, political, or civil appointment.

Increase Nowell, an original patentee and assistant, belonging to a high family at home, who came over with the charter, was a man of eminent gifts and graces, and all his life in distinguished public employment. When the church at Charlestown was planted, he was chosen a ruling or lay elder, and acted as such. The question was raised, whether he, being a magistrate, could hold office in a church. It was decided that he could not, and Nowell laid down his eldership.

Samuel Sharp was probably one of the best educated men of the first age of the colony. Bred to learning during his youth, and transferred at opening manhood to business as a merchant, he continued through life to cultivate his mind and gratify his literary tastes. He seems to have been a proficient also in military knowledge, as he was intrusted, from the first, with all that related to engineering, fortification, and ordnance, in the plantation. Colonial enterprise seems to have particularly attracted his interest. He was one of the company in London which managed the first settlement at Plymouth. The Records of the Massachusetts Company show the active part he took in its affairs, and the extent to which it availed itself of his business efficiency. When Endicott was elected temporary local governor, April 30, 1629, he divided the vote with him, was appointed one of his council, and authorized, in conjunction with Samuel Skelton, the first pastor of the Salem church, in the event of Endicott's death, to assume the government of the plantation. Although Matthew Cradock never came to America in person, he took lands, and shipped over successive cargoes of provisions, live stock, and other needful articles, selecting suitable persons to look out for their disbursement and distribution. Sharp was his chief agent, and enjoyed his full confidence. Henry Haughton was also concerned in the management of Cradock's affairs. The latter, at the formation of the Salem church, was elected its lay-elder; but, dying a few months afterwards, Sharp was chosen to his place, which he filled to his death in 1656. In consequence of holding this office, the great talents and capacity of Elder Sharp were lost to the civil service of the colony. His name, although consecrated by the memory of his various usefulness, Christian learning, and eminent piety, is seen no more on its records, except as having, with Endicott and others, been bound over to answer before the General Court, as representatives of the Salem church, for having denounced the proceedings of the Court against its minister, Roger Williams.

These instances sufficiently show how thoroughly the policy was carried out of not allowing any officers whatever of a church to hold political or civil appointments, or in any degree or shape to have share in the government.

The Fathers of Massachusetts have been ridiculed for the respect in which they held the Hebrew polity, and for bringing the authority of the Scriptures, particularly of the Old Testament, to corroborate their legislation. But it may be asked, Where else could they have gone? Not surely to precedents drawn from ancient despotisms, or European monarchies. References to the statutes of the Pentateuch were more to their purpose, and justly carried greater weight, than to feudal rolls of parliaments, basely obsequious to Tudors and Stuarts. The Hebrew government, for the ends it was designed to accomplish, was the most perfect ever contrived. It left a deeper imprint on national character than any government ever has. It gave to a people a national life which no power on earth has been able to extinguish. Subjugation, dispersion, and the scorn, hate, and persecution of all nations for two thousand years, have made no impression on it. The Jewish race has survived it all. In our day the proudest monarchs are bowing before its banking-houses, and it affords leading minds to parliaments and cabinets. Its perpetuity, as a distinct people, although scattered everywhere, and everywhere trodden down for ages, is the marvel of the world's history, and attests the greatness of Moses as a lawgiver.

The Massachusetts statesmen of the first age did not follow indiscriminately the details of the Jewish system; but, as the Records show, sought to discover and obey the requirements of eternal moral laws. They acted, in their secular administration, upon principles that will stand the test of all time; but found gratification and confirmation in the ancient Scriptures. It is wonderful to what an extent they were able to avail themselves of this resource. Any one who verifies, collates, and examines their references to the events, characters, and expressions of Holy Writ, will be surprised to find how apposite they are, and what a mine was thus opened. Verily, the volume containing the most ancient literature of the world, is worthy of being called the Book of Books. Not wholly unaware of the disparagement, in which some have indulged, of the Old Testament scriptures, I am constrained to say, that the longer I live, and the more I ponder them, the profounder is my admiration and veneration of the unapproached dignity and simplicity of style of their historical and narrative passages, and of the beauty, splendor, and sublimity of the conceptions and imagery that glorify their strains of eloquence, poetry, and prophecy, breathing an influence that expands and lifts up the soul, and is felt to be inspiration.

In support of what I have said, in reference to the legislation of the first colonial age, allow me to fall back upon the judgment of one whose name is among the ornaments of the Massachusetts Historical Society, and the memory of whose genius and scholarship is fresh in the hearts of the older members. Francis Calley Gray, in a notice of the compendium, made in 1641, of the laws of the Massachusetts colony, known as the "Body of Liberties,"[1] says, —

> "Our ancestors, instead of deducing all their laws from the Books of Moses, established, at the outset, a code of fundamental principles, which, taken as a whole, for wisdom, equity, adaptation to the wants of their community, and a liberality of sentiment superior to the age in which it was written, may fearlessly challenge comparison with any similar production, from Magna Charta itself, to the latest Bill of Rights that has been put forth in Europe or America."

The early lawgivers of Massachusetts were, indeed, in advance of their times. Before we ridicule or reproach their legislation, it becomes us to see to it that those whom we choose to make and administer law, are equally in advance of our times.

The just formation of a body-politic which these Records have now been used to illustrate, demands attention in our day. Much remains to be done, even in the most advanced and enlightened nations. Much is being done. All the light that can be obtained is needed. Men everywhere are crying out for it. Agita-

[1] Massachusetts Historical Collections, vol. viii. Third Series, p. 191.

tion and change rule the hour. The future is felt to be subject to unknown and indeterminable influences, and to depend upon the wills or fortunes or lives of individuals, or the fluctuating conflicts of parties. Who can predict what is in store for Spain, France, Italy, the German States, or the northern kingdoms of Europe? The current of events seems to be working radical changes in Great Britain and Ireland, and the dependencies of that empire. Although, in many respects the most advanced of the old forms of political civilization, it can hardly be doubted that it is doomed to pass through momentous crises; for the whole structure of its constitutional system rests upon fictions that must give way, sooner or later, to truth and right. It assumes that there are three estates essential to the composition of a nation, — king, lords, and commons. The last only has a legitimate and permanent existence. The people are the whole of a country, so far as its government is concerned, and must finally vindicate their rightful claim to power.

The framers of the Constitution of the United States are justly regarded as among the wisest statesmen of all times; but they failed, in some points, in contriving their scheme of government, to estimate aright the action of the principles of human nature, or calculate their forces. They did not foresee the operation or even the existence of what are called national parties. The arrangement they made for the election of a President was soon found utterly impracticable for the end designed. The Amendment of 1803, introducing the plan that has been subsequently followed, was only carried by the decision of the then Speaker of the House of Representatives, Nathaniel Macon, of North Carolina, who claimed the right, since conceded, of the presiding officer of that body, to vote when the House is not equally divided. His vote made the requisite two-thirds.

Indications are appearing that some further change may be demanded. The intermediate machinery of Electors is justly criticised; but great difficulty will be experienced, in contriving in any other way, to preserve the rights of the smaller States. So, also, on the elementary subject of suffrage, great enlargements have been recently made, but others are demanded. It is, indeed, evident that questions are impending that reach the foundations of political science. Let them be met, not with ridicule or reproach, but with intelligence and fairness. Having been brought to a higher stand-point, with a wider field of view than the Fathers, we ought to have a more liberal spirit; but for integrity of purpose, and independence of authority, for carefulness in deliberation, and firmness and courage in action, we may well study their example.

Pardon me for detaining you a moment longer, while summarily delineating the spectacle the early records of Massachusetts present.

Here, on a clear field, unoccupied by any organized society, with no pre-existent institutions to cumber the ground, but all as fresh as if never trodden by man before, the experiment of planting and constructing a civil government was fairly worked out. No external power was suffered to interfere, and no foreign precedents allowed to claim authority; no closet statesman or fanciful theorist formed the scheme; no lordly proprietor, or distant corporation, or board of trade, directors, or officials of any kind, dictated. The whole procedure was left, without let or hindrance, suggestion or influence, from any outside quarter, to the people on the spot. They were a select people for the work; — intelligent, thoughtful, brave, and devout. They were settled in families, and comprised all the elements of a State. Although emigrants from the Old World, they trailed none of its arbitrary, outgrown institutions or usages after them. Conversant with all the learning of ancient and feudal forms, they applied none of it here. Having a new country to dwell in, they resolved to establish nothing but what facts, as they occurred, should prove to be necessary or desirable. Oglethorpe planned a social system for Georgia, John Locke drafted a contrivance of government for the Carolinas, Lord Baltimore superintended Maryland, William Penn Pennsylvania, and other proprietors and patrons their several settlements. Not so in Massachusetts: the Fathers of this colony followed no far-off light; they moved only as experience opened the way; they tried every step as they advanced, indulged in no theories or speculations, and held fast only what was found, in their view, to be good, and thus accomplished the great end of a stable, prosperous, powerful, and permanent commonwealth. All the essential features of our present security and happiness were stamped into the fabric of society during the period of the First Charter.

The early growth of Massachusetts was natural; and the matured result as complete, as of every natural growth; but, unlike the growths of nature in other things, there was, in this, no element of decay. The institutions planted during our first fifty years withstood a century of immediately subsequent provincial endurance; and as another century under the flag of our Union is approaching its completion, they are striking their roots deeper every day. The foundation here laid can never be moved; and we owe it to the men who laid it, that, in education, arts, wealth, and power, we hold a rank second to none in the Republic. The path, here opened, other Colonies and States have travelled, and all must travel, to reach the fruition of liberty, order, justice, and the rights of man.

Of the grand Epic, Time is writing, of the Regeneration of Nations, the old charter history of Massachusetts is the First Book.

MEMORANDA,

Historical, Chronological,

&c.

PREPARED WITH THE HOPE TO AID THOSE WHOSE
INTEREST IN

PILGRIM MEMORIALS, AND HISTORY,

IS FRESHENED BY THIS JUBILEE YEAR,

And who may not have a large Historical Library at hand.

[PRINTED, *(but not Published,)* FOR THE USE OF
CONGREGATIONAL MINISTERS.]

1870.

TODD, PRINTER, 15 CORNHILL, BOSTON.

THE Convention which, on call of the Church of the Pilgrimage in Plymouth, met in the Broadway Tabernacle, in the city of New York, on the 2d March last, to "take such action as shall seem to it expedient, for ordering the Commemorative Services" of this 250th year since the landing of the Pilgrims at Plymouth, passed, among others, the following resolution, viz:

Resolved, That it be earnestly recommended that during the month of May, next, every Congregational pastor set forth from the pulpit, our obligations to the Pilgrim Fathers, the influence of their faith and polity upon the character of the nation; and the duty we owe to the memory and principles of the Fathers, to maintain, enlarge and transmit the inheritance we have received at their hands.

It was felt by that Convention to be of the highest importance that this request should be complied with, if practicable, *by every pastor and acting pastor of a Congregational church in the land;* for the possible direct relation of such preaching to the prosperity of all the Jubilee endeavors of the year, by which it is sought to put our American Congregationalism at once upon a plane of higher life and broader efficiency, not more than for its probable educational results, in giving to all Congregationalists clearer conceptions of their principles, a more precise acquaintance with their history, and a more accurate perception of the relations of their polity to the civil and religious prosperity of our own land and of the world.

As the month of May will soon be here, and the time afforded for special research upon this subject is not long; and as the books in general circulation, which treat of the Pilgrims and their history, and of the great struggle out of which sprang that Separatist faith which established itself upon the rock of Plymouth and leavened this new world, are neither numerous, exhaustive, nor always authentic; and as the sources of some of the most accurate and interesting portions of these annals have been discovered by investigations comparatively recent, whose results are as yet mainly confined to the shelves of the few great libraries, while these are not within easy reach of the majority of Congregational pastors; the Executive Committee, to whom that Convention entrusted "all matters of detail connected with the commemorative endeavors of the year," have decided—in deference to suggestions and requests received from various quarters—to publish a little pamphlet of Memoranda—historical, chronological, etc., in the hope to aid all special students of the Pilgrim history in their studies, by indicating to them where to find what they desire to refer to just now, so that their library research may perhaps be lightened, and in the hope of putting in the most condensed form within the reach of those whose circumstances do not favor their consultation of the libraries, some hints of the facts of which they are in search.

Hastily prepared, and felt to be exceedingly fragmentary and inadequate, the following pages are therefore sent forth in the hope that, while they will hinder nobody, they may possibly, in default of something better, prove helpful to some investigators, and so aid a little in the Jubilee work of the year, and the good results for the honor of the Fathers, the prosperity of the future, the benefit of man, and the glory of God, which are sought in it.

EDWARD S. TOBEY,
WILLIAM W. PATTON,
HENRY M. DEXTER,
SAMUEL HOLMES,
A. S. BARNES,
RAY PALMER,
ALONZO H. QUINT,
Jubilee Executive Committee.

BOSTON, MASS., April 25, 1870.

CHRONOLOGICAL GLANCE

AT PROMINENT FACTS OF INTEREST,

IN CONNECTION WITH THE

Pilgrim Fathers, and their History.

1380. Wycliffe completed his translation of the Bible, multiplied copies by the aid of transcribers; and, by God's blessing on His Word, thus unbound from the fetters of alien tongues, a spirit of inquiry was generated, and the seeds sown of that religious revolution, which a little more than a century later, astonished and overturned the world.

1418. Council of Constance ordered Wycliffe's bones to be ungraved and burned for those of a heretic.

1534. Henry the Eighth of England, for the reason that the Pope would not divorce him from Katharine, his wife, divorced the Church of England from its allegiance to Rome.

1550. Puritanism dates from John Hooper's "scrupling the vestments," and refusing to take the oath of supremacy, until King Edward had run his pen through a part of it.

1554. The Frankfort congregation of exiles arose, under the persecuting reign of "Bloody Mary," and the Puritan separation began with Englishmen outside of England.

1566. Date of separation in England, by Puritans who were shut out of the Church, and restrained of the press, and who thought, as separate congregations had for some time been existing at Frankfort, Geneva, and even in London, it might be right, and their duty, to come out and be separate from the corruptions and superstitions swaying the English Church, and its service.

1570. Thomas Cartwright pushed the fundamental proposition to reduce all things in reforming the Church to the apostolical way, as contained in the New Testament. For this he was expelled from Oxford, and took refuge abroad. Coming back seven years after, he maintained that government by the eldership is of divine appointment aud obligation—anticipating, mainly, the views and practices of the Presbyterian party of the time of the Commonwealth.

1582. Robert Browne threw a new element into the conflict of opinion which was agitating the English people (under Elizabeth), by evolving from the New Testament, essentially, the Democratic system of Church polity.

1591. A church of English exiles, actuated by the principles of Browne, but misliking his name, was formed at Amsterdam, of which Henry Ainsworth became pastor.

1593. Henry Barrow, John Greenwood and John Penry put to death for their Congregational principles.

1606. The Mayflower Church was formed by mutual covenant, at Scrooby in Nottinghamshire.

1607. Harried out of England, this Church begins to fly to Holland, and in the next spring, all get over to Amsterdam, where they continue about a year.

1608. The Mayflower Church removed to Leyden, where Robinson was sole pastor, and William Brewster was chosen elder.

1611. $\frac{\text{25 April.}}{\text{5 May.}}$ John Robinson and others of his church bought a house in the Kloksteeg in Leyden, near the University, which "being large," was both occupied by him, and used by them as their place of Sabbath worship.

1615. $\frac{\text{26 Aug.}}{\text{5 Sept.}}$ Robinson became matriculated in the University. Age, thirty-nine.

1620. $\frac{1}{11}$ July. The last revised conditions of the agreement of the English merchants with the intending colonists were settled, and the emigration to America finally and absolutely determined on.

1620. More particular schedule of the events of their emigration hither, and of the first six months of their settlement — in illustration of their sufferings in laying the foundations of civil and religious liberty here.

Day.	Old Style.	New Style.	
Tues.	11 *July.*	21 *July.*	Left Leyden.
Sat.	5 *Aug.*	15 *Aug.*	Sailed from Southampton, (two ships.)
Sab.	13 "	23 "	Put back to Dartmouth.
Wed.	23 "	2 *Sept.*	Sailed again.
——	——	——	Put back the second time to Plymouth, and Speedwell dismissed.
Wed.	6 *Sept.*	16 "	Sailed from Plymouth, (102 in the Mayflower.)
Mon.	6 *Nov.*	16 *Nov.*	William Butten dies at sea.
Thurs.	9 "	19 "	Saw Cape Cod.
Sat.	11 "	21 "	Anchored in Provincetown harbor, signed the compact, chose Carver Governor, and went ashore.
Mon.	13 "	23 "	Unshipped the shallop, and went ashore to wash.
Wed.	15 "	25 "	Started on first expedition inland.
Thurs.	16 "	26 "	Found springs in Truro, went as far as Pamet River, found a kettle, dug up corn, etc.
Fri.	17 "	27 "	Sunk the kettle in the pond, and went back to ship.
Mon.	27 "	7 *Dec.*	Second and larger exploring party started in shallop and get to East Harbor Creek.
Tues.	28 "	8 "	Went on to Pamet River, and inland from it.
Wed.	29 "	9 "	Revisited Cornhill, and Master Jones and a part went back to the ship.
Thurs.	30 "	10 "	Found wigwams, graves, etc., and got back to ship and found Peregrine White had been born in their absence.
Mon.	4 *Dec.*	14 "	Dies, Edward Thompson.
Tues.	5 "	15 "	Francis Billington nearly blows up the Mayflower.
Wed.	6 "	16 "	Third exploring party started in the shallop, and get as far as Eastham. Jasper Moore dies on the ship.

Day.	Old Style.	New Style.	1620.
Thurs.	7 *Dec.*	17 *Dec.*	Explored up Welfleet Bay, and inland, and slept at Great Meadow Creek; Bradford's wife falls overboard from the ship, and is drowned.
Fri.	8 "	18 "	Had first encounter with Indians, then coasted round the bay, following the shore westward and northward, went by Barnstable in a snow storm so thick they did not see its harbor, broke their rudder, split their mast into three pieces, and in a heavy northeaster ran in under the lee of Clark's Island in Plymouth harbor after pitch dark. James Chilton dies on the ship.
Sat.	9 "	19 "	Rested, refitted their mast and rudder, etc.
Sab.	10 "	20 "	*Kept the Sabbath* on Clark's Island.
Mon.	11 "	21 "	FOREFATHERS' DAY. Landed on the Rock, and explored.
Tues.	12 "	22 "	Started back for Provincetown, and the Mayflower.
Fri.	15 "	25 "	Weighed anchor for Plymouth, but a foul wind drove them back.
Sat.	16 "	26 "	Dropped anchor inside Plymouth beach.
Mon.	18 "	28 "	Party from the ship landed and explored.
Tues.	19 "	29 "	Second exploration of the shore.
Wed.	20 "	30 "	Third expedition, resulting in decision to settle near what are now Burial Hill and Town Brook.
Thurs.	21 "	31 "	Stormed, and nothing could be done, but Richard Britteredge dies on the ship.

162$\frac{0}{1}$.

Fri.	22 "	1 *Jan.*	Storm continues. Goodwife Allerton gives birth to a still-born son.
Sat.	23 "	2 "	As many as can, begin to cut and carry timber on shore for the common house.
Sab.	24 "	3 "	Those on shore hear a cry of savages — as they think, but see none. Solomon Prower dies.
Mon.	25 "	4 "	Busy on the common house. Indian alarm again, but saw none. The beer being low, they begin to drink water on board the ship.
Tues.	26 "	5 "	Foul weather, no going ashore.
Wed.	27 "	6 "	To work again.
Thurs.	28 "	7 "	Divided whole company into nineteen families, and measured out lots for them.
Fri.	29 "	8 "	Tried to work, but rainy.
Sat.	30 "	9 "	Same weather and same result. Saw Indian smokes in the distance.
Mon.	1 *Jan.*	10 "	At work again. Digory Priest dies.
Wed.	3 "	13 "	More smokes seen, but still no Indians.
Thurs.	4 "	14 "	Standish and a party go out, and find wigwams, but no Indians. Shot an eagle, and the poor hungry men likened its flesh to mutton !

Day.	Old Style.	New Style.	$162\frac{0}{1}$.
Fri.	5 *Jan.*	15 *Jan.*	A sailor found a herring, so they hoped for fish soon, but found they had no hooks small enough for cod-hooks.
Sat.	6 "	16 "	C. Martin very sick, and sends ashore for Governor Carver to see him " about his accounts."
Sab.	7 "	17 "	Carver goes on board.
Mon.	8 "	18 "	Fine, fair day. Shallop gets some fish. F. Billington discovers the pond since called by his name. Martin dies.
Tues.	9 "	19 "	Divided their lots of land by lot, laying out a street with cabins on each side.
Thurs.	11 "	21 "	William Bradford taken sick while at work.
Fri.	12 "	22 "	Rained again. John Goodman and Peter Brown lost themselves in the woods, chasing a deer.
Sat.	13 "	23 "	An armed party went out seven or eight miles in search vainly, but at night, the lost men returned, faint and frozen, so that Goodman's shoes had to be cut from his feet, and it was a long time before he was able to walk.
Sab.	14 "	24 "	More being now on shore than in the ship, they intended to have worship in the common house, but its thatch took fire and burned off, which prevented.
Mon.	15 "	25 "	Stormed again, so that there was no communication between the ship and the shore.
Tues.	16 "	26 "	Three fair, sunshiny days, like April, followed, and cheered on their work.
Fri.	19 "	29 "	Began to build a shed to store their provisions. Stormed again. Saw two wolves.
Sat.	20 "	30 "	Made their shed.
Sab.	21 "	31 "	*Kept their first Sabbath worship ashore.*
Mon.	22 "	1 *Feb.*	Fair. Stored their meal, etc., in the shed.
Mon.	29 "	8 "	Cold with sleet, but cleared, and the long-boat and shallop carried goods ashore. Miles Standish's wife Rose, dies.
Tues.	30 "	9 "	Frosty, with sleet. Could not work.
Wed.	31 "	10 "	More so. Those on the ship saw two Indians running away.
Sab.	4 *Feb.*	14 "	Wet, and so windy as almost to blow the Mayflower (now light), from her anchorage, and the windy flood almost washed the "daubing" out of the chinks of their cabins.
Fri.	9 "	19 "	Too cold to work. The cabin of the sick ones caught fire, but was put out without much damage to them. Killed five geese, and found a dead deer.
Fri.	16 "	26 "	Cold. One fowling saw twelve Indians, and heard more. The said Indians made a great fire at night in the woods, and stole some tools that had been left out.

Day.	Old Style.	New Style.	$162\frac{0}{1}$.
Sat.	17 *Feb.*	27 *Feb.*	Began to organize in a military way. Chose Miles Standish Captain. Two savages made signs on a near hill, but ran away.
Wed.	21 "	3 *Mar.*	Got the great guns out of the ship, and mounted them on what is now Burial Hill. William White, William Mullins, and two others die.
Sab.	25 "	7 "	Isaac Allerton's wife Mary dies.
Sat.	3 *Mar.*	13 "	The birds sang, and there was a thunder-storm.
Wed.	7 "	17 "	Began to sow garden seeds.
Fri.	16 "	26 "	A second meeting to arrange military affairs was broken up by *Samoset's* coolly walking in upon them "straight to the Randevous," and in tolerable English, making the brief speech of "Welcome Englishmen." He told them that all the Indians about Plymouth had died four years before by an extraordinary plague. They fed him, and lodged (and watched) him over night.
Sat.	17 "	27 "	Dismissed him with presents.
Sab.	18 "	28 "	*Samoset* came back, with five others, "to trade," and bringing the stolen tools. Tried to send them away, because it was Sunday, but *Samoset* pretended to be sick, and wouldn't go.
Mon.	19 "	29 "	Fair. Sowed seeds.
Tues.	20 "	30 "	Ditto.
Wed.	21 "	31 "	Sent *Samoset* off. Another military meeting again interrupted by the sight of Indians on the hill. The carpenter, long sick, got well enough to repair the shallop, so they could "fetch all from aboard" — so they cleaned out the ship, and their colonizing became complete.
Thurs.	22 "	1 *Apr.*	Another fine day, and another attempt at public business interrupted by the return of *Samoset*, bringing *Squanto*, (the only survivor of the Indians native to the spot,) and announcing *Massasoit*, who, with his brother, *Quadequina*, and suit, made a formal call, and concluded a treaty — which was kept by both parties, until Philip broke it in 1675.
Fri.	23 "	2 "	Visits exchanged between the colonists and *Massasoit's* party. *Squanto* went to fish for eels, which he trod out of the mud with his feet, and caught with his hands, and which the colonists thought "very fat and sweet." Concluded their military and other public business, and re-elected John Carver for Governor, for the new year, beginning on Sabbath the 25th.
Sat.	24 "	3 "	Edward Winslow's wife, Elizabeth, dies. A great mortality prevailed during this month, above the names here given. Nearly half the sailors of the Mayflower died also.

Day.	Old Style.	New Style.	1621.
Tues.	5 *Apr.*	15 *Apr.*	The Mayflower starts for England on her return voyage, but none of the diminished company wanted to go back in her.
——	— "	— "	Governor Carver died suddenly, "and his wife being a weak woman, dyed within 5 or 6 weeks after him." William Bradford was chosen Governor in his place, "and being not yet recoverd of his ilnes, in which he had been near ye point of death, Isaak Allerton was chosen to be an Assistante unto him."
Sat.	12 *May.*	22 *May.*	Edward Winslow was married to Mrs. Susanna, widow of William White, who had died, $\frac{\text{21 Feb.}}{\text{3 Mar.}}$ The first marriage in the Colony.
Mon.	18 *Jun.*	28 *Jun.*	Two servants fight a duel, each wounding the other. The company sit on their case, and adjudge them to have their head and feet tied together, and so to lie for twenty-four hours without meat or drink; but "within *an Hour*, because of their great Pains, at their own & their Master's [Stephen Hopkins] humble Request, upon Promise of better Carriage, they are released by the *Governor*."

"The spring now approaching, it pleased God the mortalitie begane to cease amongst them, and ye sick and lame recovered apace, which put, as it were, new life into them; though they had borne their sadd affliction with as much patience & contentedness, as I thinke any people could doe. But it was ye Lord which upheld them, and had beforehand prepared them; many having long borne ye yoake, yea, from their youth." — Gov. Bradford's *Hist. Plim. Plant.* 98.

VARIOUS EXTRACTS, ETC.,

ILLUSTRATING THE

RISE, CONDUCT, HISTORY, OPINIONS, TRIALS AND INFLUENCE, OF THE PLYMOUTH MOVEMENT, AND MEN.

From the rise of the Papacy to the Reformation, the theory of the Church was that of an all-embracing centralized organism; governed by the Papal Hierarchy, and whose private members had simply the right, duty, and responsibility, of submission and unquestioning obedience.

Wycliffe.

"Upwards of a century and a half before the time of Luther, Wycliffe had exposed the superstition and despotism of Rome. Born in the early part of the fourteenth century, [near Richmond, Yorkshire, 1324, died at Lutterworth, 31 Dec. 1384,] he anticipated the discoveries of his more fortunate successors, and labored with an assiduity and rectitude of purpose, which entitle him to the admiration and gratitude of posterity. Though his labors did not effect an alteration in the ecclesiastical polity of his country, they made an extensive and permanent impression. A numerous class of followers were raised up, by the Providence of God: these preserved the precious seed of the kingdom until more propitious days; and, though assailed by the fiercest persecutions, were enabled to hand down the sacred deposit to the times of the Lutheran reformation." — Price's *History of Prot. Non-Conform.* i: 4.

About 1380, Wycliffe completed a translation of the Bible into English — the first ever made public. "It was not made for his own use, but for the enlightenment of his country. His object was to throw the broad blaze of revelation upon the corruptions of the Church, to expose before his fellow-men the errors and superstitions into which they had fallen, and to disclose to their view the narrow path which they had missed. The numerous copies of Wycliffe's translation preserved for four centuries and a half, attest the early publicity of his version, and the diligent means employed for the multiplication of transcripts. It may safely be affirmed that not one of the partial versions previously made, had ever been as widely diffused as this; and it was the formation of the bold idea of its general circulation, and the execution of the daring and unexampled project, that constitute the peculiar and glorious characteristic of the reformer's enterprise." — Bagster's *English Hexapla.* 13.

"The disciples of Wycliffe were termed Lollards, and were found in most parts of the kingdom. Knighton, a canon of Leicester, and a cotemporary of Wycliffe, tells us that in the year 1382, 'their number very much increased, and that, starting like saplings from the root of a tree, they were multiplied, and filled every place within the compass of the land.' This language must undoubtedly be understood with some limitation; but we cannot mistake the inference to be drawn from it." — Vaughan's *Life of Wycliffe.* 154.

"One thing I boldly assert, that in the Primitive Church, or the time of Paul, two orders of the clergy were held sufficient — those of priests and deacons. No less certain am I, that in the time of Paul, presbyters and bishops were the same, as is shown in 1 Tim. iii, and Titus i." — Wycliffe, *Trialogue*, xiii.

"Wycliffe was the first of Puritans, as well as of Protestants." — *Bogue and Bennett*, i: 27.

"Nothing came to the birth in the 16th century, that had not lain in embryo in Wycliffe's time, under the common heart of England." — Palfrey's *Hist. New England*, i: 108.

"Hitherto, the corpse of John Wycliffe had quietly slept in his grave, about one and forty years after his death, till his body was reduced to bones, and his bones almost to dust; for though the earth in the chancel of Lutterworth in Leicestershire, where he was interred, hath not so quick a digestion with the earth of Aceldama, to consume flesh in twenty-four hours, yet such the appetite thereof, and all other English graves, as to leave small reversions of a body after so many years. But now, such the spleen of the Council of Constance, as they not only cursed his memory, as dying an obstinate heretic, but ordered that his bones (with this charitable caution, if it may be discerned from the bodies of other faithful people) to be taken out of the ground and thrown far off from any Christian burial. In obedience hereunto, Richard Flemyng, bishop of Lincoln, diocesan of Lutterworth, sent his officers, (vultures with a quick sight-scent at a dead carcass) to ungrave him accordingly. To Lutterworth they came, (sumner, commissary, official, chancellor, proctors, doctors and the servants, so that the remnant of the body would not hold out a bone amongst so many hands) take what was left out of the grave, and burnt them to ashes, and cast them into Swift, a neighboring brook running hard by. Thus this brook hath conveyed his ashes into Avon, Avon into Severn, Severn into the narrow seas, they into the main ocean; and thus the ashes of Wycliffe are the emblem of his doctrine, which now is dispersed all the world over." — Fuller's *Church Hist. Brit.* ii: 423. See also Fox's *Martyrology*, i: 606.

"Thus speaks (that voice which walks upon the wind,
Though seldom heard by busy human kind),
'As thou these ashes, little brook, wilt bear
'Into the Avon, Avon to the tide
'Of Severn, Severn to the narrow seas,
'Into main ocean they, this deed accurst
'An emblem yields to friends and enemies,
'How the bold teacher's doctrine, sanctified
'By truth, shall spread throughout the world dispersed!'" — *Wordsworth.*

Henry the VIII and the Reformation.

For the reason that the Pope would not divorce him from Katharine, his wife, when he was tired of her and wanted to marry Ann Boleyn, Henry divorced the Church of England from that of Rome, really founding a new Church in England.

"The existence of the Church of England as a distinct body, and her final separation from Rome, may be dated from the period of the divorce." — Short's *Hist. Ch. Eng.*, 102.

"Upwards of five years were employed by Henry in negotiating with the Papal Court. Wearied at length with its procrastination, he ordered Cranmer to pronounce the sentence of divorce. The Archbishop accordingly declared the marriage of the king with the lady Katherine, null and void; and on his return to Lambeth, he confirmed the marriage of Henry with Ann Boleyn, which had been privately solemnized by Dr. Lee, some months before. This step precipitated the king into a course of measures hostile to the papacy." — Price's *Hist. Prot. Non-Conf.*, i: 22.

"Henry perhaps approached as nearly to the ideal standard of perfect wickedness, as the infirmities of human nature will allow." — Sir. James Mackintosh's *Hist. of Eng.*, ii: 205.

"The doctrine of the regal supremacy in ecclesiastical matters, had been familiar to Englishmen for many generations. It had been successfully maintained up to a certain point, by the greatest of the Plantaganet kings, and had been ably vindicated by Wycliffe, one of whose cardinal heresies consisted in the denial of the supremacy of the Pope. All that Henry did was to apply and extend a doctrine that had long been filtering through the minds, both of the aristocracy and the commonalty. Hence the otherwise inexplicable circumstance, that his assumption of unlimited supremacy excited only what may be described as a professional opposition. . . . . In that age indeed, there seemed to be no alternative between the supremacy of the Pope and the supremacy of the king. The minds of the best of men, as is the case with some even in these days, were so warped by the influence of ancient ecclesiastical precedents, that none dreamed of an ultimate appeal to Holy Scripture. St. Paul, if he were consulted, was to be interpreted by Augustine, St. John by Jerome, and St. Peter by the Popes; and to the interpreters, as a matter of course, was given the principal authority. A Church of Christ, independent, as such, of human control, and existing apart from State-craft, was an idea almost impossible to that age. If entertained at all, it could only have been by men as humble in life as in spirit, such as afterwards rose to assert the spiritual character of the kingdom of Christ upon earth." — Skeats's *Hist. Free Ch's of Eng.*, 3.

"The king himself undertook to settle what the people should believe, and with this view, drew up a set of articles of religion. . . . . The new articles might have secured a much wider acceptance than it befell them to receive, but for a step altogether fatal to many of their doctrines, and almost equally fatal to the doctrine of the royal supremacy. The king not only authorized a translation of the Bible into English, but ordered a copy of it to be set up in each of the churches. This act, however, was soon felt to be, what it undoubtedly was, a political blunder, and, after seven years, was substantially recalled. Before furnishing his subjects with such a weapon of almighty power against the system which he had determined to establish, the king issued the "Injunctions." He, who was the slave of his own lusts, enjoined the clergy to exhort the people to 'keep God's commandments,' and to give themselves to 'the study of the Scriptures, and a good life.' In the 'Institution of a Christian Man,' the bishops laid down, at greater length, the creed of the Reformed Church, which was further vindicated in the 'Necessary Doctrine.' Having thus explained and apparently demonstrated the absolute truth of the new theological system, it only remained to enforce it. Some denied the corporal presence, and were accordingly sent to Smithfield. In order to strengthen his power, the king allowed his Parliament to assume the functions of a Convocation, and debate for eleven days the doctrines of the Christian religion. This debate issued in the adoption of the law of the 'Six Articles,' which set forth, in the strongest language, the presence of the natural body and blood of Christ in the Sacrament of the Lord's Supper, sanctioned Communion in one kind only, denied the right of marriage to the priesthood, enforced vows of chastity, allowed private masses, and declared auricular confession to be both expedient and necessary. The most fearful penalties were attached to any opposition to these doctrines. The least was the loss of goods; the greatest, burning at the stake — which was the punishment for denying the first of the Articles. The law was now let loose against both Protestants and Catholics, but with peculiar vengeance against the former. . . . . And so the new Church was founded. The work begun by one royal profligate was, a hundred and thirty years later, fittingly finished by another. Henry the VIIIth's natural successor in ecclesiastical politics is Charles the IId." — *Ibid*, 5.

Rise of Puritanism, etc.

John Hooper, Bishop of Gloucester, was the first father of Puritan Non-conformity. "History, while it has done justice to the character and the abilities of this eminent man, has not done similar justice to his opinions. He appears on its pages as a conscientious opponent of all ecclesiastical ceremonies and habits that are not expressly warranted by Scripture, as a sufferer for his opinions on this subject, and as a martyr for the Protestant religion; but he was more than this. All Protestants and Puritans have been accustomed to hold his name in reverence, but it belongs in a more especial manner to the English Non-conformists of the nineteenth century. It was his voice which first publicly proclaimed the principles of religious freedom. He stood alone amongst the English Protestants of his age in denying the right of the State to interfere with religion." — *Ibid*, 8.

"Touching the superior powers of the earth, it is not unknown to all them that hath read and marked the Scripture, that it appertaineth nothing unto their office to make any law to govern the conscience of their subjects in religion. Christ's kingdom is a spiritual one. In this, neither Pope nor king may govern. Christ alone is the governor of His Church, and the only law-giver." — Hooper's *Declaration of X. Com's.*, 280.

"He told the people, in words proclaimed to thousands at Paul's Cross, and throughout various parts of the kingdom, that their consciences were bound only by the Word of God, and that they might with it, judge 'Bishop, Doctor, preacher and curate.'" — Skeats *ut sup*, 9.

"Mr. Foxe [Acta et Mon, 1587,] recordeth how yt besids those worthy martires & confessors which were burned in queene Mary's days & otherwise tormented, *Many (both studients and others) fled out of ye land, to ye number of* 800. *And became severall congregations. At Wesell, Frankford, Bassill, Emden, Markpurge, Strausborough, & Geneva, &c.* Amongst whom (but especialy those at Frankford) begane yt bitter warr of contention & persecutn aboute ye ceremonies and servise booke, and other popish and anti-christian stuffe, the plague of

England to this day, which are like ye high-plases in Israell, wch the prophets cried out against, & were their ruine; which ye better parte sought, according to ye puritie of ye gospell, to roote out and utterly to abandon. And the other parte (under veiled pretences) for their ouwn ends & advancements, sought as stifly to continue, maintaine & defend. . . . . . The one side laboured to have ye right worship of God & discipline of Christ established in ye church, according to ye simplicity of ye gospell, without the mixture of mens inventions, and to have & to be ruled by ye laws of Gods Word, dispensed in those offices, & by those officers of Pastors, Teachers, & Elders, &c. according to ye Scripturs. The other partie, though under many colours & pretences, endeavored to have ye episcopall dignitie, (affter ye popish maner) with their large power & jurisdiction still retained; with all those courts, cannons & ceremonies, togeather with all such livings, revenues & subordinate officers, with other such means as formerly upheld their anti-christian greatnes, and enabled them with lordly & tyranous power to persecute ye poore servants of God." —Gov. Bradford's *Hist. Plim. Plant.*, 3.

[For a very interesting, minute and authentic history of this establishment (per force,) of separate churches on Continental soil, and the difficulties which beset them, some light from which directed later Separatists to a wiser path, see *A Briefe Discourse of the Trovbles Begun at Frankeford in Germany, An. Dom.* 1554, *About The Booke of Common Prayee and Ceremonies, and continued by the English men there, to the end of Q. Maries Raign, etc. etc.* 4to, pp. 184, published in 1575, and reprinted in London in 1642.]

The Puritan Struggle.

"During the forty-four years of the reign of Elizabeth, the whole power of the crown was exercised, in regard to ecclesiastical matters, with two distinct purposes. The first was to subject the Church to its 'governor,' the second to suppress all opinions differing from those which had received a special patent of protection. The first wholly succeeded; the second wholly failed. The Prayer-book and Articles of Elizabeth do not materially differ from those of Edward. The only difference of any importance relates to the vestments, which were ordered to be the same as those in use in the second year of Edward. This change was against a further reformation, and it was confirmed by a third Act of Uniformity. The Queen soon let it be known that this Act was not to be a dead letter. She heard of some who did not wear the habits, and who even preached against them, and Parker was at once ordered to enforce the law. Then the exiles who had returned from the Continent, flushed with hope, and ardent in the cause of the Gospel, found the paw of the lion's cub as heavy as that of the royal beast himself. . . . . So zealously did he [Parker — the Primate,] set about his work that he shocked the statesmen of his age, and at last shocked even Elizabeth herself. Not being an ecclesiastic, there was a limit to the queen's capacity of creating and afterwards enjoying the sight of human suffering. There was no such limit in Parker. The jackall's appetite was, for once, stronger even than that of the lioness. The attempt to enforce the Act of Uniformity excited instant resistance, and the Church was turned into a great shambles." — Skeats *ut sup.* 13.

"There must be a reason, apart from the character of the governing power, why Puritans within the Church have never succeeded. The reason is probably to be found in the fact that they never essentially differed from the dominant party. Both were almost equally intolerant. Parker and Whitgift persecuted the Puritans; but if Cartwright had been in Whitgift's place, he would have dealt out equal persecution to Baptists and Independents. They, who had suffered imprisonment on account of their opinions, actually remonstrated with statesmen for releasing Roman Catholics from confinement. They held a purer doctrine than their opponents held, but none the less did they require it to be enforced by the 'authority of the magistrates.' It seems strange that men who devoted so much time to the study of the Scriptures, and whose knowledge of them was as extensive as it was profound, should have missed the one study, which to a Christian, would seem to be the most obvious, the life and character of the Founder of their religion and the nature of His mission. But, habits of thought are more tyrannical than habits of action; and the habit of theological thought was then, as for generations afterwards, essentially dogmatical. The best of the Puritans looked to the Scriptures for rules rather than for principles, for propositions rather than for examples. Christianity was, with them, merely an historical development of Judaism; and therefore, while they believed in the sacrifice of Christ, they equally believed in the laws of Moses. The Sacred Writings were rough materials, out of which they might hew their own systems. The stones were taken in equal parts out of the books of the Old Testament and the New, the latter being dug for doctrine and the former for precept. Amongst all the works of the early Puritans, there is not one on the character or life of Christ, nor one which gives any indication that they had even an imagination of the wholly spiritual nature of His kingdom. Whatever that kingdom might be in the place Heaven, on the place Earth it was to be fenced and extended by pains and penalties, threatenings and slaughter. They denied the supremacy of the civil magistrate in religion, but it was only in order to assert their own supremacy. They pleaded with tears for liberty of conscience, and would have denied it to the first 'Anabaptist' whom they met. It was no wonder they did not gain their end, and no wonder that they scarcely hoped to gain it. It would seem that the English race required to be transplanted before it could bear a more perfect flower and fruit than any of which Puritanism only was capable. That service was effected by Elizabeth."—*Ibid*, 20.

The Evolution of Independency.

"There were certainly Baptist churches in England as early as the year 1589, and there could scarcely have been several organized communities without the corresponding opinions having been held by individuals, and some churches established for years previous to this date. With respect to the Independents, certain 'congregations' are spoken of by Foxe [Vol. iii: 114,] as established in London in A. D. 1555, and it is possible that they were Independent, but more probable that they were Puritan. It is now clearly established that an Independent church, of which Richard Fitz was pastor, existed in A. D. 1568 [*Congregational Martyrs*, Art. R. Fitz.] In A. D. 1580, Sir Walter Raleigh spoke of the Brownists as existing 'by thousands.' . . . . But although Richard Fitz was the first pastor of the first Independent church in England, to Robert Browne belongs the honor of founding the denomination. This man's character has been assailed with almost equal virulence by Church and Non-conformist writers; but, although he is proved to have been naturally of a passionate, dogmatic and weak nature, no charge against his piety has been successfully established. [See Fletcher's *Hist. Independ.*, ii: chap. 3.] His moral courage and his willingness to bear suffering in testimony of his sincerity, were amply shown by his life. If, like Cartwright, he eventually returned to the Church, he did what ought not to excite surprise. The wonder is, not that human nature was so weak in him, but that it was so strong in others." — *Ibid*, 22.

"The principles which Browne advocated were substantially the same as those which are now held by the majority of English dissenters. He maintained that the Christian Church is a voluntary association of believing men, that it is competent to the management of its own affairs, and is capable of existing under every form of civil government which human society can assume. He consequently repudiated its subjection to the State, and denied the possibility of its sustaining a national character. It necessarily followed from these principles, that he should denounce the hierarchy as an unscriptural institution, adapted rather to advance the designs of its political supporters, than to promote the religious welfare of mankind. He attacked the whole system of the Established Church, denying the validity of its orders, the purity of its rites, the rectitude of its worship, and the soundness of its constitution. He declaimed against it as a spiritual Babylon, loaded with many of the abominations of the popedom, equally haughty in its spirit, though less powerful to accomplish its intolerant designs." — Price's *Hist. Prot. Non-conf.*, i: 315.

The essential features of Browne's teaching were these:

1. The New Testament the source of all light on Church Government.

2. A Church a body self-associated by a "willing covenant."

3. Church Government the Lordship of Christ, whereby His people "obey to His will."

4. Separation from open and willful offenders, a duty.

5. Church officers are pastors, teachers, elders, deacons, etc., "tried to be meet, and thereto duly chosen by the church which calleth them."

6. Ordination is a pronouncing with prayer and thanksgiving, and laying on of hands "by some of the forwardest and wisest," that those receiving it "are called and authorized of God."

7. Church action is by "general inquiry and consent." — Browne's *Life and Manner of all True Christians*. A. D. 1582. 4to. pp. 112.

What this Brownism really was, as refined from the crudities and sharpnesses of Browne himself, may be excellently seen in the *Confession of Faith of Certaine English People, living in the Low Countreyes, exiled*, which was put forth in 1596, by the Church in Amsterdam, of which Henry Ainsworth was Teacher. Two or three of its articles follow:

"This Ministerie is alike given to every Christian congregation, with like and equall power and commission to have and enjoy the same, as God offereth fit men and meanes, the same rules given to all for the election and execution thereof in all places." — *Art. xxii.*

"As every Christian congregation hath power and commandment to elect and ordeine their own Ministerie acording to the rules in God's word prescribed, and whilest they shall faithfully execute their office, to have them in superabundant love for their worke sake, to provide for them, to honour them and reverence them according to the dignitie of the office they execute: so have they also power and commandment, when anie such default, eyther in their lyfe, doctrine or administration breaketh out, as by the rule of the word debarreth them from, or depriveth them of their Ministerie, by due order to depose them from the Ministerie they exercised; yea, if the case so require, and they remayne obstinate and impenitent, orderly to cut them of by excommunication."—*Art. xxiii.*

"Christ hath given this power to receive in, or to cut of, any member, to the whole body together of every Christian congregation, and not to any one member apart, or to more members sequestred from the whole, or to any other Congregation to do it for them: yet so, as ech Congregation ought to vse the best help they can heerunto, and the most meet member they have to pronounce the same in their public assembly."—*Art. xxiiii.*

"Such as yet see not the truth, may notwithstanding heare the publik doctrine and prayers of the church, and with al meeknes are to bee sought by al meanes: yet none who are growne in yeares may bee received into their communion as members, but such as do make confession of their faith, publickly desiring to be received as members, and promising to walke in the obedience of Christ. Neyther any infants, but such as are the seed of the faithfull by one of the parents, or under their education and government. And further not any from one congregation to be received members in another, without bringing certificate of their former estate and present purpose."—*Art. xxxvii.*

That these were Congregationalists, if they were Brownists, will appear from the following:

"And although the particular Congregations be thus distinct and severall bodies, every one as a compact and knit citie in it self, yet are they all to walke by one and the same rule, and by all meanes convenient to have the counsel and help one of another in all needfull affaires of the Church, as members of one body in the common faith, under Christ their onely head."—*Art. xxxviii.*

Rise and Progress of the Mayflower Church.

"Established here [as postmaster at Scrooby, near Bawtry in England] Brewster, now in the vigor of young manhood, soon took a deep interest in those religious questions which were then agitating the realm. With a mind enlarged by study and travel, he made the acquaintance of Smith, Clyfton, Robinson, and other godly ministers in that [Nottinghamshire] and the neighboring counties, who were conscientiously opposed to the Established Church; and when the policy of deprivation, confiscation, fine and imprisonment was fully entered upon by government to enforce conformity, he cast in his lot with them, and welcomed them to his house [a spacious manor-house of the Archbishop of York, leased to Brewster by Samuel Sandys, eldest son of the then Archbishop] as well as his heart, and in its ample spaces offered them that Sabbath liberty of prophesying which the churches no longer afforded. Gathering together the elect and precious few from the country round about who thought as they thought, and believed what they believed, and were willing to dare what they dared to do; he, with Clyfton and Robinson and those others, some time during 1606, formally—to use Bradford's own words—'joyned themselves (by a covenant of the Lord) into a church estate, in ye fellowship of ye gospell, to walke in all His wayes, made known, or to be made known unto them, according to their best endeavours, whatsoever it should cost them, the Lord assisting them.' "—*Sabbath at Home*, March, 1867.

"But after these things they could not long continue in any peaceable condition, but were hunted & persecuted on every side, so as their former afflictions were but as flea-bitings in comparison of these which now came upon them. For some were taken & clapt up in prison, others had their houses besett & watcht night and day, & hardly escaped their hands; and ye most were faine to flie & leave their howses & habitations, and the means of their livelehood. Yet these & many other sharper things which affterward befell them, were no other then they looked for, and therfore were ye better prepared to bear them by ye assistance of Gods grace & spirite. Yet seeing them selves thus molested, and that ther was no hope of their continuance ther, by a joynte consente they resolved to goe into ye Low-Countries, wher they heard was freedome of Religion for all men; as also how sundrie from London, & other parts of ye land, had been exiled and persecuted for ye same cause, & were gone thither, and lived at Amsterdam, & in other places of ye land. So affter they had continued togeither aboute a year, and kept their meetings every Saboth in one place or other, exercising the worship of God amongst them selves, notwithstanding all ye dilligence & malice of their adverssaries, they seeing they could no longer continue in yt condition, they resolved to get over into Holland as they could."—Gov. Bradford's *Hist. Plim. Plant.*, 10.

Emigration to Holland.

"Being thus constrained to leave their native soyle and countrie, their lands & livings, and all their freinds and famillier acquaintance, it was much, and thought marvelous by many. But to goe into a countrie they knew not (but by hearsay), wher they must learne a new language, and get their livings they knew not how, it being a dear place, & subjecte to ye misseries of warr, it was by many thought an adventure almost desperate, a case intolerable, & a misserie worse than death. Espetially seeing they were not aquainted with trads nor traffique, (by which yt countrie doth subsiste) but had only been used to a plaine countrie life, & ye inocente trade of husbandrey. But these things did not dismay them (though they did some times trouble them) for their desires were sett on ye ways of God, & to injoye his ordinances; but they rested on his providence & knew whom they had beleeved. Yet this was not all, for though they could not stay, yet were yey not suffered to goe, but ye ports & havens were shut against them, so as they were faine to seeke secrete means of conveance, & to bribe & fee ye mariners, & give exterordinarie rates for their passages. And yet were they often times betrayed (many of them) and both they & their goods intercepted & surprised, and thereby put to great trouble and charge."—*Ibid* 11.

"To be shorte, after they had been thus turmoyled a good while, and conveyed from one constable to another, they were glad to be ridd of them in ye end upon any termes; for all were wearied & tired with them. Though in ye mean time they (poor soules) indured miserie enough; and thus in ye end necessitie forste a way for them. . . . . . I may not omitte ye fruite that came hearby, for by these so publick troubls, in so many eminente places, their cause became famouss & occasioned many to looke into ye same; and their godly cariage & Christian behaviour was such as left a deep impression in the minds of many. And though some few shrunk at these first conflicts & sharp beginnings, (as it was no marvell,) yet many more came on with fresh courage, & greatly animated others. And in ye end, notwithstanding all these stormes of oppossition, they all gatt over at length, some at one time & some at an other, and some in one place & some in an other, and mette togeather againe according to their desires, with no small rejoycing." — *Ibid*, 15.

"These Provinces [the Low Countries] were of opinion not only that all religions ought to be tolerated, but that all restraint in matters of religion was as detestable as the Inquisition itself; and accordingly they maintained that nobody erred willfully, or could believe against his conscience, that none but God could inspire right notions into the minds of men; that no religion was agreeable to God, but such as proceeded from a willing heart: experience had also taught them that heterodox opinions could not so effectually be rooted out by human power or violence, as by length of time." — Brandt's *Hist. Ref. in Low Count.*, i: 308.

"Calvinism being thus the established religion of Holland, it will still be seen that entire liberty in belief and practice prevailed there; the only difference being that the followers of any peculiar faith, while they would have the most perfect freedom of worship in their own private houses, or buildings provided by themselves, would not be provided with church edifices at the public expense." — *Sabbath at Home*, March, 1867.

"Twelve or fifteen years before the Scrooby men arrived in Amsterdam, a London company had gone over, who had Francis Johnson for their pastor and Henry Ainsworth for their teacher; and also, as early as 1596, had published their 'Confession of Faith.' Four years before them (in 1604) Smyth of Gainsborough, and his company, — with whom it is not improbable that the Scrooby men were loosely affiliated before they had strength enough to form themselves into a separate church nearer home — had made good their retreat over the North Sea, and were also maintaining themselves on the Amstel. It must in sorrow be added, that these two congregations, of Johnson and Ainsworth, and of Smyth, had not found themselves able to live in that perfect peace which should have adorned their profession of the new faith which they had gathered out of the Word. No means whieh Robinson or Brewster could apply sufficed to heal the breach. Indeed it soon became evident that — would they, or would they not — the mere living in Amsterdam must involve the new comers in the ill-feeling, and the cross speech. So they prudently resolved to remove thence, before a bad matter was made worse. It is on record in Leyden that John Robinson [*Jan Robarthse*] and 'some of the members of the Christian Reformed Religion born in the kingdom of Great Britain, to the number of one hundred persons, or thereabouts, men and women,' petitioned the magistrates of Leyden for leave to come to Leyden 'by the 1st May next,' to have freedom of the city 'in carrying on their trades without being burdensome to any one.' As this petition — itself without date — is indorsed in the margin under date of 12 Feb. 1609, it seems probable that it had been presented but a few days before that time. The magistrates say in this indorsement, 'they refuse no honest persons free ingress to come and have residence in this city, provided that such persons behave themselves, and submit to the laws and ordinances; and therefore the coming of the memorialists will be agreeable and welcome.' It was beyond a doubt in connection with this cordial response to their application, that the Scrooby church, now, in itself and all its appurtenance, 'to the number of one hundred, or thereabouts,' removed, about 1 May 1609, to Leyden." — *Ibid.*

The Character of these Men in Leyden.

"I know not but it may be spoken to ye honour of God, & without prejudice to any, that such was ye true pietie, ye humble zeale, & fervent love, of this people (whilst they thus lived together) towards God and his waies, and yr single harted-nes & sinceir affection one towards another, that they came as near ye primative patterne of ye first churches, as any other church of these later times have done, according to their ranke & qualitie. . . . . . Because some of their adversaries did, upon ye rumore of their remoovall, cast out slanders against them, as if that State had been wearie of them, & had rather driven them out (as ye heathen historians did faine of Moyses & ye Isralits when they went out of Egipte) then yt it was their oune free choyse & motion, I will therefore mention a particuler or too to shew ye contrary, and ye good acceptation they had in ye place wher they lived. And first, though many of them weer poore, yet there was none so poore, but if they were known to be of ys congregation, the Dutch (either bakers or others) would trust them in any reasonable matter when yey wanted money. Because they had found by experience how carfull they were to keep their word, and saw them so painfull and diligente in their callings; yea, they would strive to gett their custome, and to imploy them above others, in their worke, for their honestie & diligence. Againe; ye magistrats of ye citie, aboute ye time of their coming away, or a litle before, in ye publick place of justice, gave this comendable testemonie of them, in ye reproof of the Wallons, who were of ye French Church in yt citie. These English, said they, have lived amongst us now this 12. years, and yet we never had any sute or accusation came against any of them; but your strifs and quarels are continuall, &c. . . . . Yea when there was speech of their [the Plymouth men's] remoovall into these parts [this was written in New England] sundrie of note & eminencie of yt nation [the Dutch] would have had them come under them, and for yt end made them large offers." — Bradford *ut sup.*, 19.

"I perswade my selfe, never people upon earth lived more lovingly together, and parted more sweetly then wee the church at Leyden did." — Edward Winslow's *Hypocrisie Unmasked*, 88.

"And that which was a crown unto them, they lived together in love and peace all their days, without any considerable differences, or any disturbance that grew thereby, but such as was easily healed in love; and so they continued until with mutuall consent they removed into New England." — Gov. Bradford's *Dialogue.*

Why they left Leyden.

"Our Reverend pastor Mr. John Robinson of late memory, and our grave Elder Mr. William Brewster, considering amongst many other inconveniences, how hard the Country was where we lived, how many spent their estate in it, and were forced to return for England; how grievous to live from under the protection of the State of England; how like wee were to lose our language, and our name of English; how little good wee did, or were like to do to the Dutch in reforming the Sabbath; how unable there to give such education to our children, as wee ourselves had received, &c. They, I say, out of their Christian care of the flock of Christ committed to them conceived, if God would bee pleased to discover some place unto us (though in America) and give us so much favour with the King and State of England, as to have their protection there, where wee might enjoy the like liberty, and where the Lord favouring our endeavours by his blessing, wee might exemplarily shew our tender Country-men by our example (no lesse burthened than our selves) where they might live, and comfortably subsist and enjoy the like liberties with us, being freed from Anti-christian bondage, keep their names and Nation, and not onely bee a meanes to enlarge the Dominions of our State, but the Church of Christ also, if the Lord have a people amongst the natives whither hee should bring us, &c. Hereby in their grave Wisdomes they thought wee might more glorifie God, doe more good to our Countrey, better provide for our posterity, and live to be more refreshed by our labours, than ever wee could doe in Holland where we were.

Now these their private thoughts upon mature deliberation they imparted to the Brethren of the Congregation, which after much private discussion came to publike agitation, till at the length the Lord was solemnly sought in the Congregation by fasting and prayer to direct us, who moving our hearts more and more to the worke, wee sent some of good abilities over into England to see what favour or acceptance such a thing might finde with the King." — Ed. Winslow, *ut sup.*, 88.

"After they had lived in this citie about some 11. or 12. years (which is ye more observable being ye whole time of yt famose truce between that state and ye Spaniards) and sundrie of them were taken away by death, & many others begane to be well striken in years, the grave mistris Experience having taught them many things, those prudent governours [Robinson and Brewster] with sundrie of ye sagest members begane both deeply to apprehend their present dangers, & wisely to foresee ye future, & thinke of timely remedy. In ye agitation of their thoughts, and much discours of things hear aboute, at length they began to incline to this conclusion, of remoovall to some other place. Not out of any newfangledness, or such like giddie humor, by which men are oftentimes transported to their great hurt & danger, but for sundrie weightie & solid reasons; some of ye cheefe of which I will hear breefly touch. And first, they saw & found by experience the hardnes of ye place & countrie to be such, as few in comparison would come to them, and fewer that would bide it out, and continew with them. For many yt came to them, and many more yt desired to be with them, could not endure yt great labor and hard fare, with other inconveniences which they underwent & were contented with. But though they loved their persons, approved their cause, and honoured their sufferings, yet they left them as it weer weeping, as Orpah did her mother in law Naomie, or as those Romans did Cato in Utica, who desired to be excused & borne with, though they could not all be Catoes. For many, though they desired to injoye ye ordinances of God in their puritie, and ye libertie of the gospell with them, yet, alass, they admitted of bondage, with danger of conscience, rather then to indure these hardships; yea, some preferred & chose ye prisons in England, rather then this libertie in Holland, with these afflictions. But it was thought that if a better and easier place of living could be had, it would draw many & take away these discouragments. Yea, their pastor would often say, that many of those wo both wrate & preached now against them, if they were in a place wher they might have libertie and live comfortably, they would then practise as they did.

"2ly. They saw that though ye people generally bore all these difficulties very cherfully, & with a resolute courage, being in ye best & strength of their years, yet old age began to steale on many of them, (and their great & continuall labours, with other crosses and sorrows, hastened it before ye time,) so as it was not only probably thought, but apparently seen, that within a few years more they would be in danger to scatter, by necessities pressing them, or sinke under their burdens, or both. And therfore according to ye devine proverb, yt a wise man seeth ye plague when it cometh, & hideth him selfe, [Prov. xxii : 3], so they like skillfull & beaten souldiers were fearfull either to be intrapped or surrounded by their enimies, so as they should neither be able to fight nor flie; and therfor thought it better to dislodge betimes to some place of better advantage & less danger, if any such could be found.

"Thirdly; as necessitie was a taskmaster over them, so they were forced to be such, not only to their servants, but in a sorte, to their dearest chilldren; the which as it did not a little wound ye tender harts of many a loving father & mother, so it produced likwise sundrie sad & sorowful effects. For many of their children, that were of best dispositions and gracious inclinations, haveing lernde to bear ye yoake in their youth, and willing to bear parte of their parents burden, were, often times, so oppressed with their hevie labours, that though their minds were free and willing, yet their bodies bowed under ye weight of ye same, and became decreped in their early youth; the vigor of nature being consumed in ye very budd, as it were. But that which was more lamentable, and of all sorowes most heavie to be borne, was that many of their children, by these occasions, and ye great licentiousnes of youth in ye countrie, and ye manifold temptations of the place, were drawne away by evill examples into extravagante & dangerous courses, getting ye raines off their neks, & departing from their parents. Some became souldiers, others tooke upon them farr vioages by sea, and other some worse courses, tending to dissolutenes & the danger of their soules, to ye great greefe of their parents and dishonour of God. So that they saw their posteritie would be in danger to degenerate & be corrupted.

"Lastly, (and which was not least) a great hope & inward zeall they had of laying some good foundation, or at least to make some way therunto, for ye propagating & advancing ye gospell of ye kingdom of Christ in those remote parts of ye world; yea, though they should be but even as stepping-stones unto others for ye performing of so great a work.

"These, & some other like reasons, moved them to undertake this resolution of their removall; the which they afterward prosecuted with so great difficulties." — Bradford, *ut sup.*, 22.

How it Looked to Them.

"The place they had thoughts on was some of those vast & unpeopled countries of America, which are frutfull & fitt for habitation, being devoyd of all civill inhabitants, wher ther are only salvage & brutish men, which range up and downe, litle otherwise than ye wild beasts of the same. This proposition being made publike and coming to ye scaning of all, it raised many varieble opinions amongst men, and cauzed many fears & doubts amongst them selves. Some, from their reasons & hops conceived, laboured to stirr up & incourage the rest to undertake & prosecute ye same; others, againe, out of their fears, objected against it, & sought to diverte from it, aledging many things, and those neither unreasonable nor unprobable; as that it was a great designe, and subjecte to many unconceivable perills & dangers; as, besids the casulties of ye seas (which none can be freed from) the length of ye vioage was such, as ye weake bodys of women and other persons worne out with age & traville (as many of them were) could never be able to endure. And yet if they should, the miseries of ye land which they should be exposed unto, would be to hard to be borne; and lickly, some or all of them togeither, to consume & utterly to ruinate them. For ther they should be liable to famine, and nakednes, & ye wante, in a maner, of all things. The chang of aire, diate, & drinking of water would infect their bodies with sore sickneses, and greevous diseases. And also those which should escape or overcome these difficulties, should yett be in a continuall danger of ye salvage people, who are cruell, barbarous, & most trecherous, being most furious in their rage and merciles wher they overcome; not being contente only to kill & take away life, but delight to tormente men in ye most bloodie maner that may be; fleaing some alive with ye shells of fishes, cutting of ye members & joynts of others by peesmeale, and broiling on ye coles, eate ye collops of their flesh in their sight whilst they live; with other cruelties horrible to be related. And surely it could not be thought but ye very hearing of these things could not but move ye very bowels of men to grate within them, and make ye weake to quake & tremble. It was furder objected, that it would require greater summes of money to furnish such a vioage, and to fitt them with necessaries, than their consumed estats would amounte too; and yett they must as well looke to be seconded with supplies, as presently to be transported. Also many presidents [precedents] of ill success, & lamentable misseries befalne others in the like designes, were easie to be found, and not forgotten to be aledged; besids their owne experience, in their former troubles & hardships in their remoovall into Holand, and how hard a thing it was for them to live in that strange place, though it was a neighbour countrie, & a civill and rich comone wealth.

It was answered, that all great & honourable actions are accompanied with great difficulties, and must be both enterprised and overcome with answerable courages. It was granted ye dangers were great, but not desperate; the difficulties were many, but not invincible. For though their were many of them likly, yet they were not cartaine; it might be sundrie of ye things feared might never befale; others by providente care & ye use of good means, might in a great measure be prevented; and all of them, through ye help of God, by fortitude and patience, might either be borne, or overcome. True it was, that such attempts were not to be made and undertaken without good ground & reason; not rashly or lightly as many have done for curiositie or hope of gaine, &c. But their condition was not ordinarie; their ends were good & honourable; their calling lawfull & urgente; and therfore they might expect ye blessing of God in their proceeding. Yea, though they should loose their lives in this action, yet mighte they have comforte in the same, and their endeavors would be honourable. They lived hear [in Leyden] but as men in exile, & in a poore condition; and as great miseries might possibly befale them in this place, for ye 12. years of truce were now out, & ther was nothing but beating of drumes, and preparing for warr, the events wherof are allway uncertaine. Ye Spaniard might prove as cruell as the salvages of America, and ye famine and pestelence as sore hear as ther, & their libertie less to looke out for remedie.

After many other perticuler things answered & aledged on both sids, it was fully concluded by ye major parte, to put this designe in execution, and to prosecute it by the best means they could."—*Ibid*, 24.

"My brethren have not the faith of our glorious Lord Jesus Christ in respect of persons. But now, if it so come to passe, (which God forbid) that the most being eyther forestalled by prejudice, or by prosperitie made secure, there be few found (especially men of learning, who will so far stoop as to look upon so despised creatures, and their cause); this alone remaineth, that we turn our faces & mouths unto thee (o most powerfull Lord, & gratious father) humbly imploreing help from God towards those, who are by men left desolate. There is with thee no respect of persons, neither are men lesse regarders of thee, if regarders of thee, for the worlds disregarding them. They who truly fear thee, and work righteousnes, although constreyned to live by leav in a forrain land, exiled from countrie, spoyled of goods, destitute of freinds, few in number, and mean in condition, are for all that unto thee (O gratious God) nothing the less acceptable: Thou numbrest all their wandrings, and puttest their tears into thy bottels: Are they not written in thy book? Towards thee, O Lord, are our eyes; confirm our hearts, & bend thine ear, and suffer not our feet to slip, or our faces to be ashamed, O thou both just and mercifull God."—John Robinson's *Just and Necessarie Apologie*, 72.

How it was at Last Arranged.

"They found God going along with them, and got Sir Edwin Sands [Sandys] a religious Gentleman then living, to stirre in it, who procured Sir Robert Nawnton then principall Secretary of State to King James of famous memory, to move his Majesty by a private motion to give way to such a people (who could not so comfortably live under the Government of another State) to enjoy their liberty of Conscience under his gracious protection in America, where they would endeavour the advancement of his Majestie's Dominions, and the enlargement of the Gospell by all due meanes. This his Majesty said was a good and honest motion, and asking what profits might arise in the part [*ie.* part of the country] wee intended (for our eye was on the most northern parts of Virginia) 'twas answered, Fishing. To which hee replyed with his ordinary asseveration, *So, God have my Soule, 'tis an honest Trade, 'twas the Apostles owne calling, &c.* But afterwards he told Sir Robert Nawnton (who took all occasions to further it) that we should confer with the Bishops of Canterbury and London, &c. Wherupon wee were advised to persist upon his first approbation, and not to entangle our selves with them, which caused our agents to repair to the Virginia Company, who in their Court demanded our ends of going; which being related, they said the thing was of God, and granted a large Patent, and one of them lent us 300*l.* *gratis* for three yeares, which was repaid."— Winslow, *ut sup.*, 89.

Bradford goes more into particulars, showing how one disappointment after another delayed, embarrassed and vexed them: especially how uncertain they were made by the course the king pursued in promising "that he would connive at them, & not molest them, provided they carried them selves peaceably." He says: "This made a dampe in ye business, and caused some distraction, for many were afraid that if they should unsetle them selves, & put of their estates, and goe upon these hopes, it might prove dangerous, and prove but a sandie foundation. Yea, it was thought they might better have presumed hear upon without makeing any suite at all, then, haveing made it, to be thus rejected. But some of ye cheefest thought other wise, and yt they might well proceede hereupon, & that ye kings majestie was willing enough to suffer them without molestation, though for other reasons he would not confirme it by any publicke acte. And furdermore, if ther was no securitie in this promise intimated, ther would be no great certainty in a furder confirmation of ye same; for if after wards ther should be a purpose or desire to wrong them, though they had a seale as broad as ye house flore, it would not serve ye turne; for ther would be means enew found to recall or reverse it. Seeing therfore the course was probable, they must rest herein on God's providence, as they had done in other things." — Bradford, *ut sup.*, 29.

"But at last, after all these things, and their long attendance, they had a patent granted them, and confirmed under ye Companies seale; but these devissions and distractions had shaken of many of ther pretended freinds, and disappointed them of much of their hoped for & proffered means. By the advise of some freinds this pattente was not taken in ye name of any of their owne, but in ye name of Mr. John Wincob (a religious gentleman then belonging to ye Countess of Lincoline) who intended to goe with them. But God so disposed as he never went, nor they ever made use of this patente, which had cost them so much labour and charge. . . . . . A right emblime, it maybe, of ye uncertaine things of this world; yt when men have toyld them selves for them, they vanish into smoke." — *Ibid*, 40.

The Hard Terms which were the Best They could Get.

The hardship of the terms to which they were reduced, shows at once the slenderness of their means, and the constancy of their purpose. It was agreed to create a joint stock company on the following plan and conditions.

1. Colonists 16 yrs. old and upwards, and persons contributing £10. each, to be owners of one share.

2. Colonists contributing £10. in money or provisions, to be owners of two shares.

3. The partnership to continue 7 years, to the end of which time all profits and benefits gotten by trade, traffic, trucking, working, fishing, or any other means, to remain as common stock.

4. The settlers, having landed, to be divided into parties to be employed in boat-building, fishing, carpentry, cultivation, and manufactures for the use of the colony.

5. At the end of 7 years the capital and profits to be divided among the stockholders in proportion to their respective shares in the investment.

6. Stockholders investing at a later period to have shares in the division proportioned to the duration of their interest.

7. Colonists to be allowed one share for each domestic dependant accompanying them (wife, child or servant) more than 16 yrs. of age; two shares for every such person, if supplied at their expense; and half a share for every dependant between 10 yrs. and 16 yrs.

8. Each child going under 10 yrs., to have at the division 50 acres of unmanured land.

9. To the estates of persons dying before the expiration of the 7 years, allowances to be made at the division proportioned to the length of their lives in the colony.

10. Till the division all colonists to be provided with food, clothing, and other necessaries, from the common stock.

Two stipulations supposed by the colonists to have been settled, to the effect that they should have two days in each week for their private use, and that at the division, they should be proprietors of their houses and of the cultivated land appertaining thereto, were ultimately disallowed by the *Merchant Adventurers* [*i. e.*, the London merchants who aided them to the money they required for the expedition] to the great disappointment and discontent of the other party. Cushman, who was much blamed for his facility in yielding these points, insisted that, if he had acted differently, the whole undertaking would have fallen to the ground. — Condensed from Palfrey's *Hist. New Eng.*, i: 153.

The Final Decision.

" Our agents returning, wee further sought the Lord by a publique and solemn Fast, for his gracious guidance. And hereupon wee came to this resolution, that it was best for one part of the Church to goe at first, and the other to stay, *viz.* the youngest and strongest part to goe. Secondly, they that went should freely offer themselves. Thirdly, if the major part went, the Pastor to goe with them; if not, the Elder onely. Fourthly, if the Lord should frowne upon our proceedings, then those that went to returne, and the Brethren that remained still there, to assist and bee helpfull to them, but if God should bee pleased to favour them that went, then they also should endeavour to helpe over such as were poore and ancient, and willing to come; these things being agreed, the major part stayed, and the Pastor with them for the present, but all intended (except a very few, who had rather wee would have stayed) to follow after. The minor part, with Mr. Brewster their Elder, resolved to enter upon this great work (but take notice the difference of number was not great)." — Ed. Winslow, *ut sup.*, 90.

The Start.

" At length, after much travell and these debats, all things were got ready and provided. A smale ship [the Speedwell, of 60 tons] was bought & fitted in Holand, which was intended as to serve to help to transport them, so to stay in ye cuntrie and atend upon fishing and shuch other affairs as might be for ye good & benefite of ye colonie when they cam ther. Another was hired at London, [the Mayflower] of burden about 9. score; [*i.e.* about 180 tons] and all other things gott in readines. So being ready to departe, they hed a day of solleme humiliation, their pastor [John Robinson] taking his texte from Ezra viii: 21. *And ther at ye river, by Ahava, I proclaimed a fast, that we might humble ourselves before our God, and seeke of him a right way for us, and for our children, and for all our substance.* Upon which he spente a good parte of ye day very profitably, and suitable to their presente occasion. The rest of the time was spente in powering out prairs to ye Lord with great fervencie, mixed with abundance of tears. And ye time being come that they must departe, they were acompanied with most of their brethren out of ye citie, unto a town sundrie miles of called Delfes-Haven, wher the ship lay ready to receive them. So they lefte yt goodly & pleasante citie, which had been ther resting place near 12. years; but *they knew they were* PILGRIMES [whence the genesis of this name as applied to them] & looked not much on those things, but lift up their eyes to ye heavens, their dearest cuntrie, and quieted their spirits. When they came to ye place they found ye ship and all things ready ; and shuch of their freinds as could not come with them followed after them, and sundrie also came from Amsterdame to see them shipte and to take their leave of them. That night was spent with litle sleepe by ye most, but with freindly entertainmente & christian discourse and other reall expressions of true christian love. The next day, the wind being faire, they went aborde, and their freinds with them, where truly dolfull was ye sight of that sade and mournfull parting ; to see what sighs and sobbs and praires did sound amongst them, what tears did gush from every eye, & pithy speeches peirst each harte ; that sundry of ye Dutch strangers y^t stood on ye key as spectators, could not refraine from tears. Yet comfortable & sweete it was to see shuch lively and true expressions of dear & unfained love. But ye tide (which stays for no man) caling them away y^t were thus loath to departe, their Reverd pastor falling downe on his knees, (and they all with him) with watrie cheeks comended them with most fervente praiers to the Lord and his blessing. And then with mutuall imbrases and many tears, they tooke their leaves one of an other ; which proved to be ye last leave to many of them." — Bradford, *ut sup.*, 58.

" And when the Ship was ready to carry us away, the Brethren that stayed having againe solemnly sought the Lord with us, and for us, and we further engaging our selves mutually as before ; they, I say, that stayed at Leyden feasted us that were to goe at our Pastors house being large [being, in fact, their usual place of Sabbath assembling] where wee refreshed our selves after our teares, with singing of Psalmes, making joyfull melody in our hearts, as well as with the voice, there being many of the Congregation very expert in Musick ; and indeed it was the sweetest melody that ever mine eares heard. After this they accompanied us to Delphs Haven, where wee were to imbarque, and there feasted us againe, and after prayer performed by our Pastor, where a flood of teares was poured out, they accompanied us to the Ship, but were not able to speake one to another for the abundance of sorrow to part : but wee onely going aboard (the Ship lying to the Key and ready to set sayle, the winde being faire), wee gave them a volley of small shot, and three peeces of Ordinance, and so lifting up our hands to each other, and our hearts for each other to the Lord our God, we departed, and found his presence with us in the midst of our manifold straits hee carryed us thorow. And if any doubt this relation, the Dutch, as I heare, at Delphs Haven preserve the memory of it to this day, [1646] and will inform them." — Ed. Winslow, *ut sup.*, 90.

The Spirit in which They Started.

" At their parting Mr Robinson wrote a letter to ye whole company. . . . as also a breefe leter writ at ye same time to Mr Carver, in which ye tender love & godly care of a true pastor appears."

In this letter Robinson laments that he is constrained for a while to be bodily absent from them, "by strong necessitie held backe for ye present," and exhorts them to special repentance in view of the circumstances of difficulty and danger surrounding them, and to provide carefully for peace with all men, and neither to give nor take offence. He suggests that, as many of them are strangers to each other, and to each other's infirmities, there will be special need of watchfulness in the matter of both giving and taking offence; and that their "intended course of ciuill communitie wil minister continuall occasion of offence and will be as fuell for that fire," except they diligently quench it with brotherly forbearance. This allusion he further explains, as follows: "Whereas you are to become a body politik, vsing amongst your selues ciuill gouenment, and are not furnished with any persons of speciall eminencie aboue the rest, to be chosen by you into office of gouernment; Let your wisedome and godlinesse appeare, not onely in chusing such persons as do entirely loue, and will diligently promote the common good, but also in yeelding vnto them all due honour and obedience in their lawfull administrations; not beholding in them the ordinarinesse of their persons, but Gods ordinance for your good; nor being like vnto the foolish multitude, who more honour the gay coate, then either the vertuous mind of the man, or glorious ordinance of the Lord. But you know better things, and that the image of the Lords power and authoritie which the Magistrate beareth, is honorable, in how meane persons soeuer. And this dutie you both may the more willingly, and oughte the more conscionably to performe, because you are at least for the present to haue onely them for your ordinary gouernours, which your selues shall make choise of for that worke."—*Mourt's Relation*, viii-xi.

"In the next place, for the wholesome counsell Mr. Robinson gave that part of the Church whereof he was Pastor, at their departure from him to begin the great worke of Plantation in New England, amongst other wholesome Instructions and Exhortations, hee used these expressions, or to the same purpose [this, by the way, is the first and only authentic version of this famous address]: We are now ere long to part asunder, and the Lord knoweth whether ever he should live to see our faces again; but whether the Lord had appointed it or not, he charged us before God and his blessed Angels, to follow him no further than he followed Christ. And if God should reveal anything to us by any other instrument of his, to be as ready to receive it, as ever we were to receive any truth by his Ministery: For he was very confident the Lord had more truth and light yet to breake forth out of his holy Word. He took occasion also miserably to bewaile the state and condition of the Reformed Churches, who were come to a period in Religion, and would goe no further then the instruments of their Reformation: As for example, the Lutherans they could not be drawne to goe beyond what Luther saw; for whatever part of Gods will he had further imparted and revealed to Calvin, they will die rather then embrace it. And so also, saith he, you see the Calvinists, they stick where he left them: A misery much to bee lamented; For though they were precious shining lights in their times, yet God had not revealed his whole will to them: And were they now living, saith hee, they would bee as ready and willing to embrace further light, as that they had received. Here also he put us in mind of our Church-Covenant (at least that part of it) whereby wee promise and covenant with God and one with another, to receive whatsoever light or truth shall be made known to us from his written Word: but withall exhorted us to take heed what we received for truth, and well to examine and compare, and weigh it with other Scriptures of truth, before we received it; For, saith he, *It is not possible the Christian world should come so lately out of such thick Anti-christian darknesse, and that full perfection of knowledge should breake forth at once.*

Another thing hee commended to us, was, that wee should use all meanes to avoid and shake off the name of *Brownist*, being a meer nickname and brand to make religion odious, and the professors of it to the Christian world; and to that end, said hee, I should be glad if some godly minister would goe over with you, or come to you, before my comming; For, said hee, there will be no difference between the unconformable [Non-conformist] Ministers and you, when they come to the practise of the Ordinances out of the Kingdome: And so advised us by all meanes to endeavour to close with the godly party of the Kingdome of England, and rather to study union then division; *viz.* how neare we might possibly, without sin close with them, then in the least measure to affect division or separation from them." — Winslow's *Hypocrisie Unmasked*, 97.

The Voyage.

"The Speedwell brought her passengers prosperously to Southampton, where they found the Mayflower, which vessel had come round from London with Cushman and others a week before. . . . . . The vessels put to sea with about a hundred and twenty passengers. . . . . Before they had proceeded far on the voyage, the Speedwell proved so leaky that it was thought prudent to return, and both vessels put in at Dartmouth. Repairs having been made, they sailed a second time. But again, when they were a hundred leagues from land, the master of the smaller vessel represented her as incapable of making the voyage, and they put back to Plymouth. This was afterwards believed to be a pretence of the master, who had been engaged to remain a year with the emigrants, and who had repented of his contract. The next resource was to divide the company, and leave a portion behind, while the rest should pursue their voyage in the larger ship. This arrangement was presently made." — Palfrey's *Hist. New Eng.*, i: 158.

"Those that went bak were for the most parte such as were willing so to doe, either out of some discontente, or feare they conceived of ye ill success of ye vioage, seeing so many croses befale, & the year time so farr spente; but others in regarde of their owne weaknes, and charge of many yonge children, were thought least usefull, and most unfite to bear ye brunte of this hard adventure; unto which worke of God, and judgmente of their brethern, they were contented to submite. And thus, like Gedions [Gideon's] armie, this small number was devided, as if ye Lord by this worke of his providence thought these few to many for ye great worke he had to doe." — Bradford, *ut sup.*, 69.

"Little is recorded of the incidents of the voyage. The first part was favorably made. As the wanderers approached the American continent, they encountered storms which their overburdened vessel was scarcely able to sustain. Their destination was to a point near Hudson's River, yet within the territory of the London Company, by which their patent had been granted. This description corresponds to no other country than the sea-coast of the State of New Jersey. At early dawn of the sixty-fourth day of their voyage, they came in sight of the white sand banks of Cape Cod. In pursuance of their original purpose, they veered to the south, but, by the middle of the day, they found themselves 'among perilous shoals and breakers' which caused them to retrace their course. An opinion afterwards prevailed, on questionable grounds, that they had been purposely led astray by the master of the vessel, induced by a bribe from the Dutch, who were averse to having them near the mouth of the Hudson, which Dutch vessels had begun to visit for trade." — Palfrey, *ut sup.*, 162.

"They put to sea again with a prosperus winde, which continued diverce days togeather, which was some incouragemente unto them; yet according to ye usuall maner many were afflicted with sea-sicknes. And I may not omite hear a spetiall worke of God's providence. Ther was a proud & very profane yonge man, one of ye sea-men, of a lustie, able body, which made him the more hauty; he would allway be contemning ye poore people in their sicknes, & cursing them dayly with greevous execrations, and did not let to tell them, that he hoped to help to cast halfe of them over board before they came to their jurneys end, and to make mery with what they had; and if he were by any gently reproved, he would curse and swear most bitterly. But it pleased God before they came halfe seas over, to smite this yong man with a greeveous disease, of which he dyed in a desperate maner, and so was him selfe ye first yt was throwne overbord. Thus his curses light on his owne head; and it was an astonishmente to all his fellows, for they noted it to be ye just hand of God upon him.

After they had injoyed faire winds and weather for a season, they were incountred many times with crosse winds, and mette with many feirce stormes, with which ye shipe was shroudly shaken, and her upper works made very leakie; and one of the maine beames in ye midd ships was bowed & craked, which put them in some fear that ye shipe could not be able to performe ye vioage. So some of ye cheefe of ye company, perceiveing ye mariners to fear ye suffisiencie of ye shipe, as appeared by their mutterings, they entered into serious consulltation with ye mr. & other officers of ye ship, to consider in time of ye danger; and rather to returne then to cast them selves into a desperate & inevitable perill. And truly ther was great distraction & differance of opinion amongst ye mariners them selves; faine would they doe what could be done for their wages sake, (being now halfe the seas over), and on ye other hand they were loath to hazard their lives too desperatly. But in examening of all opinions, the mr. & others affirmed they knew ye ship to be stronge & firme under water; and for the buckling of ye maine beame, ther was a great iron scrue ye passengers brought out of Holland, which would raise ye beame into his place; ye which being done, the carpenter & mr. affirmed that with a post put under it, set firme in ye lower deck, & otherways bounde, he would make it sufficiente. And as for ye decks & uper workes they would calke them as well as they could, and though with ye workeing of ye ship they would not longe keepe stanch, yet ther would otherwise be no great danger, if they did not overpress her with sails. So they comited them selves to ye will of God, & resolved to proseede. In sundrie of these storms the winds were so feirce, & ye seas so high, as they could not beare a knote of saile, but were forced to hull, [to float or drive on the water, like the hull of a ship without sails. — *Webster*] for diverce days togither. And in one of them, as they thus lay at hull, in a mighty storme, a lustie yonge man (called John Howland) coming upon some occasion above ye grattings [a lattice cover for the hatches of a ship. — *Webster*], was, with a seele [lurch] of ye shipe throwne into ye sea; but it pleased God yt he caught hould of ye tope-saile halliards which hunge over board, & rane out at length; yet he held his hould (though he was sundry fadomes under water,) till he was hald up by ye same rope to ye brime of ye water, and then with a boat hooke & other means got into ye shipe againe & his life saved; and though he was something ill with it, yet he lived many years after, and became a profitable member both in church & comone wealthe. In all this viage ther died but one of ye passengers, which was William Butten, a youth, servant to Samuell Fuller, when they drew near ye coast. But to omite other things (that I may be breefe) after longe beating at sea they fell with that land which is called Cape Cod ; the which being made, & certainly knowne to be it, they were not a litle joyfull. After some deliberation had amongst them selves & with ye mr of ye ship, they tacked aboute and resolved to stand for ye southward (ye wind & weather being faire) to finde some place about Hudsons river for their habitation. But after they had sailed yt course aboute halfe yt day, they fell among deangerous shoulds and roring breakers, and they were so farr intangled ther with as they conceived them selves in great danger ; and ye wind shrinking upon them withall, they resolved to bear up againe for ye Cape, and thought them selves hapy to gett out of those dangers before night overtooke them, as by Gods Providence they did. And ye next day they gott into ye Cape-harbor, wher they ridd in saftie." — Bradford, *ut sup.*, 74.

The Outlook from Cape Cod Harbor.

" But hear I cannot but stay and make a pause, and stand half amased at this poore peoples presente condition ; and so I thinke will the reader too, when he well considers ye same. Being thus passed ye vast ocean, and a sea of troubles before in their preparation (as maybe remembred by yt which wente before) they had now no freinds to wellcome them, nor inns to entertaine or refresh their weather-beaten bodys, no houses or much less townes to repaire too, [no settlement of any kind within 500 miles] to seeke for succoure. It is recorded in scripture as a mercie to ye apostle & his shipwraked company, yt the barbarians shewed them no smale kindnes in refreshing them, but these savage barbarians, when they mette with them (as after will appeare) were readier to fill their sids full of arrows then otherwise. And for ye season it was winter, and they that know ye winters of yt cuntrie know them to be sharp & violent, & subjecte to cruell & feirce stormes deangerous to travill to known places, much more to serch an unknown coast. Besids, what could they see but a hidious & desolate wildernes, full of wild beasts and willd men ? and what multituds ther might be of them they knew not. Neither could they, as it were, goe up to ye tope of Pisgah, to vew from this willdernes a more goodly cuntrie to feed their hops ; for which way soever they turnd their eys (save upward to ye heavens) they could have litle solace or content in respecte of any outward objects. For sumer being done, all things stard upon them with a wether-beaten face ; and ye whole countrie, full of woods & thickets, represented a wild & savage heiw. If they looked behind them, ther was ye mighty ocean which they had passed, and was now as a maine barr & goulfe to seperate them from all ye civill parts of ye world. If it be said they had a ship to sucour them, it is trew ; but what heard they daly from ye mr & company ? but yt with speede they should looke out a place with their shallop, wher they would be at some near distance ; for ye season was shuch as he would not stirr from thence till a safe harbor was discovered by them wher they would be, and he might goe without danger ; and that victells consumed apace, but he must & would keepe sufficient for them selves & their returne. Yea, it was mutered by some, that if they gott not a place in time, they would turne them & their goods ashore & leave them.

Let it also be considered what weake hopes of supply & succoure they left behinde them, yt might bear up their minds in this sade condition and trialls they were under ; and they could not but be very smale. It is true, indeed, ye affections & love of their brethren at Leyden was cordiall & entire towards them, but they had litle power to help them, or them selves; and how ye case stode betweene them & ye marchants at their coming away, hath allready been declared. What could now sustaine them but ye spirite of God & his grace? May not & ought not the children of these fathers rightly say: *Our faithers were Englishmen which came over this great ocean, and were ready to perish in this willdernes; but they cried unto ye Lord, and he heard their voyce, and looked on their adversitie. Let them therfore praise ye Lord, because he is good & his mercies endure for ever, etc.*" — Bradford, *ut sup.*, 78.

Their Social Compact, and its Relation to Modern Republicanism.

"The day before we came to harbour, obseruing some not well affected to vnitie and concord, but gaue some appearance of faction, it was thought good there should be an association and agreement, that we should combine together in one body, and to submit to such government and governours, as we should by common consent agree to make and chose." — *Mourt's Relation*, 2.

"I shall a litle returne backe and begine with a combination made by them before they came ashore, being ye first foundation of their govermente in this place; occasioned partly by ye discontented & mutinous speeches that some of the strangers amongst them had let fall from them in ye ship — That when they came a shore they would use their owne libertie; for none had power to comand them, the patente they had being for Virginia, and not for New-england, which belonged to an other Government, with which ye Virginia Company had nothing to doe. And partly that schuch an acte by them done (this their condition considered) might be as firme as any patent, and in some respects more sure. The forme was as followeth.

In ye name of God, Amen. We whose names are underwriten, the loyall subjects of our dread soveraigne Lord, King James, by ye grace of God, of Great Britaine, Franc, & Ireland, king, defender of ye faith, &c. haveing undertaken for ye glorie of God, and advancemente of ye Christian faith, and honour of our king & countrie, a voyage to plant ye first colonie in ye Northerne parts of Virginia, doe by these presents solemnly & mutualy in ye presence of God, and one of another, covenant & combine our selves togeather into a civill body politick, for our better ordering & preservvation & furtherance of ye ends aforesaid; and by vertue hearof to enacte, constitute, and frame such just & equall lawes, ordinances, acts, constitutions, & offices, from time to time, as shall be thought most meete & convenient for ye generall good of ye colonie, unto which we promise all due submission and obedience.

In witnes whereof we have hereunder subscribed our names at Cap Codd ye 11. of November, in ye year of ye raigne of our soveraigne Lord, King James, of England, Franc, & Ireland ye eighteenth, and of Scotland ye fiftie fourth. Ano Dom. 1620. [Signed by 41 males, as first declared in Morton's *New England Memorial*, 1669.] — Bradford, *ut sup.*, 89.

Thrown thus suddenly, by their failure to reach their chartered territory, upon their own resources, and warned by symptoms of insubordination on board ship on the part of some who had joined them in England who were not of them in spirit, of dangers which might increase upon them after they went on shore; the leading spirits of the enterprise seem to have determined at once to test the experiment whether that primitive and Divinely revealed yet self-constituted and essentially democratic government which they had found to work so well in the church, might not work equally well in the state. "Many philosophers have since appeared, who have in labored treatises, endeavored to prove the doctrine, that the rights of man are unalienable, and nations have bled to defend and enforce them; yet in this dark age, the age of despotism and superstition, when no tongue dared to assert, and no pen to write this bold and novel doctrine — which was then as much at defiance with common opinion as with actual power (of which the monarch was then held to be the sole fountain, and the theory was universal, that all popular rights were granted by the crown) — in this remote wilderness, amongst a small and unknown band of wandering outcasts, the principle that *the will of the majority of the people shall govern* was first conceived, and was first practically exemplified. The Pilgrims, from their notions of primitive Christianity, the force of circumstances, and that pure moral feeling which is the offspring of true religion, discovered a truth in the science of government which had been concealed for ages. On the bleak shore of a barren wilderness, in the midst of desolation, with the blasts of winter howling around them, and surrounded with dangers in their most awful and appalling forms, the Pilgrims of Leyden laid the foundations of American liberty."— Baylies' *Hist. New Plym. Col.* i : 29.

"These were the men who produced a greater revolution in the world than Columbus. He in seeking for India discovered America. They, in pursuit of religious freedom established civil liberty, and meaning only to found a church, gave birth to a nation, and in settling a town commenced an empire."—*Ibid.* i: 4.

"This was the birth of popular constitutional liberty. . . . In the cabin of the Mayflower humanity renewed its rights, and instituted government on the basis of 'equal laws' for 'the general government.'"— Bancroft, *Hist. U. S.* i : 310.

A Glance at the Sorrows of the New Colony.

"In these hard & difficulte beginnings they found some discontents & murmurings arise amongst some, and mutinous speeches & cariags in other; but they were soone quelled & overcome by ye wisdome, patience & just & equall carrage of things by ye Govr and better part, wch clave faithfully togeather in ye maine. But that which was most sadd & lamentable was, that in 2. or 3. moneths time halfe of their company dyed, espetialy in Jan: & February, being ye depth of winter, and wanting houses & other comforts; being infected with ye scurvie & other diseases, which this long vioage & their inaccomodate condition had brought upon them; so as ther dyed some times 2. or 3. of a day, in ye foresaid time; that of 100. & odd persons, [there were exactly 102 persons in the Mayflower company] scarce 50. remained. And of these in ye time of most distres, ther was but 6. or 7. sound persons, who, to their great comendations be it spoken, spared no pains, night nor day, but with abundance of toyle and hazard of their oune health, fetched them woode, made them fires, drest them meat, made their beads, washed their lothsome cloaths, cloathed & uncloathed them; in a word, did all ye homly & necessarie offices for them wch dainty & quesie stomaks cannot endure to hear named; and all this willingly and cherfully, without any grudging in ye least, shewing herein their true love unto their freinds & bretheren. A rare example & worthy to be remembred. Tow of these 7. were Mr William Brewster, ther reverend elder, & Myles Standish, ther Captein & military comander, unto whom my selfe, & many others were much beholden in our low & sicke condition. And yet the Lord so upheld these persons, as in this generall calamity they were not at all infected either with sicknes, or lamnes. And what I have said of these, I may say of many others who dyed in this generall vissitation, & others yet living, that whilst they had health, yea, or any strength continuing, they were not wanting to any that had need of them. And I doute not but their recompence is with y[e] Lord." — Bradford, *ut sup.*, 90.

"By that time ther corne was planted, all their victals were spente, and they were only to rest on Gods providence; at night not many times knowing wher to have a bitt of any thing y[e] next day. And so, as one well observed, had need to pray that God would give them their dayly brade, above all people in y[e] world. Yet they bore these wants with great patience & allacritie of spirite, and that for so long a time as for y[e] most parte of 2. years. . . . They haveing but one boat left and she not over well fitted, they were devided into severall companies, 6. or 7. to a gangg or company, and so wente out with a nett they had bought, to take bass & such like fish, by course, every company knowing their turne. No sooner was y[e] boate discharged of what she brought, but y[e] next company tooke her and wente out with her. Neither did they returne till they had cauight something, though it were 5. or 6. days before, for they knew ther was nothing at home, and to goe home emptie would be a great discouragemente to y[e] rest. Yea, they strive who should doe best. If she stayed longe or got litle, then all went to seeking of shel-fish, which at low-water they digged out of y[e] sands. And this was their living in y[e] somer time, till God sente y[m] beter; & in winter they were helped with ground-nuts and foule. Also in y[e] somer they gott now & then a dear; for one or 2. of y[e] fitest was apoynted to range y[e] woods for y[t] end; & what was gott that way was devided amongst them." —Bradford, *ut sup.*, 136.

When the *Anne* arrived, "the best dish they [the colonists] could presente their freinds with was a lobster, or a peece of fish, without bread or anything els but a cupp of fair spring water." — *Ibid*, 146.

Their merchant friends in London "went back on them," and their "loving freind" Thomas Weston, failed them, and each new company arriving but became largely new pensioners upon them — coming so ill supplied. As Bradford says: "As they were now fayled of suply by him [Weston] and others in their greatest neede and wants, which was caused by him and y[e] rest, who put so great a company of men upon them, as y[e] former company were, without any food, and came at shuch a time as they must live almost a whole year before any could be raised, excepte they had sente some; so upon y[t] pointe they never had any supply of vitales more afterwards (but what the Lord gave them otherwise), for all y[e] company sent at any time was allways too short for those people y[t] came with it." — *Ibid*, 116.

"But these troubls prodused a quite contrary effecte then their adversaries hoped for. Which was looked at as a great worke of God, to draw on men by unlickly means." — *Ibid*, 189.

"Brewster, the ruling Elder, lived for many months together without bread, and frequently on fish alone. With nothing but oysters and clams before him, he, with his family, would give thanks that they could 'suck of the abundance of the seas, and of the treasures hid in the sands.' Whenever a deer was taken, it was divided amongst the whole company. It is said that they were once reduced to a pint of corn, which being equally divided, gave to each a proportion of five kernels, which was parched and eaten." — Baylies's *Hist. New Plym.*, i: 121.

Reason why They Succeeded where Others had Failed.

"No trading adventurers were so capable and resolute as to be able to plant that soil. . . . . . A religious impulse accomplished what commercial enterprise, commanding money and court favor, had attempted without success. Civilized New England is the child of English Puritanism."—Palfrey, *ut sup.*, i: 101.

"Several attempts were made to plant New England from worldly motives, but they all proved abortive."—Backus's *Hist. New Eng.*, i: 33.

"And now compare this company with that of Sagadahock [Popham's colony, which landed on the Kennebec, 8 Aug., 1607.] That company, who came upon worldly designs, had an hundred men; this religious society consisted of but one hundred and one souls, men, women and children; the one arrived at the place designed for settlement in August, the other not till winter had set in. The worldly company only buried their President [Popham], and all returned the next year to their native country again; whereas this religious people, in about five months' time, buried their Governor and full half their number, and yet with fortitude and patience they kept their station; yea, though they were afterwards deserted and abused by some who had engaged to help them. We cannot now form an idea of what those pious planters endured to prepare the way for what we at this day enjoy."—*Ibid* i: 40.

"Whether Britain would have had any colonies in America at this day, if religion had not been the grand inducement, is doubtful."—Hutchinson's *Hist. Mass.*, i: 3.

"The question may very naturally be asked, how it happened that a population of adventurers without military force, and with little wealth, which is unquestionably a formidable element of power, and by which men often make their will acceptable; and with an equality as general as was possible in any country which had a government, could without the sanction of a royal charter, and without the interference of the metropolis, which in infant colonies is generally imperative and absolute, sustain themselves so long without tumults and commotions, and do everything essential to the well-being of the community? This question finds its solution in the religious character of the people. Worldly objects were with them secondary, and that curse of all small and independent communities, political ambition, found no place amongst them. The higher offices were not sought, but the services of such as were fit to sustain them were demanded as the right of the people, and they were accepted not for the sake of distinction, emolument or pleasure, but from a sense of duty; fearful of the loss of reputation, men underwent the severe and painful duties which such offices required."—Baylies's *Hist. New Plym.*, iv: 146.

Recognition of their Sufferings and Heroism at the Time.

"If ye land afford you bread, and ye sea yeeld you fish, rest you a while contented, God will one day afford you better fare. And all men shall know you are neither fugetives nor discontents. But can, if God so order it, take ye worst to your selves, with content, & leave ye best to your neighbors, with cherfullnes. Let it not be greevous unto you y^t^ you have been instruments to brake ye ise for others who come after with less dificulty, the honour shall be yours to ye worlds end. We bear you always in our brests, and our harty affection is towards you all, as are ye harts of hundreds more which never saw your faces, who doubtles pray for your saftie as their owne, as we our selves both doe & ever shall, that ye same God which hath so marvelously preserved you from seas, foes, and famine, will still preserve you from all future dangers, and make you honourable amongst men, and glorious in blise at ye last day." — Letter from some of the English adventurers, 1623, copied by Bradford, *ut sup.*, 144.

The following extract from a letter of Gov. Bradford to his wife's sister, Mary Carpenter, still in England, of date $\frac{19}{29}$Aug. 1646, will show the feeling on this subject which prevailed, when the Colony had more than attained its majority :

" We understand, by your letter, that God hath taken to himself our aged mother, out of the troubles of this tumultuous world, and that you are in a solitary condition, as we easily apprehend. We thought good, therefore, to write these few lines unto you, that if you think good to come over to us, you shall be wellcome, and we shall be as helpfull unto you as we may, though we are growne old, and the countrie here more unsettled, than ever, by reason of the great changes that have been in these late times, and what will further be, the Lord only knows, which makes many thinke of removing their habitations, and sundrie of our ministers (hearing of the peace and liberty now in England and Ireland) begin to leave us, and it is feared many more will follow. We do not write these things to discourage you, (for we shall be glad to see you, if God so dispose) but if you find not all things here according to your expectation, when God shall bring you hither, that you may not thinke we dealt not plainly with you."

The Superior Tolerance of the Plymouth Men.

" The spirit of Robinson appeared to watch over his feeble flock on the coast of New England, long after his body was moldering beneath the Cathedral church at Leyden. Again, their twelve years' residence in Holland had brought the Pilgrims in contact with other sects of Christians, and given them a more catholic spirit than pertained to those whose stay in England had been embittered by the strife of contending factions in the Established Church. Whether these reasons fully account for the superior liberality of the Plymouth Colonists, or not, the records show, that as they were distinct from the Puritans in England, and had been long separated from them in Holland, so did they preserve that distinction in some measure in America. The Pilgrims of Plymouth were more liberal in feeling, and more tolerant in practice, than the Puritans of Massachusetts Bay. The simple forms of democratic government [*i.e.*, in its absolute form, precisely as practiced in the Congregational churches] were maintained in Plymouth for eighteen years, until the growth of the Colony compelled the introduction of the representative system." — Arnold's *Hist. Rhode Island*, i : 13.

"The Plymouth Colony was more liberal in its feeling than that of the Bay, permitting a greater latitude of individual opinion." — *Ibid*, 166.

" I have shown that the Pilgrim Fathers, and their precursors, in England, Holland, and at Plymouth, were *Separatists*, and had no connection with the *Puritans*, who subsequently settled in New England, at Salem and Boston, in Massachusetts ; that the principles and practices of the two parties, confounded by some careless writers, differed essentially ; the Separatists ever contending for freedom of conscience and separation from the powers of the State, while the Puritans remained in connection and communion with the State Church, and held, both in England and New England, that the State should be authoritative in matters of religion. Hence the anti-christian and intolerant acts of the Puritan colony [Mass.] to the Separatists — Ralph Smyth, Roger Williams, Isaac Robinson, John Cudworth and Timothy Hatherley. Hence, also, on the arrival of the Friends, the cruel laws for whipping, banishing and executing, for matters of religious faith and practice. I have shown that the Separatist colony of Plymouth had no share in this intolerant conduct during the lives of the Pilgrim Fathers, and, moreover, that they acted kindly, and received into their church both Smyth and Roger Williams when forbidden to worship freely elsewhere; and that after the death of the Pilgrim Fathers, some of their sons and successors, acting up to their principles, shielded the Friends, and refused to be parties to the persecuting laws then enacted. . . . .

It may interest you to know that two eminent historians recently deceased virtually admitted the truth of that which I have thus affirmed. I refer to Lord Macaulay and Earl Stanhope (Lord Mahon), who as Commissioners for decorating, historically, the House of Lords, were appealed to respecting an erroneous inscription placed under Mr. Cope's painting of "The Pilgrim Fathers Landing in New England." The inscription stood: "Landing of a *Puritan* Family in New England," but after listening to the proofs submitted, and hearing Mr. Cope, who stated that he had taken his ideas from Bradford's Journal, the Commissioners ordered the terms "Puritan Family" to be removed, as unjust to the memory of the parties concerned, and substituted the words: 'PILGRIM FATHERS.'"— Mr. Chamberlain Benj. Scott's *The Pilgrim Fathers Neither Puritans Nor Persecutors*, 36.

"Here we may observe the great difference between our Plymouth fathers, and the Massachusetts. With all these stimulations to severity, the Court of Plymouth only charged them [the Seekonk Baptists], to desist from their practice, which others had taken such offence at, and one of them yielding thereto, the others were not so much as bound to their good behaviour, nor any other sureties required." — Backus's *Hist. New Eng.*, i: 214.

"Rigidness is a word that both Episcopalians and Presbyterians have often cast upon our Plymouth fathers. Yet the Massachusetts now discovered so much more of that temper than they, that Mr. Dunstar, in October 24, 1654, resigned his office among them and removed and spent his remaining days at Scituate in Plymouth Colony." — *Ibid*, 284.

"The Plymouth colonists of humbler rank and less excited from having been so long removed from the scene of controversy in England, were more tolerant and mild, and although much swayed by the influence of their domineering neighbors, to whom, on all great occasions, they seemed to defer, were never led into those horrible excesses of fanaticism which disgrace the early annals of Massachusetts." — Baylies's *Hist. New Plym.*, i: 203.

"More fortunate than Massachusetts, they had been undisturbed with sectarian disputes, and wiser, they exercised a liberal toleration, which increased their numbers, while the sterner temper of their neighbors could only be soothed by the banishment of their antagonists." — *Ibid*, i: 321.

"Sectarians, it is true, disturbed the tranquility of the inhabitants of this little Commonwealth; but persecution with them assumed its mildest form, and their annals have escaped that deep and indelible stain of blood, which pollutes the pages of the early history of their sterner and more intolerant brethren of Massachusetts." — *Ibid*, i: 5.

"Here may be observed to the honor of this Colony, that though the provocations of the Quakers were equally great here as elsewhere, yet they never made any sanguinary or capital laws against that sect, as some of the Colonies did." — *Appendix to Mr. Robbins' Sermon at Plymouth*, (A. D. 1760), p. 15.

Relation of the Plymouth Colony to this Republic.

"The Pilgrims brought with them to the new World a form of Christianity, which I cannot better describe than by styling it a democratic and republican religion. This contributed powerfully to the establishment of a republic and a democracy in public affairs." — *De Tocqueville*, i: 384.

"The system of town governments does not prevail in England. Nothing analogous to it is known in the Southern States, and although the system of internal government in the Middle States bears a partial resemblance to that of New England, it is in many respects dissimilar. Those who are strangers to our customs are surprised to find the whole of New England divided into a vast number of little democratic republics, which have full power to do all those things which most essentially concern the comforts, happiness, and morals of the people. . . . . Under the government of these little republics, society is trained in habits of order, and the whole people acquire a practical knowledge of legislation within their own sphere. To this mode of government may be attributed that sober and reflecting character, almost peculiar to the people of New England, and their general knowledge of politics and legislation. . . . . Now, to the Independent churches we may trace the original notion of independent communities, which afterwards assumed the name of towns, and which after having passed through an ecclesiastical state, and after the proprietaries became extinct from the special appropriation of all the lands within the bounds of their charter, assumed the shape of political corporations with municipal, and in fact legislative powers within their own limits." — Baylies's *Hist. New Plym.*, i: 240.

"The purely democratic form of government in the church at Leyden, already entrenched in the warm affections of the Pilgrims, led to the adoption of a corresponding form of civil government on board the Mayflower for the Colony at Plymouth. It has been said, and it is true, that it was a Congregational church-meeting that first suggested the idea of a New England town-meeting; and a New England town-meeting embodies all the germinal principles of our State and national government." — Wellman's *Ch. Pol. of the Pilgrims*, 68.

"The late Dr. Fishback, of Lexington, Ky., a few years since, made the following statement, which he received from the late Rev. Andrew Tribble, who died at the age of about 93 years. Mr. Tribble was pastor of a small Baptist church near Mr. Jefferson's residence, in the State of Virginia, eight or ten years before the American Revolution. Mr. Jefferson attended the meetings of the church for several months in succession, and after one of them, asked the worthy pastor to go home and dine with him, with which request he complied. Mr. Tribble asked Mr. Jefferson how he was pleased with their [purely democratic, or Congregational] church government? Mr. Jefferson replied, that its propriety had struck him with great force, and had greatly interested him; adding that he considered it the only form of pure democracy which then existed in the world, *and had concluded that it would be the best plan of government for the American Colonies*."—Belcher's *Relig. Denominations in U. S.*, 184.

"Congregationalism was, historically, the mother of our civil liberties. It was so first at Plymouth, and in the Massachusetts Colony. It was so, later, in the days of the Revolution. And it would seem a natural inference that the same polity which gave us a Republic, would be most favorable, in all its workings, to the permanent welfare of the State."—Dexter's *Congregationalism, etc.*, 290.

"The Plymouth Colony has furnished her full proportion of talent, genius, learning and enterprise in almost every department of life; and, in other lands, the merits of the posterity of the Pilgrims have been acknowledged. . . . . . In one respect they present a remarkable exception to the rest of America. They are the purest English race in the world; there is scarcely any intermixture even with the Scotch or Irish, and none with the aboriginals. Almost all the present population are descended from the original English settlers. . . . . . The fishermen and navigators of Maine, the children of Plymouth, still continue the industrious and bold pursuits of their forefathers. In that fine country, beginning at Utica (N. Y.) and stretching to Lake Erie, this race may be found on every hill and in every valley; on the rivers and on the lakes. . . . . . And in all the Southern and South-western States, the natives of the 'Old Colony,' like the Armenians of Asia, may be found in every place where commerce and traffic offer any lure to enterprise; and in the heart of the gigantic [West], like their ancestors, they have commenced the cultivation of the wilderness, like them, surrounded with savage beasts and savage men, and like them, patient in suffering, despising danger, and animated with hope."—Baylies's *Hist. New Plym.*, iv: 148.

The May-flower on New England's coast has furled her tattered sail,
And through her chafed and moaning shrouds December's breezes wail;
Yet on that icy deck, behold a meek but dauntless band,
Who, for the right to worship God, have left their native land;
And to this dreary wilderness this glorious boon they bring—
A Church without a Bishop, and a State without a King!

Those daring men, those gentle wives, say, wherefore do they come?
Why rend they all the tender ties of kindred and of home?
'Tis *Heaven* assigns their noble work, man's spirit to unbind;
They come not for themselves alone—they come for all mankind;
And to the empire of the West this glorious boon they bring—
A Church without a Bishop, and a State without a King!

Then Prince and Prelate, hope no more to bend them to your sway—
Devotion's fire inflames their breasts, while freedom points their way;
And in their brave heart's estimate, 't were better not to be,
Than quail beneath a despot, where the soul cannot be free;
And therefore o'er a wintry wave, those exiles come to bring
A Church without a Bishop, and a State without a King!

And still their spirit, in their sons, with freedom walks abroad;
The BIBLE is our only creed, our only sovereign, GOD!
The hand is raised, the word is spoke, the joyful pledge is given—
And boldly on our banner floats, in the free air of Heaven,
The motto of our sainted sires; and loud we'll make it ring—
A CHURCH WITHOUT A BISHOP, AND A STATE WITHOUT A KING!

—*Rev. Charles Hall, D.D.*

O little fleet! that on thy quest divine
Sailedst from Palos one bright autumn morn,
Say, has old Ocean's bosom ever borne
A freight of Faith and Hope, to match with thine?

Say, too, has Heaven's high favor given again
Such consummation of desire, as shone
About Columbus, when he rested on
The new-found world, and married it to Spain?

Answer—Thou refuge of the Freeman's need,
THOU for whose destinies no Kings looked out,
Nor Sages to resolve some mighty doubt,
Thou simple MAYFLOWER of the salt-sea mead!

When THOU wert wafted to that distant shore,—
Gay flowers, bright birds, rich odors, met thee not,
Stern nature hailed thee to a sterner lot,—
God gave free earth and air, and gave no more.

Thus to men cast in that heroic mold
Came Empire, such as Spaniard never knew—
Such Empire, as beseems the just and true;
And, at the last, almost unsought, came Gold.

But HE, who rules both calm and stormy days,
Can guard that people's heart, that nation's health
Safe on the perilous hights of power and wealth,
As in the straitness of the ancient ways.

—*Richard Monckton Milnes,* (*Lord Houghton.*)

Tantae Molis Erat Nov-Anglam Condere Gentem!

The First Colonization of New-England.

AN ADDRESS,

DELIVERED AT THE

ERECTION OF A MONUMENTAL STONE

IN THE

WALLS OF FORT POPHAM,

August 29th, 1862,

COMMEMORATIVE OF THE PLANTING OF THE POPHAM COLONY

ON THE

PENINSULA OF SABINO,

August 19th, O. S., 1607,

ESTABLISHING THE TITLE OF ENGLAND

TO

THE CONTINENT.

BY JOHN A. POOR.

NEW-YORK:
ANSON D. F. RANDOLPH, PUBLISHER AND BOOKSELLER,
683 BROADWAY, COR. OF AMITY STREET.

1863.

INTRODUCTORY NOTE.

The Portland *Daily Advertiser* of August 30th, 1862, published the following:

THE POPHAM CELEBRATION.

Friday, the 29th, was a most delightful day for celebrating the Two hundred and fifty-fifth Anniversary of the planting of Popham Colony on the Kennebec. Some five or six thousand people, coming from all parts of the country, assembled at Fort Popham on this occasion. In every respect the celebration was a great success.

Between eleven and twelve o'clock the ceremonies of commemoration, of erecting the Memorial Stone, commenced, Hon. Charles J. Gilman, of Brunswick, the Marshal of the day, reading the following brief statement:

"Two hundred and fifty-five years ago this day, under the auspices of a Royal charter granted by King James, there assembled on the Peninsula of Sabino, and near to this spot, a party of Englishmen, and formed the first civil Protestant government of the New World, and by formal occupation and possession, established the title of England to the continent. In the year 1607, in the month of August, on the 19th day of the month, the Commission of George Popham for the Presidency of the new Government was read. Capt. Raleigh Gilbert, James Davies, Richard Seymour, the preacher, Capt. Richard Davies, and Capt. Harlow, were all sworn assistants.

"In commemoration of this event, the Historical Society of this State, corresponding with citizens in different parts of the State, have instituted this celebration, and it is proposed from time to time, in the valley of the Sagadahoc, on the Peninsula of Sabino, to recall and to illustrate events of the past, and by this and future celebrations to assign to Maine her true historic position. On this spot, under the direction of the distinguished Chief of the Bureau of Engineers, and his accomplished assistants, a fort is in process of construction. In compliance with a petition of John

A. Poor and Reuel Williams, dated Washington, November 18th, 1861, Simon Cameron, then Secretary of War, by the advice of Gen. Totten, determined to associate this fort with the name of Popham and the history of his colony.

"In order that the record of events which have transpired may be made still more vivid and impressive, it has been thought fit and proper to insert in a wall of the fort a memorial stone. The President of the Historical Society, the President of Bowdoin College, the representative of the government of the State, the representative of the government of the United States, and the Grand Masonic Lodge of Maine, in the disposition and adjustment of this stone will participate. Before the commencement of these interesting exercises, let us imitate the example of those who stood here two hundred and fifty-five years ago this day. As the Rev. Richard Seymour, Chaplain of the Colony, was invited to perform acts of religious worship, *then*, so now do I invite Right Rev. Bishop Burgess, Bishop of the Diocese of Maine, to perform religious worship, according to the ceremonial of the Episcopal Church of that day."

Then followed the impressive services of the Episcopal Church, Right Rev. Bishop Burgess officiating, such religious services as the Popham colonists used, upon their first landing. A brief historical statement was next read by William Willis, President of the Maine Historical Society. President Woods, of Bowdoin College, Chairman of the Standing Committee of the Maine Historical Society, next solicited the consent of the State and of the United States to permit the erection of the Memorial Stone. Hon. Abner Coburn responded for the State, Capt. T. L. Casey, of the U. S. Engineers, for the United States. The erection of the Memorial Stone was then completed with Masonic ceremonies by the Grand Lodge of Maine, J. H. Drummond, Grand Master.

Following these ceremonies, which had been interspersed with appropriate music by Poppenburg's Band, of the 17th Regular Infantry, came the Oration by John A. Poor.

The Address of Mr. Poor, as now published, contains the paragraphs which were omitted for want of time, at the Celebration.

ADDRESS.

We commemorate to-day the great event of American history. We are assembled on the spot that witnessed the first formal act of possession of New-England, by a British colony, under the authority of a Royal Charter. We have come here, on the two hundred and fifty-fifth anniversary of that event, to rejoice in the manifold blessings that have flowed to us from that act, — to place on record a testimonial of our appreciation of the value of that day's work, — and to transmit to future generations, an expression of our regard for the illustrious men who laid the foundation of England's title to the Continent, and gave a new direction to the history of the world.

We meet under circumstances of deep and peculiar interest. The waters of the same broad Sagadahoc,* move onward in their majestic course to the ocean; the green summit of the beautiful Seguin still lifts itself in the distance — standing sentinel and breakwater to beat back the swelling surges of the sea; the flashing foam of the Atlantic still washes the rocky shores of the Peninsula of Sabino, and the secure anchorage of this open bay receives the tempest-tost bark, as on the day that the "Gift of God," the gallant flyboat of

* Sagadahoc, or *Sachedahock*, is Indian, and signifies, "The going out of the waters," or *the mouth of the river*. Eaton's Annals of Warren, p. 15.

George Popham, helped into port Raleigh Gilbert's good ship "Mary and John," freighted with the hopes of a new empire. Behind us rises the green summit of yonder mount, around whose sides soon clustered the habitations of the intrepid Popham and his devoted companions; and the same rocky rampart that then encircled this proud bay, stands unmoved amid the changes of two hundred and fifty-five years. *All else is changed.* The white sails of many a gallant ship now cover this broad expanse of water; a towering light-house rises high above the summit of Seguin, throwing the rays of its Fresnel lens far out into the darkness, and along these rocky shores; habitations of men dot every point of the surrounding landscape, while the stout steamer, unlike the ship of olden time, *gladly* encounters the rude waves of the ocean.

> "Against the wind, and against the tide,
> Still steady, with an upright keel." *

But the heart of man has changed less than all, in these two hundred and fifty-five years. It still bows submissive to Almighty God, and lifts its voice in prayer and praise, as when in the solemn service of his ritual their pious preacher uttered these memorable words:

"At what time soever a sinner doth repent him of his sins from the bottom of his heart, I will blot all his wickedness out of my remembrance, saith the Lord."

"I will go to my Father, and say to him, Father, I have sinned against heaven and against thee: I am no more worthy to be called thy son." †

All this was permanent and enduring. The same duty and the same dependence upon God, as then, are upon us all. We seem to see before us the faithful

* For description of the localities alluded to, see Note A, in the Appendix.

† King James's Liturgy of 1604.

Richard Seymour,* clad in the habiliments of the priesthood, as we hear the same accents of prayer and praise that he uttered,—when, before him knelt the faithful Popham and his hardy comrades, whose deep responses were borne upward to the mercy-seat. We listen to-day to the same strains of music, and to the same lessons, that first burst forth from human lips, on the shores of this great continent! That same sense of sinfulness that then found utterance in the language of the liturgy, finds expression in our hearts to-day; and may it please the Father of mercies so to mould all hearts, that these words of penitential confession shall find willing utterance from all lips, and these words of prayer and praise, raised in devout aspiration from all hearts, be continued from generation to generation through all time, till there shall be one fold and one Shepherd, and this mortal reach immortality at the final consummation of all things.

The greatness of an event is to be measured by the influence it exerts over the destinies of mankind. Acts of sublime moral grandeur, essential to the education of the race, may surpass in real magnitude the most brilliant achievements of material success, and the silent eloquence of truth, do more to conquer the fierce spirit of war, than the most imposing triumphs of warlike ambition. The ignominious execution of the Teacher of our Religion, in a remote and obscure province of the Roman Empire, was an event of so little interest at the time, as to be overlooked by the great writers of Roman history. The rise of the Christian sect in Judea, was noticed by the younger Pliny in his letter to the Emperor Trajan within the next hun-

* Who was Richard Seymour? See sketch of him by Bishop Burgess, Appendix B.

dred years;* but no human vision could then have foreseen, that their despised doctrines, would, within the next few hundred years, have become enthroned in the home of the Cæsars, and give law to the civilized world.

When Hannibal led his disciplined troops from the shores of Africa, through the perilous passes of the Pyrenees and across the Alps, into Italy, and slew more in number of the Roman youth, than the entire force of his army, we instinctively honor this sublime exhibition of martial genius and energy. When at last he failed to conquer Rome, only from the lack of succor from his own countrymen, whose jealousy of his success destroyed their country, we respect that indignant sense of justice that bequeathed his bones to a foreign resting-place, lest his unworthy countrymen should in after-times be honored, by the homage done to his remains. We weep at every fresh recital of the splendor of his achievements, and the magnitude of his misfortunes, however much we may value the superior civilization of the Roman people over that of the Carthaginians, as we reflect that the history of future times hung suspended, on the issue of that campaign. We are willing to rejoice, that at last his ungrateful nation was blotted from the earth, and Carthage lives only as a dishonor to history, while his name stands foremost, among warriors and heroes.

When the brave and accomplished Champlain returned to France after an absence of three and a half years in Acadia,† having explored all these shores, and given them the names they now bear, and placed the

* Lib. x. Epistle 99, A.D. 107.

† Champlain, with De Monts and his associates, sailed from St. Malo March 17, 1604, in two ships. They returned to St. Malo September 28, 1607. See Poor's Vindication of Gorges, and the authorities there cited, p. 20, et seq.

symbols of the authority of his sovereign, from Cape Breton to Cape Cod, confidently anticipating the future greatness of his race and nation in this their secure home in the finest portion of the new world, he found that the charter granted to De Monts under which he held and occupied the country, had been revoked,* and that the most hopeful plan of empire ever revealed to human eyes, had been marred if not destroyed. With generous valor he sought a new home amid the snows of the St. Lawrence, and in 1608 planted the flag and the power of France, upon the shores of that mighty river, where his bones now lie, in the midst of the race he there planted. But the folly of the great King Henry of Navarre, could not be overcome by any heroism on his part, for the stronger foothold of Sir Ferdinando Gorges had meanwhile been planted on the shores of this open sea, from Sagadahoc to Plymouth, and the flag of France was compelled to withdraw across the Sagadahoc, never more to return thither after 1607, and finally lay in the dust before that cross of St. George, which first floated from the rocky ramparts of Quebec on the 18th of September, 1759,† and the power of France was swept from the continent forever. But all hearts instinctively honor the immortal Champlain. The sympathy of all generous minds ever flows forth, at the utterance of his name. His monument still exists, in sight of an admiring posterity, more enduring than this stone we have this day raised in honor of another, and it shall forever remain in perpetual beauty, while the waters from the lofty summits of the Adirondac, mingling with those

* Champlain's Voyages, p. 44, 45, 99, (ed. 1632.) L'Escarbot, p. 619, 2d edition, 1612.

† The battle was fought September 13, 1759; the surrender of Quebec was agreed on in the evening of the 17th, and the English flag raised, on the morning of the 18th.

of the Green Mountains, shall fill the deep recesses of the Lake, that bears the honored name, *Champlain!**

Our duty to-day calls us to honor another, and a greater than Champlain; not greater in purpose, but in the results he achieved for humanity and his race, and more entitled to our sympathy from the blessings we owe to his labors, — the man that gave North-America to his nation, and died without even the poor reward that followed his great rival.

That colossal empire which Champlain planted on the St. Lawrence, and watched over till the close of his life,† which eventually held four fifths of the continent, was unable to regain its possession on these Atlantic shores, and from this cause alone, it finally fell beneath the power and sagacity of England's greatest war minister, Pitt, who gave to the heroic Wolfe, in his youthful prime, the noblest opportunity for fame that has yet fallen to a leader of armies. But the hero who gave the continent to England, was neither Pitt nor Wolfe, but another and greater than either, the illustrious and sagacious Knight, whose manly daring and persevering energy, upheld the drooping cause of colonization in its darkest hours, against individual jealousy and Parliamentary injustice; and saw, like Israel's great law-giver, from the top of the mountain, the goodly land that his countrymen should afterwards possess, though he was not allowed to enter it.‡ All honor, this day, to Sir Ferdinando Gorges. His praise is proclaimed by Puritan voices, after more than two hundred years of unjust reproach. His monument

* See Mrs. Sigourney's charming Sonnet to Champlain, in Note C of the Appendix.

† Champlain died in the discharge of the duties of the office of Governor-General of Canada, at Quebec, Dec. 25th, 1635.

‡ See Poor's Vindication of Gorges, p. 80, and note.

stands proudly erect among the nations, in that constitutional government of these United States which sheds blessings on the world.* His name, once perpetuated in our annals, was stricken from the records of the State, and no city, or town, or lake, or river, allowed to bear it to future times. But a returning sense of justice marks the American character, and two hundred years after his death it is heard once more in honorable renown.† Busy hands, guided by consummate skill, are now shaping into beauty and order, a work of enduring strength and national defense, that does honor to his name, and rising in sight of our chief commercial city, more beautiful in situation than any that graces the Ægean coast, or smiles from the Adriatic shore—the metropolis, too, of his ancient "Province of Mayne"—proclaims, Sir Ferdinando Gorges, *Father of English colonization in America.*‡ And in after-times,

* Gorges foresaw and predicted the independence of the colonies of North-America, of the British crown. Briefe Narration, p. 51, vol. ii. Maine Hist. Coll., also Poor's Vindication, p. 83.

† Gorges died in 1647. On the 6th of September, 1846, the Hon. George Folsom, of New-York, in an address before the Maine Historical Society, brought his claims to the public notice. See vol. ii. Maine Hist. Collections, p. 1.

‡ Fort Gorges.—The new Fort in Portland Harbor, erected by the United States Government, on Hog Island Ledge, has been named by the Secretary of War, Fort Gorges, in honor of Sir Ferdinando Gorges, "the original proprietor of the Province of Mayne and the Father of English Colonization in America."

In November last a petition was presented to the Secretary of War, as follows, namely:

To the Hon. John B. Floyd, Secretary of War:

The undersigned, citizens of Maine, respectfully ask, that the new fort now being erected in Portland Harbor by the United States Government, may be named Fort Gorges, in honor of Sir Ferdinando Gorges, "the original proprietor of the Province of Mayne, and the Father of English Colonization in America."

And as in duty bound will ever pray.

Wm. Willis,	Ether Shepley,	John A. Poor,	Jed'h Jewett,
John Mussey,	George Evans,	Ashur Ware,	Samuel Fessenden,
Samuel Jordan,	Geo. F. Emery,	Charles Q. Clapp,	Joshua Dunn,
N. Deering,	H. I. Robinson,	Samuel P. Shaw,	E. H. Elwell,
Wm. P. Preble,	P. Barnes,	Henry Willis,	Moses Macdonald,
Manasseh H. Smith,	John Neal,	Oliver Gerrish,	Jabez C. Woodman,
Geo. F. Shepley,	D. W. Fessenden,	A. W. H. Clapp,	Thomas H. Talbot,
F. A. Quinby,	Wm. Senter,	John M. Adams,	Charles A. Lord,
			and others.

Similar petitions were presented from Augusta, and the same were transmitted through Capt. Kurtz, of the Engineer Corps, in charge of the construction of the Fort.

when his race shall become not only masters of the continent, but of the earth, and his mother tongue the universal language, History shall perpetuate the deeds of his genius, and Song shall make his name immortal.*

The question that the European nations were called upon to solve, at the commencement of the seventeenth century, was, who should hereafter occupy and possess, the broad belt of the temperate zone of the New World, from the Atlantic to the Pacific seas. All previous explorations were preliminary efforts towards this one great object, but the question remained open and undecided. The voyages of the Northmen to these shores, interesting to the curious, are of no historic value, because not connected with the colonization of the country—unless it shall hereafter appear that Columbus obtained from them information, as to the extent of the Western Ocean. At the time of discovery by Columbus, the only races inhabiting the New World, north of Mexico, were tribes of wandering savages, incapable of accepting or acquiring habits of civilized life. An extinct race, had left their mounds in the West, and their deposits of oyster-beds along the shores of the Atlantic, and passed from traditionary story.

The adventurous Magellan in 1520 proved, by the *first* voyage round the world, the extent of the new continent, and in 1579, Sir Francis Drake, the first Englishman that circumnavigated the globe, in that daring

The Hon. John Appleton, Assistant Secretary of State, interested himself in the matter, and has forwarded us for publication the following note :

WASHINGTON, April 2d, 1860.

VERY DEAR SIR : I am much obliged for your note of this date.

You may say to your correspondent in Maine, that the Secretary of War has ordered the fortification he refers to to be named "Fort Gorges."

Yours, very truly, W. R. DRINKARD.

Hon. JOHN APPLETON, Asst. Sec'y of State.

—*Portland Advertiser* of April 10th, 1860.

* See in Note C, in Appendix, Mrs. Sigourney's admirable Poem on Gorges.

voyage which excited the admiration of his countrymen, gave the name of New-England to the Pacific shores of the continent, which name Captain John Smith afterwards, to strengthen the title to the country, affixed to the Atlantic slope.* But till the beginning of the seventeenth century, North-America, north of Florida, remained unpeopled by Europeans. The Spaniards, the Portuguese, the French, the Dutch, and the English, had all made voyages of discovery, and laid claims to the country. As early as 1542, it was parceled off to the three powers first named; Florida, belonging to Spain, extending as far north as the thirty-third parallel of latitude; Verrazzan, or New-France, from the thirty-third to the fiftieth parallel; and Terra Corterealis, northward to the Polar Ocean, thus named in honor of Gaspar Cortereal, a Portuguese, who explored the coast in the year 1500. The Spaniards were in pursuit of mines of gold and silver, the Portuguese in quest of slaves, and the French with hopes of profit in the fur trade, and crude but indefinite ideas of colonization.

Spain and Portugal originally claimed the New World by grant from the Pope.† England, practically abandoning all claim from the discoveries of Cabot on the Atlantic, and Drake on the Pacific coasts, laid down, in 1580, the broad doctrine, that prescription without occupation was of no avail; that possession of the country was essential to the maintenance of title. *Prescriptio sine possessione, haud valeat.*‡

Before this time, the attention of England had been turned to the northern parts of America, with a view to colonization. As early as March 22, 1574, the Queen

* John Smith's Description of New England, vol. ii. p. 2, Force's Tracts. Mass. Historical Coll. 3d series, vol. vi. p. 104.

† Bull of Pope Alexander VI. 1493.

‡ Camden's Eliz. Annales, 1580. See Poor's Vindication of Gorges, p. 9.

had been petitioned to allow of the *discovery* of lands in America "*fatally reserved to England, and for the honor of Her Majesty.*"* Sir Humphrey Gilbert's charter "for planting our people in America," was granted by Elizabeth, June 11, 1578, and in 1580 John Walker and his companions had discovered a silver mine in Norumbega. The explorations of Andrew Thevett, of John Barros, and John Walker, alluded to in the papers recently discovered in the British State Paper Office, under date of 1580, we find nowhere else recorded. The possession of Newfoundland by Sir Humphrey Gilbert, was abandoned on his loss at sea, and it was not till 1584, that the first charter to Sir Walter Raleigh was issued, by Elizabeth. Raleigh named the country VIRGINIA, in honor of his Queen. Of the two colonies sent out by him, one returned, the other perished in the country, leaving no trace of its history and no record of its melancholy fate.† Thus, at the period of Elizabeth's death, in 1603, England had not a colonial possession on the globe.

Sir Richard Whitbourne had made voyages to Newfoundland in his own ship in 1588,‡ and in 1600 there was a proposition to the Queen for planting a colony in *the North-west of America*,§ in which can be unmistakably traced the agency of Sir Ferdinando Gorges, who it now appears was also concerned in the voyage of Gosnold in 1602, of Pring in 1603, and of George Weymouth in 1605, the earliest ones of which we have any authentic record.‖ That eloquent passage in Gorges' *Briefe Narration*, in which he gives "the reasons and

* Calendar of Colonial State Papers, edited by Sainsbury, vol. i. page 1.
† Bancroft's History, vol. i. pp. 102, 107.
‡ Calendar of Col. State Papers, vol. i p. 82.
§ See this paper in full in Poor's Vindication of Gorges. Appendix.
‖ See Gorges' letter to Challons. Poor's Vindication, p. 34.

the means of renewing the undertaking of Plantations in America," deserves our highest praise; and it excites feelings of the warmest gratitude toward him, for it is a modest and touching statement, of his own heroic efforts, in the cause of American colonization.*

But the Hollanders and the French were equally aroused to the importance, and inflamed with the purpose, of seizing upon these shores. The vast wealth of the Dutch, their great commercial success prior to this time in both the East and West-Indies, gave them the advantage. Champlain, with greater knowledge of North-America than any of his rivals, had accompanied Pont Gravè to the St. Lawrence, by direction of the King, in 1603, when, on his return to France, he found Acadia granted to De Monts, a Protestant, and a member of the King's household, under date of November eighth, 1603, extending across the continent, between the fortieth and forty-sixth degrees of north latitude.†

In the spring of 1604, De Monts, accompanied by Champlain, Pont Gravè, Poutrincourt, and the learned and accomplished historian L'Escarbot, sailed from Dieppe for the occupation of the New World. They planted their colony at St. Croix, within the limits of our own State, in 1604,‡ and in the spring and summer of 1605, explored the coast under the lead of Champlain, from Campseau to Cape Malabar, twelve miles south of Cape Cod, "searching to the bottom of the bays," the same year that Weymouth explored this most excellent and beneficial river of Sagadahoc. To make sure of the country, Champlain, Champdore and L'Escarbot remained three and a half years, fishing, trading with the natives, and occupying at Boston, Pis-

* Gorges' Briefe Narration, p. 16.
† L'Escarbot, p. 432, 2d edition. 1612.
‡ See Poor's Vindication of Gorges, p. 23, note.

cadouet, (Piscataqua,) Marchin, (Portland,) Koskebee, (Casco Bay,) Kinnibequi, (Kennebec,) Pentagoet, (Penobscot,) and all east, to Campseau and Cape Breton. Returning to France in 1607, they found the charter of De Monts revoked,* on account of the jealousy of his rivals, and a small indemity from the King their only reward, for these four years of sacrifice and unremitting toil. This shortsightedness of the great Henry of Navarre, cost France the dominion of the New World. For on the return of Weymouth to Plymouth, in 1605, with five savages from Pemaquid, Sir Ferdinando Gorges gathered from them full particulars of this whole region, its harbors, rivers, natural characteristics and features, its people and mode of government.†

Associating with himself the Earl of Southampton,‡ Gorges, relying upon these circumstances as a means of inflaming the imagination of his countrymen, petitioned the King for a charter,§ which he obtained, under date of April tenth, 1606,‖ granting to George Popham, and seven others, the continent of North-America, from the thirty-fourth to the forty-fifth degrees of north latitude, extending one hundred miles into the mainland, and including all islands of the sea within one hundred miles of the shore. This charter is the basis on which rests the title of our race to the New World. It provided for a local government at home, intrusted to a

* L'Escarbot, p. 460, 2d edition. 1612. Champlain, pp. 44, 45, 99.

† Gorges' Briefe Narration. Maine Hist. Coll. vol. ii. p. 19.

‡ Henry Wriothesley, Earl of Southampton, the friend and patron of Shakspeare, was the *third* earl of that name, and grandson of Thomas Wriothesley, Lord High Chancellor of England, under Edward VI. Created a peer February sixteenth, 1547, he died in 1550. His son Henry, was Lord Treasurer, and grandfather of Lady Rachel Russell. His patent of nobility was declared forfeited, under Elizabeth, but restored by James in 1603. The third earl, Treasurer of the Virginia Company, and the patron of letters and of American colonization, died in command of an English regiment, in the Dutch service, in the Netherlands, in 1624. The fourth earl died in 1667, and the title became extinct.

§ Strachey's Travaile into Virginia, p. 161.

‖ See this charter in full in Poor's Vindication of Gorges. Appendix.

Council of Thirteen, with two companies, one of North, and the other of South-Virginia, for carrying into execution the plans of colonization in the country.* The venerable Sir John Popham,† Chief-Justice of England by the appointment of Elizabeth, a man of vast wealth and influence, became the patron of the Company; and his son, Sir Francis Popham, was appointed by the King, with Sir Ferdinando Gorges, one of the Council of Thirteen, under whom, as the Council of Virginia, the work of colonization was to be carried forward.‡ From the great fame of Chief-Justice Popham, and his interest in the matter, the colony sent by the North-Virginia Company was popularly known as Popham's Colony, though his name was not in the charter, or included among the Council. "The planting of New-England in the North, was by Chief-Justice POPHAM," said the Scotch adventurers, in their address to the King, September ninth, 1630, recently brought to our notice from the British State Paper Office.§ In a work entitled *Encouragement to Colonies*, by William Alexander, Knight, in 1625, he says: "Sir John Popham

* The COUNCIL OF VIRGINIA, appointed by King James, November twentieth, 1606, consisted of *fourteen* persons instead of thirteen. Their names are given in a subsequent note.

† Sir John Popham was born at Huntsworth, near Wellington, in Somersetshire, in 1531. He was at Oxford in 1547, became distinguished at the bar in 1560; was made Sergeant at Law, and Solicitor General, June twenty-sixth, 1579. He was Speaker of the Commons in 1581; became Attorney-General June first, 1581. He was knighted 1592; made Chief-Justice of the Queen's Bench June eighth, 1592. He assisted at King James's coronation in 1603. September fifth and sixth, 1604, King James and the Queen were entertained at Littlecote, the residence of the Chief-Justice. He was the richest lawyer of his time, having an income of ten thousand pounds per year. He died June first, 1607, and was buried at Wellington.

His eldest son was Sir Francis Popham, whose eldest son, John Popham, married June twenty-first, 1621, Mary, only daughter of Sebastian Harvey, at Stoke Newington, but had no children. The family of the Chief-Justice is supposed to be extinct.

The fact of his appointment as Chief-Justice by Elizabeth, in the later years of her life, proves him to have been a great lawyer. Elizabeth appointed the ablest men she could find to public office.

‡ See this charter in full in Poor's Vindication. Appendix.

§ This paper is now printed for the first time in the appendix to Poor's Vindication of Gorges.

sent the first colony that went, of purpose to inhabit there near to Sagadahoc."* But until the comparatively recent publication of Strachey, the history of this colony was almost unknown. Two unsuccessful attempts at planting a colony were made in 1606.†

On the thirty-first of May, 1607, the first colony to New-England sailed from Plymouth for the Sagadahoc, in two ships—one called the "Gift of God," whereof George Popham, brother of the Chief-Justice,‡ was commander; and the other, the "Mary and John," commanded by Raleigh Gilbert—on board which ships were one hundred and twenty persons, for planters. They came to anchor under an island, supposed to be Monhegan, the thirty-first of July. After exploring the coast and islands, on Sunday, the ninth of August, 1607, they landed on an island they called St. George, where they heard a sermon, delivered unto them by Mr. Seymour, their preacher, and so returned aboard again. On the fifteenth of August they anchored under Seguin, and on that day the "Gift of God" got into the river of Sagadahoc. On the sixteenth, after a severe storm, both ships got safely in, and came to anchor. On the seventeenth, in two boats, they sailed up the river—Captain Popham in his pinnace, with thirty persons, and Captain Gilbert in his long-boat, with eighteen persons, and "found it a very gallant river; many good islands therein, and many branches of other small rivers falling into it," and returned. On the "eighteenth, they all went ashore, and there made choice of a place for their plantation, at the mouth or entry of the river, on

* A copy of this rare work is in the possession of Gen. Peter Force, of Washington City.

† See Poor's Vindication, pp. 38, 39.

‡ Note by R. H. Major, editor of Strachey's Travaile into Virginia, p. 27. Published by the Hakluyt Society—one of the volumes of its series. Hubbard's History of Massachusetts Bay, p. 10.

the west side, (for the river bendeth itself towards the nor-east and by east,) being almost an island, of good bigness, in a province called by the Indians, 'Sabino'—so called of a Sagamo, or chief commander, under the grand bashaba." On the nineteenth, they all went ashore where they had made choice of their plantation, and where they had a sermon delivered unto them by their preacher, and after the sermon, the President's commission was read, with the patent,* and the laws to be observed and kept.†

* By the original charter, the company had the right to sell lands, work mines, coin money, transport thither colonists, expel by force all intruders, raise a revenue by imposts, carry out goods free of duty to the Crown, for seven years, with a denization of all persons born or residing in the country.

† A constituent code of laws was prepared, and signed by King James, in accordance with the provision to this effect set forth in the seventh section of the charter of April tenth, 1606. *Lucas's Charters of the Old English Colonies*, p. 4.

This constituent code is contained in two ordinances, or articles of instructions, from the King, namely:

I. Ordinance dated November twentieth, 1606, appointing

Sir William Wade,	Thomas Warr, Esq.,	Sir Henry Montague,
Sir Walter Cope,	Thomas James, Esq.,	John Doddridge, Esq.,
Sir Francis Popham,	Sir Ferdinando Gorges,	John Eldred, Esq.,
Sir John Trevor,	Sir George More,	James Bagg, Esq.,
Sir William Romney,	Sir Thomas Smith,	

as the Council of Virginia.

This ordinance provided that

1. Each colony may elect associates, and annually elect a President for one year; and assistants or councillors for the same time.
2. The Christian religion shall be preached and observed as established in the realm of England.
3. Lands shall descend to heirs as provided by law in England.
4. Trial by jury of twelve men, in all criminal cases. Tumults, rebellion, conspiracy, mutiny and sedition, murder, manslaughter, incest, rape and adultery, only, are capital offences.
5. In civil causes, the President and Council shall determine. They may punish excesses in drunkenness, vagrancy, etc.
6. All produce, or goods imported, to be stored in the magazine of the Company.
7 They shall elect a clerk and treasurer, or cape-merchant.
8. May make laws needful and proper, *consonant with the laws of England*
9. Indians to be civilized and taught the Christian religion.
10. All offenders to be tried in the colony.
11. Oath of obedience to be taken.
12. Records of all proceedings and judgments fully set forth and preserved, implying a right of appeal. In all criminal cases, magistrates to suspend sentence till opportunity of pardon is had by the king.

These were the laws "to be observed and kept."

(See Poor's Vindication of Gorges. Appendix.)

II. Ordinance, dated March 9th, 1607.

On the recommendation, or nomination, of the *Southern* company, the following additional members of the Council of Virginia were appointed, namely:

"George Popham, gent., was nominated President. Captain Raleigh Gilbert, James Davies, Richard Seymour, Preacher, Captain Richard Davies, Captain Harlowe, were all sworn assistants; and so they returned back again."*

Thus commenced the first occupation and settlement of New-England.

On a careful examination of this patent of King James, and of the articles, instructions and orders by him set down for the government of these colonies, we are struck with the sagacity and statesmanship every where evinced by the monarch. He rose superior to the notions of his times, reduced the number of capital offences to ten, and declared none should be capital but the more gross of political, and the more heinous of moral crimes. He gave them all the liberties they could desire.

In the subsequent charters for Virginia and New-England, the same broad principles of self-government were in the main reënacted.

In the contests with the King and Parliament of England, one hundred and fifty years later, the colo-

Sir Thomas Challoner, Kt., Sir George Kopping, Kt., Sir Edw'd Michilbourne, Kt.,
Sir Henry Nevil, Kt., Sir Thomas Rowe, Kt., Sir Thomas Smith, Kt.,
Sir Robert Mansfield, Kt., Sir Fulke Grevil, Kt., Sir Robert Croft, Kt.,
Sir Maurice Berkeley, Kt., Sir John Scott, Kt., Sir Edward Sandys, Kt.,
Sir Thomas Holcroft, Kt., Sir Oliver Cromwell, Kt., Sir Anthony Palmer.
Sir Robert Kelligrew, Kt.,

On the recommendation or nomination of the *Northern* Colony, the following additional members of the Council of Virginia were appointed:

Sir Edw'd Hungerford, Kt., Sir Richard Hawkins, Kt., Bernard Greenville, Esq.,
Sir John Mallett, Kt., Sir Bartholomew Mitchell, Kt., Edward Rogers, Esq.,
Sir John Gilbert, Kt.,* Edward Seamour, Esq., Rev. Matthew Sutcliff, D.D.
Sir Thomas Freake, Kt.,

These appointments made the Council of Virginia to consist of forty instead of thirteen. There was a further provision that "any twelve of them, at least for the time being, whereof six at least to be members of one of the said colonies, and six more at least to be members of the other colony," "shall have power to choose officers, call meetings," etc. (See Poor's Vindication of Gorges. Appendix.)

* Strachey, p. 301, Maine Hist. Coll. vol. iii.

* Oldmixon's History of British Empire in America, says Sir John Gilbert was President of the *Northern* Virginia Company, p. 41. Stith's History of Virginia, pp. 74, 75.

nists only demanded their *ancient rights*, as subjects of the British crown. From August 19, O. S., 1607, the title of England to the new world was maintained. At this place they opened a friendly trade with the natives, put up houses and built a small vessel, during the autumn and winter.

Richard Bloome, in his *History of the Present State of the Territories in America*, printed in London 1687, says:

"In the year 1607, Sir John Popham and others settled a plantation at the mouth of the river Sagadahoc. But Capt. James Davis chose a small place, almost an Island, to sit down in, when, having heard a sermon, read the patent and laws; and after he had built a fort, sailed further up the river. They call the fort St. George, Capt. George Popham being President; and the people (savages) seemed to be much affected with our men's devotion, and would say King James is a good King, and his God a good God; but our God, *Tanto*, is a naughty God.

"In January, in the space of seven hours, they had thunder, lightning, rain, frost and snow all in very great abundance."

On the 5th of February, 1608, George Popham died,* and his remains were deposited within the wall of his fort, which was named Fort St. George.

It is well known that the Popham Colony, or a portion of them, returned to England in 1608, with the ship they had built on this peninsula, the first specimen of naval architecture constructed on this continent, named the "Virginia of Sagadahoc."

But this possession of the Popham Colony proved

* Prince's New-England Chronology, p. 118; Brodhead's History of New-York, p. 14.

sufficient to establish the title. The revocation of the charter to De Monts gave priority to the grant of King James, covering the same territory, and this formal act of possession was ever after upheld, by an assertion of the title by Gorges. It was sufficient, effectually, to hold the country against the French and Spaniards alike.* When Argall, in 1613, destroyed the French settlement at Mount Desert, † the French Minister demanded satisfaction at the hands of the British nation. ‡ But no notice was taken of this

* The Spanish Secretary of State in 1612 and 1613 complained to King James for allowing his subjects to plant in Virginia and Bermuda, as the country belonged to Spain, by the conquest of Castile who acquired it by the discovery of Columbus, and the Pope's donation; to which Sir Dudley Carleton, Secretary of State, by order of King James made answer: "Spain has no *possessions* north of Florida. They belong to the crown of England by right of discovery and actual possession by *the two English colonies thither deducted, whereof the latter is yet there remaining.* These countries should not be given over to the Spanish."

Cal. of Col. State Papers, vol. i. p. 14, Nos. 28 and 29; also page 16, Nos. 31 and 32.

In the memorials of the English and French Commission concerning the limits of Nova-Scotia or Acadia, under the Treaty of Utrecht, the French Commissioners say: "The Court of France adjudged that they had the right to extend the western limits of Acadia as far as the River Kinnibequi," (p. 39.) On page 98 of the same Collections it says: "Chief-Justice Popham planted the colony at Sagadahoc."

† Mount Desert was so named by Champlain in 1605. The English named it Mount *Mansell*, in honor of Sir Robert Mansell, the highest naval officer of England, one of the grantees of the Virginia Company of 1609, and of the New-England Company in 1620. But it has retained the name of *Mount Desert*. It has always been celebrated for the excellence of its harbor and the boldness of its shores. It is the most celebrated locality on the Atlantic coast, and one of the three great harbors of the continent. The French Jesuits, who settled there in 1613, called it St. Saviour. Their precise place of settlement is described in the Relations of the Jesuits, vol. i. p. 44, 46, and has been identified by the accurate explorations of the Hon. E. L. Hamlin, of Bangor, the present year. In Poor's Vindication of Gorges, Appendix, page 103, is a translation of the Jesuit Relation, describing this place, and of its destruction by Argall.

What is of still more interest is the fact that this was the easternmost limits of *Mavosheen*, or of the English discoveries up to 1609. See Purchase, vol. iv. p. 1873. L'Escarbot, the historian of New-France and of De Monts' expedition, says the Sagamo *Marchin* was residing at their next place west of Kinnibequi, and they named the place *Marchin*, (Portland,) in honor of him. Marchin was slain in 1607, and Bessabes was chosen captain in his place. Bessabes was slain also, and then *Asticou* was chosen in his stead. According to the statement in Purchase, vol. iv. p. 1873–4, at the easternmost part of Mavosheen, at the river of Quibiquesson, dwelt *Asticou*. In 1613, *Asticou* was dwelling at Mount Desert, and the assurance given by his followers to Fathers Biard and Masse of his being sick and desirous of baptism at their hands, led them to go thither, and finally to yield to entreaties for making their settlement there, instead of at Kadesquit, (Kenduskeag,) Bangor, on the Penobscot, as they had agreed in 1611. It would seem from these facts that the authority of Asticou extended from Mount Desert to the Saco, the river of the Sagamo Olmouchin.

‡ Calendar of Colonial State Papers, vol. i. p. 15.

demand, because the French could show no claim of title. Again in 1624, M. Tillieres, the French Ambassador, claimed the territory of New-England as a portion of New-France, and proposed to yield all claim to Virginia, and the country as far south as the Gulf of Mexico; overlooking entirely the title of Spain to Florida, which had always been recognized as extending to the thirty-third parallel of north latitude. France had at this time become aware of the importance of securing the title and possession of these shores.* King James called on Sir Ferdinando Gorges to prepare a reply to the claims of the French monarch. "Whereunto," says Gorges, "I made so full a reply (as it seems) there was no more heard of their claim." † From the abstract of this reply, recently printed in the Calendar of British State Papers, it would seem that no notice was taken of the Leyden flock, who were then at Plymouth; but Sir Ferdinando Gorges based the claim of his government on the ground of the charter of 1606, and the formal occupation of the country under it, with a continued claim of title.

In 1631, Champlain, the greatest mind of his nation, ever engaged in colonial enterprise, the boldest and most wary of all his countrymen, second only to Gorges in the results he achieved, — in his memoir to his sovereign, as to the title of the two nations, says: "King James issued his charter twenty-four years ago, for the country from the thirty-third to the forty-fifth degree. England seized the coast of New-France, where lies Acadia, on which they imposed the name of New-England." ‡

The Dutch West-India Company, in their address

* Cal. of Col. State Papers, vol. i. p. 60.
† Gorges' Briefe Narration, p. 40.
‡ Doc. Hist. of New-York, vol. ix. p. 112.

to the States General, 1632, say: "In the year 1606, his Majesty of Great Britain granted to his subjects, under the names of New-England and Virginia, north and south of the river, (Manhattoes,) on express condition that the companies should remain one hundred miles apart. Whereupon the English began, about the year 1607, to settle by the river of Sagadahoc. The English place New-England between the forty-first and forty-fifth degrees of north latitude." *

In Garneau's *History of Canada*, speaking of the destruction of Mount Desert, and Port Royal, in 1613, he says: "England claimed the territory to the forty-fifth degree of north latitude." This was seven years before the date of the New-England Charter. This claim was founded on possession; for England stoutly maintained, from the time of Elizabeth onward, that without possession there was no valid title to a newly discovered country.

This view of history is overlooked by Puritan writers, and those who follow their authority. That protection of the British nation which enabled the Puritans of Massachusetts Bay, and the humble followers of Robinson, to establish, unmolested, homes in the New World, under organized forms of government, was grudgingly acknowledged by them, and the man who secured to them these blessings, and watched over them with the same jealous care as of his own colony — they always stigmatized as their great enemy,† because, among other acts of humanity, he allowed the mild and conscientious men, who could not yield implicit obedience to their fierce doctrines, and more barbarous laws, ‡ to escape into Maine, and there remain

* Holland Doc. N. Y., p. 61.

† Winthrop, vol. ii. p. 14; Bradford's Hist. of Plymouth, p. 328.

‡ None but church members shall be allowed the privileges of freemen.—Statute of 1631, Massachusetts Colony Laws, p. 117.

unharmed. When Cromwell granted to Sir Thomas Temple the country east of the Sagadahoc, at the time that the persecution of the Quakers was at its greatest height, with the design of affording them a place of refuge beyond the limits even of the Province of Maine,* which they had just conquered by violence; the anger of Massachusetts Puritans fell upon the head of the Protector, himself a Puritan, and an Independent of the straitest sect at home. But time allows no allusion to-day to historic details, except what is essential to the vindication of the truth of history. The fact that the 19th of August, Old Style, is the true date of the foundation of England's title to the continent, is all we are called upon to establish.

It may be said, that in giving this prominence to the occupation of the country by the colony of Popham, we overlook other events of importance in establishing the English title—the possession of the Elizabeth Isles by Gosnold in 1602, and the settlement of Jamestown May 13th, 1607, prior to the landing of the Popham Colony at Sagadahoc.

In reference to the occupation of Elizabeth Isles by

Any attempt to change the form of government is punishable with death.—Statute of 1641, Col. Laws, p. 59.

Absence from meeting on Sunday, fast, or thanksgiving, subjected the offender to a fine.—Col. Laws, p. 103.

Keeping or observing Christmas was punishable by fine.—Col. Laws, p. 119.

Wages to be regulated in each town by vote of the freemen of each.—Col. Laws, p. 156.

Baptists are to be punished by banishment.—Colony Laws, 1646, p. 120.

Quakers to be imprisoned and then banished, on pain of death if they returned. —Colony Laws, 1658, p. 123.

Witches shall be put to death —Colony Laws, 1641, p. 59.

Magistrates shall issue warrants to a constable, and in his absence to any person, to cause Quakers to be stripped naked from the middle upward; tied to a cart's tail, and whipped from town to town till conveyed out of our jurisdiction.—Colony Laws, p. 125.

Under these laws Baptists had their ears cropped in Boston as late as 1658, and Quakers were put to death.

* N. Y. Doc. Hist. vol. ix. p. 71, 75.

Gosnold, it is sufficient to say, that it was prior to the date of the Royal Charter, and consequently of no legal effect in establishing title. As to the settlement of Jamestown, it was south of the fortieth parallel of latitude, and therefore did not come in conflict with the French King's prior charter to De Monts. The territory between the fortieth and the forty-fifth degrees only, was in dispute. Although the maps of the time made New-France to extend from the thirty-third to the fiftieth degree of north latitude, France practically abandoned the country south of the fortieth degree from the time of the grant of the charter to De Monts, so that below that line south, it was open to any people who might have the courage to possess it; this south line of De Monts' grant, intersecting what is now Pennsylvania, just north of the city of Philadelphia, cutting Ohio, Indiana, and Illinois very nearly in their centre. Had there been no English settlement or occupancy north of the fortieth parallel of latitude prior to 1610, when Poutrincourt obtained a new grant of Acadia, the whole country north of that line must have fallen into the hands of the French.

The reason, undoubtedly, why France at this time extended her claims no further south than the fortieth parallel was, a fear of exciting the jealousy and hostility of the Spaniards. In 1562, when Ribaut and Laudonniere planted at Port Royal, Spain looked upon it as an invasion of her just domain, and promptly expelled the French invaders. Recent discoveries show that she watched with a most jealous eye the fate of the earlier voyages of Cartier from 1534 to 1541.* Spain, at that time, was the great military and naval power of Europe. There can be no doubt that the limiting of De Monts' charter to the fortieth parallel of latitude, seven degrees

* See Historical Magazine, January, 1862, p. 14.

short of all her previous claims, was induced by a dread of Spanish interference. Spanish jealousy showed itself equally in opposition to the English occupation of the country, but their prompt assertion in 1613 of their title, averring the actual occupation of the country, and the denial, on the part of King James, of any validity in the Bull of the Pope, upheld the right of England.

It was not Spain, however, but France that became the actual competitor of England in the struggle for the new dominion. The relations of Spain and France were friendly. Between Spain and England there were many irritations, and so far had this ill-feeling grown, that the capture of English ships by Spanish cruisers was not an uncommon occurrence, as in the case of Challons, and others, bound to New-England, for purposes of colonization.

The French, therefore, made no claim to that Virginia occupied by the colony at Jamestown, while Spain claimed the whole country. French plans of empire looked northward and westward, resting their base on the great inland sea, or gulf lying inside Cape Sable and Cape Cod, where, for a whole century previous, from 1504, and onward, their fishermen had found the choicest treasures of the sea.

Whoever held this region, as all now see, must eventually become the dominant power of the New World.

The national feeling was not fully aroused in either country to the greatness of the prize at stake. Champlain comprehended the true measure of the occasion, and its importance to his country; while Sir Ferdinando Gorges, with equal grasp of intellect, rested on a more secure foundation the confidence of his sovereign.

But the people of England were incapable of estimating the value of the prize, or doing justice to the man who secured it.

In the debate in the House of Commons, in 1621 and 1622, on the bill to abrogate or annul the New-England charter, and throw open the fisheries, briefly reported in the parliamentary journals, the issue was, "*Which is of most value, fishing or plantations?*" and the result showed that the enemies of colonization were in the ascendant, and a bill to this effect passed the House. By the influence of the King acting with the Lords, it was prevented from becoming a law.*

From the time of the first conflict at Mount Desert, where Father Du Thet was killed in defending his home, in 1613—the first shedding of blood between the French and English on this continent—till the fall of Quebec, in 1759, and the Treaty of Peace consequent thereon, in 1763, surrendering New-France to Great Britain, there was a strife of races, of nationalities and of religion for the territory of New-England, while Virginia, along the Atlantic slope, was never molested by the French.

The western boundary of Virginia was the Pacific Ocean, and she came into conflict with France when she crossed the Alleghanies and descended into the Mississippi Basin, and there met the French settlers, who had seized upon the western waters, claiming a continuous possession of the entire regions drained by the waters of the Mississippi and the St. Lawrence. Had England acquired nothing in the way of title in the New

* April 19, 1621, "Mr. Neale said three hundred ships, at least, had gone this year from these ports," p. 591. Nov. 20, 1621, "Mr. Glanville moved to speed the bill," etc. "Sir Ferdinando Gorges hath exhibited patent," etc. "Friday next Sir F. G., to be heard," p. 640. Dec. 1, 1621, Bill under consideration. "Mr. Guy moves a provision; debate by Mr. Neale, Mr. Secretary, Dr. Gooch, Sir Edward Gyles, Mr. Guy, and Shewell, which is of most value, fishing or plantations? £120,000 brought in annually by fishing." "Provision lost. Bill passed, p. 654."—Extracts from the Journal of the Commons.

World north of the fortieth parallel prior to the Plymouth Plantation in 1620, there is no reason to doubt that France would have swept the British power from the continent at the first clash of arms with Great Britain.

It was this possession of the shores of the Atlantic Ocean, within the limits of the fortieth and forty-fifth degrees of north latitude, prior to 1610, that settled the future destiny of the continent of North-America. The consummation of title, therefore, perfected by the act of possession of August nineteenth, O. S. 1607, by the Popham Colony, whose two hundred and fifty-fifth anniversary we this day celebrate, must, if these premises are admitted, forever remain the great fact in the history of the New World.

The Maine Historical Society, whose duty it is made, by the charter establishing it, "to collect and preserve whatever may tend to explain and illustrate the civil, ecclesiastical, and natural history of this State and the United States," was pleased to approve of the act of two of its members, then in the service of the State, who petitioned the authorities of the General Government, that this great work of national defence, then about to be undertaken, should be named Fort Popham, in honor of George Popham, the Governor, who led the first British Colony into New-England, under the charter of April 10, 1606, and who, discharging the duties of his office as President, and presenting a report in the form of a letter, to the King, dated at Fort St. George, December 13, 1607,* here laid down his life—the first man of the English race whose bones were laid beneath the soil of New-England.

* Popham's Letter in the Maine Hist. Coll. vol. v. p. 341.

The venerable Chief of the Engineer Bureau of the United States Army, to whom this petition was referred, ever jealous of the honor of his country, not only as to the character of its military structures, but as to the names, to whose honor they should attest—promptly indorsed the application, and it met the ready approval of the Secretary of War.*

To mark, with greater distinctness, the event thus commemorated, the Maine Historical Society asked permission to place within the walls of this Fort a MEMORIAL STONE, bearing on its face an appropriate inscription of the event; and that a TABLET, in memory of George Popham, so honorably associated with the great event of that period, should be allowed to form a portion of its walls.

By the favor of the Government we have this day performed that duty, with appropriate form and ceremony. The learned President of the Maine Historical Society has announced the historic facts on which this somewhat novel proceeding has taken place. The accomplished and honored Chief Magistrate of the State has given to the occasion the influence of his official

* The following correspondence, copied from the files of the War Office, shows the prompt action of the Government in the matter:

TO THE HON. SIMON CAMERON, Secretary of War:

The undersigned, citizens of Maine, respectfully request that the new Fort to be erected at the mouth of the Kenebec river, in Maine, may be named FORT POPHAM, in honor of Capt. George Popham, brother of the learned Chief-Justice Popham, of England.

Capt. George Popham, as the Governor of the first English Colony in New-England, built a fort at or near the site of the proposed fort, in the year 1607, where he died February 5, 1608, and was buried, being the first person of his race whose bones were laid beneath the soil of New-England, and whose grave will be appropriately marked by the fort that rises over his place of burial.

(Signed) JOHN A. POOR,
REUEL WILLIAMS.

WASHINGTON, November 18, 1861.

This proposal for a name was favorably received at the Engineer Bureau, by General Totten, who laid the matter before the Secretary of War.

On the 23d of November, General Cameron acted on the foregoing petition, and entered thereon: "Name approved.

"SIMON CAMERON, Secretary of War.

"WAR DEPARTMENT, Washington, November 23, 1861."

station, and the more acceptable service of eloquent words, proclaiming the importance of the event commemorated, upon the history of the country and the world, while the Episcopal Bishop of the Diocese of Maine and the President of our oldest Seminary of learning, as Chairman of the Standing Committee of the Maine Historical Society, have jointly participated in the appropriate services of this occasion, and that most ancient, Masonic Fraternity, has lent to the celebration whatever of dignity or grace the wisest of their Order have been able to embody in artistic form and expression. With the consent of the Government, these imposing ceremonies have proceeded, and finally the skillful hand of him who is charged with the construction of this Fort,* will place this stone in its final resting-place—for the information of those who come after us — proclaiming to future times, in the simple eloquence of truthful words, that

THE FIRST COLONY
ON THE SHORES OF NEW-ENGLAND
Was Founded Here,
August 19th, O. S. 1607,
under
GEORGE POPHAM.

It would ill comport with the dignity of this occasion to fail to speak of him, whose name is thus imperishably connected with the history of our State and Nation. To his family and the events of his life others may more appropriately refer. We allude to him as a public man, and to his claims to public gratitude and respect. His chief distinction is, that he was one of the eight persons named in the great charter of April 10th, 1606, and that he led to these shores the first colony under that charter. In it he is styled *gentleman*,

* Captain T. L. Casey, U. S. Engineers.

and he must have been a man of consequence and position, from the fact that he was one of its grantees. After his death, Gorges, in a few brief lines, thus sums up his character: "He was well stricken in years, and had long been an infirm man. Howsoever, heartened by hopes, willing he was to die in acting something that might be serviceable to God, and honorable to his country."* A glorious consummation of a long life, devoted to duty, to his country, and his God.†

Within the walls of this Fort, and as a companion-piece to the memorial stone, which records the historic fact of this day's celebration, the Maine Historical Society will place a tablet in memory of George Popham, expressing, in that sonorous Latin language which he employed in his communication to the King, and which was at that time used by all who wrote for enduring fame, these words:

In Memoriam
GEORGII POPHAM,
Angliæ qui primus ab oris
Coloniam collocavit in Nov. Angliæ terris,
Augusti mense annoque MDCVII.
Leges literasque Anglicanas
Et fidem ecclesiamque Christi
In has sylvas duxit.
Solus ex colonis atque senex obiit
Nonis Februariis sequentibus,
Et juxta hunc locum est sepultus.

Societate Historica Mainensi auspicante,
In præsidio ejus nomen ferente,
Quarto die ante calendas Septembres
Annoque MDCCCLXII.
Multis civibus intuentibus,
Hic lapis positus est.

* Gorges' Briefe Narration, p. 22, vol. ii. Maine Hist. Coll.

† Mrs. Sigourney has since embodied in song, in one of her happiest efforts, the heroic deeds of Popham. See Appendix C.

[TRANSLATION.]

IN MEMORY OF
GEORGE POPHAM
Who first from the shores of England
Founded a Colony in New-England
August, 1607.
He brought into these wilds
English laws and learning
And the faith and the Church of Christ.
He only of the colonists, and in his old age, died
On the fifth of the following February
And was buried near this spot.

Under the auspices of the Maine Historical Society
In the Fort bearing his name
August 29, 1862,
In the presence of many citizens
This stone was placed.

This fort, so conspicuously placed, bearing these appropriate testimonials, thus becomes a fitting monument to perpetuate the events of the early history of New-England, and transmit to future times, the memory of those illustrious men who laid the foundation of English colonies in America; to which the laws, the institutions and civilization of England were transferred, and from which, has sprung the glorious fabric of American Constitutional Government.

Standing here to-day, in sight of the spot where Popham, two hundred and fifty-five years ago, took upon himself the office of President, and near the place where, on the fifth of February following, he died, it seems our privilege to be admitted into his presence-chamber, as for the last time he had summoned around him his faithful assistants and companions, and gave commands for the future. The scene is worthy of a painter's pencil and a poet's pen. The ever-faithful and heroic Raleigh Gilbert, "a man," says Gorges, "worthy to be beloved of them for his industry and care for their well-being"—the future President of the colony—is by his side. The pious Richard Seymour administers to him words of comfort and consolation. Captain Richard Davies, of all his assistants, was absent in England. His devoted companions stand around their dying chief, when, in the language of Israel's great law-giver, laying the burden of the government on Joshua, he might well say to Raleigh Gilbert: "Be strong and of a good courage, for thou must go with this people into the land which the Lord hath sworn unto their fathers to give them: and thou shalt cause them to inherit it. And the Lord he it is that doth go before thee: he will be with thee, he will not fail thee, neither forsake thee: fear not, neither be dismayed."

"So Moses, the servant of the Lord, died there, in the land of Moab, according to the word of the Lord. And he buried him in a valley in the land of Moab, over against Bethpeor; but no man knoweth of his sepulchre unto this day."

In the far-distant future, not two hundred and fifty-five years from this day, the period of time that has intervened since his death, but in that period of more than three thousand years to come, like that from the death of Israel's law-giver, to that of Popham, these stones which are here builded, shall mark the place of his sepulture, and the myriads of thronging pilgrims, led by eager curiosity, to tread the soil of this peninsula of Sabino, hereafter made classic by song and story, shall pause and read, on that memorial stone, the record of his great work; and when we who are now here, shall have passed away, and beyond the reach of story or tradition, Popham's name shall live in the history of the mighty race, who have changed this continent from one vast wildernesss to a marvel of refinement and beauty, fitted for the enjoyment of civilized man.

His sagacity and ability are best evidenced by the fact, that after the experience of two hundred and fifty-five years, the highest military skill has confirmed the wisdom of his choice of a place of settlement, by the adoption of it as the proper site of the great work of defence for the Kennebec River.*

To this spot multitudes shall annually repair, for this region will continue to be, what it ever was, to the early navigators and colonists of both France and England—a chief point of interest. The French historian L'Escarbot, speaking of this river, says "*it shortened the way*" to the great river of Canada.† Gosnold's landfall, in 1602, was at Sagadahoc.‡ Pring, in 1603, made it the chief point of his discoveries; and the great voyage of Weymouth was to "the most excellent and beneficyall river of Sagadahoc."§ Here the English remained in 1608 and 1609, as related by the French Jesuits.‖ Here Vines pursued his voca-

* See Note A, with its accompanying Map.

† L'Escarbot, p. 497.

‡ Strachey, Hakluyt Society edition, p. 155; caption at the head of the chapter. See Poor's Vindication of Gorges, p. 30, note 2.

§ Much controversy and discussion have arisen as to the route of Weymouth, and as to the river he explored. Belknap's authority was generally accepted, fixing it at the Penobscot, till the critical eye and more ample knowledge of the late John McKeen, Esq., detected its errors. He maintained that the Kennebec was the true river. Mr. George Prince and Rev. Mr. Cushman have argued in favor of the river St. George. Mr. R. K. Sewall and Rev. Mr. Ballard maintain the views of Mr. McKeen. Hon. W. Willis adheres to Belknap's authority. Strachey's positive statement that it was the Sagadahoc, was unknown to Belknap.

I find in Purchase, a fact not alluded to by any of these writers, that may aid in solving the difficulty. John Stoneman, of Plymouth, who went out with Weymouth, in 1605, sailed as pilot in the ship Richard, of Plymouth, in charge of Henry Challons commander, in Gorges' employ, to found the colony at Sagadahoc, in 1606. Nicholas Hine, of Cockington, near Dartmouth, was master. Although Challons failed of his object, by disregarding his instructions, and was taken captive by the Spaniards, his purpose of going to Sagadahoc is expressly stated, and his pilot was of Weymouth's party in 1605.

This discovery of the name of *Hine*, as master under Challons, also relieves us of the difficulty in the apparent contradiction between Gorges and Strachey; the former using the name of Challons as master, the latter calling the master's name Haines, leading us to suppose there were two several voyages, instead of one in fact.

‖ Relations of the Jesuits, vol. i. p. 36.

tion,* and hither all the fishing vessels came, because the finest fish were taken in this region. The salmon of the Kennebec are to this day known in all our cities.

The Council of New-England, on the twenty-fourth of July, 1622, set apart "two great islands in the river of Sagadahoc to be reserved for the public plantation," and "a place between the branches of the two rivers" "*for a public city*."† Though the strife of races and of nationalities has kept back the settlement of this whole region, and the still more disastrous conflicts of rival grants and hostile occupation, destroyed for generations all plans of improvement, who shall dare to say that these plans shall not be realized?

When this Acadian peninsula, with its one hundred and fifty thousand square miles of territory, and its abundant resources, shall contain a population equal to that now peopling the British Isles,—this magnificent estuary, with its deep sea-soundings, discharging a larger volume of water than any river of the Atlantic coast, between the St. John and the Mississippi, may become the chief seat of wealth and power, of the mighty race who inhabit the continent,—why then *may* not the history of other lands become ours, and another Liverpool here rival the great commercial city of New-England; and Boston become to the city of the Sagadahoc, what Bristol is to the great shipping port of the Mersey? ‡

We miss from our celebration to-day, one who was instrumental in creating the immediate occasion of it, and in affixing the name of Popham to this great pub-

* Gorges' Briefe Narration, p. 24.

† Minutes of the Council of New-England, July twenty-fourth, 1622. Calendar of Col. State Papers, vol. i. p. 32. This paper is given in full in Poor's Vindication of Gorges, in the Appendix.

‡ The extraordinary advantages of Bath for a naval and military dépôt, are admitted by all military engineers, but no effort adequate to such a consummation has yet been made.

lic work, and who looked forward with prophetic eye to this day's proceedings.

The propriety of associating important historic events with works of national defence, and of attesting thereby to the fame of the actors therein, met the approval of his mature judgment, and his last act of public duty was an appeal to the Secretary of War for the erection of this fort, and affixing to it the name it now bears.* His stern countenance relaxed into a smile at the first suggestion of this anniversary celebration, and the placing within the walls of this fort of this memorial stone.

Born on the banks of this river, the place of his birth continued for fourscore years to be his home; and without the aid of anything but his strong character and his indomitable will, he reached wealth and eminence early in life, and bore at the close of it, the title of "the first citizen of Maine." †

This is not the time or place to pronounce his eulogy; an abler pen at the appointed hour shall perform this pleasing duty. But among the many memorials of his enterprise and public spirit that adorn the banks of the Kennebec, this fort attests and will attest the praise of Reuel Williams, while it is made by this day's celebration a fitting monument to preserve in remembrance the greater events of an earlier time.

We must not, in this connection, forget our obligations to the people of the colony of Massachusetts, and the early settlers of Plymouth, for their share in conquering the continent for our race, though dealing harshly with Maine. ‡ These Massachusetts Puri-

* By appointment of Governor Washburn, Mr. Williams visited Washington, November first, 1861, as one of the Commissioners of Maine, in reference to the public defences of the State, his first visit after eighteen years' absence. He retired from the Senate in 1843, resigning after having been reëlected for six years. He left Washington November eighteenth, 1861, after a personal interview on that day with the Secretary of War.

† Hon. I. Washburn, Jr., Governor of Maine.

‡ See petition of Edward Godfrey and other inhabitants of Maine, to the Parliament of the Commonwealth. Cal. Col. State Papers, vol. i. p. 479.

tans of the Saxon type, inheriting all the gloomy errors of a cruel and bloody period, under the iron rule of the Tudors, were ready to demand of Elizabeth the enforcement of the Act of Uniformity against Papists, but refused obedience to it themselves. Nor would they yield to the decision of a majority of the clergy, who in 1562, in full convention, voted to retain the priestly vestments and the forms of a liturgy. While agreeing to all the doctrines of its creed, they grew restless under the forms of the church service, elevated non-essentials into the dignity of principles, and stigmatized the Prayer-Book and the priestly robes as badges of Popery.

They imagined that by a severe austerity they secured the favor of God, and became his chosen people. They mistook their hatred of others for hatred of sin. They set up their own morbid convictions as the standard of right, and rather than submit to the laws of their own land, they endured their penalties, or sought escape from them by expatriation.

Once planted on the shores of New-England, the Puritans of Massachusetts Bay endeavored to exterminate every thing that stood in the way of their ambition. * Hence, after their conquest of Maine, they

Also, Godfrey's Letters in Mr. Geo. Folsom's Catalogue of Papers in the English State Paper Office in relation to Maine, pp. 52, 54.

* The charter of the Massachusetts Company of March 4th, 1629, authorized them to make laws and ordinances for their government, "*not contrary to the laws of England.*" Notwithstanding this they proceeded at once to frame a code of laws designed for the purpose, abrogating the laws of England whenever they stood in the way of their own wishes. The obvious purpose of the charter was to allow such minor regulations to be made as might meet the peculiar wants of the local population. A similar provision is inserted in charters in modern times, designed to allow the recipients of such grants to exercise their rights in any way they choose, not infringing any of the general laws of the State. These Puritans construed their grant differently from all others, because they designed to establish a religious community on a plan of their own, discarding all portions of the English law, unless reënacted by themselves.

Their be-praised Body of Liberties enacted in 1641, but not printed till within about thirty years since, virtually abrogated the laws of England.

Equally striking was their claim to the territory of Maine. The political troubles at home, from 1637 to the restoration of Charles II., in 1660, withdrew public gloried in extirpating every trace of title granted to others, making war on whatever was opposed to them, aiming at unlimited despotism. True, they planted other men's fields, instead of devastating them, and seized upon the territory of others by the same authority and in the same spirit as the Israelites drove out the tribes, that formerly possessed the valley of the Jordan.

It is hardly necessary to remind the student of American history that, at the close of the seventeenth century, as at the beginning, the two great geographical divisions of English dominion on this continent, north of the Delaware, were "the Provinces of New-York and Sagadahoc." Such are the definitions employed in the grant of that dominion by King Charles II. to his brother, the Duke of York; and such are the titles under which the Duke of York, when he ascended the throne as James II., commissioned his Governor, Col. Thomas Dongan, afterwards Earl of Limerick, to exercise authority over these countries. In England, a country of precedents, where the law advisers of the Crown always scrupulously adhered to ancient records in the preparation of official documents, such recognition, eighty years after the death of George Popham, is another proof, if any were wanting, of the legal establishment of England's claims in these latitudes being inseparable from the foundation of the first settlement, which to-day we commemorate.

To review, in the most hurried manner, the events

attention almost entirely from America, and it was not till 1676 that the heirs of Gorges, nearly worn out in the controversy, obtained a decision in their favor against her usurpations. Thereupon March 13, 1677, for £1250 they purchased the title of Gorges' heirs.

Finally in 1684, on *scire facias*, the Court of Chancery declared their charter forfeited, and thereby put an end to the Massachusetts theocracy.

A new charter protecting all Protestant Christians in the exercise of their religion, was granted by William and Mary, in 1691, including the colony of Plymouth and of Massachusetts, the Province of Maine, and Sagadahoc, under one government, and Sir William Phipps, a native of Maine, was appointed Governor.

affecting our race, that have transpired within the two hundred and fifty-five years since it was planted here, would transcend the proper limits of this occasion. Less than five millions of people, at that time engaged in the ruder forms of labor, were shut up in the narrow limits of the British Isles,—those who speak the English language to-day in the two hemispheres, hold dominion over one fifth of the earth's surface, and govern one fourth of the human species.*

Their material greatness commenced with colonizing North-America. Slowly, patiently and in much suffering, our fathers gained possession of this soil. The title was secured by the act of possession of the Popham Colony. Others came in to help to hold it; political troubles at home favored emigration hither; and one hundred years after Popham, three hundred thousand people of the Saxo-Norman race inhabited the then eleven existing colonies. During the next sixty years they had mastered the French, and gained the Atlantic slope from the St. Lawrence to Florida. Before the end of the next one hundred years the same people had grown into the Colossal Empire of the West, embracing thirty-four States, and regions yet unpeopled of still greater extent, including, in all their dominions, a territory equal to the continent of Europe, inhabited by more than thirty millions of human beings, speaking one language; while a new power has arisen in North-America, the Colonial Empire of Great Britain, extending over a larger, but less valuable territory than the United States, and containing more than three millions of inhabitants.

Temporary differences and periods of alienated feeling, will from time to time arise, but nothing can prevent the gradual and cordial union of the English-speaking people, of this continent in every thing essen-

* See Appendix D.

tial to their highest welfare. Though divided into various governments, each pursuing its own lawful ends, in obedience to that principle of political harmony, that allows each to revolve, in its own appropriate orbit, around its common centre, an enlightened sense of justice, and obedience to the Divine law, as the highest of all good to communities and states, is the daily lesson of their life. Let, then, each returning anniversary of this day's commemoration draw closer and closer the bonds of fraternal fellowship, and strengthen those ties of lineage that shall gradually encircle the earth, and constitute all mankind of various races and nationalities, one final brotherhood of nations.

Two hundred and fifty-five years have sufficed to change this wilderness continent, as if by enchantment, into the home of a refined civilization. Cultivated fields, clustering villages, the refinements of city life, rise to our immediate view; stretching from this point eastward to Ascension Bay,—northward to the Laurentian Hills, — southward to the Gulf of Mexico, and westward to the Pacific seas, where San Francisco, at the Golden Gate, at the touch of the telegraph, sends to us kindly greetings for this hour.

The improvement in agricultural implements, the wonders of the power-loom and the spinning-jenny, the marvels of the steamship, the mysteries of the photograph, the magic of the telegraph, and the omnipotent power of the locomotive railway, have since been made our ever-willing ministers, so that man seems almost invested with ubiquity and omnipotence; yet each revolving year brings forth new marvels, till the finite mind is overwhelmed at any attempt to forecast the future.

And the historian of our race traces back this development to the two first acts in the great drama of American history by which the title of England to the Continent was established; the first, closing with the grant of the Great Charter of April 10th, 1606; the second, with the formal act of possession of the New World under it, August 19th, O. S. 1607, thereby making the title, forever clear and unquestionable.

On that day, and upon this peninsula of Sabino, was unfurled that proud flag that had so long braved the battle and the breeze; then our fathers' flag—and now the flag of the Fatherland—and beneath its waving folds were proclaimed, for the first time, the political principles which lie at the foundation of free government, in ever memorable words.

"I give," said King James, "to my loving subjects, liberty to settle Virginia, in the north of America, between the thirty-fourth and forty-fifth degrees of north latitude. I authorize them to transport thither any of my own people, or those of other lands, and appoint over them a government of their own choice, subject to my approval, according to the laws of this kingdom. I authorize them to work mines, coin money, collect duties by imposts, and to expel all intruders therefrom by military force; and I declare, that all children born therein, and all persons residing therein, are, and shall always remain citizens, entitled to all the rights, privileges, and immunities of the loyal subjects of the British realm.

"And I do further declare, that these, my loving subjects, shall have the right annually to elect a President, and other officers; that the Christian Religion, established in this our kingdom, shall be therein preached and observed; that lands shall descend to heirs, according to the provisions of our ancient laws; that trial by jury of twelve men is established in all criminal cases, with a right of pardon by the King; that in civil causes the President and Council shall determine between party and party, keeping full records of all proceedings and judgments, with a right of appeal to the King in council; that no man shall be tried as an offender outside of the Colony where the alleged offence was committed, and no offences shall be capital except tumult, rebellion, conspiracy, mutiny, and sedition, murder, manslaughter, incest, rape, and adultery. And I do further declare, and ordain, that my loving subjects in America shall forever possess and enjoy the right to make all needful laws for their own government, provided only, that they be consonant to the laws of England. And these, my loving subjects, shall be, and forever remain, entitled to the protection of the British Crown, and I establish over them the government of the King of Great Britain, France, and Ireland."*

This charter of liberties was never revoked. It was a decree of universal emancipation, and every man of any color, from any clime, was by this act of King James redeemed, regenerated, disenthralled, the moment he touched the soil of America, between the thirty-fourth and forty-fifth degrees of north latitude; and he at once became entitled to all the rights of citizenship — one hundred and fifty years before the decree of Lord Mansfield struck off the chains and fetters from the African in England. This ordinance also established the right of the people to self-government, subject only to the paramount authority of the Crown and Laws of England.

These solemn formalities, unknown to any other of the early colonies, counselled by the Lord Chief-Justice of England, whose brother, as President of the infant commonwealth, planted on these shores the emblems of the authority of his nation,—proclaimed in no doubtful accents to all other nations, that here, the title

* See Poor's Vindication of Gorges, Appendix, for this constituent Code of Laws of King James.

of England was established. That pledge of the protection of his government, which every Englishman has always felt when he planted his foot on any portion of the empire of his sovereign, gave strength and courage to this colony,—and when the humble settlers of Plymouth, thirteen years later, impressed with their feet the sandy shores of Cape Cod, the claim of England to the country had been vindicated and established, against the asserted claims of both Spain and France.

The power of England remained undisturbed west of Sagadahoc, and southward, till it was finally yielded on the third of September, 1783—one hundred and seventy-six years from the time it was first planted—when all political connection with Great Britain was dissolved, on the conclusion of the Definitive Treaty of Peace. In announcing that fact, King George the Third said: "In thus admitting their separation from the Crown of these kingdoms, I have sacrificed every consideration of my own, to the wishes and opinions of my people. I make it my humble and earnest prayer to Almighty God, that Great Britain may not feel the evils which might result from so great a dismemberment of the empire; and that America may be free from the calamities which have formerly proved, in the mother country, how essential monarchy is to the enjoyment of constitutional liberty. Religion, language, interest, affections may, and I hope will yet prove a bond of permanent union between the two countries. To this end neither attention nor disposition on my part shall be wanting."

Memorable words, for they admit the national error.

But the repentance of the King had come too late. The loyal subjects of King James had planted on these shores the principles of civil and religious liberty, under his guidance and his express authority, and it was not in the power of King or Parliament, after one hundred and seventy-six years of the exercise of these rights, to reclaim them by force of arms.

It was in defence of rights granted by King James that our fathers took up arms, against the arbitrary enactments of King George the Third and his Parliament, under the lead of Sir George Grenville, then first Minister of the Crown. They defended a principle since made universal in its application, in every part of the British Colonial Empire. They claimed only their rights as loyal subjects of Great Britain.

Our fathers charged the acts of oppression, commencing in 1763, and ending in the Revolution of 1776, on the King, as the responsible head of the British government, but the exact truth still remains obscured, from want of public access, till a recent date, to the state papers of that period. If the odium of these acts shall justly fall on the head of the Minister rather than on the King, to what an eminence of guilt did Sir George Grenville attain, and how different the award of future over cotemporary times and opinions, as to the claims to veneration of the two men of England most intimately associated with American affairs, Sir Ferdinando Gorges, the father of English Colonization in America, a private citizen,—and Sir George Grenville, the highest officer of state, who inaugurated those measures that caused the final separation of the thirteen North-American Colonies from the British Crown,—an event, under the circumstances in which it was achieved, every day seen to have been most disastrous to humanity and our race.

The mind of each one present instinctively turns back to-day, over this long line of history, pausing to survey, in this broad sweep, the great epochs that mark its progress. It lingers longest in contemplating the initiatory steps that gave title and possession to the country,—and delights to loiter, here, around this cherished spot, and recall to present view the deeds of Gorges and Popham, and those who assisted them to transport hither the Saxo-Norman race; for that race, planted on this new continent, has favored and illustrated every thing that tends to the advancement of freedom and humanity, whatever may have been its occasional errors.

We have established our power as a people, developed the natural resources of our country, and demonstrated the ability of our government to resist foreign aggression. One further duty remains—the vindication of its principles in reference to ourselves. Can a government, resting for its strength and support on the consent of the governed, so far maintain its power as to suppress insurrection without weakening the safeguards to personal liberty? Can popular elections fill the highest offices of the state, and insure that strength and stability to the government, that can vindicate its power in times of domestic insurrection, or open rebellion, like that, now shaking it to its foundations?

Putting our trust in that power that alone can save us, invoking that arm that can alone be stretched forth for our deliverance, we bow our wills to the Divine teaching.

What though at this hour clouds and darkness hang like a thick pall over our country, and in the excess of our marvellous prosperity, we are called for a time to self-abasement and trial, the race shall survive all shocks of civil strife and of foreign invasion, and rise superior to both; this free government emerge into the full strength and measure of its giant proportions; and "the gorgeous ensign of the Republic," known and honored throughout the earth, shall once more float, full and free, as in former days, over a united and prosperous people.

APPENDIX.

NOTE A.

To enable those not familiar with the localities of Sabino, to understand the allusions made to them, a map and a brief description are given.

The Sagadahoc river, so famous in the early history of the country, is formed by the junction of two large rivers, the Androscoggin and the Kennebec, at Merrymeeting Bay,* twenty-five miles from the sea, from which junction the Sagadahoc is a deep estuary of very irregular width, often contracted into narrow limits, but carrying a large volume of water to the ocean.

At its mouth, between Stage Island on the eastern shore, and the lower end of the Peninsula of Sabino on the west, it is about a mile and a half in width. One mile above this, is its narrowest point, where the north-east point of the Sabino Peninsula projects far out into the channel, nearly opposite which point, only a few rods higher up the river, the lower end of a sharp rocky isle, called Long Island, narrows the main channel to less than a third of a mile. There is no navigable passage on the eastern side of this island. This outermost north-eastern point of the Sabino Peninsula is the site of Fort Popham. It was occupied by a small fort in the war of 1812. Above this point opens out Adkins Bay, extending south-west for a mile or more, where formerly it evidently connected with the ocean. In De Barre's chart, made for the British government between 1764 and 1774, it is laid down as flats, subject to the overflow of the tide, between this Bay and the ocean. At the present time, there is enough of earth formed by action of the sea, to afford a good road-bed, free from overflow, connecting Sabino with the mainland.

From Merrymeeting Bay south to the ocean, there is a constant succession of narrows, formed by high, sharp, projecting points of rock, alternating into broad reaches or bays. A reach of some miles in front of the city of Bath, varying from one half to a mile in width, having abundant depth of water, forms one of the noblest landlocked harbors in the world, when the river turns, first east, at right angles, then again south, between high, rocky shores, with great depths of water. Nothing can be more beautiful or picturesque than the sail between Merrymeeting Bay and the sea.

As you descend towards the mouth of the river, the Island of Seguin, a high, rounded, rocky ridge, rising one hundred and forty feet above the sea-level, stands directly in front, apparently closing the mouth of the river, though three miles distant from it, clothed with a native growth of evergreen to its summit. Above this, rises a first-class lighthouse, holding in its spacious iron lantern a Fresnel lens of the largest size, seen for more than twenty miles at sea, and for a very great distance from the high lands of the interior.

The Peninsula of Sabino is the outer point of the mainland, on the right

* Marimitin. See Father Dreuilletts' Journal of an Embassy from Canada to New-England, in 1650, published from a translation of John G. Shea, with valuable notes, in the Collections of the New-York Historical Society, 1857, vol. iii. Second Series, part i. page 303. The country was then occupied from Cushnoc (Augusta) to Merrymeeting Bay.

or west bank of the river, three miles from Seguin. It is very nearly an irregular triangle in shape, its shortest line fronting the Sagadahoc—the other two side-lines formed, one by Adkins Bay, and the other by the ocean. It rises into two rocky ridges, lying nearly east and west of each other, with a deep depression running north and south the bulk of the land, lying west of it, where it rises from two to three hundred feet into two considerable peaks in a ridge running north and south. In the valley, or narrow depression running north and south, the land is free from stones, and the soil is made up chiefly of sand. Toward its southern end there is a beautifully clear lake or pond of fresh water sufficient for the wants of the Peninsula. The level of this lake is only about thirty or forty feet above the sea, and is said at times to be reached by the flashing spray which is dashed with prodigious force at times upon this rocky shore.

Near the shore of Adkins Bay is a spring of water half a mile from the site of Fort Popham, near which, are remains of ancient habitations; and those who have explored the localities profess their belief that the principal fort was in the "vicinity of this spring." There is an old gentleman still living, more than ninety years of age, who was present at the celebration, who testifies to the ploughing across a covered way between the ruins of an old fort and this spring of water, in his early days.

The whole Peninsula was originally covered with a forest growth, and materials would have been abundant for the building of houses and a stockade fort.

As to the probable site of their fort, that must depend upon the purpose of its construction. If an European foe, Spaniard or French, was dreaded, the site of the present fort would naturally be chosen. If, on the other hand, the enemy they feared was the Indian, they would naturally select a spot convenient to fresh water, where they could best guard the approach of the foe, coming across the neck, that alone connected the peninsula with the main. The site pointed out as that of their fort, would, in that view of the case, be at once determined on the southern shore of Adkins Bay, near to the neck, in the vicinity of this spring.

No one can fail to perceive the wonderful foresight of the men who selected this spot for their plantation. Easily approached at all times by water, capable of being defended at all points, those in possession of this peninsula hold complete control of the country and the rivers above, one of the finest agricultural districts in New-England. It was also the finest river for fish on the coast. When the Pilgrims of Plymouth were considering the question of abandoning their home, from the poverty of the soil and the want of means of subsistence, Sir Ferdinando Gorges gave them a valuable tract of land on the Kennebec in 1629, at the time he established their boundaries at Plymouth, which they farmed out to advantage, deriving thence, and from the fisheries their chief means of support. The facts stated by Father Dreuilletts, at the time of his visit in 1650 and 1651, are of great historic interest.

At the time of the celebration, the level floor or parade of the fort was occupied by the large assemblage of people. A platform facing east, overlooked the fort and the Sagadahoc river, resting for its background against the end of the large shed occupied for dressing stone. This platform was occupied by the distinguished guests from abroad, the members of the Historical Society, the Masonic fraternity, and those taking part in the celebration. The various steamers and barges in attendance, the United States revenue cutter, and a large fleet of smaller craft, all gaily dressed in flags, lay at anchor in Adkins Bay. A strong tidal current swept past the fort, aided by a stiff north-west wind. The speaker's stand commanded a complete view of all the localities alluded to.

Half a mile from the fort, a few rods north of the pond or lake before spoken of, on a ridge rising fifty feet above the ocean-level, the large canvas Pavilion was spread, stretching east and west, looking like one vast cathedral in the distance, all its masts crowded with flags. At the conclusion of the services at the fort, the company marched in procession to the Pavilion, where, with refreshments and speeches, the remainder of the day was occupied.

NOTE B.

RICHARD SEYMOUR.

At the Pavilion, after a few introductory words, connecting the sentiment proposed with the name of the Chaplain of the Colony, Bishop Burgess read the following paper:

Mr. President: Who was Richard Seymour? And why should he be remembered with honor?

The house of Seymour, the second among the English nobility, first rose to eminence through the elevation of Queen Jâne, the daughter of Sir John Seymour, the favorite wife of Henry the Eighth, and the mother of Edward the Sixth. Her brother, Sir Edward Seymour, became Earl of Hertford, and in the minority of his nephew, King Edward, was created Duke of Somerset, and governed the realm as Lord Protector. He was twice married, and his second wife, Anne Stanhope, being a lady of high descent, it was made a part of his patent of nobility, that his titles should first be inherited in the line of her children, and only in the event of the failure of that line, should pass to his children by his first wife, Catherine Fillol, and their descendants. Accordingly, the honors forfeited when "the Good Duke," as the Protector was called, perished on the scaffold, being afterwards restored, passed down in the younger line, till it expired in Algernon, Duke of Somerset, in 1750, when they reverted to the elder line, in which they continue till this day.

In the mean time, this elder branch had been seated, all along, at Berry Pomeroy, in Devonshire, a few miles from Totness, from Dartmouth, and from the sea. The eldest son of the Protector, Sir Edward, a Christian name which continued in the eldest sons for eight generations, died in 1593. This son, Sir Edward, the grandson of the Protector, was married in 1576, and died in 1613, having had, according to one account, five sons; according to another, three, besides four daughters. The youngest son, according to both accounts, bore the name of Richard, and this great-grandson of the Protector Somerset, was, I suppose, the Richard Seymour who was the Chaplain of the Popham Colony. The case is sustained as follows:

There is no other person of the name known in genealogical history. Amongst sixty-nine male descendants of the Protector, he is the only Richard.

His age corresponds with the chronology of the occasion. His father having married in 1576, the youngest of three or even of five sons might well have been born within ten years after, so as to have been, in 1607, a young clergyman, just from the University. What more probable than that such a young man should be attracted by this noble adventure, as it happened to be in the hands of his immediate friends?

His residence corresponds with the locality of the enterprise. It was within fifteen or twenty miles of Plymouth, and amongst those gentlemen of Devonshire, who chiefly formed the company with whom this undertaking originated. Of the Plymouth company of 1620, his brother, Sir Edward Seymour, was one of the incorporated members.

This brings us to the most decisive circumstances, which are not a little interesting in the light which they cast upon the history of the colony. At Dartington, close by Berry Pomeroy, was then, and still is, the seat of the old family of Champernoun, which "came in with William the Conqueror." Francis Champernoun, who came to Maine as one of the Councillors under the patent of Gorges, and settled at Kittery, was the nephew of Sir Ferdinando Gorges. Therefore, either Gorges himself, or his sister, or his sister-in-law, must have married a Champernoun. Gorges was Governor of Plymouth, and was the soul of these expeditions long after.

The mother of Sir Walter Raleigh was also a Champernoun; and as she was of course the mother also of his half-brother, the gallant Sir Humphrey Gilbert, it follows that his son, Raleigh Gilbert, the admiral of this expedition, was the grandson of a Champernoun, and had an affinity with Gorges through that family.

Sir John Popham had several children, amongst whom was a daughter Elizabeth, who was married to Sir Richard Champernoun; and thus there was affinity between the families of Gorges, Gilbert, and Popham through the household at Dartington.

Sir Edward Seymour, the father of Richard Seymour, was married, as has been said, in 1576, and his wife was Elizabeth, daughter of Sir Arthur Champernoun; and thus the chain of relationship is complete between the families of Gorges, Raleigh, Gilbert, Popham and Seymour.

Richard Seymour, therefore, the son of Edward Seymour, was related to Gorges, the projector of the colony, to Popham, its patron, to Popham, its President, and to Gilbert, its admiral, all through the common link of the family of his mother. When they sought a Chaplain, they found one in Richard Seymour; and no other Richard Seymour is known except this relative of theirs. May we not regard the identity as, I will not say demonstrated, but fairly established, to the extent of a reasonable conviction?

The connection between the families of Seymour and Popham ceased not with that generation. Sir John Popham, though Wellington, in Somersetshire, was his birth-place and burial-place, purchased from the family of Darell, to which the grandmother of the Protector belonged, the seat of Littlecote, in Wiltshire, on the borders of Berkshire, and here resided his descendants. Sir Edward Seymour, grand-nephew of Richard Seymour, married Letitia Popham, daughter of Francis Popham, Esq., of Littlecote, and had a son named Popham Seymour; and the next Sir Edward, his eldest son, married another Letitia, daughter of Sir Francis Popham, also of Littlecote. This hereditary friendship accords with the association on this spot.

But Richard Seymour has his honor, this day, not from his memorable descent, but from the place assigned him by the Providence which presided over the destinies of this now Christian land. He was not the first English clergyman who ever preached the Gospel or celebrated the Holy Communion in North-America; that honor fell to Wolfall, in 1578, on the shores of Newfoundland or Labrador. He was not the first English clergyman in the United States; for Hunt had already begun his pastoral office on the banks of the James. He was not even the first Christian teacher within the limits of Maine; for L'Escarbot, a Huguenot, had instructed his French associates in 1604, on an island in the St. Croix.

But Seymour was the first preacher of the Gospel in the English tongue, within the borders of New-England, and of the free, loyal and unrevolted portion of these United States. Had he inherited all the honors of his almost royal great-grandsire, they would have given him a far less noble place than this, in the history of mankind.

NOTE C.

THE SETTLEMENT OF MAINE BY GOVERNOR GEORGE POPHAM, AUGUST, 1607.

Before the Mayflower's lonely sail
Our northern billows spanned,
And left on Plymouth's ice-bound rock
A sad-eyed pilgrim band;

Ere scarce Virginia's forest proud
The earliest woodman hewed,
Or gray Powhatan's wondering eyes
The pale-browed strangers viewed;

The noble Popham's fearless prow
Essayed adventurous deed;
He cast upon New-England's coast
The first colonial seed;

And bade the holy dews of prayer
Baptize a heathen sod;
And 'mid the groves a church arose
Unto the Christian's God.

And here, on green Sabino's marge,
He closed his mortal trust,
And gave this savage-peopled world
Its first rich Saxon dust.

So, where beneath the drifted snows
He took his latest sleep,
A faithful sentinel of stone
Due watch and ward shall keep;

A lofty fort, to men unborn,
In thunder speak his name,
And Maine, amid her thousand hills,
New-England's founder claim. L. H. Sigourney.

Hartford, Ct., Sept. 3, 1862.

LE SIEUR DE CHAMPLAIN.

Onward o'er waters which no keel had trod,
No plummet sounded in their depths below,
No heaving anchor grappled to the sod
Where flowers of ocean in seclusion glow;
From isle to isle, from coast to coast he prest
With patient zeal and chivalry sublime,
Folding o'er Terra Incognita's breast
The lilied vassalage of Gallia's clime.
Though Henry of Navarre's profound mistake
Montcalm must expiate and France regret;
Yet yonder tranquil and heaven-mirrored lake,
Like diamond in a marge of emerald set,
Bears on its freshening wave, from shore to shore,
The baptism of his name till time shall be no more.

Hartford, Ct., Oct. 1, 1862. L. Huntley Sigourney.

SIR FERDINANDO GORGES.

Not 'mid Ambition's sterner sons, inspired with restless rage,
Whose wreaths of laurel stain with blood the snow of History's page,
Nor 'mid those sordid hordes who wrap their souls in cloth of gold,
And smother every generous aim in that Laocoon fold;
But with the men whom age on age complacently shall view
Unostentatious in their course, and like the pole-star true,
Who nobly plan, and boldly aid the welfare of their race—
Sir Ferdinando Gorges' name shall find an honored place.

On the new Western Continent, his earnest eye was bent,
Nor rising cloud, nor rolling storm obscured his large intent;
Though Raleigh, that chivalrous friend, upon the scaffold bled,
And many an unexpected foe upreared the hydra head;
Though adverse fortune ruled, and loss his flowing coffers drained,
And monarchs vacillated sore, and parliaments complained;
Yet with a persevering zeal that no defeat impaired,
When others failed, he onward pressed—where others shrank, he dared.

Then colonizing ships went down beneath the engulfing main,
Or on their cargoes fiercely fed the pirate power of Spain,
And homeward from their rude abodes the baffled planters steer,
Discouraged at the hardships dire that vex the pioneer;
The wily Aborigines* his proffered kindness grieved,
And the great Bashaba himself all Christian trust deceived:
Still as the beacon rises brave o'er desolation's flood
Sir Ferdinando Gorges, firm in faith's endurance stood.

He ne'er beheld New-England's face that woke such life-long toil,
Nor traversed with exploring foot his own manorial soil,
Nor gazed upon those crested hills where misty shadows glide,
Nor heard her thundering rivers rush to swell old ocean's tide,
Nor like the seer on Pisgah's cliff one distant glance enjoyed
Of those delightful vales that oft his nightly dreams employed;
Yet still with deep indwelling thought and fancy's graphic art
He bore her strongly-featured scenes depictured on his heart.

She gave him no memorial stone 'mid all her mountains hoar,
Nor bade one islet speak his name along her sounding shore,
Nor charged a single mirrored lake that o'er her surface spread
To keep his image on its wave till gratitude was dead:
The woodman in the forest hews, the kingly mast to rear,
And forth the fearless vessel goes to earth's remotest sphere;
But who of all the mariners upon the watery plain
Gives praise to that unswerving knight, who loved the hills of Maine?

Hartford, Ct., Nov. 5, 1862. L. H. S.

* Some native Indians being brought to England, were kindly received by Sir Ferdinando Gorges into his family, from whom he acquired much information of their country, its scenery and productions. One of them, a native of Martha's Vineyard, named Epinow, artfully invented a story of a mine of gold in that region.

A vessel having been fitted out for the coast of New-England by Sir Ferdinando Gorges and the Earl of Southampton, Epinow went in it, and when it approached his native island leaped into the sea and swam ashore. Soon a shower of arrows from about twenty canoes was discharged on deck, much disconcerting the crew. This expedition, like several other unsuccessful ones, returned without having performed any service adequate to the equipment.

NOTE D.

ESTIMATED TERRITORY AND POPULATION OF THE GLOBE.

	Square miles.	Population.
Europe,	3,500,000	275,000,000
Asia,	16,800,000	720,000,000
Africa,	11,700,000	100,000,000
America,	16,000,000	70,000,000
Oceanica,	4,000,000	35,000,000
	52,000,000	1,200,000,000

ENGLISH SPEAKING OR ENGLISH GOVERNED.

	Square miles.	Inhabitants.
United States of America,	3,250,000	31,445,080
United Kingdom of Great Britain and Ireland,	122,556	29,334,788
British Colonies and Dependencies,	8,124,528	189,610,665
Total,	11,497,084	250,390,533

THE FOLLOWING TABLE GIVES IN DETAIL THE

BRITISH TERRITORY AND POPULATION IN 1861.

COUNTRIES, ETC.	AREA. SQ. M.	POPULATION.
Europe.		
England,	50,922	18,949,930
Wales,	7,398	1,111,795
Scotland,	31,324	3,061,251
Ireland,	32,518	5,764,542
Channel Islands:		
Man,	282	52,339
Jersey,	62	56,078
Guernsey, with adjacent Islands,	42	29,846
Alderney,	6	4,933
Sark,	2	583
Army, Navy, and Sailors,	..	303,491
United Kingdom,	122,556	29,334,788
Gibraltar,	2	17,750
Maltese Islands,	115	136,271
Ionian Islands,	1,045	229,726
Heligoland,	5	2,800
Total in Europe,	123,723	29,721,355
Asia.		
Bengal Presidency,	221,969	40,852,397
Madras "	132,090	22,437,297
Bombay "	131,544	11,790,042
North-West Provinces,	105,759	33,655,193
Punjab,	73,535	10,435,710
As-Sutlej States,	8,090	2,282,111
Oude,	25,000	5,000,000
Nagpore or Berar,	76,432	4,650,000
Pegu,	32,250	570,180
Tenasserim Provinces,	29,168	115,431
East'n Straits Settlem'ts:		
Penang and Wellesley,	251	90,688
Malacca and Naning,	1,049	19,103
Singapore,	275	92,749
Native States subordinate		
to Bengal,	515,535	38,702,206
to Madras,	51,809	5,213,671
to Bombay,	60,575	4,470,370
British India,	1,465,331	180,377,148
Ceylon,	24,700	1,759,528
Labuan,	50	1,163
Hong-Kong,	29	75,503
Aden,	10	80,000
Total in Asia,	1,490,120	182,293,342
Africa.		
Gambia,	2,000	5,693
Sierra Leone,	3,000	38,318
Gold Coast,	6,000	151,346
Cape Colony,	104,921	267,096
Caffraria,	22,000	120,000
Natal,	18,000	121,068
St. Helena,	47	5,490
Mauritius,	708	238,368
Seychelles,	200	8,276
Total in Africa,	156,876	955,650
Oceanica.		
New South-Wales,	356,480	350,553
Victoria,	86,940	544,677
South-Australia,	898,830	117,967
Western Australia,	988,980	14,823
Queensland,	450,780	30,115
North-Australia,	698,770	6,987
Australia,	2,980,780	1,065,122

BRITISH TERRITORY AND POPULATION IN 1861.—Continued.

COUNTRIES.	AREA. SQ. M.	POPULATION.	COUNTRIES.	AREA. SQ. M.	POPULATION.
Tasmania,..............	22,629	89,977	St. Vincent,............	132	30,128
New-Zealand,...........	95,500	129,477	Tobago,................	144	16,363
Norfolk Island,..........	18	600	St. Lucia,..............	296	26,471
Auckland Island,........	500	100	Nevis,..................	21	9,601
Feejee Islands,.........	8,034	133,500	St. Christopher,........	68	23,177
			Antigua,................	108	37,757
Total in Oceanica,...	3,107,461	1,418,776	Montserrat,............	47	7,653
			Virgin Islands,..........	92	6,689
America.			Dominica,..............	274	25,230
Vancouver,.............	12,756	25,000	Barbuda,..............	72	1,707
British Columbia,........	237,250	64,000	Anguilla,................	34	3,052
Hudson Bay Co.'s Ter....	2,250,000	71,000			
Labrador,..............	170,000	1,650	West-Indies,........	15,663	942,245
Canada West,...........	147,832	1,396,091			
Canada East,............	209,990	1,111,566	Guayana:		
New-Brunswick,.........	27,704	252,047	Essequibo,...........	44,000	22,925
Nova Scotia, etc.,........	18,746	330,699	Berbice,.............	25,000	29,003
Prince Edward,..........	2,134	80,648	Demerara,...........	27,000	75,767
Newfoundland,..........	35,913	122,958	Falkland Islands,........	6,297	539
Bermuda Islands,........	19	11,612			
Balize, (Honduras,)......	18,600	18,600	South-America,......	102,297	128,234
North-America,......	3,250,944	3,485,871	Total in America,....	3,368,904	4,556,350
Bahama Islands,.........	5,094	31,402	European,..............	123,723	29,721,355
Turk's Isl. and the Caicos,	430	4,428	Asiatic,...............	1,490,120	182,293,342
Jamaica,...............	6,250	441,264	African,...............	156,876	955,650
Cayman Islands,.........	260	1,760	Oceanic,...............	3,107,461	1,418,776
Trinidad,............ .	2,020	78,845	American,..............	3,368,904	4,556,350
Barbadoes,..............	166	161,201			
Grenada,..............	155	35,517	GRAND TOTAL,.......	8,247,084	218,945,453

The oldest of the present Colonies of Great Britain is Newfoundland, obtained by settlement in 1608; Bermuda was obtained in 1609; St. Christopher, in 1623; Barbadoes, in 1625; Nevis, in 1628; Bahamas, in 1629; Gambia, in 1631; and Antigua, in 1632. There are fifty distinct colonial governments over the British possessions.

NOTE E.

From the N. Y. Christian Times of Nov. 20, 1862.

THE POPHAM CELEBRATION.

ACTION OF THE NEW-YORK HISTORICAL SOCIETY.

Among the pleasing incidents not remotely connected with the meeting of the General Convention, was the gathering of a number of the members of that body, both clerical and lay, of acknowledged interest in historical pursuits, at the October meeting of the New-York Historical Society, to notice appropriately the late celebration of the Popham settlement at the mouth of the Kennebec. Invitations were extended by the courtly and accomplished President of the New-York Historical Society, the Hon. Luther Bradish, in behalf of the Society, to a number of the Bishops, to the delegation from the Diocese of Maine, and to several prominent members of the Maine and Massachusetts Historical Societies at that time in New-York, to be present on this interesting occasion. The invitation was very generally responded to; and, among others, the Rev. James Craik, D.D., of Kentucky, President of the House of Clerical and Lay Deputies; the Hon. R. C. Winthrop, President of the Massachusetts Historical Society; Prof.

Shattuck, of Boston; the Rev. Dr. Edson, of Lowell; the Hon. John A. Poor, and the Rev. William Stevens Perry, of Portland, members of the Maine Historical Society, were received by a large and brilliant assembly, consisting of prominent historical and literary characters of New-York and vicinity, in the elegant hall of the Society, on Second Avenue.

After the paper of the evening was read, the Hon. Luther Bradish, President of the Society, said, that in reporting upon the miscellaneous business of the Society, it was his pleasing duty to refer to an interesting event that had taken place during the vacation—the celebration in Maine of the founding of the English race in the New World. In many particulars, this celebration was one of the most memorable and successful historical commemorations that had yet taken place. On the Peninsula of Sabino, at the mouth of the ancient Sagadahoc, the modern Kennebec river, in the State of Maine, the two hundred and fifty-fifth anniversary of the founding of the first English colony on the shores of New-England was celebrated on the 29th of August, 1862, at which, after the use of the old words of prayer and praise of the English Prayer-Book of that time, an eloquent and appropriate oration, with speeches, was delivered, and other proceedings took place, at the erection of a monumental stone in the walls of Fort Popham. The New-York Historical Society, through its President, was honored with an invitation to participate in that celebration. Absence from home prevented his receiving the invitation in time to be present, had his health permitted. He had replied in what he trusted were appropriate terms. He was glad to know that other members of this Society had responded for our city and State. He regretted that we had not been able to do full justice to our sense of obligation to our sister Society in Maine. He trusted the Society would in some form take notice of it in an appropriate manner.

The Hon. George Folsom, a son of Maine, and well known as the learned historian of one of Maine's cradle homes of civilization and Episcopacy, rose, and said he fully sympathized in all that had fallen from the President; he regretted that absence in Canada, with his family, prevented his acceptance, in person, of the honor done him by an invitation. He asked leave to introduce the following resolution:

"*Resolved*, That the New-York Historical Society has observed with pleasure the efforts of the Historical Society of Maine to perpetuate the earliest history of their State, by associating important historic events with the great works of national defence of the United States Government; that they acknowledge with satisfaction the courtesy extended by the Historical Society and citizens of Maine, inviting the Society and its officers to participate in the commemorative celebration of the founding of the first colony on the shores of New-England, on the two hundred and fifty-fifth anniversary of that event, on the 29th of August, 1862, at which time a memorial stone was placed in the walls of Fort Popham commemorating the establishment of the first Protestant civil government on the shores of New-England; that this Society cordially approves the act of its President, in his reply to the invitation to participate in that celebration, and the good-will therein expressed; that all such efforts to preserve and illustrate the history of our race in the new world are worthy of general notice."

The Hon. J. Romeyn Brodhead said he seconded the resolution with great pleasure. He was pleased further to learn that several members of the Maine Historical Society had honored our meeting by their presence this evening, as had the President of the Historical Society of Massachusetts. Among others from Maine, the orator of the Popham Celebration, the Hon. Mr. Poor, was present, and he trusted this resolution would be adopted and that Mr. Poor would be called on to favor us with some reply thereto.

The resolution was unanimously adopted. In reply to a call from the

President, Mr. Poor said his associates of the Maine Historical Society and other friends from Maine present, with himself, felt personally complimented by the action here taken, in reference to the Popham Celebration. He rose with a feeling of embarrassment to return thanks for this cordial and unlooked for compliment. He doubted not that the Historical Society of Maine would, in its own befitting manner, return appropriate acknowledgments for this generous courtesy on the part of the New-York Historical Society.

The Popham Celebration, so courteously alluded to, had already borne fruits, in awakened attention to the study of the early history of the country, and we are largely indebted to eminent historical minds of New-York for much of the interest already attached to it. The fact so happily alluded to by your own historian, Mr. Brodhead, the political connection between New-York and Maine under the charter of Charles II., in his most interesting and appropriate reply to the invitation to speak for *the great metropolis of the New World*, cannot fail to excite a feeling of mutual sympathy, at this day, with the more recent but increasing commercial intimacy of the two States. It is certainly refreshing to revive and recall, for this brief hour, the kindly intercourse of other days. It is a fact, almost forgotten, even by the active men of this time, that much the largest portion of Maine was at one time under the same government as that of New-York, and that Gyles Goddard, the renowned representative from *Pemaquid*, sat in the Legislature of New-York in 1684, chosen by the free-holders of the county of Cornwall, in ancient Sagadahoc. This letter of Mr. Brodhead, already published in the Maine papers, will be preserved in our memorial volume as one of the choicest of the many interesting contributions to its pages. The courteous and appropriate letter of your President is already published in the papers of Maine.

One from the Hon. Mr. Bancroft, the most eminent of living American historians, and another from one of Maine's honored sons, Mr. Folsom, are promised for this volume. Mr. Folsom's invaluable labors in bringing to light and preserving the earliest history of his native State, have been publicly acknowledged by formal resolutions of the Maine Historical Society.

New-York, therefore, will have a foremost position, if not, in fact, the post of honor, in the records of that commemorative festival.

That celebration was well calculated to attract attention, for in its purpose it appeals at once to the sympathy of all who speak the English language, or share in any proper measure a feeling of pride at the achievements of our race. It had for its object the due observance of the great fact, the planting of our race in North-America, with the language, literature, laws, and religion of England, an event, if rightly comprehended in its relations and consequences, of as much importance as any one that has taken place since the establishment of the Roman Empire.

Eight years before the Leyden Church had been gathered in Holland, under the charge of the pious Robinson, twenty years before they set foot on Plymouth sands, the purpose of "planting colonies in the north-west of North-America" had been set forth in a paper on file in the British State Paper Office. More than thirteen years prior to the voyage of the May Flower, the title of Old England to New England had been secured by a formal act of possession and occupation at the mouth of the Sagadahoc by Governor Popham's colony.* No Frenchman ever set foot on the Atlantic

* The Seven Articles of the Leyden Flock, signed by Robinson and Brewster, sent to King James before their departure from Holland, signifying their full assent to the authority of the English Church, form a striking contrast to their subsequent pretensions, under the guidance of such men as Bradford and Winslow. See Poor's Vindication of Gorges, p. 108, for this remarkable document in full.

shore, claiming title west of the Kennebec, after the planting of Popham's colony in 1607.

The Colonial Empire of Great Britain, the wonder of this age, had its root in the charter of April tenth, 1606, and its development in the New-England charter of 1620, both granted on the petitions of Sir Ferdinando Gorges. The great idea of a strong central government, having extended dominions in distant lands, divided into separate provinces, communities, and states, each enjoying equal and just laws, suited to the local wants of each, fully developed in action under the rule of Cromwell, originated in an earlier day, and in the mind of him who secured those great charters, and maintained them till the soil of the New World was planted with our race, where it has gradually advanced toward universal dominion.

The failure of Sir Humphrey Gilbert, of Sir Walter Raleigh, and of Sir Richard Grenville to comprehend the geographical and commercial laws that control the destiny of races and of empires, imposed on Sir Ferdinando Gorges, or rather left to him, the task of occupying the continent of North-America, from the fortieth to the forty-eighth parallel of north latitude, in which limits, in spite of individual jealousy and parliamentary injustice, he achieved the great work of English colonization in America. In their zeal against monopolies, in 1621 and 1622, the Commons of England declared "*fishing is of more value than plantations in America*," and would have abandoned the continent to the French but for the pertinacity, foresight, and enlightened views of Gorges, and his favor with the King, from the possession of these great qualities.

But the chief significance of the Popham Celebration, undoubtedly, is the introduction of a new principle in the naming of our forts, making them serve the double purpose of national defence and of preserving the memory of the great events in our history.

We have seen the national honor tarnished, and the moral sense of the nation shocked, by the bestowal of unworthy names—names of mere partisan leaders—upon national vessels, forts, and other public works. This form of coarse flattery panders to the lower tastes of men and destroys the independence of official men, who are made the recipients of it.

It was, therefore, with a feeling of relief that Gen. Totten was pleased to accept the proposal of affixing to the great work in Portland harbor the name of Fort Gorges, in honor of Sir Ferdinando Gorges, the father of English colonization in America, and naming the new work at the mouth of the Sagadahoc or Kennebec Fort Popham, in a similar spirit, and we hope to see this rule made universal. Especially do we look forward to the construction of a new fort, to guard the entrance to Portland harbor, to be named Fort Gosnold, and placed on the shore of Cape Elizabeth, the first point of the northern main of New-England, touched by that great English navigator, who has left on record the details of his discovery of the New-England coast in 1602.

The fitness of the policy proposed will be readily appreciated by all men endowed with any share of that quality we call the historic sense; for all know that the reputation of no public man is secure within the first hundred years after his death. Personal ambition, partisan motives, and narrow views characterize the popular movements of every age—our own as of all past ones—and the value of no man's life can be justly measured in his own time. We build monuments, we name towns, cities, and counties, for men that a future age will hold in disfavor. We almost execrate the memory of men to-day, that a later time shall honor. We rear in affected grandeur an obelisk in devotion to the demon of war, that the calmer reason of the coming centuries will demolish or condemn. We do homage to popular partisan leaders to-day, whose doctrines have undermined the foundations of our Government and brought upon us civil war.

Thanks to the good sense of the people of the Empire State, they have preserved the name of their great navigator, Hudson, from any possibility of forgetfulness or decay, by affixing it to the great *river of the mountains* that must forever bear to this great metropolis the treasures of an expanding commerce with the interior.

Looking back to the first dawnings of American history, we are beginning to discover the superior lustre of the great lights that guided hitherward the adventurous and heroic spirits of that great age. Under their benignant glow we revisit the spots made sacred by self-denying labors. We hope to strengthen our love of what is noble and heroic by an annual pilgrimage to that spot where, in prayer and faith, the foundations of empire in the New World were laid.

Associating the history of Maine with New-York, so appropriately done by Mr. Brodhead, may serve to increase your interest in our State. Maine — so rich in historic interest, so full of legendary romance, so marked by the fascinations of its scenery;* the territory claimed by the great European powers, Spain, Holland, France, and England; the home of the earliest French settlers and of the first English colonists; the *Norumbega* of Milton's *Paradise Lost*, the *Mavosheen* of Purchase's strange narration; "discovered by the English in 1602, '3, '5, '6, '7, '8, and '9;" the *New-England* of John Smith in 1614, and of later times—obeys the law of historic as of commercial gravitation and gladly finds sympathy, "without reservation," in the great metropolis of the Western World.

Maine, too, builds the ships that fill the docks of the East River and the Hudson. She lifts from her quarries the granite columns that form the ornaments and support of your public edifices, and the rich colonnades and solid walls of the Treasury Extension at Washington. She needs, most of all, the pen of the historian and the pencil of the painter, to be made as familiar as household words in the private residences of the Fifth Avenue and Madison Square, by means of landscapes that shall equal in beauty the richest scenery of the Rhine and the Alps; true to nature from the sea-shores, the valleys, and the mountains of Maine. With her summer retreats thus laid open, she shall annually attract pleasure tourists of other lands than our own.

Rejoicing in the success of your Society, and grateful for your generous courtesy, I may be allowed to close, as I began, by expressing for our Society and its members, here present, the assurance of our hearty thanks.

* "We, Americans, neglecting both the surpassing magnificence—nay, often sublimity—and the rare loveliness of various districts of our own Continent, wander forth across the seas, to seek, at great expense, and amid physical and moral dangers, scenery in foreign lands, which falls short of the attractions of much we possess at home. Thus, how few are alive to the glorious and varied beauty of that zone of islands, which, commencing with the perfection of Casco Bay, terminates with the precipitous, seal-frequented shores of Grand-Menan, at the entrance of the Bay of Fundy. Of all the Archipelagoes sung by the poet, described by the historian, and depicted by the painter, there is none which can exceed, in its union of charms, those two hundred miles of intermingling land and ocean, where, lost in each other's embrace, the sea seems in love with the land, and the shore with the foam-frosted waves!"—*General J. Watts de Peyster's Dutch in Maine*, p. 44.

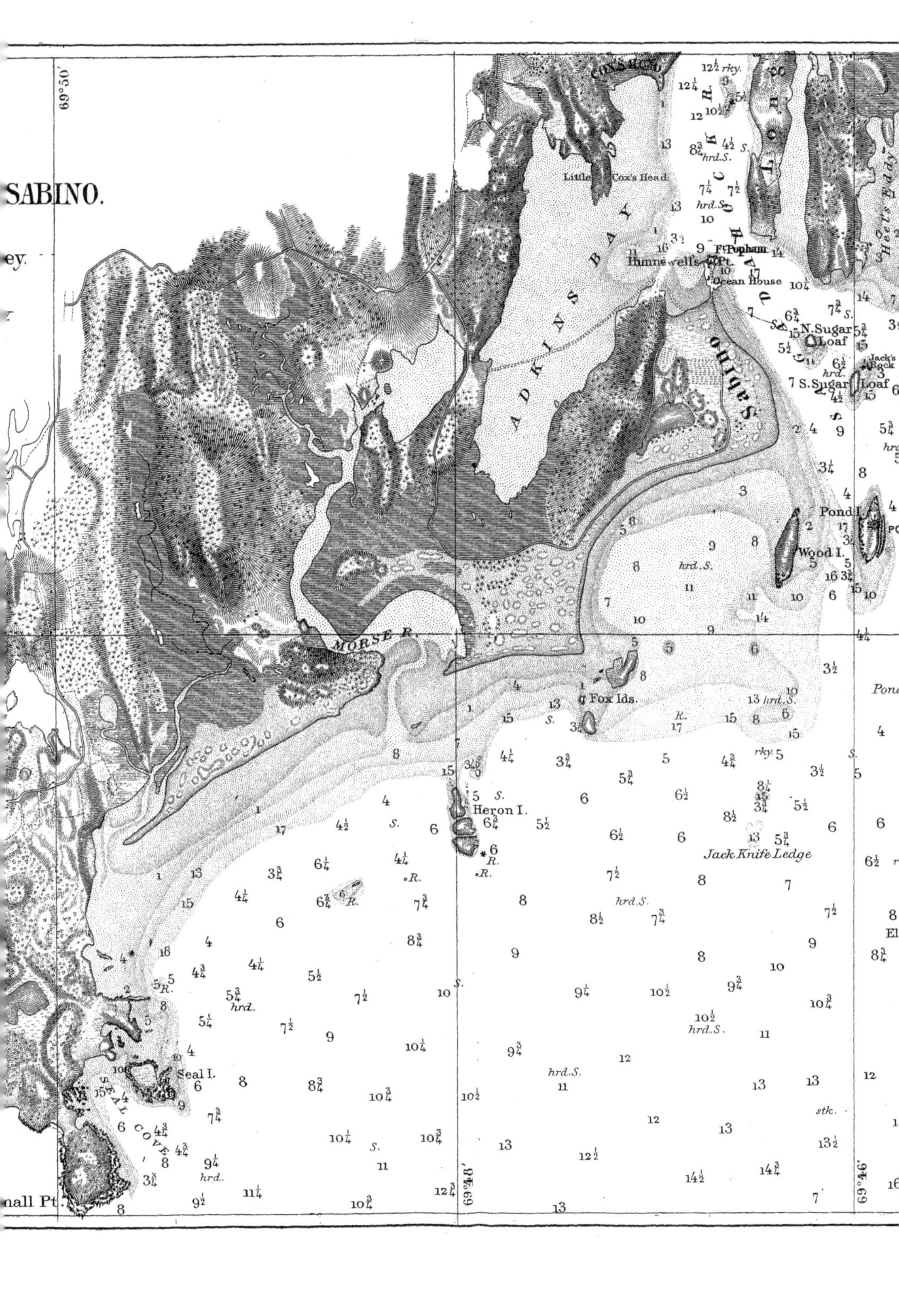

SABINO.
69°50'
ADKINS BAY
Little Cox's Head
Hunnewell's Pt.
Ft Popham
Ocean House
N. Sugar Loaf
S. Sugar Loaf
Jack's Rock
Pond I.
Wood I.
Fox Ids.
MORSE R.
Heron I.
Jack Knife Ledge
Seal I.
SEAL COVE
69°48'
69°46'

THE

DISCOVERY

AND

COLONIZATION OF AMERICA,

AND

IMMIGRATION TO THE UNITED STATES.

A LECTURE DELIVERED BEFORE THE NEW YORK HISTORICAL SOCIETY, IN METROPOLITAN HALL, ON THE 1ST OF JUNE, 1853.

BY

EDWARD EVERETT.

BOSTON:
LITTLE, BROWN, AND COMPANY.
1853.

CAMBRIDGE:
METCALF AND COMPANY, STEREOTYPERS AND PRINTERS.

LECTURE.

Mr. President and Gentlemen of the Historical Society: —

Although I appear before you at the season at which the various religious, moral, and philanthropic societies usually hold their annual meetings to discuss the stirring and controverted topics of the day, I need not say to you that the proprieties of this occasion require me to abstain from such subjects; and to select a theme falling, to some extent at least, within the province of an historical society. I propose, accordingly, this evening, to attempt a sketch of the history of the discovery and colonization of America and of immigration to the United States. I can of course offer you, within the limits of a single address, but a most superficial view of so vast a subject; but I have thought that even a sketch of a subject, which concerns us so directly and in so many ways, would suggest important trains of reflection to thoughtful minds. Words written or spoken are at best but a kind of short-hand, to be filled up by the reader or hearer. I shall be gratified if, after honoring my hasty sketch with your kind attention, you shall deem it worth filling up from your own stores of knowledge and thought. You will forgive me, if, in the attempt to give a certain completeness to the narrative, I shall be led to glance at a few facts, which, however interesting, may seem to you too familiar for repetition.

In the last quarter of the fifteenth century, an Italian mariner, a citizen of the little republic of Genoa, who had hitherto gained his livelihood as a pilot in the commercial marine of different countries, made his appearance successively at various courts in the South and West of Europe, soliciting patronage and aid for a bold and novel project in navigation. The state of the times was in some degree favorable to the adventure. The Portuguese had for half a century been pushing their discoveries southward upon the coast of Africa, and they had ventured into the Atlantic as far as the Azores. Several conspiring causes, and especially the invention of the art of printing, had produced a general revival of intelligence. Still, however, the state of things in this respect was at that time very different from what we witness in the middle of the nineteenth century. On the part of the great mass of mankind, there was but little improvement over the darkness of the Middle Ages. The new culture centred in the convent, the court, and the university, places essentially distrustful of bold novelties.

The idea of reaching the East by a voyage around the African continent had begun to assume consistency; but the vastly more significant idea, that the earth is a globe and capable of being circumnavigated, had by no means become incorporated into the general intelligence of the age. The Portuguese navigators felt themselves safe as they crept along the African coast, venturing each voyage a few leagues farther, doubling a new headland, ascending some before unexplored river, holding a palaver with some new tribe of the native races. But to turn the prows of their vessels boldly to the west, to embark upon an ocean, not believed, in the popular geography of the day, to have an outer shore, to pass that bourne from which no traveller had ever returned, and from which experience had not taught that any traveller could return, and thus to reach the East by sailing in a western direction, — this was a conception which no human being is known to have formed before Columbus, and which he proposed to the governments of Italy, of Spain, of Portugal, and for a long time without success. The state of science was not such as to enable men to discriminate between the improbable and untried on the one hand, and the impossible and absurd on the other. They looked upon Columbus as we did thirty years ago upon Captain Symmes.

But the illustrious adventurer persevered. Sorrow and disappointment clouded his spirits, but did not shake his faith nor subdue his will. His well-instructed imagination had taken firm hold of the idea that the earth is a sphere. What seemed to the multitude even of the educated of that day a doubtful and somewhat mystical theory; what appeared to the uninformed mass a monstrous paradox, contradicted by every step we take upon the broad, flat earth which we daily tread beneath our feet; — that great and fruitful truth revealed itself to the serene intelligence of Columbus as a practical fact, on which he was willing to stake all he had, — character and life. And it deserves ever to be borne in mind, as the most illustrious example of the connection of scientific theory with great practical results, that the discovery of America, with all its momentous consequences to mankind, is owing to the distinct conception in the mind of Columbus of this single scientific proposition, — the terraqueous earth is a sphere.

After years of fruitless and heart-sick solicitation, after offering in effect to this monarch and to that monarch the gift of a hemisphere, the great discoverer touches upon a partial success. He succeeds, not in enlisting the sympathy of his countrymen at Genoa and Venice for a brave brother sailor; not in giving a new direction to the spirit of maritime adventure which had so long prevailed in Portugal; not in stimulating the commercial thrift of Henry the Seventh, or the pious ambition of the Catholic King. His sorrowful perseverance touched the heart of a noble princess, — worthy the throne which she adorned. The New World, which was just escaping the subtle kingcraft of Ferdinand, was saved to Spain by the womanly compassion of Isabella.

It is truly melancholy, however, to contemplate the wretched equipment, for which the most powerful princess in Christendom was ready to pledge her jewels. Floating castles will soon be fitted out to convey the miserable natives of Africa to the golden shores of America, and towering galleons will be despatched to bring home the guilty treasures to Spain; but three small vessels, two of which were without a deck, and neither of them probably exceeding the capacity of a pilot-boat, and even these impressed into the public service, compose the expedition, fitted out under royal patronage, to realize that magnificent conception in which the creative mind of Columbus had planted the germs of a new world.

No chapter of romance equals the interest of this expedition. The most fascinating of the works of fiction which have issued from the modern press have, to my taste, no attraction compared with the pages in which the first voyage of Columbus is described by Robertson, and especially by our own Irving and Prescott, the last two enjoying the advantage over the great Scottish historian of possessing the lately discovered journals and letters of Columbus himself. The departure from Palos, where a few years before he had begged a morsel of bread and a cup of water for his way-worn child; his final farewell to the Old World at the Canaries; his entrance upon the trade-winds, which then, for the first time, filled a European sail; the portentous variation of the needle, never before observed; the fearful course westward and westward, day after day and night after night, over the unknown ocean; the mutinous and ill-appeased crew;— at length, when hope had turned to despair in every heart but one, the tokens of land; the cloud-banks on the western horizon; the logs of drift-wood; the fresh shrub floating with its leaves and berries; the flocks of land-birds; the shoals of fish that inhabit shallow water; the indescribable smell of the shore; the mysterious presentiment that ever goes before a great event;— and, finally, on that ever memorable night of the 12th of October, 1492, the moving light seen by the sleepless eye of the great discoverer himself from the deck of the Santa Maria, and in the morning the real, undoubted land, swelling up from the bosom of the deep, with its plains, and hills, and forests, and rocks, and streams, and strange, new races of men; — these are incidents in which the authentic history of the discovery of our continent excels the specious wonders of romance, as much as gold excels tinsel, or the sun in the heavens outshines that flickering taper.

But it is no part of my purpose to dwell upon this interesting narrative, or to follow out this most wonderful of histories, sinking as it soon did into a tale of sorrow for Columbus himself, and before long ending in one of the most frightful tragedies in the annals of the world. Such seems to be the law of humanity, that events the most desirable and achievements the most important should, either in their inception or progress, be mixed up with disasters, crimes, and sorrows which it makes the heart sick to record.

The discovery of America, I need hardly say, produced a vast extension of the territory of the power under whose auspices the discovery was made. In contemplating this point, we encounter one of the most terrible mysteries in the history of our race. "Extension of territory!" you are ready to exclaim; "how could Spain acquire any territory by the fact that a navigator, sailing under her patronage, had landed upon one or two islands near the continent of America, and coasted for a few hundred miles along its shores? These shores and islands are not a desert on which Columbus, like a Robinson Crusoe of a higher order, has landed and taken possession. They are occupied and settled, — crowded, even, with inhabitants, — subject to the government of their native chiefs; and neither by inheritance, colonization, nor as yet by conquest, has any human being in Europe a right to rule over them or to possess a square foot of their territory." Such are the facts of the case, and such, one would say, ought to be the law and equity of the case. But alas for the native chiefs and the native races! Before he sailed from Spain, Columbus was furnished with a piece of parchment a foot and a half square, by Ferdinand and Isabella, creating him their Viceroy and High-Admiral in all the seas, islands, and continents which he should discover, his heirs for ever to enjoy the same offices. The Viceroy of the absolute monarchs of Aragon and Castile!

Thus was America conquered before it was discovered. By the law of nations as then understood, (and I fear there is less change in its doctrines at the present day than we should be ready to think,) a sovereign right to the territory and government of all newly discovered regions inhabited by heathen tribes was believed to vest in the Christian prince under whose auspices the discovery was made, subject to the ratification of the Pope, as the ultimate disposer of the kingdoms of the earth. Such was the law of nations, as then understood, in virtue of which, from the moment Columbus, on that memorable night to which I have alluded, caught, from the quarter-deck of the Santa Maria, the twinkling beams of a taper from the shores of San Salvador, all the territorial and political rights of its simple inhabitants were extinguished for ever. When on the following morning the keel of his vessel grated upon the much longed for strand, it completed, with more than electric speed, that terrible circuit which connected the islands and the continent to the footstool of the Spanish throne. As he landed upon the virgin shore, its native inhabitants, could they have foreseen the future, would have felt, if I may presume thus to apply the words, that virtue had gone out of it for ever. With some of them the process was sharp and instantaneous, with others more gradual, but not less sure; with some, even after nearly four centuries, it is still going on; but with all it was an irrevocable doom. The wild and warlike, the indolent and semi-civilized, the bloody Aztec, the inoffensive Peruvian, the fierce Araucanian, — all fared alike; a foreign rule and an iron yoke settled or is settling down upon their necks for ever.

Such was the law of nations of that day, not enacted, however, by Spain. It was in reality the old principle of the right of the strongest, disguised by a pretext; a colossal iron falsehood gilded over with the thin foil of a seeming truth. It was the same principle which prompted the eternal wars of the Greeks and Romans. Aristotle asserts, without qualification, that the Greeks had a perpetual right of war and conquest against the barbarians,—that is, all the rest of the world; and the pupil of Aristotle proclaimed this doctrine at the head of the Macedonian phalanx on the banks of the Indus. The irruption of the barbarous races into Europe, during the centuries that preceded and followed Christianity, rested on as good a principle,—rather better,—the pretext only was varied; although the Gauls and Goths did not probably trouble themselves much about pretexts. They adopted rather the simple philosophy of the robber chieftain of the Scottish Highlands:—

> "Pent in this fortress of the North,
> Think'st thou we will not sally forth,
> To spoil the spoiler as we may,
> And from the robber rend the prey?"

When the Mohammedan races rose to power, they claimed dominion over all who disbelieved the Koran. Conversion or extermination was the alternative which they offered to the world, and which was announced in letters of fire and blood from Spain to the Ganges. The states of Christian Europe did but retort the principle and the practice, when, in a series of crusades, kept up for more than three hundred years, they poured desolation over the West of Asia, in order to rescue the sepulchre of the Prince of Peace from the possession of unbelievers.

Such were the principles of the public law and the practice under them, as they existed when the great discoveries of the fifteenth and sixteenth centuries took place. When the Portuguese began to push their adventures far to the south on the coast of Africa, in order to give to those principles the highest sanction, they procured of Pope Nicholas the Fifth, in

1454, the grant of the right of sovereignty over all the heathen tribes, nations, and countries discovered or to be discovered by them, from Africa to India, and the exclusive title thus conferred was recognized by all the other nations of Christendom.

On the return of Columbus from his first voyage, the king of Spain, not to fall behind his neighbors in the strength of his title, lost no time in obtaining from Pope Alexander the Sixth a similar grant of all the heathen lands discovered by Columbus, or which might hereafter be discovered, in the west. To preclude as far as possible all conflict with Portugal, the famous line of demarcation was projected from the north to the south, a hundred leagues west of the Azores, cutting the earth into halves, like an apple, and, as far as the new discoveries were concerned, giving to the Spaniards all west of the line, and confirming all east of it to the Portuguese, in virtue of the grant already mentioned of Pope Nicholas the Fifth.

I regret that want of time will not allow me to dwell upon the curious history of this line of demarcation, for the benefit of all states having boundary controversies, and especially our sister republics of Nicaragua and Costa Rica. It is sufficient to say, that, having had its origin in the papal bull just referred to of 1454, it remained a subject of dispute and collision for three hundred and sixty-one years, and was finally settled at the Congress of Vienna in 1815!

The territorial extension of Portugal and Spain, which resulted from the discovery of America, was followed by the most extraordinary effects upon the commerce, the finances, and the politics generally, of those two countries, and through them of the world. The over-land trade to the East, the great commercial interest of the Middle Ages, was abandoned. The whole of South America, and a considerable part of North America, were, in the course of the sixteenth century, settled by those governments; who organized in their Transatlantic possessions a colonial system of the most rigid and despotic character, reflecting as far as was practicable in distant provinces beyond the sea the stern features of the mother country. The precious metals, and a monopoly of the trade to the East, were the great objects to be secured. Aliens were forbidden to enter the American viceroyalties; none but a contraband trade was carried on by foreigners at the seaports. To prevent this trade, a severe right of search was instituted along the entire extent of the coasts, on either ocean. I have recently had an opportunity, in another place, to advert to the effects of this system upon the international relations of Europe.* Native subjects could emigrate to these vast colonial possessions only with the permission of the government. Liberty of speech and of the press was unknown. Instead of affording an asylum to persons dissenting from the religion of the state, conformity of belief was, if possible, enforced more rigidly in the colonies than in the mother country. No relaxation in this respect has, I believe, taken place in the remaining colonies of Spain even to the present day. As for the aboriginal tribes, after the first work of extermination was over, a remnant was saved from destruction by being reduced to a state of predial servitude. The dejected and spiritless posterity of the warlike tribes that offered no mean resistance to Cortés and Pizarro, are now the hewers of wood and the drawers of water to Mexico and Peru. In a word, from the extreme southern point of Patagonia to the northernmost limit of New Mexico, I am not aware that any thing hopeful was done for human improvement by either of the European crowns which added these vast domains to their territories.

If this great territorial extension was fruitless of beneficial consequences to America, it was not less so to the mother countries. For Spain it was the commencement of a period, not of prosperity, but of decline. The rapid influx of the precious metals, in the absence of civil liberty and of just prin-

---

* Speech on the affairs of Central America, in the Senate of the United States, 21st of March, 1853.

ciples and institutions of intercourse and industry, was productive of manifold evils; and from the reign of Philip the Second, if not of Charles the Fifth, the Spanish monarchy began to sink from its haughty position at the head of the European family. I do not ascribe this downfall exclusively to the cause mentioned; but the possession of the two Indies, with all their treasures, did nothing to arrest, accelerated even, the progress of degeneracy. Active causes of decline no doubt existed at home; and of these the Inquisition was the chief.

"There was the weight that pulled her down."

The spirit of intolerance and persecution, the reproach and scandal of all countries and all churches, Protestant as well as Catholic, (not excepting the Pilgrim Fathers of New England,) found an instrument in the Holy Office in Spain, in the sixteenth century, such as it never possessed in any other age or country. It was not merely Jews and heretics whom it bound to the stake; it kindled a slow, unquenchable fire in the heart of Castile and Leon. The horrid atrocities practised at home and abroad, not only in the Netherlands, but in every city of the mother country, cried to Heaven for vengeance upon Spain; nor could she escape it. She intrenched herself behind the eternal Cordilleras; she took to herself the wings of the morning, and dwelt in the uttermost parts of the sea; but even there the arm of retribution laid hold of her, and the wrongs of both hemispheres were avenged in her degeneracy and fall.

But let us pass on to the next century, during which events of the utmost consequence followed each other in rapid succession, and the foundations of institutions destined to influence the fortunes of Christendom were laid by humble men, who little comprehended their own work. In the course of the seventeenth century, the French and English took possession of all that part of North America which was not preoccupied by the Spaniards. The French entered by the St. Lawrence; followed that noble artery to the heart of the continent; traced the great lakes to their parent rivulets and weeping fountains; descended the Mississippi. Miracles of humble and unavailing heroism were performed by their gallant adventurers and pious missionaries in the depths of our Western wilderness. The English stretched along the coast. The geographer would have pronounced that the French, in appropriating to themselves the mighty basins of the Mississippi and the St. Lawrence, had got possession of the better part of the continent. But it was an attempt to compose the second volume of the "Fortunes of America," in advance of the first. This it was ordained should be written at Jamestown and Plymouth. The French, though excelling all other nations of the world in the art of communicating for temporary purposes with savage tribes, seem, still more than the Spaniards, to be destitute of the august skill required to found new states.* I do not know that there is such a thing in the world as a colony of France growing up into a prosperous commonwealth. Half a million of French peasants in Lower Canada, tenaciously adhering to the manners and customs which their fathers brought from Normandy two centuries ago, and a third part of that number of planters of French descent in Louisiana, are all that is left to bear living witness to the amazing fact, that in the middle of the last century France was the mistress of the better half of North America.

It was on the Atlantic coast, and in the colonies originally planted or soon acquired by England, that the great work of the seventeenth century was performed, — slowly, toilsomely, effectively. A mighty work for America and mankind, of which even we, fond and proud of it as we are, do but faintly guess the magnitude! It could hardly be said, at the time, to prosper in any of its parts. It yielded no return to the pecuniary capital invested. The political relations of the

---

* "La France saura mal coloniser et n'y réussira qu'avec peine." — Victor Hugo, *Le Rhin*, Tom. II. p. 280.

colonies from the first were those of encroachment and resistance; and even the moral principle, as far as there was one, on which they were founded, was not consistently carried out. There was conflict with the savages, war with the French and Spaniards, jarring and feud between neighboring colonies, persecution of dissenting individuals and sects, perpetual discord with the crown and the proprietaries. Yet, in the main and on the whole, the WORK was done. Things that did not work singly worked together; or if they did not work together, they worked by reaction and collision. Feeble germs of settlement grew to the consistency of powerful colonies; habits of civil government rooted themselves in a soil that was continually stirred by political agitation; the frame of future republics knit itself, as it were in embryo, under a monarchical system of colonial rule; till in the middle of the eighteenth century the approach of mighty changes began to be dimly foreseen by gifted spirits. A faint streak of purple light blushed along the eastern sky.

Two things worth mentioning contributed to the result. One was the absence of the precious metals. The British colonies were rich in the want of gold. As the abundance of gold and silver in Mexico and Peru contributed, in various ways, to obstruct the prosperity of the Spanish colonies, the want of them acted not less favorably here. In the first settlement of a savage wilderness the golden attraction is too powerful for the ordinary routine of life. It produces a feverish excitement unfavorable to the healthy growth and calm action of the body politic. Although California has from the first had the advantage of being incorporated into a stable political system, of which, as a sister State, she forms an integral part, it is quite doubtful whether, looking to her permanent well-being, the gold is to be a blessing to her. It will hasten her settlement; but that would at any rate have advanced with great rapidity. One of the most intellectual men in this country, the author of one of the most admirable works in our language, I mean "Two Years before the Mast," once remarked to me, that "California would be one of the finest countries in the world to live in, if it were not for the gold."

The other circumstance which operated in the most favorable manner upon the growth of the Anglo-American colonies was the fact, that they were called into existence less by the government than the people; that they were mainly settled, not by bodies of colonists, but by individual immigrants. The crown gave charters of government and grants of land, and a considerable expenditure was made by some of the companies and proprietors who received these grants; but upon the whole, the United States were settled by individuals, — the adventurous, resolute, high-spirited, and in many cases persecuted men and women, who sought a home and a refuge beyond the sea; and such was the state of Europe in the seventeenth and eighteenth centuries, that it furnished a succession of victims of a long series of political and religious disasters and persecutions, who found, one after another, a safe and a congenial retreat in some one of the American colonies.

This noble theme has been treated with a beauty and a power, by one whom I need not name in this presence, (the historian of the United States,) which, without impairing their authenticity, have converted the severe pages of our history into a magnificent Odyssey of national adventure. I can but glance at the dates. The first settlement, that of Virginia, was commenced in the spirit of worldly enterprise, with no slight dash, however, of chivalry and romance on the part of its leader. In the next generation this colony became the favorite resort of the loyal cavaliers and gentlemen who were disgusted by the austerities of the English Commonwealth, or fell under its suspicion. In the mean time, New England was founded by those who suffered the penalties of non-conformity. The mighty change of 1640 stopped the tide of emigration to New England, but recruited Virginia with those who were disaffected to Cromwell. In 1624 the island of Manhattan, of which you have perhaps heard, and if not, you will find its history related with learning, judgment, and good taste, by a loyal descendant of its early settlers (Mr. Brodhead), was purchased of the Indians for twenty-four dollars; a sum of money, by the way, which seems rather low for twenty-two thousand acres of land, including the site of this great metropolis, but which would, if put out at compound interest at seven per cent. in 1624, not perhaps fall so very much below even its present value; though I admit that a dollar for a thousand acres is quite cheap for choice spots on the Fifth Avenue. Maryland next attracted those who adhered to the ancient faith of the Christian world. New Jersey and Pennsylvania were mainly settled by persecuted Quakers; but the latter offered an asylum to the Germans whom the sword of Louis the Fourteenth drove from the Palatinate. The French Huguenots, driven out by the revocation of the Edict of Nantes, scattered themselves from Massachusetts to Carolina. The Dutch and Swedish settlements on the Hudson and the Delaware provided a kindred home for such of their countrymen as desired to try the fortune of the New World. The Whigs of England who rebelled against James the Second in 1685, and were sent to the Transatlantic colonies, lived long enough to meet in exile the adherents of his son, who rebelled against George the First, in 1715. The oppressed Protestants of Salzburg came with General Oglethorpe to Georgia; and the Highlanders who fought for Charles Edward, in 1745, were deported by hundreds to North Carolina. They were punished by being sent from their bleak hills and sterile moors to a land of abundance and liberty; they were banished from oatmeal porridge to meat twice a day. The Gaelic language is still spoken by their descendants, and thousands of their kindred at the present day would no doubt gladly share their exile.

There is no doubt that the hardships which awaited the

emigrant at that early day were neither few nor slight, though greatly exaggerated for want of information. Goldsmith, in "The Deserted Village," published in 1769, gives us a somewhat amusing picture of the state of things as he supposed it to exist beyond the ocean at that time. As his local allusion is to Georgia, it is probable that he formed his impressions from the accounts which were published at London about the middle of the last century by some of the discontented settlers of that colony. Goldsmith, being well acquainted with General Oglethorpe, was likely enough to have had his attention called to the subject. Perhaps you will allow me to enliven my dull prose with a few lines of his beautiful poetry. After describing the sufferings of the poor in London at that time, reverting to the condition of the inhabitants of his imaginary Auburn, and asking whether they probably shared the woes he had just painted, he thus answers his question: —

"Ah, no! To distant climes, a dreary scene,
Where half the convex world intrudes between,
Through torrid tracts with fainting steps they go,
Where wild Altama murmurs to their woe.
Far different there from all that charmed before,
The various terrors of that horrid shore:
Those blazing suns that dart a downward ray,
And fiercely shed intolerable day;
Those matted woods, where birds forget to sing,
But silent bats in drowsy clusters cling;
Those poisonous fields with rank luxuriance crowned,
Where the dark scorpion gathers death around, —
Where, at each step, the stranger fears to wake
The rattling terrors of the vengeful snake, —
Where crouching tigers wait their hapless prey,
And savage men more murderous still than they;
While oft in whirls the mad tornado flies,
Mingling the ravaged landscape with the skies."

In this rather uninviting sketch, it must be confessed that it is not easy to recognize the natural features of that thriving State, which possesses at the present day a thousand miles of railroad, and which, by her rapidly increasing population, her liberal endowment of colleges, schools, and churches, and all the other social institutions of a highly improved community, is fast earning the name of the "Empire State" of the South.

After repeating these lines, it is scarcely necessary to say that there was much ignorance and exaggeration prevailing in Europe as to the state of things in America. But a few years after Goldsmith's poem appeared, an event occurred which aroused and fixed the attention of the world. The revolt of the Colonies in 1775, the Declaration of Independence in 1776, the battles of the Revolutionary war, the alliance with France, the acknowledgment of American Independence by the treaty of 1783, the establishment of a great federative republic, the illustrious career of Lafayette, the European reputation of Franklin, and, above all, the character of Washington, gave to the United States a great and brilliant name in the family of nations. Thousands in every part of Europe then probably heard of America, with any distinct impressions, for the first time; and they now heard of it as a region realizing the wildest visions. Hundreds in every walk of life began to resort to America, and especially ardent young men, who were dissatisfied with the political condition of Europe. Among these was your late venerable President, Albert Gallatin, one of the most eminent men of the last generation, who came to this country before he attained his majority; and the late celebrated Sir Isambert Brunel, the architect of the Thames Tunnel. He informed me that he became a citizen of the State of New York before the adoption of the Federal Constitution, and that he made some surveys to ascertain the practicability of the great work which afterwards united the waters of Lake Erie with the waters of the Atlantic, and gave immortality to the name of your Clinton.

Before the Revolution, the great West was shut even to the subjects of England. A royal proclamation of 1763 forbade the extension of the settlements in North America beyond the Ohio. But without such a prohibition, the still unbroken power of the Indian tribes would have prevented any such extension. The successful result of the Revolutionary war did not materially alter the state of things in this respect. The native tribes were still formidable, and the British posts in the Northwestern Territory were retained. So little confidence was placed in the value of a title to land, even within the limits of the State of New York, that the enterprising citizens of Massachusetts, Messrs. Gorham and Phelps, who bought six millions of acres of land on the Genesee River, shortly after the Peace, for a few cents the acre, were obliged to abandon the greater part of the purchase from the difficulty of finding under-purchasers enough to enable them to meet the first instalments.

On one occasion, when Judge Gorham was musing in a state of mental depression on the failure of this magnificent speculation, he was visited by a friend and townsman, who had returned from a journey to Canandaigua, then just laid out. This friend tried to cheer the Judge with a bright vision of the future growth of Western New York. Kindling with his theme, he pointed to a son of Judge Gorham, who was in the room, and added, "You and I shall not live to see the day, but that lad, if he reaches threescore years and ten, will see a daily stage-coach running as far west as Canandaigua!" That lad is still living. What he has seen in the shape of travel and conveyance in the State of New York, it is not necessary before this audience to say.

It was the adoption of the Constitution of the United States, in 1789, which gave stability to the Union and confidence to the people. This was the Promethean fire, which kindled the body politic into vital action. It created a national force. The Indians on the southwest were pacified. On the northwestern frontier the troops of the general government were at first defeated; but after the victory of Wayne, and the peace of Greeneville, in 1795, the British posts were surrendered, and the tide of emigration began to pour in. It was rather, however, from the older States than from foreign countries.

The extensive region northwest of the Ohio had already received its political organization as a territory of the United States by the ever-memorable Ordinance of 1787.

While Providence was thus opening on this continent the broadest region that ever was made accessible to human progress, want, or adventure, it happened that the kingdoms of Europe were shaken by the terrible convulsions incident to the French Revolution. France herself first, and afterwards the countries overrun by her revolutionary armies, poured forth their children by thousands. I believe there are no official returns of the number of immigrants to the United States at the time, but it was very large. Among them was M. de Talleyrand, the celebrated minister of every government in France, from that of the Directory, in 1797, to that of Louis Philippe, in whose reign he died. I saw at Peale's Museum, in Philadelphia, the original oath of allegiance, subscribed by him in 1794.* Louis Philippe himself emigrated to this country, where he passed three years, and is well remembered by many persons still living. He habitually spoke with gratitude of the kindness which he experienced in every part of the Union.

As yet, no acquisition of territory had been made by the United States beyond the limits of the British colonies; but in 1803 a most important step was taken in the purchase of

---

* Since this lecture was delivered, I have been favored with a copy of this paper by Edward D. Ingraham, Esq., of Philadelphia. It is in the following words: —

"I, Charles Maurice Talleyrand Perigord, formerly Administrator of the Department of Paris, son of Joseph Daniel de Talleyrand Perigord, a General of the Armies of France, born at Paris and arrived at Philadelphia from London, do swear that I will be faithful and bear true allegiance to the Commonwealth of Pennsylvania and to the United States of America, and that I will not at any time wilfully and knowingly do any matter or thing prejudicial to the freedom and independence thereof.

"CH. MAU. DE TALLEYRAND PERIGORD.

"Sworn the 19th May, 1794,
Before MATTH. CLARKSON, *Mayor.*"

Louisiana, by which our possessions were extended, though with an unsettled boundary both on the south and the north, to the Pacific Ocean. The war in 1812 reduced the Indian tribes in the Northwestern States; and the campaigns of General Jackson a few years later produced the same effect on the southern frontier. Florida was acquired by treaty from Spain in 1819; and the Indians in Georgia, Alabama, and Mississippi were removed to the west of the river Mississippi ten or twelve years later. Black Hawk's war in Wisconsin took place in 1833, and a series of Indian treaties, both before and after that event, extinguished the Indian title to all the land east of the Mississippi, and to considerable tracts west of that river. Texas was annexed to the Union in 1845, and in 1848 New Mexico and California came into our possession.

I have, as you perceive, run rapidly over these dates, compressing into one paragraph the starting-points in the history of future commonwealths, simply in their bearing on the subject of immigration. These acquisitions, not inferior in extent to all that there was solid in the Roman conquests, have resulted in our possession of a zone of territory of the width of twenty degrees of latitude, stretching from ocean to ocean, and nearly equal in extent to the whole of Europe.* It is all subject to the power of the United States; a portion of it has attained the civilization of the Old World, while other portions shade off through all degrees of culture, to the log-house of the frontier settler, the cabin of the trapper, and the wigwam of the savage. Within this vast domain there are millions of acres of fertile land, to be purchased at moderate prices, according to its position and its state of improvement, and there are hundreds of millions of acres in a state of nature, and gradually selling at the government price of a dollar and a quarter per acre.

---

* Square miles in the United States, 3,260,073; in Europe, 3,700,971. — *American Almanac* for 1853, pp. 315 and 316.

It is this which most strikes the European imagination. The Old World is nearly all appropriated by individuals. There are public domains in most foreign countries, but of comparatively small amount, and mostly forests. With this exception, every acre of land in Europe is private property, and in such countries as England, the Netherlands, France, Germany, and Italy, what little changes hands is sold only at a high price. I presume the number of landholders in England is far less than in the State of New York. In the course of the French Revolution the land has been greatly divided and subdivided in France and in Germany, and is now held in small farms; but owing to the limited quantity of purchasable land, these farms, when sold, are sold only at high prices. Generally speaking, the mass of the inhabitants of Europe regard the ability to hold and occupy a considerable landed property as the summit of human fortune. The suggestion that there is a country beyond the ocean, where fertile land is to be purchased, in any quantity, at a dollar and a quarter per acre, and that dollar and a quarter to be earned in many parts of the country by the labor of a single day, strikes them as the tales of Aladdin's lamp or Ali Baba's cave would strike us, if we thought they were true. They forget the costs and sacrifices of leaving home, the ocean to be traversed, the weary pilgrimage in the land of strangers after their arrival. They see nothing with the mind's eye but the " *land* of promise "; they reflect upon nothing but the fact, that there is a region on the earth's surface where a few days' unskilled labor will purchase the fee-simple of an ample farm.

Such an attraction would be irresistible under any circumstances to the population of an old country, where, as I have just said, the land is all appropriated, and to be purchased, in any considerable quantity, only at prices which put its acquisition beyond the thought of the masses. But this is but half the tale. It must not be forgotten that in this ancient and venerable Europe, whose civilization is the growth of two thousand years, where some of the luxurious refinements of life are carried to a perfection of which we have scarcely an idea in this country, a considerable part of the population, even in the most prosperous regions, pass their lives in a state but one remove from starvation, — poorly fed, poorly clothed, poorly housed, without education, without political privileges, without moral culture. The average wages of the agricultural laborer in England were estimated a year ago at 9*s.* 6*d.* sterling — about $ 2.37½ — per week. The condition of the working population on the continent of Europe is in no degree better, if as good. They eat but little animal food either in England or on the Continent. We form romantic notions at a distance of countries that abound in wine and oil; but in the best governed states of Italy, — in Tuscany, for instance, — the peasantry, though they pass their lives in the vineyard and the olive-orchard, consume the fruit of neither. I have seen the Tuscan peasants, unable to bear the cost of the most ordinary wine from the vineyards in which their cottages are embowered, and which can be bought at retail for a cent a flask, pouring water over the grape-skins as they come from the press, and making that their beverage.

Even for persons in comparatively easy circumstances in Europe, there are strong inducements to emigrate to America. Most of the governments are arbitrary, the taxes are oppressive, the exactions of military service onerous in the extreme. Add to all this the harassing insecurity of life. For sixty or seventy years the Continent has been one wide theatre of scarcely intermitted convulsion. Every country in it has been involved in war; there is scarcely one that has not passed through a revolution. We read of events like these in the newspapers, we look upon them with curiosity as articles of mere intelligence, or they awaken images of our own revolution, which we regard only with joyous associations. Far different the state of things in crowded Europe, of which the fairest fields are trampled in every generation by mighty armies into bloody mire! Dazzled by the brilliancy of the military exploits of which we read at a safe distance, we forget the anxieties of those who grow up within the sound of the cannon's roar, whose prospects in life are ruined, their business broken up, their little accumulations swept away by the bankruptcy of governments or the general paralysis of the industry of the country, their sons torn from them by ruthless conscriptions, the means of educating and bringing up their families consumed in a day by disastrous emergencies. Terrified by the recent experience or the tradition of these miseries, thousands emigrate to the land of promise, flying before, not merely the presence, but the "rumor of war," which the Great Teacher places on a level with the reality.

Ever and anon some sharp specific catastrophe gives an intense activity to emigration. When France, in the lowest depth of her Revolution, plunged to a lower depth of suffering and crime, when the Reign of Terror was enthroned, and when every thing in any way conspicuous, whether for station, wealth, talent, or service, of every age and of either sex, from the crowned monarch to the gray-haired magistrate and the timid maiden, was brought to the guillotine, hundreds of thousands escaped at once from the devoted kingdom. The convulsions of San Domingo drove most of the European population of that island to the United States. But beyond every thing else which has been witnessed in modern times, the famine which prevailed a few years since in Ireland gave a terrific impulse to emigration. Not less, probably, than one million of her inhabitants left her shores within five years. The population of this island, as highly favored in the gifts of nature as any spot on the face of the earth, has actually diminished more than 1,800,000 since the famine year; * the only example, perhaps, in history, of a similar result in a country not visited by foreign war or civil convulsion. The population ought, in the course of nature, to have increased within ten years by at least that amount; and in point of fact, between 1840 and 1850, our own population increased by more than six millions.

---

* *London Quarterly Review* for December, 1851, p. 191.

This prodigious increase of the population of the United States is partly owing to the emigration from foreign countries, which has taken place under the influence of the causes general and specific, to which I have alluded. Of late years, from three to four hundred thousand immigrants are registered at the several custom-houses, as arriving in this country in the course of a year. It is probable that a third as many more enter by the Canadian frontier. Not much less than two millions of immigrants are supposed to have entered the United States in the last ten years; and it is calculated that there are living at the present day in the United States five millions of persons, foreigners who have immigrated since 1790, and their descendants.

There is nothing in the annals of mankind to be compared to this; but there is a series of great movements which may be contrasted with it. In the period of a thousand years, which began about three or four hundred years before our Saviour, the Roman republic and empire were from time to time invaded by warlike races from the North and East, who burst with overwhelming force upon the South and West of Europe, and repeatedly carried desolation to the gates of Rome. These multitudinous invaders were not armies of men, they were in reality nations of hostile emigrants. They came with their wives, with their "young barbarians," with their Scythian cavalry, and their herds of cattle; and they came with no purpose of going away. The *animus manendi* was made up before they abandoned their ice-clad homes; they left their Arctic allegiance behind them. They found the sunny banks of the Arno and the Rhone more pleasant than those of the Don and the Volga. Unaccustomed to the sight of any tree more inviting than the melancholy fir and the stunted birch, its branches glittering with snowy crystals,—brought up under a climate where the generous fruits are unknown, — these children of the North were not so much fascinated as bewildered "in the land of the citron and myrtle"; they gazed with delighted astonishment at the spreading elm, festooned with Falernian clusters; they clutched, with a kind of frantic joy, at the fruit of the fig-tree and the olive; — at the melting peach, the luscious plum, the golden orange, and the pomegranate, whose tinted cheek outblushes every thing but the living carnation of youthful love.

> " With grim delight the brood of winter view
> A brighter day and heavens of azure hue,
> Scent the new fragrance of the breathing rose,
> And quaff the pendent vintage as it grows."

By the fortune of war, single detachments and even mighty armies frequently suffered defeat; but their place was immediately taken by new hordes, which fell upon declining Rome as the famished wolves in one of Catlin's pictures fall upon an aged buffalo in our Western prairies. The imperial monster, powerful even in his decrepitude, would often scatter their undisciplined array with his iron tusks, and trample them by thousands under his brazen feet; but when he turned back, torn and bleeding, to his seven hills, tens of thousands came howling from the Northern forests, who sprang at his throat and buried their fangs in his lacerated side. Wherever they conquered, and in the end they conquered everywhere, they established themselves on the soil, invited new-comers, and from their union with the former inhabitants, the nations of the South and West of Europe, at the present day, for the most part, trace their descent.

We know but little of the numbers thus thrown in upon the Roman republic and empire in the course of eight or ten centuries. They were, no doubt, greatly exaggerated by the panic fear of the inhabitants; and the pride of the Roman historians would lead them to magnify the power before which their own legions had so often quailed. But when we consider the difficulty of subsisting a large number of persons in a march through an unfriendly country, and this at a time when much of the now cultivated portion of Europe was covered with forest and swamp, I am disposed to think that the hosts which for a succession of centuries overran the Roman empire did not in the aggregate exceed in numbers the immigrants that have arrived in the United States since 1790. In other words, I am inclined to believe, that within the last sixty years the Old World has poured in upon the United States a number of persons as great, with their natural increase, as Asia sent into Europe in these armed migrations of barbarous races.

Here, of course, the parallel ends. The races that invaded Europe came to lay waste and to subjugate; the hosts that cross the Atlantic are peaceful immigrants. The former burst upon the Roman empire, and by oft-repeated strokes beat it to the ground. The immigrants to America from all countries come to cast in their lot with the native citizens, and to share with us this great inheritance of civil and religious liberty. The former were ferocious barbarians, half clad in skins, speaking strange tongues, worshipping strange gods with bloody rites. The latter are the children of the countries from which the first European settlers of this continent proceeded, and belong, with us, to the great common family of Christendom. The former destroyed the culture of the ancient world, and it was only after a thousand years that a better civilization grew up from its ruins. The millions who have established themselves in America within sixty years are, from the moment of their arrival, gradually absorbed into the mass of the population, conforming to the laws and moulding themselves to the manners of the country, and contributing their share to its prosperity and strength.

It is a curious coincidence, that, as the first mighty wave of the hostile migration that burst upon Europe before the time of our Saviour consisted of tribes belonging to the great Celtic race, the remains of which, identified by their original dialect, are still found in Brittany, in Wales, in the Highlands of Scotland, and especially in Ireland, so by far the greater portion of the new and friendly immigration to the United States consists of persons belonging to the same ardent, true-hearted, and too often oppressed race. I have heard, in the villages of Wales and the Highlands of Scotland, the Gospel preached in substantially the same language in which Brennus uttered his haughty summons to Rome, and in which the mystic songs of the Druids were chanted in the depths of the primeval forests of France and England, in the time of Julius Cæsar. It is still spoken by thousands of Scotch, Welsh, and Irish immigrants, in all parts of the United States.*

This great Celtic race is one of the most remarkable that has appeared in history. Whether it belongs to that extensive Indo-European family of nations, which, in ages before the dawn of history, took up a line of march in two columns from Lower India, and, moving westward by both a northern and a southern route, finally diffused itself over Western Asia, Northern Africa, and the greater part of Europe; or whether, as others suppose, the Celtic race belongs

---

* A learned and friendly correspondent, of Welsh origin, is of opinion that I have fallen into a "gross error, in classing the Irish, Welsh, and Scotch as one race of people, or Celts, whose language is the same. The slightest acquaintance," he adds, "with the Welsh and Irish languages would convince you that they were totally different. A Welshman cannot understand one word of Irish, neither can the latter understand one word of Welsh."

In a popular view of the subject this may be correct, in like manner as the Anglo-Saxon, the Teutonic, and Scandinavian races would, in a popular use of the terms, be considered as distinct races, speaking languages mutually unintelligible. But the etymologist regards their languages as substantially the same; and ethnographically these nations belong to one and the same stock.

There are certainly many points, in reference to the ancient history of the Celts, on which learned men greatly differ, and at which it was impossible that I should even glance in the superficial allusions which my limits admitted. But there is no point on which ethnographers are better agreed, than that the Bretons, Welsh, Irish, and Highland Scotch belong to the Celtic race, representing, no doubt, different national families, which acquired each its distinctive dialect at a very early period.

Dr. Prichard (the leading authority on questions of this kind), after comparing the remains of the ancient Celtic language, as far as they can now be traced in proper names, says: 'We must hence conclude that the dialect of the ancient Gauls was nearly allied to the Welsh, and much more remotely related to the Erse and Gaelic." — *Researches into the Physical History of Mankind*, Vol. III. p. 135. See also Latham's *English Language*, p. 74.

to a still older stock, and was itself driven down upon the South and into the West of Europe by the overwhelming force of the Indo-Europeans, is a question which we have no time at present to discuss. However it may be decided, it would seem that for the first time, as far as we are acquainted with the fortunes of this interesting race, they have found themselves in a really prosperous condition in this country. Driven from the soil in the West of Europe, to which their fathers clung for two thousand years, they have at length, and for the first time in their entire history, found a real home in a land of strangers. Having been told, in the frightful language of political economy, that at the daily table which Nature spreads for the human family there is no cover laid for them in Ireland, they have crossed the ocean, to find occupation, shelter, and bread on a foreign but friendly soil.

This "Celtic Exodus," as it has been aptly called, is to all the parties immediately connected with it one of the most important events of the day. To the emigrants themselves it may be regarded as a passing from death to life. It will benefit Ireland by reducing a surplus population, and restoring a sounder and juster relation of capital and labor. It will benefit the laboring classes in England, where wages have been kept down to the starvation-point by the struggle between the native population and the inhabitants of the sister island for that employment and food, of which there is not enough for both. This benefit will extend from England to ourselves, and will lessen the pressure of that competition which our labor is obliged to sustain, with the ill-paid labor of Europe. In addition to all this, the constant influx into America of stout and efficient hands supplies the greatest want in a new country, which is that of labor, gives value to land, and facilitates the execution of every species of private enterprise and public work.

I am not insensible to the temporary inconveniences which are to be offset against these advantages, on both sides of the water. Much suffering attends the emigrant there, on his passage, and after his arrival. It is possible that the value of our native labor may have been depressed by too sudden and extensive a supply from abroad; and it is certain that our asylums and almshouses are crowded with foreign inmates, and that the resources of public and private benevolence have been heavily drawn upon. These are considerable evils, but they have perhaps been exaggerated.

It must be remembered, in the first place, that the immigration daily pouring in from Europe is by no means a pauper immigration. On the contrary, it is already regarded with apprehension abroad, as occasioning a great abstraction of capital. How the case may be in Great Britain and Ireland, I have seen no precise statement; but it is asserted on apparently good grounds, that the consumption and abstraction of capital caused by immigration from Germany amounts annually to twenty millions of rix-dollars, or fifteen millions of our currency.*

No doubt, foreign immigation is attended with an influx of foreign pauperism. In reference to this, I believe your system of public relief is better here in New York than ours in Massachusetts, in which, however, we are making important changes. It is said, that, owing to some defect in our system, or its administration, we support more than our share of needy foreigners. They are sent in upon us from other States. New York, as the greatest seaport, must be exposed also to more than her proportionate share of the burden. However the evil arises, it may no doubt be mitigated by judicious legislation; and in the mean time Massachusetts and New York might do a worse thing with a por-

---

* In an instructive article relative to the German emigration in Otto Hübner's *Jahrbuch für Volkswirthschaft und Statistik*, the numbers who emigrated from Germany, from 1846 to 1851 inclusive, are estimated to have amounted to an annual average of 96,676, and the amount of capital abstracted by them from the country to an average of 19,370,333 rix-dollars (about fifteen million Spanish dollars) per annum.

tion of their surplus means than feed the hungry, clothe the naked, give a home to the stranger, and kindle the spark of reason in the mind of the poor foreign lunatic, even though that lunatic may have been (as I am ashamed, for the credit of humanity, to say has happened) set on shore in the night from a coasting-vessel, and found in the morning in the fields, half dead with cold, and hunger, and fright.

But you say, "They are foreigners." Well, do we owe no duties to foreigners? What was the founder of Virginia, when a poor Indian girl threw herself between him and the war-club of her father, and saved his life at the risk of her own? What were the Pilgrim Fathers, when the friendly savage, if we must call him so, met them with his little vocabulary of kindness, learned among the fishermen on the Grand Bank, — "Welcome, Englishmen"? "They are foreigners." And suppose they are? Was not the country all but ready, a year or two ago, to plunge into a conflict with the military despotisms of the East of Europe, in order to redress the wrongs of the oppressed races who feed their flocks on the slopes of the Carpathians, and pasture their herds upon the tributaries of the Danube, and do we talk of the hardship of relieving destitute foreigners, whom the hand of God has guided across the ocean and conducted to our doors?

Must we learn a lesson of benevolence from the ancient heathen? Let us then learn it. The whole theatre at Rome stood up and shouted their sympathetic applause, when the actor in one of Terence's plays exclaimed, "I am a man; nothing that is human is foreign to me."

I am not indifferent to the increase of the public burdens; but the time has been when I have felt a little proud of the vast sums paid in the United States for the relief of poor immigrants from Europe. It is an annual sum, I have no doubt, equal to the interest on the foreign debt of the States which have repudiated their obligations. When I was in London, a few years ago, I received a letter from one of the interior counties of England, telling me that they had in their house of correction an American seaman, (or a person who pretended to be,) who from their account seemed to be both pauper and rogue. They were desirous of being rid of him, and kindly offered to place him at my disposal. Although he did not bid fair to be a very valuable acquisition, I wrote back that he might be sent to London, where, if he was a sailor, he could be shipped by the American Consul to the United States, if not, to be disposed of in some other way. I ventured to add the suggestion, that if her Majesty's Minister at Washington were applied to in a similar way by the overseers of the poor and wardens of the prisons in the United States, he would be pretty busily occupied. But I really felt pleased, at a time when my own little State of Massachusetts was assisting from ten to twelve thousand destitute British subjects annually, to be able to relieve the British empire, on which the sun never sets, of the only American pauper quartered upon it.

Ladies and gentlemen, my humble tale is told. In thanking you for your most kind attention, let me remind you that its first incident is Columbus, begging bread for his child at the gate of a convent. Its last finds you the stewards of this immense abundance, the almoners of this more than imperial charity, providing employment and food for starving nations, and a home for fugitive races.

AN ADDRESS

BEFORE THE

NEW ENGLAND SOCIETY,

ANN ARBOR,

BY REV. AZARIAH ELDRIDGE.

AN ADDRESS

DELIVERED BEFORE THE

NEW ENGLAND SOCIETY,

IN ANN ARBOR, MICH.,

ON

Fore - Fathers Day,

DECEMBER 22, 1860,

BY

REV. AZARIAH ELDRIDGE,

OF DETROIT.

ANN ARBOR:
ELIHU B. POND, PRINTER,
1861.

CORRESPONDENCE.

ANN ARBOR, Dec. 31, 1860.

REV. A. ELDRIDGE,

DEAR SIR:—A number of our citizens are desirous of circulating the very eloquent Address which you delivered at the late anniversary of the New England Society. I therefore take this opportunity of requesting a copy for publication.

Yours Respectfully,

J. L. TAPPAN, *Cor. Sec'y.*

MR. J. L. TAPPAN,

DEAR SIR:—Your kind note of a recent date in respect to my Pilgrim Address at Ann Arbor has been duly received; and enclosed herewith you will find a copy of the same.

Yours, very truly,

AZARIAH ELDRIDGE.

January 2nd, 1861.

PILGRIM ADDRESS.

MR. PRESIDENT, LADIES AND GENTLEMEN :

IT IS pleasant and profitable to look upon the past; and among by-gone experiences, no event is more important and interesting than the commencement of individual, or national existence. Our present stature, as a united people; the wonderful run of success and development, by which we have grown to this greatness and power, help to render that small and forlorn beginning, on the bleak shore of New England, which we are now here to celebrate, peculiarly significant and attractive. Our minds and hearts are drawn to it, on the seasonable recurrence of these filial and patriotic festivities, as to a point where providence was planting and causing to germinate, among rocks and sterility, a mighty plan to change the face of this Western Continent, and turn the destinies of the whole World. There was no parade, pomp, nor circumstance about it; and there seldom is, where great events are coming to pass. The nation was born, in those colonial scenes, as it were, in a manger; and with as little demonstration as when an acorn, presse'd into the earth by a heedless tread among the trees, begins to take root; or a rivulet, turned by some obstruction, trickles at a new point from the hillside.

But a singular interest, especially for those in the true line of descent, attaches to those remarkable men, and to their more remarkable work. Every incident, from the day they left Holland, or rather England, to the time the colony was recognized as a success, has a charm for us which is ever new. Who, that has Puritan blood in him, but loves to think and feel how calmly they endured reproach; how nobly, gave up the comforts of home; how steadily, passed through the perils of the sea; how bravely, took hold of and mastered the difficulties of their new position, and the problem they had undertaken to solve?

What an address was that, from the learned and saintly Robinson, to which they listened, on casting off from the old world! Was there ever such an occasion! Ever such a body of men and women assembled! Ever such words of wisdom and courage spoken by uninspired man! In vain I search the pages of history and literature for the like. So tender, and yet firm; so solemn, and cheering; so well fitted to make heroes of the hearers, and martyrs, if need should be. How thoughtful and timely, that remarkable passage, to liberate the more rigid from undue bondage to dogma and the letter, wherein he said, so much in advance of his age, "And, if God reveal anything to you, by any other instrument of his, be as ready to receive it as ever you were to receive anything by my ministry; for I am verily persuaded that the Lord has more truth yet to break out of his holy word."

But at length they were ready, and upon the eve of final departure. Having finished their preliminary sojourn in Holland, and made preparation to sail, the Speedwell had started and returned, and her crew been some of them transferred to the May Flower, when, on the 6th of September, this vessel of one hundred and eighty tons burthen finally set sail from Dreft-Haven alone. The days had already begun to shorten; autumnal storms, to visit the Atlantic; and the voyage, proved a tempestuous one. In the wrenching of the ship one day, a strong timber threatened to break, "but a great iron screw was found," and the ship saved. While they were at sea one man died, whose name was William Button; and one child was born, to Mrs. Hopkins, which they named Oceanus. So that the number of one hundred and two, with which they put forth, was preserved until they came to land.

On the 11th of November they cast anchor, within the sheltering arm of Cape Cod, which seemed to come down from the rocky interior of New England, and extend itself far into the sea, to meet them and encircle them within its embrace. They were aiming to go farther south, and find the Hudson, if possible, but were caught and detained by this out-reaching arm of the old Bay State. Within what is now Provincetown harbor, they found themselves enclosed from the winds and waves of the Atlantic, in one of the finest roadsteads known to the sons of the Ocean. This was on Saturday afternoon. Sixty-seven weary days had they passed in the ship.—On Sunday they rested, and on Monday, the 13th, they sent ashore sixteen men armed with musket, sword and corslet, and headed by Miles

Standish. Very sandy, they found it, and sterile. Few signs of life were discovered until the fourth day, when they saw five or six Indians, with a dog; who ran away swiftly, and whistled the dog after them. This whistling of the dog, one historian thinks, must have done something towards assuring the wanderers. They sent parties along the shore, and into the woods, to explore. At length, on a plain, they came to what looked like a grave and "musing what it might be," they resolved to examine, and found, under some mats, a bag, with a bow by it; and not far off, a smaller bag, with a little bow. In the first, there was a quantity of fine red powder, together with the skull and bones of a man; in the second, more of the powder, with the skull and bones of a child. Here then, was an Indian grave. In another, which was subsequently opened, there was a quantity of corn, in a little old basket; and on digging further, they came to a fine large basket, full of fair corn, with thirty-six goodly ears at the top, which two of them could scarcely lift, but which they added to the common stock, promising, "so soon as we could meet any of the inhabitants of that place, to make them large satisfaction."

So they spent a week or two, while their boat was repairing, and during that time, being compelled to wade much to and from the ship, some of them caught the "original of their death." Then, having ascertained that the point where they were was not the one at which to establish themselves permanently, Carver, Bradford, Winslow, Standish, and ten more started forth with the boat, on an exploring trip, along the shore. They followed the coast round on the inside of Cape Cod, for some seventy miles. It was very cold; the sea broke over them repeatedly; the water froze to their garments and "made them many times like coats of iron." At a certain point one of their party, who had gone up from the shore, soon ran back, crying, "Indians," and was followed by a flight of arrows. But Standish was ready; and returning the fire, which checked the savages, they again put to sea. Then a storm came on, with snow and hail; the mast was carried away by the wind; and they knew not which way to turn; but at length, gained the land, and found it to be an island Clark's Island—secure from Indians. That was Saturday, again, and there they resolved to spend the Sabbath, which was their first one ashore, and they had such service as the circumstances would permit, with only

> A screen of leafless branches
> Between them and the blast.

On Monday, the 11th, old style, the 22d, as we reckon it, of December, they sounded the harbor, near the mouth of which they found themselves, and finding it good, they went over to a rock, on the shore of the main land, and stepping upon it from their boat, marched up from the water's edge. There were corn-fields before them. That rock was Plymouth Rock! That Monday is what we now know and celebrate as Fore-Fathers Day!

The rest of their company were sent for, and came to them, with the ship. Soon the sound of axes, and saws, and hammers was heard. Their blows were heavy, their hearts were earnest, and their hands strong. The arrangement was for each man to build his own house. These were planted near together, in two parallel rows, for purposes of defence. So they toiled on, during the winter, without interruption from the natives. The latter were hostile, owing to the kidnapping enterprise of a slave trader named Hunt, but had been mostly swept away from the neighborhood of Plymouth, by a pestilence. Their ordinary labors were relieved, occasionally, by expeditions for hunting and fishing.

I find on record the trying experience of two Pilgrims, who lost themselves while hunting, with a great female mastiff, and wandered about all night, "They heard in the night, as they thought, two lions roaring exceedingly for a long time together, and a third that they thought very near them. Not knowing what to do, they resolved to climb up in a tree, as their safest refuge, though that would prove an intolerably cold lodging; so they stood at the tree's root, that when the lions came they might take their opportunity of climbing up. The bitch they were fain to hold by the neck, for she would have been gone to the lion; but it pleased GOD so to dispose that the wild beasts came not, so they walked up and down under the tree all night; it was an exceedingly cold night."

But those trials and perils, alas! were not many of them imaginary. When Spring came, death had been busy among them. The wife of Bradford was drowned in Province-town harbor; and, of the remaining one hundred and one, six died in December; eight, in January; seventeen, in February; and thirteen, in March. The women suffered most, as might be expected, but there was no murmuring or complaint. Miles Standish, the warrior, was seen passing from house to house, an angel of tenderness and mercy. Quietly they suffered and died, as in a holy cause; and the living suppressed their tears and sighs. The dead, they buried in the hillside, near the rock, and smoothed the graves away, and sowed them over with grass, that the Indians might not infer, by counting them, the weakness of the colony, which kept at work as before. The summit of the ascent was graded, and a fortification begun there. It soon bristled with cannon, and beneath the platform which supported these, was the room in which they worshiped God on Sunday, marching to it armed, and leaving their weapons stacked at the entrance.

But at length Spring came, as I have said, after the long winter; and it is on record how sweetly the singing of the birds sounded in their ears. There was also a pleasanter sound still came to some of them, one day in the middle of March, in the fine English word, "Welcome, Welcome," kindly, though imperfectly, uttered by a savage, who suddenly stood before them. It was Samoset. He told them of Hunt and the pestilence. In a few days he returned, with more savages, including Squanto, who had been one of those slaves and escaped. And so intercourse with the natives began.

With fine weather, the time for planting arrived, and also, for the departure of the May Flower. This was a trying separation. The good ship, lying in the harbor, visited from time to time, was a comforting feature of the scene, and seemed like a link of connection, if not a dernier means of escape, between them and the Father land. When that vessel was gone, the wide ocean would be before them, a continent of wild beasts and savages behind them, yet not one of them thought to return in her. Not a man, woman, or child, of those who had come to remain, went back to England in the May Flower. Her work was done in bringing them out. They had come to remain and establish themselves, and were not the people to abandon an enterprise once undertaken. And yet the prospect was far from promising, to an ordinary set of men, engaged in an ordinary expedition. The London Merchants, who had put in a small venture, were very much disheartened, but not so the Pilgrim Fathers themselves. They were not discouraged, when their first crop proved a short one. They did not think of being so, when the summer of the second year proved unpropitious; nor when the ship Fortune came, bringing more men and no provisions; nor even when an Indian messenger appeared among them, and, dropping a bundle of arrows tied up in a rattle-snake's skin, fled swiftly out of their village. It was a declaration of war, from Canonicut the chief of five thousand Narraganset warriors. But Miles Standish took up the skin, filled it with powder and ball, and caused it to be sent back. And they calmly waited the result. Not so calmly either, for hearing that Squanto, their man Friday, had been killed by a Narraganset Chief, ten men armed themselves, plunged into the forest, and surrounded the Chief's cabin; when they found that Squanto was not dead, and so they came back. This, while they knew of the massacre at Jamestown, of four hundred whites in a single hour. But they were different men from those Virginia colonists, and went on prospering and victorious in spite of everything.

At length, as time passed, they gave up the common stock principle. Bradford who had succeeded Carver, at his death, as Governor of the Colony, expressly says that it did not work well. Each man began to set up for himself, and they only paid in enough to support the officers and fishermen. After that, a new and larger division of land took place, of twenty acres to the man. Then also, a division of the live stock, except some belonging to the town, according to the children and families of each; and cattle, in those days, were used, not only for purposes of draught, but ridden as beasts of burden. We are told, for example, that "when John Alden went to Cape Cod to marry Priscilla Mullens, he covered his bull with broad-cloth and rode upon his back:" and that "when he returned he placed his wife there, and led the bull home by the ring in his nose." He first went, you remember, according to the story which Longfellow has helped to render immortal, to plead for Priscilla, in behalf of his friend Miles Standish, and being referred by her father, whom he first approached according to custom, if not to law—for they soon had a law, that any young man who did not do that, before he made advances to the girl herself, should be fined, or suffer corporal punishment—being referred to Priscilla, by her respected parent, Mr. Mullens, Alden argued so heartily for his friend Standish, and had so pleasing a person and so handsome a face, that, fixing her eyes on him, and then on the ground, she said, "Prythee, John, why do you not speak for yourself?" Upon that hint he spoke, probably considering the old gentleman's permission covered this new aspect of the case, and so took her home as aforesaid; which entire performance, Standish finally forgave him, in the version given by the poet, but for my own part, I very much doubt if he ever did.

But years rolled on, another colony sprang up, at the north of them, under Roger Conant, the patriarch of Dorchester, and ancestor of our good old judge at Detroit, and whose cordial reception of John Endicott, sent out from England to succeed him, caused them to name the place near Boston where it occurred Salem. Then the New Haven colony began, in the year 1638, under Davenport and Pruden. And, about the same time, the Connecticut colony, with John Hooker and others at the head of it. Each one of these colonies came to adopt very much the same government for itself. Neither of them made any definite reference to any superior authority in England. In all four the freemen were the sole fountain of power. And who should be admitted to exercise the right of suffrage was decided, in the Massachusetts and New Haven colonies, by the male members of the church; and in Plymouth and Connecticut colonies, by all the freemen in mass meeting.

At length, in Massachusetts, after justice had been administered for years, without any system of Statutes, or any recognition of the common law of England, but according to the principles of manifest equity, and to the law of God, which they would use, they said, until they had time to make better, a "body of liberties," so called, was prepared by Mr. Nathaniel Ward, and adopted in General Court. It consists of one hundred fundamental laws, and is a most wonderful production, to come from any one man of any age. Among the remarkable things about it, is its definition of treason, which is silent respecting all allegiance, on the part of the people, except to Massachusetts, and is so drawn as to threaten with death all who should take even the King's part against her. That was in 1631, when they had only been going alone about twenty years. How far back the spirit of independence dates in that State you can see. In Connecticut they adopted, the next year, almost a copy of the same instrument, being then, perhaps some four thousand persons strong. And when Cromwell came to power, while these colonists admired him, they carefully abstained from acknowledging his authority; and when England made him Protector, they preserved a steady silence; and when he died, the event is not so much as referred to in their public records. Yet Cromwell always liked and valued them. He allowed the navigation laws, which pressed hard upon the Southern Colonies, to become a dead letter, as against them. They received the commodities of all nations free of duty, and sent their ships at will to the ports of continental Europe. And when he had conquered Ireland, and began to consider how to keep it in subjection and in order, he bethought him of these Puritans in New England, then some thirty thousand in number, and straightway sent over most liberal propositions, if they would be removed in a body to Ireland. But they declined, in a most peculiar letter, which John Endicott wrote, for the General Court, promising not to hinder any persons, or families, from going to any part of the world where God called them; but on the whole, while very much obliged to him, they did not think they cared to change their abode.

The Protector seems to have taken their pious and polite rebuff in good part, yet not to have abandoned his idea of bringing their remarkable qualities into play, for the furtherance of his mighty enterprises. When the Island of Jamaica was reduced by his fleet, and found to contain too small a number of white inhabitants,—only about fifteen hundred,—he thought of these Puritans again, and conceived the idea of giving it them, to possess and defend. Daniel Larkin, a colonist then in London, was sent back with a document proposing liberal things, as to land rent, privilege, duties, &c; only he, Cromwell, to name their Governor, and Commander of forces. What did they do with the communication? Waited eight months before it was read, and considered, by the General Court. Then a letter was ordered "to his Highness from this Court;" which it took five months to draw up; but which was very short, wordy and devotional; thanking him, again, for his offer, and promising never to cease praying for His Highness, that the Lord would long continue him to carry on his work, overthrow the enemies of his truth, and to enlarge the kingdom of his dear Son. Here that matter ended, and with it I shall conclude my enumeration of incidents illustrative of the character of our Forefathers.

Take them, for all in all, we shall not look upon their like again.

John Robinson, who is to be reckoned their leader, although like Moses, he never reached the promised land, would be a rare man in any age, or country; learned, wise, polished and modest; and of such scholarly tastes and acquirements, that the chief preachers of Leyden, chose him to defend their doctrines, at the University, against the Arminians, led on by the celebrated Episcopius, whom he is thought to have thoroughly defeated.

William Brewster was a gentleman by birth, educated as a scholar at Cambridge, had lived in early life,—for he was older than most of the Pilgrims,—at the Court of Queen Elizabeth, and was the confidential friend and assistant of the renowned Davidson, when the latter was her Secretary of State.

John Carver was well educated, and possessed of a good estate, which he spent in the cause, and died shortly after being chosen first Governor of the Colony.

William Bradford, his successor, was also a man of property and mark; the master of several languages, German, French, Latin and Greek, and especially the Hebrew. He was familiar with literature and with general history. He had a large library for the time; was no mean poet, when he chose to exercise his gifts in that direction, and few names come down to us associated with more of the distinctive attributes of a noble soul.

Edward Winslow was a man of good family and education. Had traveled over Europe, moved among the gentlemen of the British Parliament, and on revisiting England, was commissioned to superintend the English fleet at the West Indies.

These things, I mention to show, that those stern Forefathers of ours were not mere men of bone and muscle, on the one hand, nor wild, hot-headed fanatics on the other; but well bred, intelligent, conscientious persons, who had been accustomed to a different experience, and were making great sacrifices in what they did.

Such was the work, the beginning of which we celebrate. These are some of the attending circumstances. These are the men, sifted from three Kingdoms, and bolted again by the return of the Speedwell, who planted themselves and their new idea, two hundred and forty years ago, on the edge of a then howling wilderness.

But why, after all, do their names stand so high upon the pillar of human renown? Is it solely the justice of mankind to the sterling virtues they cherished, and the heavy sacrifices they made, for freedom to worship God? Why so faithfully honored and applauded, the part they took, when so much good and true service has been forgotten? Because of its relation to providence. That was the turning point. There the current changed in favor of civil and ecclesiastical liberty. That was the scene, and they, the chosen instruments, for inaugurating a new era in religious and governmental affairs. There freedom of conscience began. There constitutional government first had a being in the annals of time. That compact framed and signed with forty one names, in the cabin of the May Flower, riding at anchor, by which they bound themselves before going on shore to be governed by each other as a body politic, and not the document penned by Thomas Jefferson, was the first Declaration of Independence. That "body of liberties" drawn up by Mr. Ward, and not the Constitution of the United States, was our earliest attempt, and the first one among mankind, at constitutional self government. Those deliberate answers, suggesting to Oliver Cromwell himself, the idea of hands off, as to selecting Governors and Generals, and not the casting of taxed tea into Boston harbor, was the first indication in America of resistance to Royal authority and will. What did it mean, when they declined to go to Ireland, and declined to go to Jamaica? That they were free, and designed to remain so! The spirit of freedom was already in them! There the thing commenced! There the tree of liberty began to grow. Its roots are entwined about the bones of the Pilgrim Fathers in the old Bay State. With them it was, at the start, a religious sentiment. They sought freedom to worship God, which they knew belonged to them, and, in achieving it, freed themselves from civil domination, both in feeling, and for the time, in fact. So it was ordered to be. The great Disposer permitted and encouraged this result. Every providential advantage needful, and preventive necessary, to give their enterprise the right direction, and make it an advance in human history, was wonderfully supplied. The hand of the Lord was in it. This could only be done, the true character and quality imparted to the whole movement, and its consequences in this land and to the world only be secured, by such forefathers as they were. Therefore, he raised them up and sent them. Therefore he kept them as they were, true to themselves, by preserving them from admixture, and guarding them from contamination. Cromwell had a purpose, and would have sent them where they soon had been spoiled. The Lord had a higher purpose, and kept them there, and what he wished them to be, by the bracing quality of the climate, by the barrenness of the soil which he cleared of natives and guided them to, and by the rigor of those habits which expelled the worthless and troublesome, and repelled gay and fashionable adventurers. When the London Merchants, desirous of large returns for the little money invested, sent men to change all this to overrule these Fathers of a strong, orderly and well-educated Christian nation, and transform the colony into a company of enterprising, fur-traders; how quickly was the plan set aside, in the good providence of God, and did things go on as before in the way preordained for them!

It is from this view of the case, wherein the mind of God concerning these friends and their early work comes to light, that we may derive assurance of hope for the country. Too much interest has been betrayed from the first, too many blessings have all along been invested in this national enterprise, by Him who sees the end from the beginning, for it to be abandoned now! The position we occupy, on the surface of the earth, with heathen Africa on one side, and heathen China and India on the other, has been too wisely selected; the incipient stages of our existence, as a people, too carefully watched over; the strides of progress, too rapid and regular, for nothing to come of it! God does not so work. I feel in regard to the ruin of this country, as I do when they tell of the second advent of Christ, and the destruction of the world, that it is too early yet. The world was four thousand years in preparing for him, and the gospel has been presented as yet to only one eighth of the people. So this country has just begun to be what it has so long been preparing for. It is now just beginning to enter on the high career, which He has marked out for it far—far into the future; and it is altogether too early to talk of dissolution and decay. Do nations die in mid-career, as a man is smitten down in middle life? Do nations come apart, and when the dew of youth is still upon them? Never. Will he who has blessed and favored no other one, since the birth of time, so lavishly, now suffer this nation to come to any serious harm, by a junto of selfish men, scheming for a confederacy in which South Carolina may be the banner State, and Charleston the great Metropolis? Never. Never. They can't make me believe it, by their threatening, but harmless, ordinances. They can't make me believe it, by their crocodile tears and sighs, or proposals from whatever quarter, to humble ourselves before God, with fasting and prayer that He may prevent such a calamity. He has no idea of bringing it upon us, or of suffering it to be done. There is no occasion to fear any such thing, but abundant occasion for thanksgiving and praise, that He has bestowed upon us such blessings, together with the power to retain them that He is granting us such rewards of industry, and such returns from the soil, as the world has never seen; that there has been no time, since the Fathers landed on Plymouth Rock, when we were any thing like so strong as now, as against foreign aggression, or the elements of internal trouble. But let us not abuse our power. Let us not think to tyrannize over any portion of our fellow countrymen, and interfere with their peculiar institutions. Let us bear and forbear, as the worthy sons of calm, firm, clear headed, strong willed, conscientious sires, in whom a Cromwell at the head of England found his match. And when we do pray, as all often should, upon this subject; let it be that the God of our Fathers, may still be the God of their children, to the latest generation; and that He may lead us and them into the adoption of all private virtues and public measures which will lift the country higher and higher as a model of successful and glorious Republicanism.

OFFICERS OF THE SOCIETY FOR 1861.

ENOCH JAMES, *President.*

Vice Presidents,

GEORGE D. HILL, JOHN M. WHEELER,
SOLOMON MANN, C. B. COOK,
GEORGE DANFORTH.

RANSOM S. SMITH, *Rec. Sec'y.*
JOHN L. TAPPAN, *Cor. Sec'y.*
WILLIAM N. STRONG, *Treasurer.*

Executive Committee,

LUTHER DODGE, EBENEZER WELLS,
CHAUNCEY H. MILLEN.

A Finger-Point from Plymouth Rock.

REMARKS

AT THE

PLYMOUTH FESTIVAL,

ON

THE FIRST OF AUGUST, 1853.

IN COMMEMORATION OF

THE EMBARKATION OF THE PILGRIMS.

BY

CHARLES SUMNER.

BOSTON:
CROSBY, NICHOLS, AND COMPANY,
111 WASHINGTON STREET.
1853.

CAMBRIDGE:
METCALF AND COMPANY, PRINTERS TO THE UNIVERSITY.

REMARKS.

The President, in giving the next toast, said they had already been delighted with the words of a distinguished member of the Senate of the United States. They were favored with the presence of another; and he would give as a sentiment: —

"*The Senate of the United States*, — The concentrated light of the stars of the Union."

Hon. Charles Sumner responded as follows: —

Mr. President, — You bid me speak for the Senate of the United States. But I cannot forget that there is another voice here, of classical eloquence, which might more fitly render this service. As one of the humblest members of that body, and associated with the public councils for a brief period only, I should prefer that my distinguished colleague [Mr. Everett], whose fame is linked with a long political life, should speak for it. And there is yet another here [Mr.

Hale], who, though not at this moment a member of the Senate, has, throughout an active and brilliant career, marked by a rare combination of ability, eloquence, and good humor, so identified himself with it in the public mind, that he might well speak for it always, and when he speaks all are pleased to listen. But, sir, you have ordered it otherwise.

From the tears and trials at Delft Haven, from the deck of the "Mayflower," from the landing at Plymouth Rock, to the Senate of the United States, is a mighty contrast, covering whole spaces of history, hardly less than from the wolf that suckled Romulus and Remus to that Roman Senate which, on curule chairs, swayed Italy and the world. From these obscure beginnings of poverty and weakness, which you now piously commemorate, and on which all our minds naturally rest to-day, you bid us leap to that marble Capitol, where thirty-one powerful republics, bound in indissoluble union, a Plural Unit, are gathered together in legislative body, constituting a part of One Government, which, stretching from ocean to ocean, and counting millions of people beneath its majestic rule, surpasses far in wealth and might any government of the Old World when the little band of Pilgrims left it, and now promises to be a clasp between Europe and Asia, bringing the most distant places near together, so that there shall be no more Orient or Occident. It were interesting to dwell on the stages of this grand procession; but it is enough on this occasion merely to glance at them and pass on.

Sir, it is the Pilgrims that we commemorate to-day; not the Senate. For this moment, at least, let us tread under foot all pride of empire, all exultation in our manifold triumphs of industry, of science, of literature, with all the crowding anticipations of the vast untold Future, that we may reverently bow before the forefathers. The day is theirs. In the contemplation of their virtue we shall derive a lesson, which, like truth, may judge us sternly; but, if we can really follow it, like truth, it shall make us free. For myself, I accept the admonitions of the day. It may teach us all never, by word or act, although we may be few in numbers or alone, to swerve from those primal principles of duty, which, from the landing at Plymouth Rock, have been the life of Massachusetts. Let me briefly unfold the lesson; though to the discerning soul it unfolds itself.

Few persons in history have suffered more from contemporary misrepresentation, abuse, and persecution, than the English Puritans. At first a small body, they were regarded with indifference and contempt. But by degrees they grew in numbers, and drew into their company men of education, intelligence, and even of rank. Reformers in all ages have had little of blessing from the world which they sought to serve; but the Puritans were not disheartened. Still they persevered. The obnoxious laws of conformity they vowed to withstand till, in the fervid language of the time, "they be sent back to the darkness from whence they came." Through them the spirit of modern Freedom made itself potently felt, in its great warfare with Authority, in Church, in Literature, and in the State; in other words, for religious, intellectual, and political emancipation. The Puritans primarily aimed at religious Freedom; for this they contended in Parliament, under Elizabeth and James; for this they suffered; but so connected are all these great and glorious interests, that the struggles for one have always helped the others. Such service did they do, that Hume, whose cold nature sympathized little with their burning souls, is obliged to confess that to them alone "the English owe the whole freedom of their constitution."

As among all reformers, so among them there were differences of degree. Some continued within the pale of the National Church, and there pressed their ineffectual attempts in behalf of the good cause.

Some at length, driven by conscientious convictions and unwilling to be partakers longer in its enormities, stung also by the cruel excesses of magisterial power, openly disclaimed the National Establishment and became a separate sect, first under the name of Brownists, from the person who had led in this new organization, and then under the better name of *Separatists.* I like this word, sir. It has a meaning. After long struggles in Parliament and out of it, in Church and State, continued through successive reigns, the Puritans finally triumphed, and the despised sect of Separatists, swollen in numbers, and now under the denomination of Independents, with Oliver Cromwell at their head and John Milton as his Secretary, ruled England. Thus is prefigured the final triumph of all, however few in numbers, who sincerely devote themselves to Truth.

The Pilgrims of Plymouth were among the earliest of the Separatists. As such, they knew by bitter experience all the sharpness of persecution. Against them the men in power raged like the heathen. Against them the whole fury of the law was directed. Some were imprisoned; all were impoverished, while their name became a by-word of reproach. For safety and freedom the little band first sought shelter in Holland, where they continued in indigence and obscurity for more than ten years, when they were inspired to seek a home in this unknown Western world. Such in brief is their history. I could not say more of it without intruding upon your time; I could not say less without injustice to them.

Rarely have austere principles been expressed with more gentleness than from their lips. By a covenant with the Lord, they had vowed to walk in all his ways, according to their best endeavors, *whatsoever it should cost them,* — and also to receive whatsoever truth should be made known from the written word of God. Repentance and prayers, patience and tears, were their weapons. "It is not with us," said they, "as with other men, whom small things can discourage or small discontentments cause to wish themselves at home again." And then, again, on another occasion, their souls were lifted to utterance like this: "When we are in our graves it will be all one, whether we have lived in plenty or penury, whether we have died in a bed of down or on locks of straw." Self-sacrifice is never in vain, and they foresaw, with the clearness of prophecy, that out of their trials should come a transcendent Future. "As one small candle," said an early Pilgrim Governor, "may light a thousand, so the light kindled here may in some sort shine even to the whole nation."

And yet these men, with such sublime endurance and such lofty faith, are among those who are sometimes called "Puritan knaves" and "knaves-Puritan," and who were branded by King James as the "very pests in the Church and Commonwealth." The small company of our forefathers became the jest and gibe of fashion and power. The phrase "men of one idea" had not been invented then; but, in equivalent language, they were styled "the pinched fanatics of Leyden." A contemporary poet and favorite of Charles the First, Thomas Carew, lent his genius to their defamation. A masque, from his elegant and careful pen, was performed by the monarch and his courtiers, wherein the whole plantation of New England was turned to royal sport. The jeer broke forth in the exclamation, that it had "purged more virulent humors from the politic bodies than guaiacum and all the West Indian drugs from the natural bodies of the kingdom."

And these outcasts, despised in their own day by the proud and great, are the men whom we have met in this goodly number to celebrate; not for any victory of war; not for any triumph of discovery, science, learning, or eloquence; not for worldly success of any kind. How poor are all these things by the side of that divine virtue which made them, amidst the reproach, the obloquy, and the hardness of the world, hold fast to Freedom and Truth! Sir, if the honors of this day are not a mockery; if they do not expend themselves in mere selfish gratulation; if they are a sincere homage to the character of the Pilgrims, — and I cannot suppose otherwise, — then is it well for us to be here. Standing on Plymouth Rock, at their great anniversary, we cannot fail to be elevated by their example. We see clearly what it has done for the world and what it has done for their fame. No pusillanimous soul here to-day will declare their self-sacrifice, their deviation from received opinions, their unquenchable thirst for liberty, an error or illusion. From gushing multitudinous hearts we now thank these lowly men that they dared to be true and brave. Conformity or compromise might, perhaps, have purchased for them a profitable peace, but not peace of mind; it might have secured place and power, but not repose; it might have opened a present shelter, but not a home in history and in men's hearts till time shall be no more. All will confess the true grandeur of their example, while, in vindication of a cherished principle, they stood alone, against the madness of men, against the law of the land, against their king. Better be the despised Pilgrim, a fugitive for freedom, than the halting politician, forgetful of principle, "with a Senate at his heels."

Such, sir, is the voice from Plymouth Rock, as it salutes my ears. Others may not hear it. But to me it comes in tones which I cannot mistake. I catch its words of noble cheer: —

> "New occasions teach new duties; Time makes ancient good uncouth;
> They must upward still and onward, who would keep abreast of Truth:
> Lo, before us gleam her camp-fires! we ourselves must Pilgrims be,
> Launch our Mayflower, and steer boldly through the desperate winter sea."

A BRIEF SKETCH OF A LECTURE

DELIVERED BEFORE THE

ESSEX INSTITUTE, MAY 12, 1856,

RESPECTING THE FOUNDERS OF

Salem and the First Church.

SALEM:
WILLIAM IVES AND GEORGE W. PEASE, PRINTERS.
OBSERVER OFFICE.
1856.

BRIEF SKETCH

OF A LECTURE

DELIVERED BEFORE THE

ESSEX INSTITUTE, MAY 12, 1856,

RESPECTING THE FOUNDERS OF

Salem and the First Church.

By Daniel A. White

SALEM:
WILLIAM IVES AND GEORGE W. PEASE, PRINTERS.
OBSERVER OFFICE.
1856.

Monday, May 12, 1856.

Evening Meeting. The President, Hon. D. A. WHITE, in the chair. After reading records, list of donations and correspondence since the last meeting, the President occupied the hour with a lecture upon certain important matters of record and history pertaining to the Fathers of Salem and the First Church. A brief sketch only will be presented here.

Judge W., referring to a remark of the late Mr. Adams, the "old man eloquent," in his Address on the New England Confederacy, before the Massachusetts Historical Society, that it was one of their pre-eminent duties to preserve the good name of our forefathers, observed that it became our more especial duty to protect that of the fathers of Salem from all injurious representations as we ever might with the broad shield of truth. With such views he had explored some of our ancient church records and other historical documents as faithfully as he could, and now brought the results of his humble labor, octogenarian labor—and to be appreciated accordingly. Yet he could truly say that it had been a labor of love from his grateful veneration of our forefathers—a veneration that had grown upon him as he more nearly approached the world where they are. It was a trite remark, because so obvious and just, that no people on earth owed more to their ancestors than the people of New England; and Salem, perhaps, of all New England, was the most deeply indebted. Here they had exerted, in a signal manner, their wisdom and energy in planting the seeds of freedom, piety, and learning, the fruits of which we so richly enjoyed. We were bound to study their principles and institutions, and to preserve them unimpaired.

The main purpose of the lecture was to correct certain errors contained in two recent publications in relation to the institution of the First Church in Salem, the first organized church in New England; and more especially the very important error that instead of the one truly scriptural "confession of faith and covenant," adopted by the First Church at its foundation, there was established together with the covenant a test creed, or sectarian articles of faith, to which subscription or assent was required in order to church membership. These publications were,—"The Ecclesiastical History of New England," by Mr. Felt,* and a new edition of "Morton's New England's Memorial," containing an appendix, so arranged as to misrepresent the real meaning of the author as well as that of Cotton Mather, the two original and indubitable authorities on the subject.† The correction of these errors was demanded of us in justice to the memory of our forefathers, as well as by the sancity of history and the importance of the principles involved in the question. The fundamental rule inculcated by Cicero, that "the historian must never dare to utter what is false, or to suppress anything that is true, and must always keep his mind above prejudice or partiality," had been sanctioned and enforced by the highest Christian authorities; "truth being the very life and soul of history." The publications referred to having been issued by the "Congregational Board of Publication," and one of them highly extolled for its "thoroughness of research and accuracy of statement," it became the more necessary to correct their misrepresentations concerning the First Church, as otherwise error might supplant truth at the very foundation of our ecclesiastical history.

There were three sources of evidence, each of which was conclusive, to prove that the First Church had never adopted any such test creed, or articles of faith.

1. The avowed principles of the founders of the church.
2. The authentic history of its foundation.
3. The ancient records of the church.

---

* The Ecclesiastical History of New England, by Jos. B. Felt. Boston. 1855—p. 115 and 267.

† New England's Memorial—6th ed. Boston: 1855—p. 459.

1. The principles of the founders were purely congregational, and as understood by themselves required their strict adherence to the Scriptures in constituting the church. This too was their declared purpose. Great wrong was done them in confounding their principles with their opinions; things essentially distinct. Opinions were variable and transient; principles, fixed and eternal. Opinions belonged exclusively to the individual holding them; principles, to the whole community in common. Opinions could not be a guide for any but the holder of them, nor always a safe guide for him; but fixed principles safely guided all, both in forming their conduct and their opinions also. This distinction was well understood by the fathers of Salem, and nobly manifested by them in constituting their church, according to their genuine congregational principles, and not in perpetuation of their peculiar opinions.

2. This glorious fact was confirmed by authentic history. The foundation of the First Church, being a memorable transaction, had been recorded with more fullness and accuracy than that of any other church. Governors Endicott and Bradford, with the ministers Higginson and Skelton and other eminent characters, were earnestly engaged in their inquiries to ascertain the true scriptural foundation of a Christian church. "And accordingly it was desired of Mr. Higginson to draw up a confession of faith and covenant in scripture language; which being done, was agreed upon." So stated Secretary Morton, in his New England's Memorial, and Cotton Mather, in the Magnalia, recorded it at length, omitting the preamble of its renewal in 1636, and the postscript added in 1660, giving the true original "Confession and Covenant" of 1629. Though variously termed, and most commonly "the covenant" simply, one and the same instrument was always intended;—"the instrument," as Judge Davis called it, "venerable for its antiquity, and estimable for its mild and benignant spirit;"* which was published in London in 1644, and included by Han-

* Morton's Mem. Davis's ed. p. 391

bury among his select "Memorials of the Independents," and which Dr. Bentley, in his History of Salem, said, had been "recorded in every History of New England." Yet in the recent copious Ecclesiastical History of New England, it found no place excepting some mutilated sentences introduced apparently to disprove its authenticity. And in the appendix to the new edition of Morton's Memorial it was treated in a way still less worthy and more perversive of its true character.

Morton and Mather entirely agreed as to the manner of admission into the church, particularly described by the latter as follows:—"Some were admitted by expressing their consent unto their Confession and Covenant; some were admitted after their first answering to questions propounded unto them; some were admitted, when they had presented in writing such things, as might give satisfaction to the people of God concerning them; and some, that were admitted, orally addressed the people of God in such terms as they thought proper to ask their communion with; which diversity was perhaps more beautiful than would have been a more punctilious uniformity. But none were admitted without regard unto a blameless and holy conversation."*

The accounts of both Morton and Mather were expressly sanctioned by Rev. John Higginson, an eye witness of the foundation of the church and perfectly acquainted with its discipline and history.† The facts stated by Mather had doubtless been furnished by Mr. Higginson himself; and they demonstrated that no test creed, or prescribed form of confession, could have been used in the admission of members.

3. The records of the church afforded the same clear demonstration. These records, as contained in the present old church book, consisted of transcript records from 1636 to 1659, and of original records from the settlement of John Higginson in 1660, to the dismission of Samuel Fisk in 1735. The transcript records, copied from a former book, comprised the

---

* Magnal. 1. 19. fol. ed. † See Appendix and Note.

original covenant as given by Dr. Mather, under the sanction of Mr. Higginson, with the preamble of its renewal in 1636, and the postscript, or Quaker clause, added in 1660 by Mr. Higginson, and a marginal note in the hand writing of Mr. Fisk;* also, the names of the first thirty members of the church, and those afterwards added before the settlement of Mr. Higginson, together with an account of baptisms from 1636 to 1659.

As regarded the present question the records might be considered complete. It sufficiently appeared from the proceedings of the church, at its first meeting, after Mr. Higginson's settlement, Sept. 10, 1660, that all important matters must have been copied from the former book. A committee, then appointed "to review the church book," &c., consisting of "Major Hawthorn, Mr. Battis, Mr. Price, the two deacons, together with the pastor,"—represented, "That they conceived the book itself and the paper of it being old, not well bound, and in some places having been wet and torn and not legible, is not like to continue long to be of use for posterity; therefore they thought it best if it were kept in safety by the elders, *by that means it may be of good use so long as it will last.* Only some few passages in it which do reflect upon particular persons, or upon the whole church without any church vote, and without due proof, they did mark in the book as thinking they should be struck out."

Mr. Higginson thus had possession of the whole former book as well as the transcripts from it. He was very exact in his church records, especially in what related to the admission of members. But no intimation was to be found in the whole church book of any test creed, or prescribed articles of faith, having ever been adopted, or used, in the First Church.

A single instance from his records of admission was enough to show the spirit of the whole. "1678, at a church meeting, March 9, (after naming eight persons)—these eight having been

---

* See Appendix.

propounded a month, no exception coming against them, they making their profession of faith and repentence in their own way, some by speech, others by writing, which was read for them, they were admitted to membership in this church, by consent of the brethren, they engaging in the covenant."

Thus appeared the entire agreement of authentic history and church records with the principles of the founders in proving the freedom of candidates for church membership in making confession of their own faith in their own way. The Cambridge Platform, of 1648, showed the spirit in which such confessions were to be met on the part of the church; inculcating "such charity and tenderness to be used as the weakest christian, if sincere, might not be excluded nor discouraged."

It might be asked, as it sometimes had been, "what possible difference," whether such candidates were required to subscribe to "a written confession," or to make in some other satisfactory mode a profession of their faith? The difference in the two modes was self evident and manifestly essential. One accorded with the right of private judgment and the acknowledged sufficiency of the Scriptures; the other contravened these fundamental principles of protestantism. The one was in harmony with the spirit of congregationalism; the other adverse to it. The one in its tendency was beneficent; the other, pernicious. The one led to increasing knowledge and love of Christian truth; the other tended to stifle the spirit of free inquiry. The one, in short, was a delightful privilege, the other an odious imposition.

Our forefathers, of the first generation, were, indeed, "noble Bereans" in settling their principles of church polity,—searching the scriptures daily for divine guidance. We all venerated their principles, though in following them out we might now be led to different conclusions and reject some of their opinions. So too, we all admired the spirit which actuated them, and blessed God for its glorious results, while we felt obliged to disapprove some parts of their conduct; for where on earth was to be found human perfection! Charity would gladly throw her mantle over errors, which our fathers might have committed in common with other great and good men of their day, while gratitude delighted to indulge her warmest admiration of the wisdom, energy, and fidelity to principle, which raised them above the spirit of their age, above all sectarian influence, and even above the bias of their own darling opinions, in their steadfast adherence to the scriptures as their only guide and standard in the constitution of their churches.

APPENDIX.

—o—

Here is presented a transcript of the two first pages of the old Church book: all in italics excepting the original Covenant of 1629.

Gather my Saints together unto me that have made a Covenant with me by sacrifyce. Psa. 50: 5:

6. of 6th Month, 1629, *This Covenant was publickly Signed and Declared, as may appear from page* 85, *in this Book.*

Wee whose names are under written, members of the present Church of Christ in Salem, having found by sad experience how dangerous it is to sitt loose to the Covenant wee make with our God: and how apt wee are to wander into by pathes, even to the loosing of our first aimes in entring into Church fellowship: Doe therefore, solemnly in the presence of the Eternall God, both for our own comforts, and those which shall or maye be joyned unto us, renewe that Church Covenant we find this Church bound unto at theire first be inning, viz: That we covenant with the Lord and one with an other; and doe bynd ourselves in the presence of God, to walke together in all his waies, according as he is pleased to reveale himself unto us in his Blessed word of truth. And doe more explicitely in the name and feare of God, profess and protest to walke as followeth through the power and grace of our Lord Jesus.

1. First wee avowe the Lord to be our God, and ourselves his people, in the truth and simplicitie of our spirits.

2. Wee give ourselves to the Lord Jesus Christ, and to the word of his grace, for the teaching, ruleing and sanctifyeing of us in matters of worship, and conversation; resolveing to cleave to him alone for life and glorie; and oppose all contrarie wayes, cannons and constitutions of men in his worship.

3. Wee promise to walke with our brethren and sisters in this Congregation with all watchfullness and tendernes, avoyding all jelousies, suspitions, backbyteings, censurings, provoakings, secrete risings of spirit against them; but in all offences to follow the rule of the Lord Jesus, and to beare and forbeare, give and forgive as he hath taught us.

4. In publick or private we will willingly doe nothing to the ofence of the Church, but will be willing to take advise for ovrselves and ours as occasion shalbe presented.

5. Wee will not in the Congregation be forward eyther to shew oure owne gifts or parts in speaking or scrupling, or there discover the fayling of oure brethren or sisters, butt atend an orderly cale there unto; knowing how much the Lord may be dishonoured, and his Gospell in the profession of it, sleighted, by our distempers, and weaknesses in publyck.

6. Wee bynd our selves to studdy the advancement of the Gospell in all truth and peace, both in regard of those that are within, or without, noe waye sleighting our sister Churches, but useing theire counsell as need shalbe: nor laying a stumbling block before any, noe not the Indians, whose good we desire to promote, and soe to converse, as wee may avoyd the verrye appearance of evill.

7. Wee hearby promise to carrye our selves in all lawful obedience, to those that are over us, in church or commonweale, knowing how well pleasing it will be to the Lord, that they should have incouragement in theire places, by our not greiveing theryre spirites through our iregularities.

8. Wee resolve to approve our selves to the Lord in onr perticular calings, shunning ydlenes as the bane of any state,

nor will wee deale hardly, or opressingly with any, wherein we are the Lord's stewards: alsoe promysing to our best abilitie

9. to teach our children and servants, the knowledg of God and his will, that they may serve him also; and all this, not by any strength of our owne, but by the Lord Christ, whose bloud we desire may sprinckle this our covenant made in his name.

This Covenant was renewed by the Church on a sollemne day of Humiliation 6 *of* 1 *moneth* 1660. *When also considering the power of Temptation amongst us by reason of ye Quakers doctrine to the leavening of some in the place where we are and endangering of others, doe see cause to remember the Admonition of our Saviour Christ to his disciples, Math.* 16. *Take heed and beware of ye leaven of the doctrine of the Pharisees, and doe judge soe farre as we understand it yt ye Quakers doctrine is as bad or worse than that of ye Pharisees: Therefore we doe covenant by the help of Jesus Christ to take heed and beware of the leaven of the doctrine of the Quakers.*

After a single blank leave in the Church book comes the "Catalogue" of Church Members extending to 1659. The names of the first thirty only are here given:

A Catalogue of the Names of those that are joined in full communion.

Samuel Sharp,	John Sibly,
John Endecott,	John Baulch,
Phillip Veren,	Samuel Moore,
Hugh Larkin,	John Holgrove,
Roger Conant,	Ralph Fogge,
Lawrence Leach,	John Horne,
William Auger,	John Woodberye,
Francis Johnson,	William Traske,
Thomas Eborne,	Townsend Bishop,
George Williams,	Thomas Read,
George Norton,	Richard Rayment,
Henry Herricke,	Jeffry Massy,
Peter Palfrye,	Edmond Batter,
Roger Maurye,	Elias Stileman,
Thomas Gardener,	Edmond Giles.

NOTES.

Cotton Mather, in his Magnalia, says, "Mr. J. Higginson and Mr. W. Hubbard have assisted me and much obliged me with information for many parts of our history."

In his "Attestation," prefixed to Mather's Magnalia, or "Church History of New England," dated "Salem, 25th of the first month, 1697," Mr Higginson says,—"As for myself, having been by the mercy of God, now above sixty-eight years in New England, and served the Lord and his people in my weak measure, sixty years in the ministry of the Gospel, I may now say in my old age, I have seen all that the Lord has done for his people in New England, and have known the beginning and progress of these churches unto this day, and having read over much of this history, I cannot but in the love and fear of God bear witness to the truth of it." "JOHN HIGGINSON."

Dr. Mather, having given the original covenant, here printed in Roman letters, immediately subjoins the following remarks:

"By this instrument was the covenant of grace explained, received, and recognized by the First Church in this colony, and applied unto the evangelical designs of a church-estate before the Lord. This instrument they afterwards often read over, and renewed the consent of their souls unto every article in it; especially when their days of humiliation invited them to lay hold on particular opportunities for doing so.

"So you have seen the nativity of the First Church in Massachusetts Colony.

"As for the circumstances of admission into this church, they left it very much unto the discretion and faithfulness of the Elders, together with the condition of the persons to be admitted. Some were admitted by expressing their consent unto their confession and covenant;" &c., as before quoted on the 6th page.

As Morton's Memorial, first published in 1669, also bears the sanction of the venerable Higginson as to its "truth of matter," we here continue the passage, commenced on page 5th, marking in italics the words which prove that the confession of faith and covenant was but one instrument. Indeed, a formula of faith distinct from the covenant was a thing unheard of in the formation of the early congregational churches of New England.

" Accordingly it was desired of Mr. Higginson to draw up a confession of faith and covenant in scripture language; which being done, *was* agreed upon. And because they foresaw that this wilderness might be looked upon as a place of liberty, and therefore might in time be troubled with erroneous spirits, therefore they did put in one article into the confession of faith, on purpose, about the duty and power of the magistrate in matters of religion: Thirty copies of the aforesaid confession of faith and covenant being written out for the use of thirty persons who were to begin the work. When the 6th of August came, it was kept as a day of fasting and prayer, in which, after the sermons and prayers of the two ministers, in the end of the day, the aforesaid confession of faith and covenant being solemnly read, the forenamed persons did solemnly profess their consent thereunto; and proceeded to the ordaining of Mr. Skelton pastor, and Mr. Higginson teacher, of the church there. Mr. Bradford, the Governour of Plimouth, and some others with him, coming by sea, were hindered by cross winds, that they could not be there at the beginning of the day, but they came into the assembly afterward, and gave them the *right hand of fellowship*, wishing all prosperity, and a blessed success unto such good beginnings. After which, at several times, many others joined to the church in the same way. The confession of faith and covenant forementioned *was* acknowledged only as a direction, pointing unto that faith and covenant contained in the holy scripture, and therefore no man was confined unto that form of words, but only to the substance, end and scope of the matter contained therein. And for the circumstantial manner of joining to the church, it was ordered according to the wisdom and faithfulness of the elders, together with the liberty and ability of any person. Hence it was, that some were admitted by expressing their consent to *that* written confession of faith and covenant; others did answer to questions about the principles of religion that were publicly propounded to them; some did present their confession in writing, which was read for them; and some, that were able and willing, did make their confession in their own words and way; a due respect was also had unto the conversations of men, viz: that they were without scandel."—*New England's Memorial, Davis's Ed. p.* 145.

Rev. W. Hubbard and Rev. J. Higginson, referred to by Dr. Mather as his assistants in compiling the Magnalia, having been intimate friends, the former doubtless received from Mr. Higginson much of his information respecting the institution of the First Church. The following brief extracts from Hubbard's History of New England are therefore added to the preceding:

" But they had not as yet waded so far into the controversy of church discipline, as to be very positive in any of those points wherein the main hinge of the controversy lay between them and others ; yet aiming as near as they well could, to come up to the rules of the gospel in the first settling of a church state, and apprehending it necessary for those who intended to be of the church solemnly to enter into a covenant engagement one with another in the presence of God to walk togethey before him according to the word of God, and then to ordain their ministers unto their several offices, to which they were by the election of the people designed, scil. Mr. Skelton to be their pastor, and Mr. Higginson to be their teacher. In order to the carrying on of that work, or preparation thereunto, the said Mr. Higginson, according as he was desired, drew up a confession of faith and form of church covenant according to the Scriptures; several copies whereof being written out, they publicly owned the same, on the day set apart for that work, a copy of which is retained at this day by some that succeed in the same church..... There were at that time thirty persons joined together in that church covenant; for which end so many copies being prepared aforehand, it was publicly read in the assembly, and the persons concerned solemnly expressing their assent and consent thereunto, they immediately proceeded to ordain their minister.....Those that were afterward admitted unto church fellowship, were with the confession of their faith required to enter into a like covenant engagement with the church, to walk according to the rules of the gospel, as to the substance, the same as at the first ; but for the manner and circumstances, it was left to the wisdom and faithfulness of the elders, to be so ordered as was judged most conducing to the end, respect being by them always had to the liberty and ability of the person."—*Hubbard's Hist. of N. E. p.* 119.

John Horne, one of the first thirty members of the Church, deserves a special notice. He was deacon from 1629 to 1684. Mr. Higginson, in 1680, says of him in the church records,—" Our bro. Horne, having been Deacon of this Church above this 50 years, being now very Antient, the Church proceeded and agreed to choose 2 Deacons to be added unto him." He finally dropped the H from his name, signing it, in his will Orne. From him have descended all the Salem Ornes. He left four sons, John, Symon, Joseph and Benjamin. Joseph was the great grandfather of the late Capt. William Orne, and Dr. Joseph Orne who graduated at H. C. 1765.

COMMEMORATIVE DISCOURSE.

A COMMEMORATIVE DISCOURSE

PRONOUNCED AT

QUINCY, MASS., 25 MAY, 1840,

ON THE

SECOND CENTENNIAL ANNIVERSARY

OF THE

ANCIENT INCORPORATION OF THE TOWN.

WITH

AN APPENDIX.

By GEORGE WHITNEY.

BOSTON:
JAMES MUNROE AND COMPANY.
M DCCC XL.

CAMBRIDGE PRESS:

METCALF, TORRY, AND BALLOU.

Quincy, June 16, 1840.

To the Rev. George Whitney,

Dear Sir, — In behalf of the Committee of Arrangements, I have the honor to communicate to you the annexed vote, expressing the thanks of the Committee for the Discourse delivered by you on the 25th of May last, and requesting a copy of the same for publication.

Voted, unanimously, That the thanks of the Committee of Arrangements be presented to the Rev. George Whitney of Roxbury, for the interesting and valuable Discourse, which he delivered on the 25th of May last, in commemoration of the Second Centennial Anniversary of the ancient Incorporation of the Town, and that he be requested to furnish a copy for the press.

In obedience to my instructions I cheerfully communicate this vote, and cordially express my individual desire that you will acquiesce in their request.

Accept, dear Sir, the warmest good wishes of the Committee, and of

Your friend and servant,

John A. Green,

Chairman of the Committee of Arrangements.

TO

THE YOUNG MEN OF QUINCY,

AT WHOSE REQUEST

THIS DISCOURSE WAS DELIVERED,

AND TO ALL WHO CONTRIBUTED TO OUR INTERESTING CELEBRATION,

THESE PAGES

Are Respectfully Dedicated.

DISCOURSE.

FRIENDS, FELLOW-NATIVES, AND DESCENDANTS
OF THIS ANCIENT INCORPORATION.

We meet this day, in obedience to the dictates of the highest sentiments in man. We have gathered together, scattered as we are in our various pursuits, in the spirit of a filial and dutiful reverence, to commemorate the times that have passed, and our Fathers, who made them what they were. We come to testify our admiration of all that was elevating and ennobling in those who first stepped upon these shores, and who in later periods contributed their part towards the good institutions and manifold privileges with which we are surrounded. We come, amidst comforts and ever newly opening blessings, — such as their fondest hopes never dared to dream of, — to be grateful for their patience and sacrifices, and trust in God in times of peril and darkness and deprivations, such as we may try to describe, but can never adequately conceive. We come, after two centuries and six generations of men have passed away, to stand around their graves, yet among the works, where they most emphatically live, that we may attempt to do some feeble justice to their principles and example, and to our own feelings also, in the tribute we thus pay to their memories.

With this day, two hundred years have elapsed, and

a new century commences, since an act was passed by the General Court incorporating a town in this place. Previously to this period, as is almost too well known to be repeated, a settlement here of civilized men had already been begun, following rapidly in the wake of the Pilgrims at Plymouth. In 1625, fifteen years before the time alluded to, Captain Wollaston, with about thirty in his company, as is supposed, — the number being nowhere, so far as I am acquainted, definitely designated, — landed somewhere on the shore near the mount, which afterwards received his name, and in the language of the old historians "sat down," either upon the mount, or in the region round about. In other words, they came and fixed their abode and planted a colony here. From subsequent events we are left to infer that there were no very exalted aims, like those which actuated many of the early pilgrims, either in the heart of Wollaston or his comrades. And yet with regard both to himself and some who accompanied him, it may possibly have been otherwise. We are sure, there was little to commend in Thomas Morton, or in those who were ready to sympathize with him. At any rate, we learn that after "spending much labor, cost, and time in planting the place," * things did not answer Wollaston's expectation, and he departed to Virginia. This can be considered, to be sure, no positive proof that Wollaston's aims were not so elevated as the noblest of that long line of self-exiled men, who came out to these distant shores, but the great mass of them were not in the habit of calculating profit and loss in any such way, nor did they think

* Hubbard's History of New England, p. 103.

their hardships and disappointments, where once they had planted themselves, of sufficient moment to urge them to try new locations. Wollaston's enterprise bore strong marks, to say the least, of being merely a pecuniary speculation.

The fifteen years, which elapsed from the landing of Wollaston to the incorporation of the town, were somewhat eventful ones, and appear to have been of considerable moment in the annals of those times. Thomas Morton, already alluded to, and one who accompanied Wollaston, proved a disorganizer, and a ringleader of such as were disposed to sympathize with him. It would be difficult, with an eye the most indulgent, and making liberal allowances, in the extreme, for the sanctimonious views and rigid discipline of the Puritans, to apologize for his own private irregularities, his conduct to the Indians, whether friendly or inimical, and specially for the contempt with which he treated all order and authority. He became indeed the source of great trouble to the early settlers here and elsewhere, a constant annoyance to those in authority, and withal, in his disposition and conduct, about as incorrigible a subject as they could well desire for their management. Among his notorious acts of dissipation and riot, he set up a May Pole to be danced and sung round, than which, it would not have been easy to have devised anything more odious to the scrupulous Puritans, short of the actual introduction among them of the Evil One himself. Subsequently, also, in various ways, his conduct was exceedingly reprehensible. After repeated measures had been enforced against him, some of them military and violent, all equally indicative of the displeasure of the Government and their decided purposes in regard to him ; after he had once been sent to England in 1628, and had returned to Mount Wollaston, or, as Governor Bradford somewhere says, to "his old nest at Merry Mount," the name he had himself given it, we find a record left in these words, "September 7, 1630, Second Court of Assistants held at Charlestown. Present, Governor Winthrop, Deputy Governor Dudley, Sir Richard Saltonstall and others. Ordered, 'That Thomas Morton of Mount Wollaston shall presently be set in the bilbowes, [long bars or bolts of iron used to confine the feet of prisoners and offenders on board ships,] and after sent to England by the ship called the Gift, now returning thither: that all his goods shall be seized to defray the charge of his transportation, payment of his debts, and to give satisfaction to the Indians for a canoe he took unjustly from them, and that his house be burnt down to the ground in sight of the Indians, for their satisfaction for many wrongs he has done them.' " *

This was enforced, and in pursuance of the order he was again sent to England. But his annoyances did not end here. He urged complaints to the king, which were likewise sources of difficulty: he returned again to Mount Wollaston, and afterwards in repeated forms disturbed and harassed the colony, so that at last, as Hutchinson says, "Nothing but his age saved him from the whipping-post." † He died at Agamenticus — the town of York, in the state of Maine, about 1643 — if not in obscurity, as he resolved not to die, at least in disgrace, and to the promotion of the public tranquillity.

* Prince's Chronology, Vol. I. p. 248.

† Hutchinson's History, Vol. I. p. 32, London Edition, Note.

A source of still more ardent and general excitement, if possible, to the people of those early times, was the supposed heretical preaching of Mr. John Wheelwright, a connexion in kindred, and a zealous friend in opinion of the memorable and gifted Mrs. Anne Hutchinson. To some, this latter circumstance was of far deeper interest than the preceding one, as, in their view, no radicalism in politics, no disorderly conduct could compare with heresy on that absorbing topic, to which their eyes and hearts were so steadily directed. This gentleman came out and ministered to the people of the Mount, by the permission, if not at the instigation of the First Church in Boston, as early as 1636 — the residents here, on account of their distance from Boston, having previously petitioned to have the benefit of a preacher. The chief excitement, which with all innocence, and sincerity of purpose, too, he seems to have been the cause of brewing up, was that apparently simple thing, the preaching of a Fast sermon. Already the clergy, as a body, and some of the laity had begun to look upon him with fearful and suspicious eyes. But the larger portion of the laity, we have reason to think, went not a little beyond an ordinary sympathy with him. It was in consonance with what, in my opinion, was the prevalent spirit of the times, as, with your patience, in the sequel we may hope to see illustrated. He was apparently an innovator and reformer: he took one step aside from the trodden way; and the conservatives sounded the trumpet of alarm. His seemingly humble instrument, the Fast sermon, set the whole community into a blaze. From such small beginnings do great things grow. Thus does God choose the weak things of the world to confound the things that are mighty. He was pursued and arraigned, disfranchised and banished. Fortunate in his time, that he came off even thus lightly, and escaped the block. A little earlier period would have counted him less venial. A slighter matter, persisted in with the firmness he manifested, might but shortly before his day have crowned him with the honors of martyrdom.

It comes within my present plan only to take this passing notice of Mr. Wheelwright, and the excitement which followed him, as one of the remarkable events, which had taken place previously to the incorporation of the town. This event alone would afford an almost interminable field for remark and discussion, were it to be pursued, and more than absorb all the time I ought to claim on the present occasion. Inviting as it is, I leave it with the less regret, as it has recently been so ably and satisfactorily presented to the public in the discourses * consequent upon the return of the second century since the gathering of the first church, to which its further consideration might in every view appear more pertinent.

Other incidents likewise are to be noticed of inferior but still not very slight consequence, considering the circumstances of the times. Intimately connected with much that has already been stated, and in part the cause of it, were first the highly probable fact, that after the departure of Wollaston, some of his company had become stationary at the Mount, thus affording us, at least, the venerable distinction of being the oldest permanent † settlement in Massachusetts; and secondly, the indisputable fact, that men both of eminence and

* See Lunt's Second Century Discourses.

† See Winthrop's Journal, Vol. I. p. 43.

industry came out here from the metropolis and had allotments of land made to them, already cleared and inviting their labors, and thus giving us the less questionable distinction of having had some of the earliest, if not the very earliest, cultivated farms in the colony, possibly in New England. These all rendered the Mount conspicuous — lifting it up before the eyes of the sparse community far above its humble physical elevation. It had early a name, notoriety, and character. It was a cherished spot both to the Bostonians, to whom in fact it belonged, being by order of court early annexed to it, and to the magistrates and the early settlers generally.

Accordingly, the way was naturally and easily and early prepared for an application, on the part of the residents here, and for a ready acquiescence on the part of the magistrates, that the inhabitants at Mount Wollaston should be incorporated into a town. The benefits of such a measure must be too obvious to be enlarged upon. It it natural that we should turn with some curiosity and interest to the early document — to wit, the petition which was presented to this effect. No very musty antiquarian fondness would seem to be essential in order to reap gratification from its perusal. But that privilege is denied us. It has shared the fate of many more valuable things. It is not extant.

In the first volume of the Massachusetts Colony Records, under date of 13 May, 1640, is the following account of the action that was had in reply to the application from the Mount.

"The Petition * of the Inhabitants of Mount Wool-

* Massachusetts Colony Records, Vol. 1. p. 277.

laston was voted and granted them to be a Town according to the agreement with Boston; provided, that if they fulfil not the covenant made with Boston and hearto affixed, it shall be in the power of Boston to recover their due by action against the said inhabitants or any of them, — and the town is to be called Braintree."

Pretty rigid principle this, on which to base their conditions, whatever the amount or extent of those conditions might have been! It was, in fact, the very principle, involving the question, which, in our own time, has been mooted, with so much earnestness and cogent reasoning on both sides, whether individuals shall be holden for the liabilities of the corporation, of which they are a component part.

It is not necessary to quote these conditions, extending to considerable length, and being rather minute. They are principally the payment of certain yearly assessments on special parcels of land. One item it is curious at this distant day to observe. Boston resigns* to Braintree, probably as hardly worth the keeping, the rocky hill extending west from where we are assembled, far into the granite quarries, "together with another parcel of rocky ground near to the Knight's Neck."

* The language of the record runs thus, — "All that rocky ground lying between the Fresh brook and Mr. Coddington's brook, adjoining to Mr. Hough's farm, and from the west corner of that farm to the southmost corner of Mr. Hutchinson's farm, to be reserved and used in common forever." Mr. Coddington's farm, we know, was the present Mount Wollaston farm. Where Mr. Hutchinson's farm was we have no means of determining. But guided by the two brooks mentioned, in all probability the two principal ones which pass through the town at the present day, I have supposed the parcel alluded to would be likely to lie in the direction stated. If I am right in this conjecture it included Mount Ararat, (so called,) with the hilly portion stretching south of it as far as the brook.

It was reserved for a period, long after their very names had passed from among men, amidst the growing improvements of advancing time, to affix to the worthless rocks a value surpassing all that could have entered their imagination.

The origin of the name of our ancient town, as thus incorporated, is traced in this way. In 1632, according to Winthrop,* a company from Braintrey in England, near Chelmsford, where Mr. Hooker was the preacher, begun to settle at Mount Wollaston. They removed afterwards to Newton, but, as has been conjectured, it appears to me with good reason,† a part of the company must have returned again, perhaps about 1634, and settled permanently. Unquestionably at their request or suggestion, the name of their former residence was given to the new place of their adoption.

It is far from common, I suppose, that in the division of towns, the movement for separation occurs with the old settlement. Such, however, was the fact here; and in the issue, whether from necessity or not, the ancient name was resigned and the present one was taken, in honor of Colonel John Quincy, who had occupied the Mount Wollaston farm. As we have come up, however, to commemorate the original incorporation, there seems a special propriety in doing it where the first settlement and incorporation were actually made, rather than follow the name to a spot where only a feeble settlement, if any, had been begun, and no church gathered till more than half a century afterwards.

* See Winthrop's New England, p. 87, note by Savage.

† See Lunt's Second Century Discourses, Appendix, p. 66.

I now take leave of the history, which, commencing with the period to which I have arrived, has been steadily accumulating for two hundred years, and pass to other considerations, of a more practical bearing, and in which we shall be far more likely to find some end. It would be as preposterous as it would be fearfully tedious, to pursue the history through all the details of two centuries, down to the present hour. This is more properly the work of the annalist. Let us turn, therefore, to matters of a more comprehensive character.

And here we may well remark how little history in general has done to elevate our conceptions of man. Something it could hardly fail to accomplish of good, as from age to age it affords us records of what advancement has been made upon the past. But it tells us little of human capacity. It is, for the most part, the dismal catalogue of man's animal conflicts, and the exhibition of his worst passions. War, conquest, ambitious triumphs, purchased at the cost of wholesale suffering; selfish accumulation at the expense of monstrous and revolting miseries, awful and unjust impositions; these, and the things like them, are what stand out glaringly on its pages. It does no justice to the better part of man. It is no index in itself alone of what he is destined to accomplish. He who looks to history in the light of so many facts only, as so many items alone in the amount of mortal action, and takes them for his guide, will be about certain to err. He must of necessity be narrow in his expectations of human advancement. The true philosopher will go behind history and analyze the picture it presents, find its real elements, and place them in their rightful order. He will sift out the chaff, and set down to the lower propensities what belongs exclusively to them. After wading through a century of disheartening events, he will not, therefore, grow hopeless of man; for he can perceive that scarcely one of the higher powers of his nature has been called into action. Man has not himself been before him, but the deformity of man, which we may justly complain history has been so lavish in portraying.

Hence the difference among men in their visions of the future. One takes history for his exclusive guide, its bare, dark chapters. Another takes his stand upon principles — the elements and capacities of human nature, what man was evidently designed by his Creator to be. Can we doubt how meagre, unsatisfactory, and delusive in comparison history thus becomes? An Egyptian colony, we are told, planted Athens; a band of robbers and outcasts laid the foundations of Rome, — her sons in time left Carthage a heap of ashes, and transferred her glory to the beautiful Italian shores. William the Conqueror invaded and overran Britain; the Turks, during more than double the centuries we have had a name on the earth, planted their feet with a gigantic power on the neck of Grecian valor, refinement, and unsurpassed literary fame; meanwhile the mighty sway, and the feeble are ground in the dust. Where do we get the intimation that the feeble band of the Puritans, at very sight of whom the imposing court of Charles curl their lips in scorn, shall one day push off to these ends of the earth, and here kindle up on new principles the dawn of a better hope for man? The convents of the middle ages, the castle-crowned cliffs of Lords and Barons ministered, in part, to the physical wants of the human race. It was their pride and glory that the beggar knocked never at their gates in vain. But nothing was done, nothing even attempted to lift the unfortunate or the indigent above the necessity of beggary. Let him, who counts history thus all-sufficient, lay his finger upon those hopeful premises, whence we may safely make the glad deduction that, far in the distant future, a better almsgiving shall call forth the sympathies of humanity, — that all their bounties and charity shall look poor and shallow, the merest surface work by the side of a truer benevolence, which, striking deeper than physical want, aims at individual self-respect and social elevation.

Nevertheless, history in its place is not to be disparaged. It has its lessons, and it is fruitful of instruction. Only let not man grow faithless under it. They who left the smiling scenes of England, and built up in this wilderness, first the humble towns, and, through their growing strength, our present wide domain, till "the little one has become a thousand, and the small one a strong nation," came forth here and conquered and took the victory, as had been done times without number before. History records for us their doings, fortunately also some of the elevated objects at which they were aiming. What was there in their coming forth here, and in the prosperity that has followed them, differing from those of all other conquests or colonizations? Let us briefly look into this, and trace, as I think we may, to the same cause the success of their enterprise at the beginning, and the surpassing prosperity that has risen up to honor their memories since.

If we step for a moment behind history and look at it as it passes before us, we shall perceive that there have been two preëminently distinct and prominent classes of principles, which have prevailed among men, and by which communities and the world in general have been swayed. These are the binding and the dissevering principles, founded the one upon the moral sentiments, the other upon the animal propensities in man. Neither of these has as yet ever existed, without any alliance with the other. The latter has prevailed in by far the largest measure. The binding principles, founded as they are upon the moral sentiments, have reference to the everlasting laws of rectitude, and to a conformity with the will and designs of the Creator. The dissevering principles, on the contrary, founded upon what is low, are shallow, superficial, extraneous, — they are attendant upon arbitrary will or artificial circumstances or temporary necessity, or what is worse, error, folly, ignorance, or crime. Thus, for example, all the principles which go to the support of a despotism are dissocial, dissevering, and shattering in their very nature. They tend naturally and inevitably to nurture passions and promote objects, which must as certainly divide men, as a decree of fate. They set one against another, and bring on opposing interests and factions, weakness and downfall. On one side, the side of the despot, there are pride, arrogance, indolence, oppression, inordinate selfishness, the idea of inherited or inalienable right over the property, persons, freedom, and happiness of others; and on the other, the side of the overpowered, envy and hatred, the desire of liberty, the chafing feeling of rights trampled on and human nature abused. In these there is no permanent germ, no bond of union. They can no more coexist eternally, they can no more draw naturally and willingly in any harmonious fellowship, than the hungry tiger can gambol with the lamb. Those principles, on the contrary, which are at the foundation of a true republic, are naturally binding; never as yet, indeed, have we seen them anything like generally prevailing, or freely and fully acted out. Whenever we do see them, we shall find them exercising this influence; as far as we witness them at all, we perceive this to be their character; — and reasonably, for their object is to call out individual action in its legitimate and noblest sphere, and to respect, develop, defend all human rights. The disconnection of religion from the state, the union of taxation and representation, the right of private judgment, the principle of toleration, and in morals the principle of doing unto others what we would wish they should do to us,— these all are binding principles. The more they get into operation, the more will they cement men and prosper their union, — fixing their eyes and hearts on one common good, the highest happiness, the greatest and universal elevation of the human race.

Taking this key with us, the history of the past assumes a new face. We read it with an alphabet that makes it intelligible. It is not only not discouraging, but crowded with lessons of warning, with incitements to new effort, and hopeful promises of good. What cause for wonder, so often expressed, when we look back to nations or cities of antiquity, and perceive that under seemingly prosperous circumstances, fortune smiling, they could not be held together beyond a certain point, — that after a time they have shattered to pieces like some vast edifice, outwardly adorned, but within which the perilous elements of explosion have been all the while concealed, ready fuel for the fatal spark! The truth was, their overthrow and downfall were inevitable; — in most instances, because the prominent principles by which they were governed were dissocial, not only not binding, but altogether dissevering. And in the same connexion, though in a different sphere, we see why it was that such a man as Howard could go on his self-devoted mission and fulfil it so well, why it was that success and triumph seemed so marvellously to run before him, that, in the striking language of the Scriptures, he appeared "to have power to tread on serpents and scorpions and over all the power of the enemy, nothing by any means hurting him." It was because his whole heart and soul were allied with, and all he did was done upon these binding principles, — principles, which draw men to one common object, the sublimest services that can engage the human soul, and cement all their sympathies, hopes, and affections with it.

If now, we inquire again what there was in the coming out of the first settlers of New England so distinctive and hopeful in its very nature, — if we ask, again, what was the peculiar character of the seed here sown, whence sprung up these flourishing towns, whence came the unparalleled prosperity, which in less than two centuries, nay in far less than one, converted a wilderness into more than a blooming garden, here we find the reply. It was their alliance with these elevating principles, blessed by the overruling Providence of God, which did it all. Coiled up here, lay hidden, as I conceive, the great moving spring, which first drove our fathers from their pleasant abodes, and founded here these new manifestations of freedom and hope. It was the same, which, as it gradually uncoiled, gave a new impulse to human action, scattered far and wide hitherto unimagined blessings, and handed down to distant ages an inheritance surpassing — with the exception of Christianity, of which it might be called in part a new development — surpassing in value the most precious legacy of the past.

It might be useful, only that it would lead me into too wide a field, to consider somewhat in detail, by what operation of their opposites these better principles gradually found root in the hearts of the Puritans, and by what oppressions and excesses our fathers grew more and more enamored of them, till they found an asylum and a new sphere for them here. In their day and previously to their day, the selfish and dissevering principles had gained almost entire sway in their own and other lands. The civil, moral and religious, and intellectual aspect of the times were each and all singularly odious and hateful. All refinement had a low aim. Correct modes of philosophizing were buried up under metaphysical obscurities. Expansive and elevated principles were wanting. Few, if any, among the higher elements of man, were recognised as having any foundation in himself. Religion was practically regarded as an outward mechanism, to be used only for worldly purposes. To complete the dark picture, the civil power came down in the form of infringements upon property and personal liberty. Those unpleasant ministers, those unconciliating peace-makers, confiscation and imprisonment, torture and the stake, were everywhere busy. Wisdom above man's overruled them all for good. Strange to tell, their very contraries grew up on the uncongenial soil. Out of adversity gems of virtues glistened brightly. The old curse was again a blessing; and in these elevated principles they took refuge with high and animating hope.

It has been common to ascribe the first movement of the founders of New England, and their subsequent action and success to religion; and in its very broadest acceptation, undoubtedly, this term would embrace the wide circle of incitements by which they were moved. But let us beware lest, in our application of it, we fail to do justice to all their springs of action. Religion has been narrowed, and made a technical thing. Little else does it express to the minds of many but the unfolding and right direction of the sentiment of reverence alone. It speaks to them only of pious sentiments, and affectionate and confiding trust in God. They had all these, but they had more. The Jews present to us a remarkable specimen of this sort of development. The devotional and pious element, — religion in this restricted sense was signally displayed in their character. But what did they comparatively accomplish, even with all this, in the way of civil and social institutions, in the sense of laying the foundation of a comprehensive and enduring national prosperity? What have the various tribes and nations accomplished, — the long catalogue of whom we need not stop to recapitulate, — in whom the same element has predominated? We may readily reply, without injustice, little or nothing. Contrast the founders of New England with such as these, and how obvious is it that by such an estimate we reach to no adequate appreciation of their wide spirit, their far reaching principles. A much nearer approach do we make to it, by saying that they were looking to the foundation of a Christian commonwealth. That end was most assuredly in their hearts, and for its accomplishment all that I have set forth, as their guiding principles, was indispensably necessary. It *was* religion, under the direction of which they moved, but religion in its most comprehensive sense; reverence presiding over the right development of all the higher faculties. Hence the principles, with which they were accompanied, all the subsidiary action became of the character we have been considering. They were those binding principles, which elevate at the same time that they honor humanity. They were those which, in proportion as they prevail in their perfection, give success and permanency to any undertaking.

Mighty principles these! And yet say now, ye who calculate the chances of success of human enterprises, say, what chances have these exiles as the dim outline of their loved land fades from their view! By all worldly calculation, they would be set down as destined to certain and irretrievable failure. So might we say of almost every great undertaking, in which man has ever engaged. Judged by the maxims of worldly prudence, scarcely one great achievement of all the myriads that man has brought to pass, would have been marked antecedently with any likelihood of success. But tested by the principles on which we perceive the Pilgrims started, we see good reason why beginnings so inauspicious as theirs have grown so illustrious; and, on the other hand, why schemes, that arrayed on their side wealth and power and numbers and public opinion, have dwindled into insignificance, and left no other trace that they ever were, but the story of their early promise and almost as early and signal defeat.

We * are not to look back to the Pilgrims, even in all our admiration of what they were and what they did, with the expectation of finding a full and perfect exemplification of the principles, the general character of which have rendered them and their cause so illustrious. They manifested them, perhaps, about as fully as could be expected from humanity, under their circumstances. Their perfect manifestation would have realized the Utopian commonwealth. They gave their hearts to the higher order of principles, the highest that can actuate the souls of men, — and that was enough. That they were not perfect only reminds us that they were mortal. They took hold of principles in sympathy with man's better elements, principles that had been despised and rejected of men, and with their adherence to them the institutions of society could not but be remodelled and safely founded. They poured a fresh spirit into religion by claiming the rights of conscience; and even cramped, as it undeniably was, it stood forth among them as if raised from the dead. They defended the principle of self government, and vested the right of electing their own magistrates in the hands of the people. This also breathed into the civil condition the breath of life. They recognised all the right of individual action they felt to be consistent with safety; and that set all the wheels of industry in motion, on which public prosperity relies so much. They drew out the religious sentiment, and kept it uppermost like a presiding Deity. They founded the free schools, and thus rocked an infant Hercules as

* This and the next paragraph, on account of the unavoidable length of the Discourse, were omitted in the delivery.

among the first-born children of the youthful commonwealth.

We may pardon some few imperfections to men who in a dark age could accomplish such things as these. Is it asked, why they could not have carried out some of their professed principles a little more fully, — toleration, for example? "Tolerate! tolerate whom?" let me reply in the words of a descendant of one of the first settlers of the Mount and some of the earliest natives of this ancient town, whose name has been given to our soil, "Tolerate whom? the legate of the Roman Pontiff, or the emissary of Charles the First and Archbishop Laud? How consummate would have been their folly and madness, to have fled into the wilderness to escape the horrible persecutions of those hierarchies, and at once to have admitted into the bosom of their society men brandishing and ready to apply the very flames and fetters from which they had fled! Those, who are disposed to condemn them on this account, neither realize the necessities of their condition, nor the prevailing character of the times. Under the stern discipline of Elizabeth and James, the stupid bigotry of the first Charles, and the spiritual pride of Archbishop Laud, the spirit of the English hierarchy was very different from that which it assumed, when, after having been tamed and humanized under the wholesome discipline of Cromwell and his commonwealth, it yielded itself to the mild influence of the principles of 1688, and to the liberal spirit of Tillotson."*

We would honor the memories of those, who first trod these shores, and founded our towns in all their

* Quincy's Centennial Address, Boston, p. 26.

allegiance to these elevating and binding principles. We would honor their patience and perseverance, their magnanimous endurance and trust in God, in all the days of darkness and discouragement they saw, of which there were many. And we would devoutly bless God, that to causes so honorable to themselves, so elevating and enduring in their very nature, we may trace the success that crowned their day of small things, their feeble but magnanimous enterprise.

If now we have been able to find an interpretation to the prosperity that attended the original enterprise of our Fathers, in the very principles on which they started, equally also to the same cause are we to ascribe the rapid growth of the towns, which soon sprung up upon their footsteps, and the almost startling and constantly accelerating progress they have made since in all that improves and honors man.

1. In the first place, as to their government. It was the same order of principles, carried out into practice here, that bound them together and gave them stability. Actually it might seem it could be no otherwise at the first; for the very men, who in the beginning brought to this wilderness the principles we have been considering, were those who peopled the ancient towns. They must be expected to breathe the spirit of the principles they cherished. But in this we overlook the important distinction between being merely resident in the towns,—the general government being, meanwhile, administered over all,—and the transmission of all the vital principles they held so sacred, so far as they could be transmitted, down to the towns themselves. In a word, it would have been one thing, as it

might have been, to have made the towns actual dependencies, — subject in every particular to the discretion and management of the general government, having their officers all appointed by authority, amount of taxes fixed and assessed abroad, enactments passed as to the regulation of all matters connected with public roads, instruction, and so forth, descending to the very lowest details, — and another thing, as it was, to commit all this to their entire management and control, with an undoubting confidence as to the wisdom and success of entrusting it to their care.

In doing this, the very principles were put in action in all the towns for which the Pilgrims had crossed the ocean. The roots of the liberty they sought to realize went down to the smallest communities among them. It was the right they claimed of governing themselves, and having a voice in every law they were called to obey, which was the one thing essential, the beginning, middle, and end of their civil prosperity. We see its good effects in its cementing and elevating character, turn where we will, in their early history; — nowhere are these good effects more apparent than in the growing prosperity of the towns. The prevalence of this principle, in particular, — and of a similar character, more or less, were all upon which they acted, — tended to make at once a common interest for all. It served as a stimulant upon individual exertion. Where each one does something to determine measures, and who shall enforce them, it is natural that each one should feel some incitement and call to that service. It is natural that, in devising the best means of bringing about desirable objects, the higher intellectual qualities should be called forth and exercised, such as invention, prudence, and forethought. A generous spirit and liberal views spring up likewise in the same connexion and from the same cause, — and in every byway where we trace its operation, the principle becomes a blessing. Hence it is, that accumulating funds and legacies, whether for schools or religious institutions, become so often dead weights upon a community; not so much by any direct influence of evil, as because they go, — precisely in proportion to the ground they cover, — to palsy all those qualities in man, which ought to be roused to do for the community just that amount they are trying to do for them. The real good in the world is accomplished by individual exertion and sacrifice; and these the free principles, planted in all our towns, have been singularly well calculated to draw out.

Now all these qualities, thus stirred into action, are the sure elements of prosperity. The rocky and sterile soil of New England, — girdled almost uninterruptedly by breakers on the sea and mountains on the main, — whose natural productions, as has been strikingly said, are nothing but rocks and ice, yet dotted all over with these flourishing communities, most satisfactorily corroborates the assertion. It is vain to place man under the most genial sky, and amid all the favorable circumstances of outward condition, warm suns and balmy breezes and a fruitful soil, without those manly qualities, which enable him to make them tributary to great ends; and on the contrary, with these, what are the most forbidding and dreary wildernesses but the fields of his prosperity and glory? Let some of the sunny Italian lands with their lazy, stupid, decaying population attest the first. Our own time-honored municipality, imbedded in her granite quarries, with her long and flourishing sisterhood, the smiling towns of New England, shall be the diagram for the last.

> "Man is the nobler growth our realms supply,
> And souls are ripened in our northern sky."

2. So much for the principles, which have entered into the government of the towns. Then next in relation to their social interests. Some provision must be made to foster these, or any community will dwindle away. Instead of taking a prosperous course, it will in time die out. Our progenitors took the most decidedly effectual measures towards this object, that human ingenuity could devise, and by doing nothing, actually did everything. They might, indeed, be said to have taken off all the old impediments and restrictions, which had been previously wound round the social condition, as if artfully contrived to put an end to all healthy circulation, inasmuch as they never, for a moment, renewed, on this side of the water, what had been amply tested to their satisfaction on the other. But it was only in such a sense that they could be said to have done anything. They virtually left the social condition to itself. They gave it all it asked, — the field of a fair opportunity.

It was a wide stride in the advancement of human affairs, and in the elevation of the social condition, thus to do nothing. With the laws already based upon justice, and looking to the support of equal rights, all the fruits of industry were at once made secure and permanent; — all property, in short, however acquired, became sacred and safe. Beyond this, to drop all the old props of society, the crazy framework on which they had relied so much, wasting their energies in sustaining what, instead of strengthening, only made society the weaker, was, we must confess, in their day, an experiment, as bold as to the philosophic eye it was profound, as in the event it has proved successful. What mad scheme would you be venturing upon? might have inquired the crafty politician of those times, — and the inquiry would not have sounded either shallow or unmeaning, — what mad scheme would you be venturing upon, thus to cut loose from the protecting laws, the safe mooring places of primogeniture and entail? What will become of all the family distinctions of wealth and power, we have found so essential to preserve the government and the social state what it is? Hold on, — rather the more firmly amidst the gathering commotions that are brewing up, — to what time has proved such efficient instruments to check and regulate human affairs. — Unfortunately, they have checked and regulated us a little too much, — might have been the sagacious reply, — and that too at the cost of the real interest and happiness of those who have been only dreaming that they were served. In reality, all of us have fared alike. All of us have suffered. The social circulations have been dead. We want free action. Let us lay the social foundations anew. Let us put them on the free exercise of the native sentiments of the soul. — There they were laid. There they have prospered.

In this result, in this new experiment of the Pilgrims, we come back again to the prevalence of the same elevated and binding principles which governed them from the first, and all along. The towns flourished under these new social privileges. The sympathies of men were called out, we might almost say, as they had never before been in the history of Christian civilization. There was nothing to impede or counteract them. They were free. They worked spontaneously. If to any one thing more than another we are to ascribe the healthy and unexampled growth of the towns, I know not to what we could turn more readily than to this. Lay back, at this hour, upon the most prosperous of these communities, the old burden of social embarrassments, and who can doubt, for one moment, their certain and rapid decay?

3. Then, too, in still another department, — never to be overlooked or forgotten, — may we trace, in the growth and prosperity of our towns, the prevalence and operation of the same exalted and elevating principles. The system that was early adopted for the diffusion of good learning; and the means that were taken to develop and direct the religious sentiment, were alike honorable to our Fathers, and fruitful of unspeakable blessings to their posterity. We sometimes lose sight of the actual dimensions of great privileges enjoyed; — on the one hand, by our familiarity with their constant contributions to our comfort or prosperity; and on the other, by never ceasing panegyric or fulsome eulogy. Let us take care that neither of these makes us insensible to the institutions in question. Let me not be thought especially to be falling in with any formal commendation. If much has been said, in times past, on these topics, it has been because they could rightfully claim so much. In connexion with all their other wise provisions, these prospective measures, — for beyond dispute they were eminently that, — stood out foremost, and engaged their most devoted attention. They sprung beyond the narrow calculations of utility. They were neither bread, nor houses, nor weapons of

defence against their ever watchful and insidious foes. The first settlers could hardly be said to have required these institutions for themselves, — certainly not those for the promotion of learning. Their great distinction was that they came charged with the treasures of learning, — an overflowing stock for the youthful commonwealth. But they looked forward to the generations that were to follow on after them. Or rather, let us say, actuated by higher considerations still, feeling the strong claims and necessity of disciplining and storing the mind, impressed with the infinite importance of religion to human well-being, they gave expression to these convictions. Their anticipations were far-reaching and hopeful, we know; but there were deeper fountains in their own souls than they. They did their duty to themselves, and confided in God that their fruits would appear in their children. So it came to pass that in poverty and straits they built their churches and supported their ministers, established the free schools and founded the university.

The fruits, for which they trusted in God, have appeared in their children. In those fruits the towns have been strong and prosperous. Of what avail were all other blessings without the fruits of these institutions? What were all our glorious rivers, our granite hills, our mines of coal, our protecting harbors, opening into the wide bosom of the ocean, and ready to lay the treasures of distant climes into the lap of the stretching main, — what were industry, toiling from early morn till latest eve, without mind directing all these, and intelligent enterprise turning them into a richer value, a truer worth, than Peruvian gold? The free schools, aided by the higher institutions and colleges, have done this, and far more than I may even hint at, throughout New England. And of what avail were all the acuteness of intellect, all the unfolded powers and stored wisdom of the mind, unsanctified by higher considerations, — unless guarded, made safe and strong by moral and religious influences? Possibly might they prove only the greater curse. The sons of the Pilgrims, in these our towns, have fully exemplified the worth of these institutions. Nothing can be truer than the assertion often made and in many forms, that these institutions have cost us nothing. They have borrowed nothing, they have not more than twice over paid back. But rising above all such considerations as these is the more grateful and ennobling reflection, that from the churches of New England has shone forth a steady light, guiding her sons in all their homes and walks, and opening to their aspiring vision a higher world beyond the sorrows and allurements of this.

I have spoken of the character of the principles, by which the first settlers of New England were actuated, in their original enterprise, on their fidelity to which, under the smiles of a beneficent Providence, their success was founded; and to the prevalence of the same order of principles have traced the prosperity of our towns. In their growing and flourishing condition, New England herself has been honored. With the matron of old, presenting them as her offspring, she has been ready to exclaim, "these, these are my jewels."

On a day like this, when the children of this our household have gathered home, — when, with a filial reverence and glowing affections we have come to sit once more by the family hearth-stone, and to enjoy the social pleasures of the paternal birth-day, — when we have come to mingle our gladness and our grief together in many of the proud and happy, no less than the tender and affecting remembrances of the past, we shall be indulged, I trust, without the accusation of an attempt to glorify the family name, in recurring, as a dutiful service, to some of the venerable portraits that honor our walls, whose lives were eminent in their day, and many of whose names have become illustrious in the history of the world.

In doing this, we may well rejoice that we still keep within the circle of the elevated principles that have guided us thus far. It has been by their adherence to whatever is ennobling in man, to whatever meliorates and exalts the human condition, devotion to freedom and truth and God, that the native and adopted sons of this ancient town have earned the laurels of their fame and become eminent, some of them, in all the earth. To us have they bequeathed an imperishable renown,— our least return will be to call up their names, that we may pay some feeble tribute to their memories. Let us begin with the days of the Mount, with *John Wheelwright*, the bold and acute thinker. No time-serving conformist, no timid one to grow pale before councils or decrees. Fit companion for Sir Henry Vane, a reserve in the noble army of martyrs. Honor now to thy name, who for thy character and long ministry wouldst have been honored at the death, had not thy persecutors been in power.* — *William Coddington*, a fellow pilgrim with Winthrop, munificent and upright, "with the chiefest in all public charges," the friend of Wheel-

* See Hutchinson.

wright, peace-maker, judge, and governor. He should be remembered here where he did something for learning, and everything for a good example.—*Henry Adams.* Of him little is left to us but his epitaph. That tells us that "he took his flight from the Dragon persecution in Devonshire in England, and alighted at Mount Wollaston," (we may add, perhaps as early as 1630.) Would that we knew more of the intrepid Pilgrim. But we know this, and for this let him be remembered, that a century and a half afterwards, he turned round upon that Dragon, in his mighty descendant, and bearded him in his den. — *Edmund Quincy,* dying early, but worthy in his youth to be one of the first representatives of Boston, in the first General Court in the Province. He left those who came after him to complete his work, a long line of descendants, the magistrate, the judge, officers civil and military, among whom the glory of the children were their Fathers. They had freedom and the good of the country at heart. It was seen in their own doings and in the confidence of the people. — *Henry Flynt* breaks in upon the line, yet allied with them in kindred, a descendant of the Godly first teacher here. He has the memorable distinction of having labored longest on the roll of Harvard, — fellow and tutor among her servants and sons. Mirthful yet grave, he could mingle the "*suaviter in modo* with the *fortiter in re.*" Preacher and scholar! thou didst well in thy day. — *Lemuel Briant,* — let us pause here. He is not to be passed by as a common name. He stood out before his age where there were few to be at his side. High authority * pronounced him "the learned,

* President Adams, sen.

ingenuous, and eloquent pastor." He was all that. His distant successor assigns him his place to walk with Wheelwright in the grand procession of bold and thinking men. Posterity gives him fame in measures his own age had no censer they could burn it in. — Next comes *Richard Cranch*, born at the beginning of the last century, living into this. His tall person, like his upright mind, is still familiar to many of us. He was the son of a Puritan, and, in all that made such an one great, a Puritan himself. He loved science and adorned it. He was a profound theologian in everything but the name; and his life and his practice were better than that. Representative, senator, judge among the people, his integrity was a rock that could not be moved. He was honored by Harvard College, though he sat not in her seats or mused in her groves. The pillar he was, was missed when he fell where few like him have been left or risen up. — *John Adams* follows in the order of time, — the bold champion of freedom, the asserter of human right, the vindicator of the oppressed, by the power of his eloquence starting from their seats as august an assembly as the world ever saw. He was the son of one who served at this communion table. He was an ornament to religion and his race, faithful to his age and his God, great among the greatest. I will add no further feeble words of mine to a name that is written where it cannot die. Behold the man! approach and read! "This house will bear witness to his piety: This town, his birth-place, to his munificence: History to his patriotism: Posterity to the depth and compass of his mind." * — The next year

* By the side of the pulpit, in the First Church, where the present Discourse was delivered, is a mural monument, surmounted by a bust of John

after him, but not four months younger, is born *John Hancock*, the minister's son: the literary and polished gentleman, favorite of the people, liberal merchant, eloquent orator, courteous and dignified, representative and governor, member of the first congress, president of the second, first to write his name on the memorable scroll, the Declaration of Independence, where it stands bold and finished like his character and manners. He gave an immortality of littleness to General Gage, who sentenced him to condign punishment, and denied him pardon on any terms as a rebel, by showing in his triumphant cause how contemptible was his threat. — Eight years more, and there comes the youthful patriot, *Josiah Quincy, jr.*, another in the bright line we have already passed, eminent in the law, bold for freedom, both as a writer and actor. He stood up for justice, with his co-patriot John Adams, amidst the furious excitement of the Boston massacre; a stand as fearless as it was righteous. Like Regulus of old, his life was given to his country, but in a better way. Already enfeebled in health, he died returning from England, whither he had privately sailed for her good. No cheering tidings fell upon his dying ear, announcing her dawning glories. The battle of Lexington had been fought only seven days before. He sleeps in our burial yard. Peaceful be his rest! How befitting him, as we dwell upon the memory of his early promise, is that exquisite monumental inscription!

"Heu! quanto minus est cum reliquis versari quam tui meminisse."

Time would fail me to speak of all that might be

Adams, beneath which is an inscription from which the few words quoted in the text are taken.

added to the brilliant constellation, — the eminent dead, the more illustrious living. They will brighten the glittering galaxy at last. May they be mentioned with more becoming eulogy a hundred years from this day.

Such are some of the honorable and inspiring reminiscences of the past. There are other emotions that cannot but be awakened in us, — tender and more affecting. Two hundred years have passed away since the foundation of the town; and what joyful scenes and sorrowful ones have come and gone in all her habitations! Generation after generation have followed each other, like wave rolling upon wave, alike swallowed up together, — but time and its changes have neither of them stopped for them, nor have the divine appointments been altered or set aside. The cradle with its infant smiles, watched over by parental fondness; the bridal with its garlands and its hopes, each of them rosy and bright; the grave with its breaking hearts and tearful eyes; sickness with its own pains, and the watchful solicitude of those who have bent over it; merry gladness and withering gloom knocking side by side at countless doors; prayers of thanksgiving, and prayers imploring comfort, ascending from the same and different scenes; sunny prosperity and times that tried the soul; battle and peace, with all their terrors and rejoicings, who shall recount all these? In what thronging numbers do these affecting remembrances thicken round us, as we turn to the scenes of home, to the burial yard, to these worshiping courts, where in all their varied character they have been acted out, — how do they rise to our imaginations, as through the dim aisles of the past fancy pictures to us the retreating footsteps of the passing generations!

Meanwhile, on a wider field, what changes have been witnessed through the earth! For every one that landed with Wollaston more than two hundred may be rallied within the limits of the ancient incorporation, where three flourishing towns are opening day by day new avenues of enterprise and improvement. The feeble band of the Pilgrims — feeble only in numbers — have swollen to fifteen millions, and twenty-six independent republics have sprung up on the soil where they confided their hopes. The despised principles, for which they dared and bore everything, have been unfolding every hour, in new and more perfect manifestations, winning men to their embrace and practice. Intolerance has dropped her unseemly garments, and flung away, at least professedly, all her weapons of abuse and persecution. Their spirit has gone back and reacted upon the old world with its conciliating and elevating influences, — awing despotism and lifting the burdens of the social condition from despairing humanity. The university, on which they doated, rears her venerable head, amidst half a hundred, which her own sons almost alone have established. Learning has found channels for diffusing itself through society, of which they never dreamed, and is fast undermining social evils and demoralizing recreations, which open hostility had only fortified the more. Laws have been humanized and simplified, and barbarous and revolting practices have been banished from society as degrading to Christian men. Art, science, philosophy, into what hitherto unexplored regions have they penetrated, since the morning of New England first dawned! what treasures have they brought back to the waiting generations, increasing comfort, lessening toil, contracting the wide separations of the human family, scattering intelligence, awakening the higher faculties of man, banishing low pursuits and pleasures, and thus directing all their tributaries to swell the great tide of human improvement and progress!

What remains to us, descendants of the early emigrants, in helping forward this progress, on these shores so auspiciously begun, but more and more to copy their sympathy with, their allegiance to those higher principles, on which their enterprise was built? On our fidelity to these depends everything that is ennobling in the hopeful anticipations of the future. Nothing great or glorious lives, the roots of which have been planted in the lower propensities of man. Everything triumphs at last, which is based upon right, and religion, and truth. The applause of the passing hour, the shouts of the multitude may give a temporary prosperity to the wrong; black night may shut down for a while round the righteous cause; — but by the fidelity of human endeavor the final consummation is sure, and the steady progress towards it is as certain. Fathers of New England, may your sons learn this of you! Let the inheritance of your children be your trust in God, your never faltering faith in the capacities of man. "Thou carriest Cæsar," said the world's conqueror to the trembling boatman, as he ferried him in fear through the perilous tempest; "never despair with such a burden." Thou art bearing forward the purposes of God, is a nobler reflection, yet appealing to the same sentiment, to swell and sustain our souls. He, who despairs with such a burden, deserves not to know what he carries. Let patience, perseverance, and diligence be in all time to come as in all time past the cardinal virtues in the land of the Pilgrims. Smitten with the memory of the great and good, who have lived and labored for our benefit, measuring justly what man is and what he has done, watching the steady growth of the ages, worshiping the divine power of truth, and still more adoringly Him who gives truth its power, — thus may we, and those who come after us, aim to catch some ennobling sense of the true destiny of our race. Springing beyond the fences of our own time, living faithfully and hopefully, let us commit the cause of man, without a fear, to the advancing generations, to the irresistible laws and the presiding care of God.

APPENDIX.

APPENDIX.

Measures taken in regard to the Centennial Celebration at Quincy, Mass., 25 May, 1840, and the proceedings on that occasion.

In October and November, 1839, two or three meetings were held by the Town, as may be seen by reference to the Town Records, to take into consideration the propriety and the means of celebrating the Two Hundredth Anniversary of the Incorporation of the ancient Town in this place, which, dating from 1640, 13th May, (old style,) in the course of events was to come round on the 25th May, 1840. In the progress of this design, various perplexities and inauspicious circumstances occurred, which as they were not foreseen could neither in the event be avoided nor surmounted. The well intended attempt lingered along, with no final action, and there seemed little prospect of getting so far extricated from the embarrassment as to arrive at any successful termination.

At length, as the recurrence of the Anniversary was rapidly hastening on, the young men of Quincy were moved to engage in the matter, and pursuant to a notice to that effect a meeting was held by them, at the Centre District School room, on Monday evening, 27th April, 1840, to consider the whole subject. Mr. Caleb Gill, jr., was called to preside, and Captain Samuel White was appointed secretary.

After remarks from several gentlemen, it was resolved to commemorate the return of this interesting event. The following Committee of Arrangements was accordingly chosen, namely, John A. Green, James F. Brown, Nathan White, Rufus Foster, Alvin Rodgers, William Whitney, Edward A. Spear, James Penniman, Charles N. Souther, Edwin N. Willet, Waldo Nash, Philip Carver, who were instructed to report, at an adjourned meeting, such measures as they might deem proper for a suitable observance of the day.

Wednesday evening, 29th April. At the adjourned meeting it was recommended by the Committee of Arrangements that the Rev. George Whitney of Roxbury, a native of Quincy, be invited to deliver a Commemorative Discourse on the approaching interesting occasion; which recommendation was unanimously adopted.

It was also voted to invite the Rev. John Gregory, minister of the First Universalist Church in Quincy, to deliver an Address to the Young Men.

And upon the suggestion of the Chairman of the Committee of Arrangements, it was likewise voted, that Mr. Christopher Pearse Cranch, a descendant from Quincy, be invited to deliver a Poem on the same occasion.

Other suggestions of the Committee of Arrangements, in reference to the observance of the day, were duly considered and adopted. Whereupon the meeting was dissolved.

Caleb Gill, Jr., *Moderator.*

Samuel White, *Secretary.*

The Committee of Arrangements engaged with alacrity in making those preparations which the occasion required, receiving likewise such suggestions, as were from time to time offered, with readiness and a desire to meet the reasonable wishes of all interested in the celebration. The inhabitants of the town, with great unanimity, and the natives and descendants, scattered far and wide, more especially those in the neighboring metropolis, came forward cordially to the good work. A large pavilion was erected on the Hancock Lot, capable of accommodating from six to eight hundred people; and at the earnest desire very generally expressed of having the Ladies at the dinner, such measures were speedily taken as should secure their cheering presence and elevating influence on the occasion. This circumstance, rather novel in these days, yet marking, we think, an era in the progress of Christian civilization, we may well hope will be more a matter of course in all public festivities, among those who shall assemble to celebrate the third centennial anniversary.

Soon after the celebration had been decided upon, the following notice was published in some of the Boston papers.

QUINCY CENTENNIAL CELEBRATION.

Preparations are now making suitably to commemorate the two hundredth Anniversary since the incorporation of the Town of Braintree, (Quincy then being a part of said town, and the place of original settlement,) on MONDAY, the 25th instant.

The day will be ushered in by a National salute. The procession will be formed in the morning, and, after marching through several streets, will repair to the Adams Temple, where appropriate Religious services will take place, and a Commemorative Discourse be pronounced by the Rev. George Whitney, of Roxbury. The Rev. John Gregory, of Quincy, will deliver an Address to the Young Men. A Poem will also be given on the occasion, by Mr. C. P. Cranch.

After these exercises, a procession will be formed of the subscribers to the Dinner and invited guests, who will then proceed to the pavilion erected for the occasion.

The Quincy Light Infantry will perform escort duty, accompanied by an excellent Band of Music.

Tickets for the Dinner may be procured, in Boston, of Jeffrey R. Brackett, 69 Washington Street, and of Farnsworth & Baxter, Kilby street. Those gentlemen, who intend to take tickets for the Dinner, are particularly desired to purchase them on or before the 22d instant.

The Committee of Arrangements, in compliance with their instructions, hereby extend an invitation to the *natives* of Quincy and their *descendants*, residing in other places, to unite in the festivities of the occasion. It is to be hoped that all the widely scattered sons of Quincy, with their children, will again return once more to meet each other at home.

By order of the Committee of Arrangements,

JOHN A. GREEN, Chairman.

JAMES F. BROWN, Secretary.

Quincy, May 13, 1840.

In consequence of this invitation, a meeting was called by an advertisement in the Daily Evening Transcript of May 13th, as follows.

CENTENNIAL CELEBRATION AT QUINCY. The citizens of Quincy have determined to celebrate the completion of the second Century of the Incorporation of that Town, on Monday, the 25th day of the present month, and invite the coöperation of the descendants of that Town, who are now located in other places. A meeting of the natives of Quincy and their descendants, residing in this city, will be held in the Old Supreme Court room, in the Court House in School Street, at 8 o'clock this evening, to adopt such measures as may be necessary to aid in this celebration, and evince their attachment to this time-honored spot of their origin.

The result of this meeting comes next in course, and is given as it appeared in several of the Boston papers.

QUINCY CENTENNIAL CELEBRATION.

Agreeably to a call in the papers of the 13th instant, the natives of Quincy and their descendants in Boston assembled at the Old Court House in School street. The meeting was called to order by Lewis G. Pray, Esq., and organized by the choice of Hon. Josiah Quincy, Jr., for Chairman, and Jeffrey R. Brackett, Secretary. Mr. Quincy, on taking the Chair, made a short address, and was followed by Charles F. Adams, Esq., who offered the accompanying Resolutions, which were unanimously adopted.

Resolved, That the perpetuation of the principles of freedom in New England depends, under God, most upon the extent to which the knowledge of the origin and history of their supporters during the period of two centuries now elasped since the first settlements, can be generally spread among us.

Resolved, That no occasions present themselves which can be more fitly used for this purpose than commemorations of the anniversaries of the original foundations of the various towns of our Commonwealth.

Resolved, That the citizens of Boston, natives of or otherwise connected with Quincy, have seen with great pleasure the manifestation on the part of their fellow citizens in the latter town of an intention to celebrate in a proper manner the 25th day of May, as the day upon which two hundred years ago their town was originally incorporated; and that they will cheerfully coöperate with them in all suitable arrangements to promote the same.

Resolved, That a committee be appointed from this meeting who shall have power to communicate with any committee that shall be raised in Quincy, and to aid them in making all the necessary preparations which are contemplated for the due solemnization of this anniversary.

In accordance with the last resolution, the following named gentlemen were chosen, to constitute a committee:

Josiah Quincy, Jr.,
Lewis G. Pray,
William Hayden,
Edward Miller,
Nathaniel Faxon,
R. C. Greenleaf,
William Phipps,
Edmd. Burke Whitney,
Zabdiel B. Adams,
James B. Richardson,
Benjamin Guild,
Charles F. Adams,
Charles Arnold,
Francis Adams,
Jeffrey R. Brackett.

After addresses from several gentlemen, among whom were Dr. Adams, William Hayden, and Edward Miller, Esqrs., the meeting was adjourned.

JOSIAH QUINCY, Jr., Chairman.

Jeffrey R. Brackett, Secretary.

Information, as to the places where Tickets for the Centennial Dinner could be procured, was published in the Quincy Patriot of May 9th, in the annexed

NOTICE.

Tickets to the Centennial Dinner will be ready for sale on Tuesday next, and may be purchased at the following places; — In Quincy, at the stores of E. Packard & Co., John Whitney, Justin Spear, Caleb Gill. In Braintree, at Atherton's store and Arnold's Tavern. In Randolph (West), Howard's Hotel; (East), Lincoln's store. In Weymouth, Wales's Hotel. In Milton, Babcock's store. In Dorchester, Neponset Hotel. In Boston, at the stores of Jeffrey R. Brackett, 69 Washington street; Farnsworth & Baxter, in Kilby street. Persons, intending to purchase, are requested to do so previously to the 22d instant.

Subscription papers were opened both in Quincy and in Boston, and liberal sums raised to defray the incidental expenses. The natives and descendants in Boston furnished the Boston Brass Band to play upon the occasion. The Quincy Light Infantry were invited to perform escort duty; the Quincy Union Singing Society, likewise to sing at the services in the church.

In the Quincy Patriot of May 23d the following gentlemen were announced as officers of the day.

President — Hon. Josiah Quincy, jr.

Vice Presidents of Quincy — Josiah Brigham, John Whitney, Adam Curtis, Ebenezer Bent, William Torrey, James Newcomb.

Vice Presidents of Boston — Edward Miller, Charles F. Adams, Jeffrey Richardson.

Chief Marshal — Ibrahim Bartlett.

Assistant Marshals of Quincy — William Seaver, Caleb Gill, jr., Lloyd G. Horton, John Faxon 2d, Clift Rogers, George Newcomb, Justin Spear, Jonathan French, Josiah Babcock, jr., John C. Edwards, Jacob F. Eaton, Charles H. Brown, Joseph Whiting, Benjamin Hinckley, jr., Cyrus Goss, Joseph Field, Henry West.

Assistant Marshals of Boston — Charles F. Baxter, James Brackett, Henry Adams, Charles E. Miller, George Savil, Charles Adams.

In the same paper appeared the following announcement.

CENTENNIAL CELEBRATION.

Quincy, May 25, 1840.

The committee of arrangements, and those gentlemen to whom have been assigned offices for the day, and all who have become subscribers to the dinner and intend to join in the procession, will assemble *in* the Universalist Church, and all other citizens who intend to join in the procession are requested to assemble *at* said church, at a quarter before *nine* o'clock in the morning. A procession will be formed precisely at *nine* o'clock, by the marshals, and when formed will move through Elm Street, down Hancock Street, into Sea Street, to the house of the Rev. Peter Whitney, where they will receive the orators, chaplains, invited guests, &c. of the day, and from thence proceed through Sea Street to Washington Street, to the church where the exercises will take place. The hour of assembling at the Meeting-house to form in procession will be announced by ringing the bell.

Per order. IBRAHIM BARTLETT, *Chief Marshal.*

Order of the first Procession from the Universalist Meeting-house to the Stone Temple.

Escort.
Chief Marshal and Aids.
President of the Day.
Marshal. Orators and Chaplains. Marshal.
Invited Guests.
State Officers.
Marshal. Vice Presidents. Marshal.
Committee of Arrangements.
Municipal Officers
of the Towns of Quincy, Braintree, and Randolph.
Marshal. Subscribers to the Dinner. Marshal.
Citizens who wish to join in the Procession.

Second Procession.

The committee of arrangements, invited guests, and gentlemen who have accepted offices on the occasion, and gentlemen accompanied by ladies, will assemble at the Meeting-house in the body pews, and all others, who are provided with tickets to the dinner, will assemble in the wall pews at the ringing of the bell soon after the exercises, when a procession will be formed immediately, which will be divided into seven or more divisions, as circumstances may require, each to be headed by a marshal and numbered by lot corresponding to the tables.

The following will be the order of the second procession.

From the Stone Temple to the Pavilion.

Escort.
Chief Marshal and Aids.
Marshal. President of the Day. Marshal.
Orators and Chaplains.
Invited Guests.
Marshal. Vice Presidents. Marshal.
Chairman of the Committee of Arrangements.
Marshal. Gentlemen accompanied by Ladies. Marshal.
Citizens who have Tickets to the Dinner.

The marshals are all requested to meet at the Hancock House, Saturday evening, May 23d, at half past seven o'clock.

Per order. IBRAHIM BARTLETT, *Chief Marshal.*

The following gentlemen will be in attendance at the Meeting-house to conduct ladies to seats, viz., Benjamin Page, William B. Duggan, Abner Willett, Lewis Bass, Francis Williams.

All persons who intend to dine must provide themselves with tickets previously to joining the procession.

Tickets for the Ball in the evening are for sale at Gill's Book-store.

By order of the Committee of Arrangements.

JOHN A. GREEN, *Chairman.*

JAMES F. BROWN, *Secretary.*

CENTENNIAL CELEBRATION.

Monday, 25th May, 1840.

The day dawned clear and beautiful. The weather was unusually warm for the season, being at noon about 85° of Fahrenheit's thermometer. A few scudding clouds were observed about six o'clock, A. M., and afterwards in the southwest, which excited some apprehension that the day would turn out to be rainy. But they soon disappeared, and scarcely another cloud was visible in the broad heavens till the sun went down. The morning was ushered in by the ringing of the bells on the Stone Temple and the Universalist Church, and by the discharge of cannon in front of the gun house on President's Hill. A flag waved its broad folds likewise from the same eminence, and from the pavilion below. The roads were dry and dusty, but not a breath of wind prevailed to make the dust annoying. A more lovely day for the interesting occasion could not have been chosen by man. The smiles of heaven seemed to favor the hour. Natives and descendants, friends and strangers soon gathered in throngs, to exchange congratulations and to share in the interesting associations and festivities of the day.

At a quarter before nine o'clock the bell of the Universalist Church summoned all together to form the procession. A numerous concourse gathered up. The Quincy Light Infantry, attended by the Boston Brass Band, made a glittering and imposing appearance; and the delightful martial music falling on the ear was not among the least of the pleasant circumstances of the day. As they passed along from their armory to the appointed place of assembling, Mount Wollaston lying off beyond them towards the sea, one might be forcibly impressed by the contrast between these prosperous days and those feeble and trying ones, when Captain Standish came from Plymouth with his small military band, to quell the riotous proceedings of Thomas Morton around his May-pole.

By the promptness and judicious arrangement of the Chief Marshal and his aids, Charles F. Baxter and Thomas Adams, jr., appointed by him, together with the assistant marshals, the procession was soon formed, and moved in the course already described a few minutes after nine. Meanwhile, at nine o'clock, the bell of the Stone Temple had given notice that the doors were opened for the admission of ladies. A little longer time was occupied by the procession in passing through the route prescribed than had been anticipated. The procession reached the church about a quarter past ten. The ladies occupied the galleries and some of the wall pews below. The immense area of the church was filled by the procession. At half past ten all were seated and the services commenced.

ORDER OF EXERCISES IN THE CHURCH.

CENTENNIAL CELEBRATION AT QUINCY,

25 MAY, 1840.

1. VOLUNTARY — *On the Organ.*

GLEE — *By the Choir.*

Hail smiling morn that tips the hills with gold,
Whose rosy fingers ope the gates of day,
Who the gay face of nature doth unfold,
At whose bright presence darkness flies away.

2. PRAYER OF INVOCATION. By the Rev. W. P. Lunt, of Quincy.

3. ODE — Landing of the Pilgrims. — *Hemans.*

[Sung by Mr. John Hollis, of Braintree.]

The breaking waves dashed high
On a stern and rock-bound coast,
And the woods against a stormy sky
Their giant branches tost;

And the heavy night hung dark
The hills and waters o'er,
When a band of exiles moored their bark
On the wild New-England shore.

Not as the conqueror comes,
They, the true hearted came,
Not with the roll of the stirring drums,
And the trumpet that sings of fame;

Not as the flying come,
In silence and in fear —
They shook the depths of the desert's gloom
With their hymns of lofty cheer.

Amidst the storm they sang,
And the stars heard, and the sea!
And the sounding aisles of the dim woods rang
To the anthem of the free!

The ocean-eagle soared
From his nest by the white wave's foam,
And the rocking pines of the forest roared —
This was their welcome home!

What sought they thus afar?
  Bright jewels of the mine?
The wealth of seas, the spoils of war?
  — They sought a faith's pure shrine!

Ay, call it holy ground,
  The soil where first they trod!
They left unstained what there they found —
  Freedom to worship God!

4. PRAYER. By the Rev. Peter Whitney, of Quincy.

5. HYMN — *By the Rev. Dr. Flint.*

In pleasant lands have fallen the lines
  That bound our goodly heritage,
And safe beneath our sheltering vines
  Our youth is blest, and soothed our age.

What thanks, O God, to thee are due,
  That thou didst plant our fathers here;
And watch and guard them as they grew,
  A vineyard, to the planter dear.

The toils they bore our ease have wrought;
  They sowed in tears — in joy we reap;
The birthright, they so dearly bought,
  We'll guard, till we with them shall sleep.

Thy kindness to our fathers shown,
  In weal and wo through all the past,
Their grateful sons, O God, shall own,
  While here their name and race shall last.

6. COMMEMORATIVE DISCOURSE.
By the Rev. George Whitney, of Roxbury.

7. VOLUNTARY — *By the Band.*

GLEE — *By the Choir.*

Land of our fathers, wheresoe'er we roam —
Land of our birth, to us thou still art home;
Peace and prosperity on thy sons attend,
Down to posterity their influence descend.

Though other climes may brighter hopes fulfill,
Land of our birth, we ever love thee still!
Heaven shield our happy home from each hostile band,
Freedom and plenty ever crown our native land.

9. ADDRESS TO THE YOUNG MEN.
By the Rev. J. Gregory, of Quincy.

10. VOLUNTARY — *By the Band.*

11. HYMN.

Thou Lord, through every changing scene
Hast to thy saints a refuge been;
Through every age, eternal God,
Their pleasing home, their safe abode.

In thee our fathers sought their rest;
In thee our fathers still are blest;
And, while the tomb confines their dust,
In thee their souls abide and trust.

Lo, we are come, a feeble race,
Awhile to fill our fathers' place;
Our helpless state with pity view,
And let us share their refuge too.

To thee our infant race we leave;
Them may their fathers' God receive;
That voices yet unformed may raise
Succeeding hymns of humble praise.

12. POEM. By Mr. C. P. Cranch, of Boston.

13. ANTHEM.

Let us with a joyful mind
Praise the Lord, for he is kind,
For his mercies shall endure —
Ever faithful, ever sure.
Hallelujah, Amen.

14. BENEDICTION. By the Rev. Mr. Wolcott, of Quincy.

The exercises in the Church occupied three hours and a half. The singing in all its parts was uncommonly fine. At the close of the services, the Chief Marshal gave notice that an intermission of fifteen minutes would take place, after which, at the ringing of the bell, the second procession would be formed in the order already stated, to proceed to the pavilion.

The company were relieved by this respite, and at three o'clock were again formed in procession and on their way to the Pavilion. About a quarter before four all were seated at the tables, the Ladies affording a beautiful and pleasant relief to the large collection of men, which would otherwise have presented, as on all similar occasions, a dark and monotonous appearance. Between five and six hundred were comfortably seated at the tables. The Rev. H. G. O. Phipps, of Cohassett, a native of Quincy, invoked the divine blessing.

The dinner was prepared by Messrs. Daniel French & Son, of the Hancock House, creditable to them and satisfactory to the guests.

It may be worth while to mention that a company of youths, from Braintree and Randolph, paraded all day on horseback, arrayed in fantastic dresses, and attracting some attention. They fell into the rear of the procession, as it passed from the Church to the Pavilion, and during the dinner performed a variety of manœuvres upon the Hancock Lot to the amusement of the spectators. To the antiquarian eye, they might have been mistaken for a deputation from Morton's jovial crew, on the Merry-Mount, two hundred years ago. Unlike them, however, they caused no disturbance to the seriously disposed. In fact, in regard to all who were gathered together upon the occasion, — although a much larger number were doubtless assembled in the town than ever before,— it may be said with pride and satisfaction, that the utmost order and propriety prevailed, — and that no single circumstance, neither accident nor disorder, occurred to mar the harmony, good fellowship, and pleasures of the day.

After the company had been refreshed by a substantial and grateful repast, the Hon. Josiah Quincy, jr., President of the day, rose and said: —

Ladies and Gentlemen, — We are assembled to commemorate our Fathers. Let me propose to you, therefore, as the most suitable sentiment, with which we should commence,

The memory of our Fathers.

They to life's noblest end
Gave up life's noblest powers,
And bade the legacy descend
Down, down to us and ours.

The President then proceeded to say, — We have spoken of our Fathers, let me next propose to you

The memory of our Mothers.

But not alone, nor all unblessed,
Our Fathers sought a place of rest;
One dared with him to burst the knot
That bound her to her native spot;
In life in death with him to seal
Her kindred love, her kindred zeal.

In introducing the next sentiment, the President observed, — The distinguished honor belongs to us of having furnished the name of our Commonwealth. The Sagamore who governed the Indians in these parts had his residence upon a hill, near Squantum, in their language denominated Moswetuset, from whence with a slight variation came Massachusett. Let us say, then,

Chickatabut, the Sachem of Moswetuset, the friend of our Fathers. Our state has taken her appellation from his council fire in Quincy, and has made that name a name and a praise in all the earth.

Music by the Band, and occasional songs by Messrs. Knight, Dempster, and others were interspersed among the sentiments and speeches. The following Ode, written for the occasion by Mrs. L. H. Sigourney, was next sung.

ODE,

On the Two Hundredth Anniversary of the Incorporation of Braintree.

Two hundred years! Two hundred years!
  Mount Wollaston could say,
What wondrous scenes their fleeting wings
  Have brought, and borne away!

The pilgrim band, the council fire,
  The war dance circling round,
Town, tower, and spire, emblazoned bright,
  Where rock and forest frowned.

Speak forth, speak forth — ye ancient trees,
  Whose green heads drank the dew,
While old Naponset's ripening corn
  In slender furrows grew;

Or while his arrows winged with death
  From subtle ambush flew,
Where now in sainted tombs repose
  The noble and the true.

Beneath your shade the roving tribes
  Concerted 'gainst the foe,
Or held their pagan ritual wild,—
  Red Sachem! was it so?

He answereth not. His buried race
  Have like shorn grass decayed;
No baying of their hunter's hound
  Disturbs the green-wood glade.

They rear their simple roofs no more,
  Nor o'er the waters blue
With sinewy arm and venturous oar
  Propel the bark canoe.

But ye, who in their places rise,
  With every blessing fraught,—
Give praise for all the glorious change
  Two hundred years have wrought.

Governor Morton, who had been invited to attend, remarked in his letter declining the invitation, that the sentiment, which John Randolph once gave of the town of Albemarle, might well apply to Quincy; —

The ancient Town of Braintree; — That prolific soil, which bears Presidents of the United States.

The next sentiment from the chair was as follows: —

The Schools endowed by John Adams and William Coddington at Quincy, and the one founded by John Harvard at Cambridge. — A century hence may the school of the patriots stand second only to the school of the prophets.

In reply to this President Quincy of Harvard College rose and said, that reminiscence seemed to be the appropriate object of the hour. In truth, he proceeded, my own mind is more filled with a company which is gone and by most forgotten, than with that which is present. Of this number is one among the earliest of my recollections, an individual who deserves to be remembered on this occasion, second to none if not first of all.

It is now fifty-six years since, being a boy I attended my mother on a visit to her friend, a lady who then dwelt in that humble mansion which yet stands at the foot of Pen's hill, and who was destined in future time to be the wife of one President of the United States, and the mother of another. I remember her, a matronly beauty, in which respect she yielded to few of her sex, full of joy, and elevated with hope. Peace had just been declared, Independence attained, and she was preparing to go from that humble mansion to join the husband whom she loved, and by whom she was little less than adored, at the court of St. James; possessed with the consciousness as she doubtless was, that she had been by his side in every trial, encouraged him in every danger, and that her spirit had sustained him and been of his council in every vicissitude. Though then very young, I was impressed with the sentiment which frequent opportunities of acquaintance and observation in subsequent life confirmed, that of her it might be as truly said as ever it could be of woman — she was of her own sex the glory, and of the other the admiration.

Mr. Quincy then proposed —

The memory of Abigail Adams — who to a soul chastened and elevated by Christian principle united the spirit of a Grecian, and the virtues of a Roman matron.

A letter had been received from Ex-Governor Everett, declining an invitation to attend, and giving the following sentiment:

The Ancient Town of Quincy; — venerable parent of men, whom the country venerates as Fathers.

The attention of the company was next called to the following song.

OUR FOREFATHERS' SONG.

Composed in the year 1630, — *author unknown.*

New England's annoyances you that would know them,
Pray ponder these verses which briefly do show them.

I.

The place where we live is a wilderness wood,
Where grass is much wanting that's fruitful and good:
Our mountains and hills and our valleys below,
Being commonly covered with ice and with snow:
And when the northwest wind with violence blows,
Then every man pulls his cap over his nose:
But if any 's so hardy and will it withstand,
He forfeits a finger, a foot, or a hand.

II.

But when the Spring opens we then take the hoe,
And make the ground ready to plant and to sow;

Our corn being planted and seed being sown,
The worms destroy much before it is grown;
And when it is growing some spoil there is made,
By birds and by squirrels that pluck up the blade;
And when it is come to full corn in the ear,
It is often destroyed by raccoon and by deer.

III.

If fresh meat be wanting, to fill up our dish,
We have carrots and turnips as much as we wish;
And is there a mind for a delicate dish,
We repair to the clam banks, and *there* we catch fish.
Instead of pottage and puddings and custards and pies,
Our pumpkins and parsnips are common supplies;
We have pumpkins at morning and pumpkins at noon;
If it was not for pumpkins we should be undone.

IV.

If barley be wanting to make into malt,
We must be contented and think it no fault;
For we can make liquor to sweeten our lips,
Of pumpkins and parsnips and walnut tree chips.
But you whom the Lord intends hither to bring,
Forsake not the honey for fear of the sting;
But bring both a quiet and contented mind,
And all needful blessings you surely will find.

After this song the President said he had a living witness to its authenticity, and he would call on the Attorney General to sustain him and to propose a sentiment.

Mr. Austin thereupon rose and said that, being thus called upon, he could not hesitate to say that he had, when a boy, often heard an ancestor of his — a lady in direct descent from the company who landed at Salem with Gov. Endicott in 1628 — repeat the same lines as she had heard them when a child, with no other difference, that he could recollect, from the present version, than in some peculiarities of pronunciation, which conformed to a more ancient system of orthoepy.

And this incident — said Mr. Austin — as every other on this occasion, is calculated to carry back the mind to the times of the Pilgrims, and to draw before us, for new reverence and love, the principles and character of those worthy men, who laid the foundation of whatever is most estimable in the glorious character of New England. Particularly are we drawn to these considerations, on this spot, because the settlement at Mount Wollaston, which undoubtedly took place not long after the landing at Plymouth, is not without claim to be considered the oldest continuous plantation within the original chartered limits of Massachusetts. But it is not from mere local feeling that this sentiment arises. There is a general, universal sympathy excited by this reference to antiquity, in which the whole people, the friends of civil and religious liberty, wherever they may be, all who cherish in their hearts a veneration for free institutions and the rights of man deeply enter. The cause of it may be stated in a word.

It is to the age of the Colonists, to the first planters of New England, that not only New England, but the nation of the United States owes its present possession of constitutional liberty; and the civilized world the amelioration of political government.

Having illustrated this sentiment at considerable length, and attempted in a pleasant manner to introduce to the company, and enjoy the astonishment of some of those ancient adventurers, and especially that old soldier, Miles Standish, and "*his army of twelve men,*" who once came on a hostile expedition against Morton of Merry-Mount, Mr. Austin adverted to the legend, most worthy to be remembered on this occasion, that of all that band of Pilgrims, who landed from the Mayflower, it was a woman's foot that *first* pressed the rock of Plymouth; that it was a woman, from that glorious company, who, with high constancy and firm faith, *began* in an act of adventurous heroism the settlement of this mighty empire; as it has been, in every subsequent period of its history, the fortitude and affection of the sex, and the purity of their domestic character, which have encircled it with glory. I know — said Mr. Austin — that the incredulous spirit of antiquarian research has affected to throw doubts on this romantic incident; but tradition sustains it; the learned Annotator * of the times confirms it. I believe it. I go for the beauty of the thing, for its poetry, its brilliancy, its chivalry, its romance. Yes, — take it to be true. It is but an original of the energy, the fortitude, the courage of the daughters of New England.

* Judge Davis, Editor of Morton's Memorial.

Passing from these scenes — said Mr. Austin — there is another incident of deep interest connected with this occasion. This day is not only the second centennial of the settlement, but the second celebration of a centennial ! ! —

Where are they, who rejoiced in this place, at the first revolution of an hundred years ? Gone : — passed away ! No survivor can tell us of the remembrances, the fears, or the hopes of that memorable day. Imagination, indeed, pictures to us the generous and patriotic crowd of Christian men and women at the holy altar, with their thanks and their prayers for their country and their race.

That first centennial was the last day of a most memorable period ; the first day of an era equally wonderful. The former had witnessed the actual settlement of the country. Its inhabitants were Colonists. The latter was to establish its independence. Its citizens were to be free. But this future was all unknown to the thronged assembly. They, like us, stood on that narrow isthmus, which separated the century of the dead from the interminable succession of living men. No prophetic vision assured them — as the revolution of time has assured us — that from their public and private virtues, and that of the age they had celebrated, would be produced a harvest of national happiness and glory, as certainly as the oak of the forest from the acorn whence it sprung.

One individual might have been present on that occasion, to whom was to be entrusted an eminent share in the magnificent enterprise. From the venerable preacher of that day, [Rev. Mr. Hancock,] himself the ancestor of a distinguished family, this child may have acquired the rudiments of a character, which was materially to secure the independence of his country, and establish the immortality of his fame.

Yes, Sir, John Adams, — to whom we now look back as to a colossal monument of our country's glory, — was then a child of five years old, destined to bear onward and upward, in all the storms of political dissention, and in the earthquake of revolution, the ark of his country's independence.

It is glory enongh for any portion of our land to have been the birth-place of John Adams. It is something to tell of and to boast of, by those of us, who had the good fortune personally to know him, that we have sat at the feet of Gamaliel, and drank of the inspiration of his lips.

My first recollection of Quincy — said Mr. Austin — was in the good fortune, which, soon after my college life, brought me into an acquaintance — so far as a boy might hold the relation — with this eminent statesman; and I have never ceased to regret, that, when afterwards I was domiciliated in a family where he was a familiar visitor, I had not preserved a record of the thousand anecdotes, which enlivened his profound remarks on politics and men. They would have formed a volume more interesting than Boswell, and more profitable than Waverley. We look, Sir, for some authentic record of the debates in Congress on the question of Independence. One of the eminent statesmen of our own age has attempted, in the manner of the classic historians, to supply the want by an imaginary speech of Mr. Adams.

"Sink or swim, live or die, survive or perish, I give my heart and hand to this vote."

It has the force, directness, energy, and abruptness of the man; but it is only an imitation. There is extant a speech, which, Mr. Austin said, he had good reason to believe, was delivered by Mr. Adams, and written out from his own notes at the time, full of argument, abounding in illustration, sparkling with classic beauty and poetical quotation, equally nervous, direct, impassioned, and abrupt.

"The great God, Sir, who is the searcher of all things, will witness for me, that I have spoken to you in the fulness and purity of my heart."

It is not compatible, Mr. Austin said, with any reasonable time he could ask, to follow out the life of this distinguished citizen of Quincy. While the reverend preacher of the first century looked back with a laudable pride on the fame of Carver and Endicott and Winthrop, it is not probable his imagination suggested to him, that "a greater than these were there." The eloquent and learned speaker, who addressed us this day, and who warmed our hearts with gratitude for the unnumbered blessings of Providence in every exigency of our country, could not foresee the occasions nor the men, who, in the coming century, are to be rivals to the patriots and statesmen of the past. But we may trust, humbly indeed, but yet with becoming confidence, that in any circumstances there may arise from the virtues of our ancestors some kindred spirits worthy to claim alliance with such glorious progenitors.

Mr. Austin then proposed as a sentiment —

The respect of POSTERITY for the memory of JOHN ADAMS.

The President next proposed —

John Wheelwright, the first minister of Quincy, the friend of Sir Henry Vane. He was exiled for that liberty from this land, for which his friend expired on the scaffold.

In reply to this, the Rev. Wm. P. Lunt, junior minister of the First Congregational Church, rose and acknowledged the honor paid to the first preacher at the Mount. He then glanced at several circumstances presenting an amusing contrast between the present and the past, — alluded to Morton's May-pole and to the decorations of the pavilion, in which the company were seated, and closed by offering

The May-pole of 1627 *and the May-pole of* 1840 — the opposite poles of festivity.

The next sentiment was from the Chair : —

John Adams, a native of Quincy. The glory of his life, like the day of his death, shall never fail from the remembrance of the sons of men.

The following letter, received from the Hon. J. Q. Adams, was then read by the President.

JOHN A. GREEN,

Chairman of the Committee of Arrangements.

Washington, 18 May, 1840.

SIR, — I have received your letter of the 7th inst., containing the obliging invitation to me to attend the celebration of the centennial anniversary of the incorporation of the town of Braintree, on the 25th of this month. The necessity of my attendance upon my public duties at this place, deprives me of the power of complying with this invitation, for which I am duly grateful. I pray the company to accept instead of my presence my best wishes for the health and happiness of them all.

I am, very respectfully, Sir,

Your obedient serv't,

J. Q. ADAMS.

After which he proposed —

John Quincy Adams — This is not an occasion to praise the living; and distant be the day when any inscription shall bear his name, or any tongue pronounce his eulogy.

And following this

The name of John Hancock, a native of Quincy, — With American Liberty it arose — with American Liberty alone it can perish.

The following letter was received from Professor John G. Palfrey.

Boston, 23d May, 1830.

Dear Sir, — I am unexpectedly deprived, by an unavoidable engagement, of the pleasure which I promised myself, when I accepted the invitation, with which I was honored by the citizens of Quincy, to attend the very interesting occasion of Monday next. If a convenient opportunity occurs, will you do me the favor to submit, in my behalf, the following sentiment to the attention of the company?

The Town of Quincy — The home of Wheelwright and Coddington; the birth place of Hancock, the Adamses, and the Quincys; a spot to be held in everlasting remembrance in the history of religious and civil liberty.

The following sentiment was received from Hon. Robert C. Winthrop, who was prevented by other engagements from complying with the invitation to attend: —

Braintree and Quincy — Their men and their hills — their *scions* and their *sienite;* the first have furnished some of the ablest *hands* by which our Revolution was *achieved;* the last has supplied the materials of the proudest *monument* by which it will be *commemorated.*

The President then proposed

John Adams and Josiah Quincy, Jr. — The defenders of Preston. Together they stood as the advocates of Liberty and Law, — together they sleep amid the graves of their Fathers;

"Thus joined in fame, in friendship tried, —
No chance could sever, nor the grave divide."

The Rev. George Whitney of Roxbury, being requested to give a sentiment, rose and said: — It will not be expected of me, Mr. President, after the long and I am afraid sufficiently tedious utterance I have already put forth, to make anything like a set speech here, but I will ask your patience and that of our friends in recurring to a brief incident of former times.

As I passed, a day or two since, the place where we are now assembled, and saw the Pavilion going up in preparation for this interesting occasion, an anecdote occurred to me I had heard a long time ago in reference to the elder Adams, the point of which may be turned with singular force to this spot and the distinguished personages associated with it. It is said that when President Adams, senior, was minister to the Court of St. James, he was called upon, at his lodgings, by Sir Benjamin West, who invited him to a morning walk. They went out together as far as Kensington Gardens, conversing on various topics. Upon their arrival at the spot already named, Sir Benjamin West thrust his cane into the ground, and with a strong expression of patriotic feeling, turning at the same time to Mr. Adams, exclaimed, "Here, Sir, was the origin of the American Revolution." "How so?" said Mr. Adams. "It was thus," replied Sir Benjamin. "When George III. was about to take to himself Queen Charlotte, following the wisdom of the old adage — first your cage and then your bird — he summoned one of his ministers into his presence, and informed him that it was his purpose to have a new Palace for the Queen: and that the necessary funds must forthwith be supplied. 'We have nothing in the Treasury,' replied the minister, 'not a penny.' 'That will be no impediment,' replied the King; 'the Palace we must have; we have only to tax the Colonies.' — The Colonies were taxed. The stamp act was imposed. We see what they got by it. Here, Sir, was the origin of the American Revolution." *

When we come to speak of the secondary causes of that great

* The reader may find a little different version of this anecdote in Tudor's Life of James Otis, p. 206. The main incidents, however, are the same. Hyde Park and Kensington Gardens join each other: and it was somewhere thereabouts, — on the spot occupied by Sir Benjamin West, — where the King had proposed to locate the palace. Possibly the pleasing of the Queen might have concerned him less than the pleasing of himself or even of his courtiers.

event, Mr. President, — for independent of all that might be gathered up, we cannot but feel that from the development of the original principles on which the Pilgrims started, the Revolution and the Declaration of Independence were both sooner or later certain to come forth, — it seems to me, that it turns out to be our privilege with singular propriety and force, on this very spot, to imitate the action of Sir Benjamin West, and to say with emphasis, in his own words also — *Here, here,* Sir, was the origin of the American Revolution.

This spot, Sir, was the birth-place of John Hancock, whose name is first on the scroll of the Declaration of Independence. The house that gave him birth, and in which his cradle was rocked, stood but a few yards from the head of this Pavilion. The remains of the cellar are visible yet. In after times this place became first the residence of the glowing patriot, Josiah Quincy, Jr., and down further still a part of the landed property of the illustrious John Adams, "*par nobile fratrum.*" When we consider what were the signal and successful efforts of these eminent champions of liberty in the great cause alluded to, we can hardly find room for a doubt, that but for their agency the American Revolution might not and the Declaration of Independence certainly would not have occurred as early as they did. *Here*, then, may we also be permitted to say was the origin of these great events.

I have already, in another place, alluded to some of the eminent personages who in earlier and later times have honored our soil. Fabulous history tells us that Cadmus, having slain the Dragon that guarded the fountain sacred to Mars, sowed his teeth, and there sprung up from them armed men. Our fathers, if they did not slay the Dragon of persecution, would not at least suffer themselves to be slain by him. Instead of his teeth, they sowed here their own principles, which in time were destined to grind him to powder.

In conclusion, I will give you as a sentiment,

Our beloved native soil — May there be springing up from it, in all the future as in the two hundred years that are past, armed men, — armed neither with sword, helmet, nor buckler, but with those exalted principles, the hope of the world, which elevate at the same time that they adorn humanity.

Dr. Z. B. Adams next rose, at the request of the President, and gave

The Granite Rocks of Quincy, as connected with her prosperity and wealth: — In the words of the eloquent orator of the day, I would say, " he who despairs under such a burden deserves not to know what he carries."

The President then requested a sentiment from Charles F. Adams, Esq., who began by remarking that, although entirely unused to any public appearance on occasions of this kind, he could not resist the feeling which prompted him to express to all who were here assembled, the deep sense of gratitude he entertained for the very kind notice that had been this day taken of those with whom nature had connected him.

Yet, in considering whatever share of merit it was the present disposition to award to their public services, the reflection ought at once to suggest itself, that it was the offspring of the soil of this old town and the natural consequence of the principles early inculcated and long adhered to. And when Mr. Adams looked around him and thought of the names of many of the persons who sat here, and compared them with those which are recorded in the annals of the town, even from the day of its settlement, it was matter of gratification to him to find how often they proved the same. These might indeed be regarded as the good old roots (if he could be allowed the expression) first planted in a healthy soil, which had been going on from generation, shooting forth new and green and healthy branches, conducing at one and the same moment to be the pride, the ornament, and the support of our common country.

It had been already remarked, in another place, this day, how fruitful this town was in associations, and this Mr. Adams took to be the great use of celebrations of the sort. They revived the recollections of the past, and presented ideas which could not fail to produce a beneficial action of the mind for the future. Indeed, how could it be otherwise, when there was hardly a spot in Quincy to which a young man could look, without thinking of something in connexion with it to improve his heart or to rectify his head? Here, on this very site we were now occupying, it was that a worthy pastor lived, who passed his days not merely in teaching his flock the principles of faith, but gave the best evidence of his success in instilling rules of practical conduct, by educating a son, (John Hancock,) who, when he came of age and the day of trial arrived and he was called upon to choose between the probable loss of fortune and adherence to his country, never hesitated, but bravely stuck to his country and let the fortune go.

And here, too, on this same spot, succeeded to him another father, who brought up another son, (Josiah Quincy, Jr.) And this son as he advanced in life devoted his strength to the cause of his country. And when it pleased God that this strength should depart from him, and he fell into weakness of body, then came the trial for his patriotism. He was told by his physicians in England that, if he wished to recover, he must abandon his duties and go to recruit his exhausted powers at certain medicinal springs — yet notwithstanding this, he chose to go on, to stick to his country and to give up his life.

After such examples, it was not fit that the dwelling, which knew them both, should stand the risk of desecration by successors of less exalted purposes. And it had been the will of Heaven, as if designing to prevent it, that a fire should soon after break forth and sweep it from the face of men. Yet the land remains and will continue, it is to be hoped, in hands ever anxious to provide that it shall be put only to noble uses.

Again, there was still at the foot of a hill yonder, an old house which had been the dwelling of a worthy farmer — and he had given little to his son (John Adams) but right notions. Yet, even these proved to him in after life an ample inheritance, for he followed them out, and as God was pleased to grant to him a moderate competency and long life, he went straight forward in his course, and died as he had lived with independence on his lips.

These were instances of a more extended reputation than fell to the lot of most of our other citizens, but it was not for a moment to be supposed that the same feeling, which made itself so visible to the world in them, did not glow with equal ardor in the breasts of their fellows of this town. Why, it was but a few days ago that Mr. Adams was reading a letter — yes, a letter from a Quincy woman to her husband, dated in the second year of the revolutionary struggle, in which she writes to him that even then more than half of the male population of the town, between the ages of fifteen and sixty, was acting in the field or on the water against the British, and that if this went on much further the women would have to gather the harvest; and she adds, that for her own part she thinks she could help to gather the corn and husk it, but she fears she should make a poor figure at digging potatoes.

Mr. Adams concluded by again exhorting the young men of the town to be mindful of these facts, for they could be turned to useful account even in the regulation of the daily industry of life. In allusion to the incident quoted from the letter, he would propose for a toast —

The harvest of 1776 *in the town of Braintree* — When the corn and potatoes were left to be gathered by the women, because a more precious crop, matured from the seedtime of 1640, demanded the labor of all the men.

Mr. C. P. Cranch, poet of the day, at the solicitation of the chair, presented the following sentiment: —

The New England character; — Like our Granite hills, may it long continue to clothe over the everlasting rock of principle with the evergreen of the best and most beautiful affections.

I rise — said Mr. Frederic A. Whitney — at your request, Mr. President, by the side of the poet of the day, but failing to catch the inspiration of his fancy and beauty with which he has entertained us, turn to the musty rolls of tradition for an incident which may be recalled as we commemorate the Fathers of our Town and those eminent in character and life, who have trodden its soil. Of this latter class, one has been passed over, whom, two centuries since, the court and ministers of the second Charles would hardly have spared. It has been reputed that our forest and rocks became the shelter and resting place of one of that large body, who, favoring the sect of the Independents, brought Charles I. to the block, and at the restoration of his son to the throne, fled for their lives from England.

Some years since, I gathered from the lips of an aged citizen of this town, whose numerous descendants are yet with us, who was remarkable for his retentive memory and exceeding accuracy in all matters of fact, this tradition. His childhood, he told me, had been with those who had conversed with this lonely exile for liberty. Within his own memory, there had stood on a hillock, not far from the spot on which we are assembled, the humble abode of the old refugee. Here, as said tradition, under the assumed name of Revel, he lived and died; and his funeral was honored by the attendance of his Excellency, the Provincial Governor, and of distinguished men from the neighboring metropolis of Boston.

I stand not up to claim for this ancient personage a place among the Regicide Judges. The historian of the United States, whom we hoped to have seen with us this day, has not written his name with those of Whalley, Goffe, and Dixwell, *known* to have been three of the Judges who found shelter in America, dwelling first in Massachusetts and afterwards fleeing to Connecticut. But the restoration of Charles II. made other victims than the Judges a sacrifice to the memory of his beheaded father; else Peters, for instance, the friend, 'honored and beloved' of Roger Williams, might have escaped the gallows. And if not one of those who sat in judgment on King Charles I., doubtless our exile was one who for their principles and in their cause fled to our shores.

It was enacted concerning the oracle of Pythos, that though it uttered doubtful responses, they should not be utterly disregarded. So without blindly reverencing, should we ever regard the voice of tradition. On the strength of the tradition now cited, and for the sake of adding another name to those whom this day brings to mind, I will propose, Sir,

The Memory of Thomas Revel, an Exile for civil liberty from his own land to this place — May the principles of freedom, for which with the Stuarts he contended, live ever on the soil that became the home of the Puritan and the English Independent.

Hon. B. L. Wales of Randolph next proposed

William Coddington — familiarly known to the youngest schoolboy of Braintree as the munificent donor of the Coddington School Fund: his memory will be cherished, and his name hallowed by all future generations, so long as common schools continue the pride of New England, — the right-arm of our national defence.

John Whitney, Esq., in proposing a sentiment, remarked — that in reflecting upon the great and good men who had been reared upon our soil, and casting our thoughts forward to the ages that should follow, the great question rose before us to be settled, — whether, so far as depended upon our exertions, the long line of eminent individuals should be continued, or a broken link should fall out in the chain connecting the present with the future. This question — he continued — rests for its decision upon the young men of our town. I will, therefore, Mr. President, offer as a sentiment —

The Young Men of Quincy: — When they recollect the statesmen and patriots who have claimed this as their birth-place, may they be emulous to follow them in all that is great and good, and thus become the ornaments and the pride of our land.

Captain Josiah Brigham, one of the former commanders of the Quincy Light Infantry, addressed the chair as follows: —

Mr. President, — Having been called on for a sentiment, I would merely remark, that it was not my privilege to be born in Quincy. But, Sir, it has been my fortune to spend the largest portion of my life in this ancient and distinguished town. I have lived here very happily with the inhabitants for about thirty years, and I feel as though I had a right to share, in some degree, in that just pride which the native born inhabitants feel, from the circumstance that this town can justly boast of having given birth to a greater number of Presidents and eminent men than any other town in the State, or in the United States. It gives me great pleasure, on this interesting occasion, to meet with so many of the inhabitants of Quincy, and with those who originated here, but whose fortunes have caused them to locate in other places. And it gives me additional pleasure, at this time, to meet again with the military Company who have this day performed escort duty. It was my fortune, in the early part of my life, to be associated with that Company; and consequently I have ever since felt an interest in its continued existence and prosperity, — a gratification also in meeting with them, as it always brings to my mind fresh recollections of past feelings and associations. That Company is now one of the oldest, if not the very oldest, Light Company in the Commonwealth. It is now fifty years old, and but a few weeks since it celebrated the fiftieth anniversary of its incorporation. — In the time of the last war between the United States and Great Britain, in the fall of 1814, that Company was called out by the State authorities, and ordered to march to Boston. It was stationed at South Boston, where it remained in the service of its country for about two months. It was my lot to be a member of the Company at that time. Since then the Company has passed into other hands. At this hour it is one of the best disciplined and most respectable Independent Companies in the State. Sir, I will on this occasion give as a sentiment,

The Quincy Light Infantry — Now fifty years old. Its members always ready to answer the call of their country — always ready to perform escort duty. May the Company continue to exist in prosperity from generation to generation, until it shall perform escort duty on the *Third* Centennial Anniversary of the incorporation of this ancient and honored town.

The Rev. John Gregory proposed the following sentiment: —

The sons and daughters of Quincy — May they mingle with their patriotism the social and domestic virtues, and may their firesides be the calm retreat of every heartfelt enjoyment of "*sweet home.*"

Mr. John A. Green, chairman of the committee of arrangements, offered —

The Fair Sex — Our joy in youth, — our companions in manhood, — our solace in age.

Mr. James F. Brown proposed

Quincy, Braintree, and Randolph — May they become united in sentiment and feeling as when combined under one act of Incorporation.

The President announced the following sentiment from James Newcomb, Esq. of Quincy, which he said the gentleman preferred not to deliver himself, for a reason which would be obvious to the ladies when they heard it.

Woman — the friend and guide of man — Her sphere is the *domestic circle* — her influence the "*still small voice.*"

The ladies being applied to for a sentiment, presented the following in reply.

The gentleman who first voted to admit the ladies to a public dinner — May his table never want the comfort and graces, not omitting the still small voice, which it is their vocation to furnish.

After this followed a number of volunteer sentiments.

VOLUNTEER SENTIMENTS.

Fair Harvard — A contemporary of the pilgrim fathers — with the experience of two centuries, she intrusts her literary treasures and her historical inscriptions to the Quincy granite.

The Blue Hill — The first landmark hailed by the mariner as he approaches the still bay of the Massachusetts. May the principles of those who first settled at its foot be as permanent as its color and as enduring as its base.

John Wheelwright and Oliver Cromwell — They set a ball in motion which the whole civilized world cannot stop.

The blessings we derive from our fathers — Like the light of the source of day reflected from every object we forget the fount from which it flowed.

The shadows of the past — They leave no trace behind, but they give grace and beauty to the spot over which they hover.

Those who take their drop from the bucket; — they will never be found with the drop in their eye.

The day — When we make a pastime out of past time.

The first settler of Quincy — Although a man cannot always be merry and wise, at proper times it is wise to be merry.

The Farmers of Quincy — May they suffer no root of bitterness to spring up among us, nor any to show the cloven foot, except they be neat cattle.

Those who live on Rock Common — May they soon be again able to make their bread out of stone.

The first Railroad in the United States — It connected the rocky mountain in Quincy with the Atlantic. The last Railroad in the United States — it shall connect the Rocky Mountains of the West with both the Atlantic and the Pacific tide.

The City of Quincy in Adams County, Illinois, and the towns of Quincy in Florida, Mississippi, and Tennessee —May their prosperity be as lasting as our own, although it is not like ours, founded upon a rock.

Our Fathers — Fishermen before they were shepherds — they got along by hook as well as by crook.

Independence — Its first germ appeared on Mount Wollaston; and when, one hundred and fifty years after, it was publicly proclaimed, a son of Braintree, one of its most distinguished advocates, urged its annual celebration with bonfires and illuminations; this son is now its fearless supporter even on the floor of Congress; may it be held sacred in our country "till rolling years shall cease to move."

Dr. Z. B. Adams then addressed the chair as follows: —

Mr. President, — We have alluded with great propriety to our Fathers and our Mothers, — the early settlers of New England. It appears to me there is still a very interesting class, whom it would be wrong in us to pass by with neglect, — the young ladies. And I will venture to add, therefore, even at this late hour,

The Young Ladies, emigrants to this country in 1620; — they must have been possessed of energy and true fire, for they caught their sparks from the "*Leyden Jar.*"

Dr. Lewis Joseph Glover followed Dr. Adams with some very entertaining professional remarks in allusion to Quincy, his native place, — his interest in her welfare, and the healthy state in which, in her advanced age, her symptoms evidently discovered her to be. But the lateness of the hour, and the movement already making towards an adjournment, did not enable him to say all that he intended.

The sun was already rapidly declining. The President of the day, early in the course of the dinner, had presented to the attention of the company a piece of parchment, headed with a part of the closing paragraph in the Discourse of the Hon. Daniel Webster at Plymouth in 1820, on which it was his wish that the names of those present should be written; — the parchment then to be deposited in some safe place and handed down to those who should come up to celebrate a similar occasion, one hundred years hence.

This suggestion was readily complied with, and two hundred and eighty-six names were subscribed.

The President likewise suggested in closing, that in order to connect the present more particularly with the coming century, and to honor the day, the young men of Quincy should form a society, for the purpose of ornamenting the town with trees, especially the burial yard, which, growing for a century, should appear in perfection to the company on the 25th of May, 1940. This suggestion likewise met with a cheerful and ready response.

The President then further suggested that as the meeting was about to be broken up, they should adjourn, to meet in the same place, to celebrate the Third Centennial Anniversary on the 25th of May, 1940, which was adopted without a dissenting voice.

The company then left the pavilion, and might be seen wending their ways towards their various homes, — the bells on the churches ringing out their merry peals, — the cannon on President's Hill pouring its echoing roars over hill and valley, and the sun with his retiring rays gilding the distant hill tops as with glittering gold.

The evening was spent in social and family intercourse, recounting the interesting events and associations of the day, and by a party of young ladies and gentlemen in a Ball at the Hancock House.

We cannot close this imperfect sketch of the Celebration, some account of which we were anxious to transmit to those who should come after us, better than in the beautiful language of the orator at Plymouth, and so happily inscribed, by the President of the day, at the head of the parchment already alluded to. Including the whole matter it runs thus.

HANCOCK LOT — QUINCY — MASSACHUSETTS.

We who celebrate the 25th of May, 1840, would welcome you, who a century hence shall fill the places we now fill, " to this pleasant land of the Fathers. We bid you welcome to the healthful skies and the verdant fields of New England. We greet your accession to the great inheritance, which we have enjoyed. We welcome you to the blessings of good government and religious liberty. We welcome you to the treasures of science and the delights of learning. We welcome you to the transcendent sweets of domestic life, to the happiness of kindred and parents and children. We welcome you to the immeasurable blessings of rational existence, the immortal hope of Christianity, and the light of everlasting truth!"

www.ingramcontent.com/pod-product-compliance
Lightning Source LLC
LaVergne TN
LVHW020602110826
845149LV00002B/354

* 9 7 8 1 4 1 8 1 8 8 1 2 2 *